Ao Haru Ride

The scent of air after rain...
In the light around us, I felt your heartbeat.

12

IO SAKISAKA

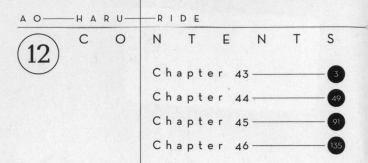

C O N T E N T S

S T O R Y   T H U S   F A R

Futaba Yoshioka was quiet and awkward around boys in junior high, but she's taken on a tomboy persona in high school. It's there that she once again meets her first love, Tanaka (now Kou Mabuchi), and falls for him again. But a series of missed connections and problems with timing have kept the two apart...

During the class trip, Kou shares that he wants to make new memories in Nagasaki, so Futaba accompanies him as a friend. She isn't sure how to tell Toma about sneaking off with Kou, but it turns out that he has known all along. When Futaba realizes that simply avoiding Kou isn't enough, she tells Kikuchi she wants to be more honest with him in their relationship. Meanwhile, Kou finally has a chance to talk to Yui in person...

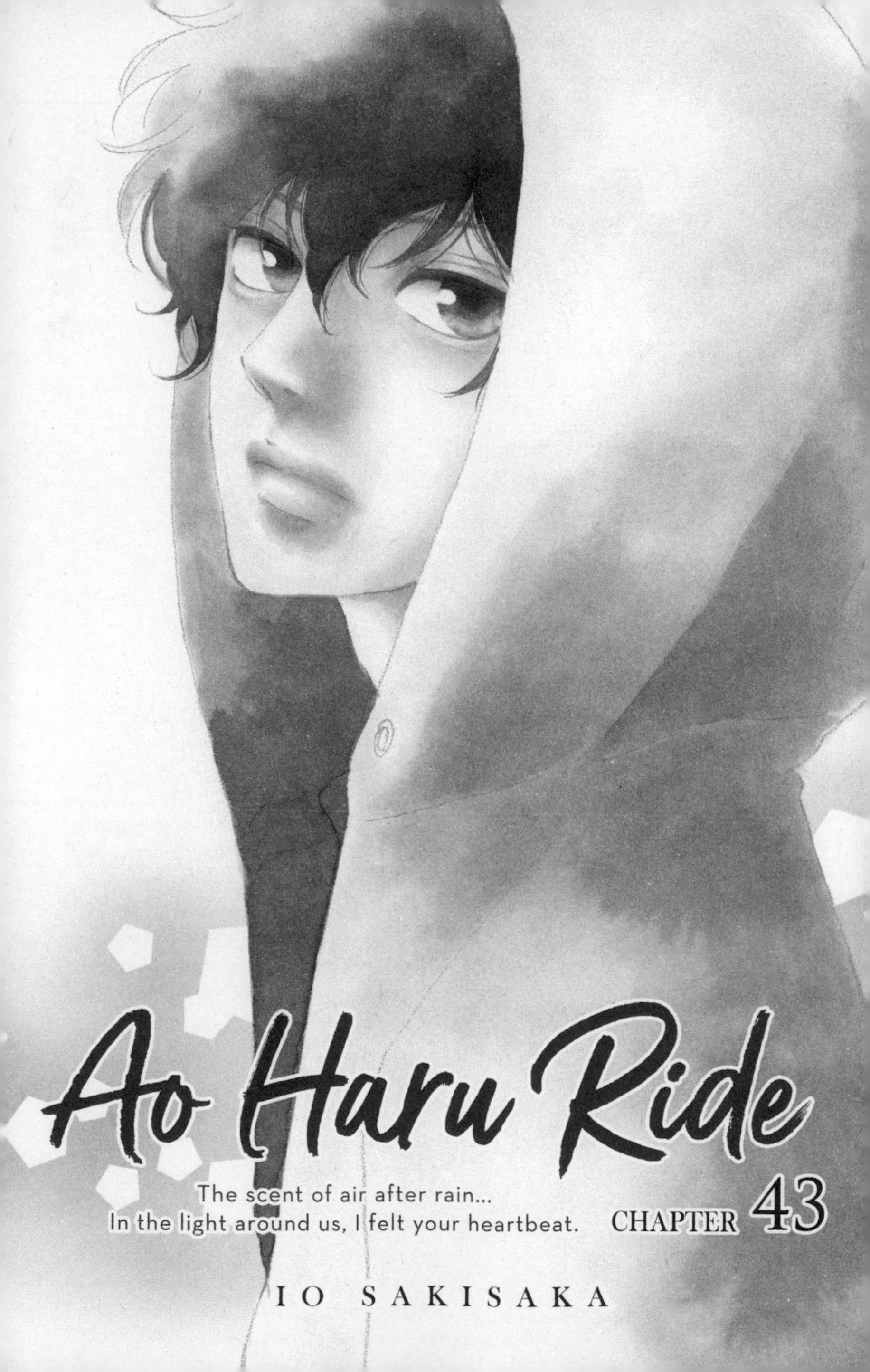
Ao Haru Ride
The scent of air after rain...
In the light around us, I felt your heartbeat.
CHAPTER 43
IO SAKISAKA

HELLO

Hi! I'm Io Sakisaka. Thank you for picking up a copy of
Ao Haru Ride, volume 12.

In letters you've sent me, many of you have written about
your own love lives, and without fail, I feel a pang in my
heart when I read them. ♡ I'm always reminded of how
love takes so many shapes, and that there are so many
perspectives out there. Each story is so different, and I
sense that each one is right. I feel like I can relate to them
all. Love is just so mysterious and exciting! I find that the
actions, worries, and all the feelings you write to me about
are no different from what I experienced during my school
years. (Though the tools you use are different now.)

With that in mind, I try to be confident about the work I do.
Just as I feel the pang in my heart when I read your stories,
I hope you'll feel the same as you read *Ao Haru Ride*. With
that, I hope you enjoy this volume all the way through!

 Io Sakisaka

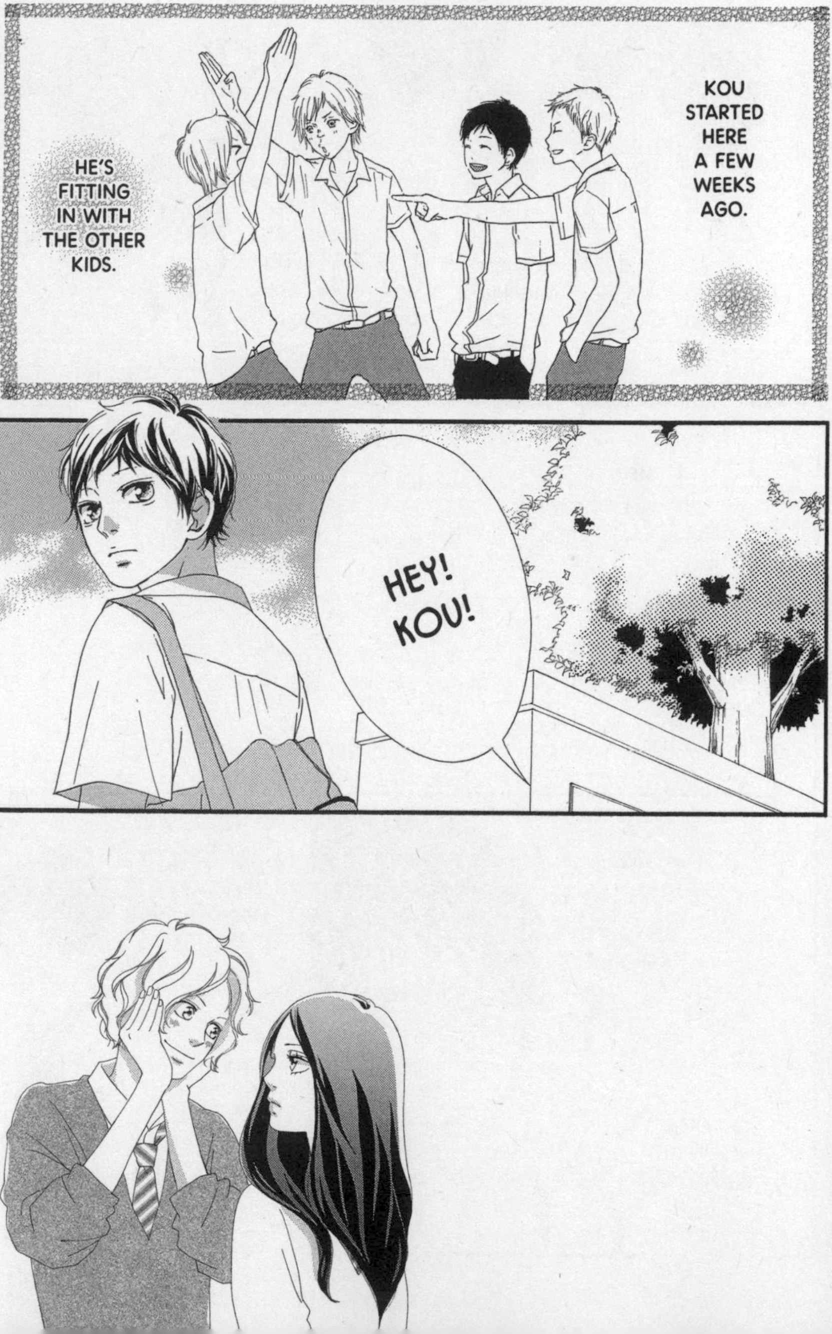
KOU STARTED HERE A FEW WEEKS AGO.
HE'S FITTING IN WITH THE OTHER KIDS.
HEY! KOU!

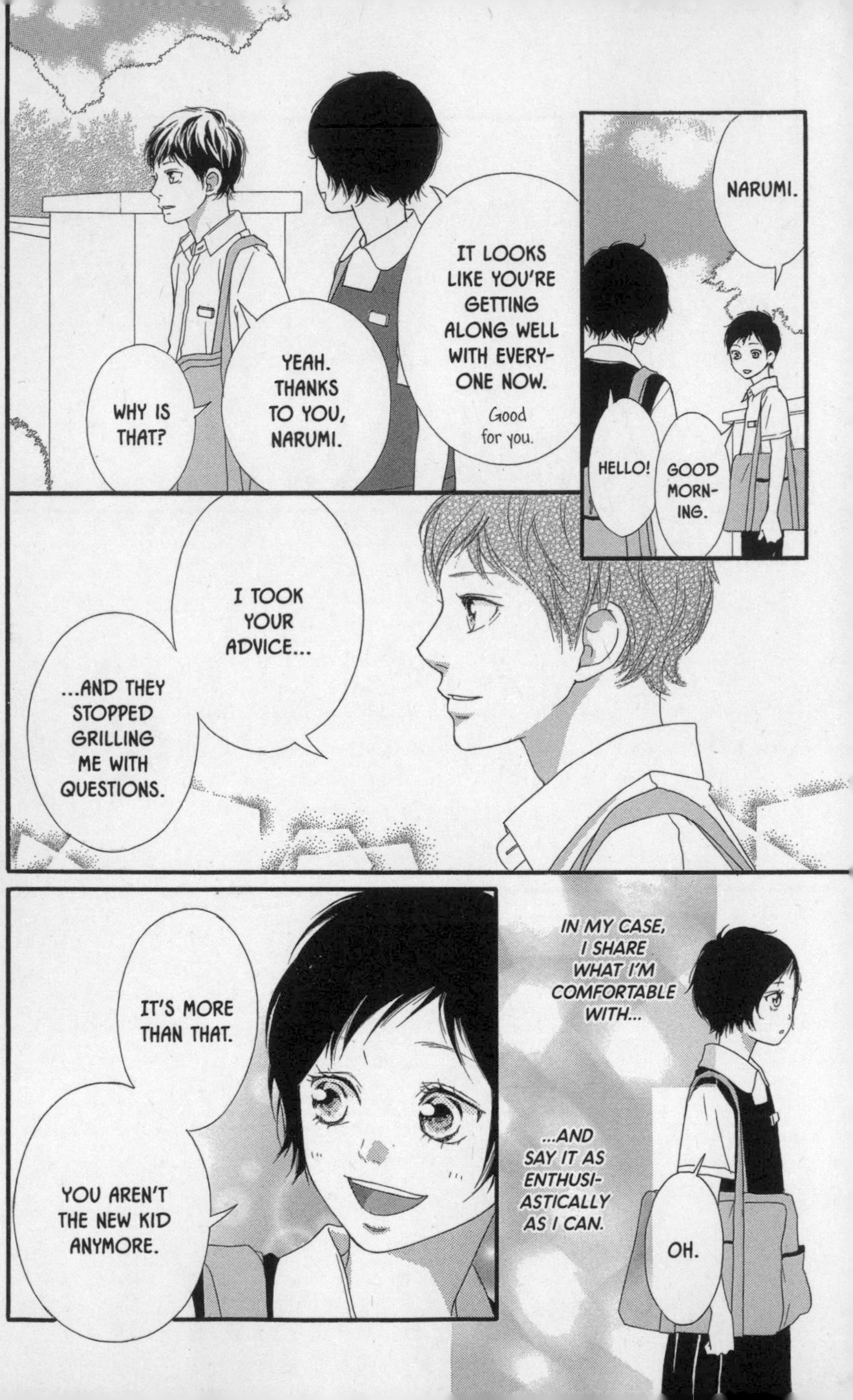
NARUMI.
GOOD MORNING.
HELLO!
IT LOOKS LIKE YOU'RE GETTING ALONG WELL WITH EVERYONE NOW.
Good for you.
YEAH. THANKS TO YOU, NARUMI.
WHY IS THAT?
I TOOK YOUR ADVICE...
...AND THEY STOPPED GRILLING ME WITH QUESTIONS.
IN MY CASE, I SHARE WHAT I'M COMFORTABLE WITH...
...AND SAY IT AS ENTHUSIASTICALLY AS I CAN.
OH.
IT'S MORE THAN THAT.
YOU AREN'T THE NEW KID ANYMORE.

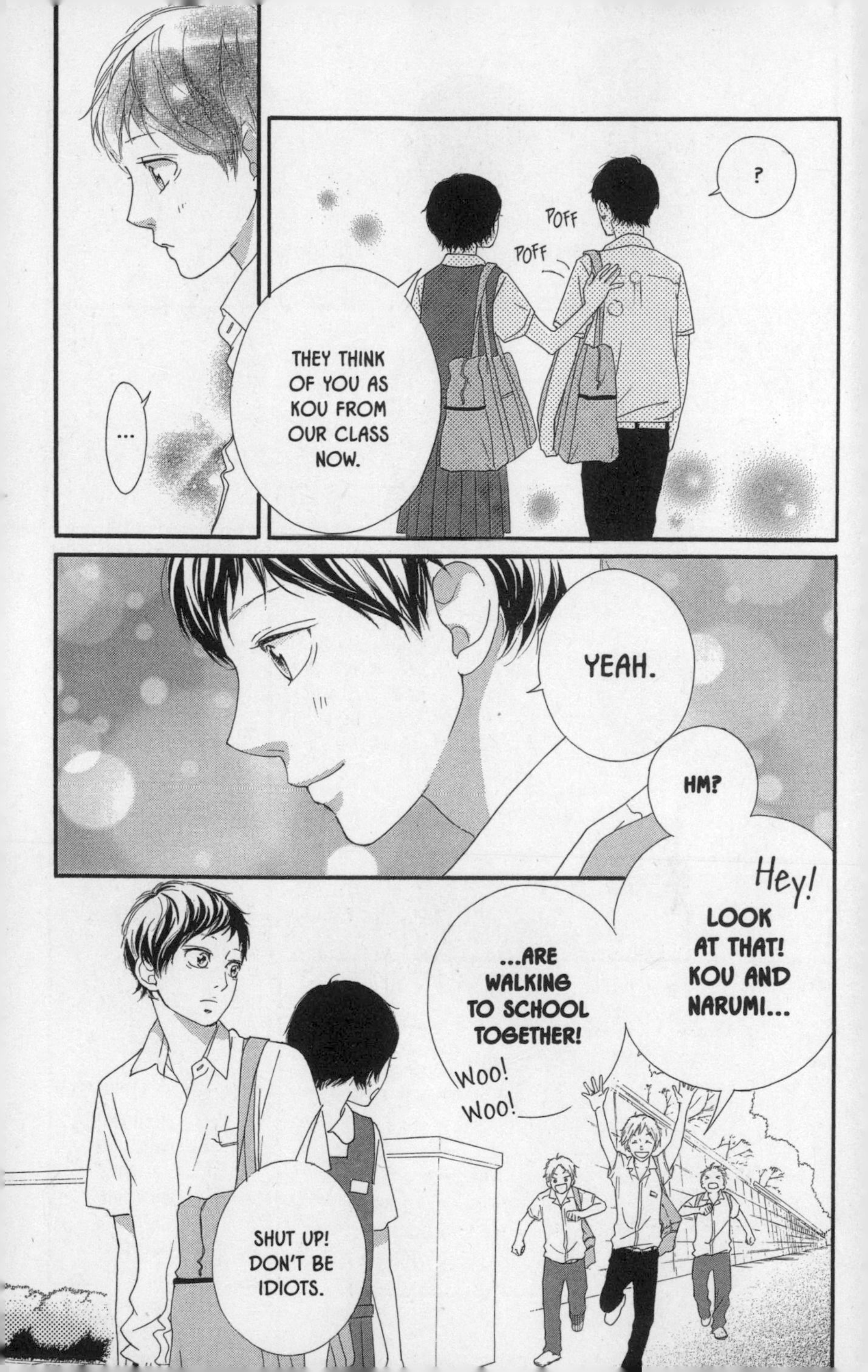
?
POFF
POFF
THEY THINK OF YOU AS KOU FROM OUR CLASS NOW.
...
YEAH.
HM?
Hey!
LOOK AT THAT! KOU AND NARUMI...
...ARE WALKING TO SCHOOL TOGETHER!
Woo!
Woo!
SHUT UP! DON'T BE IDIOTS.

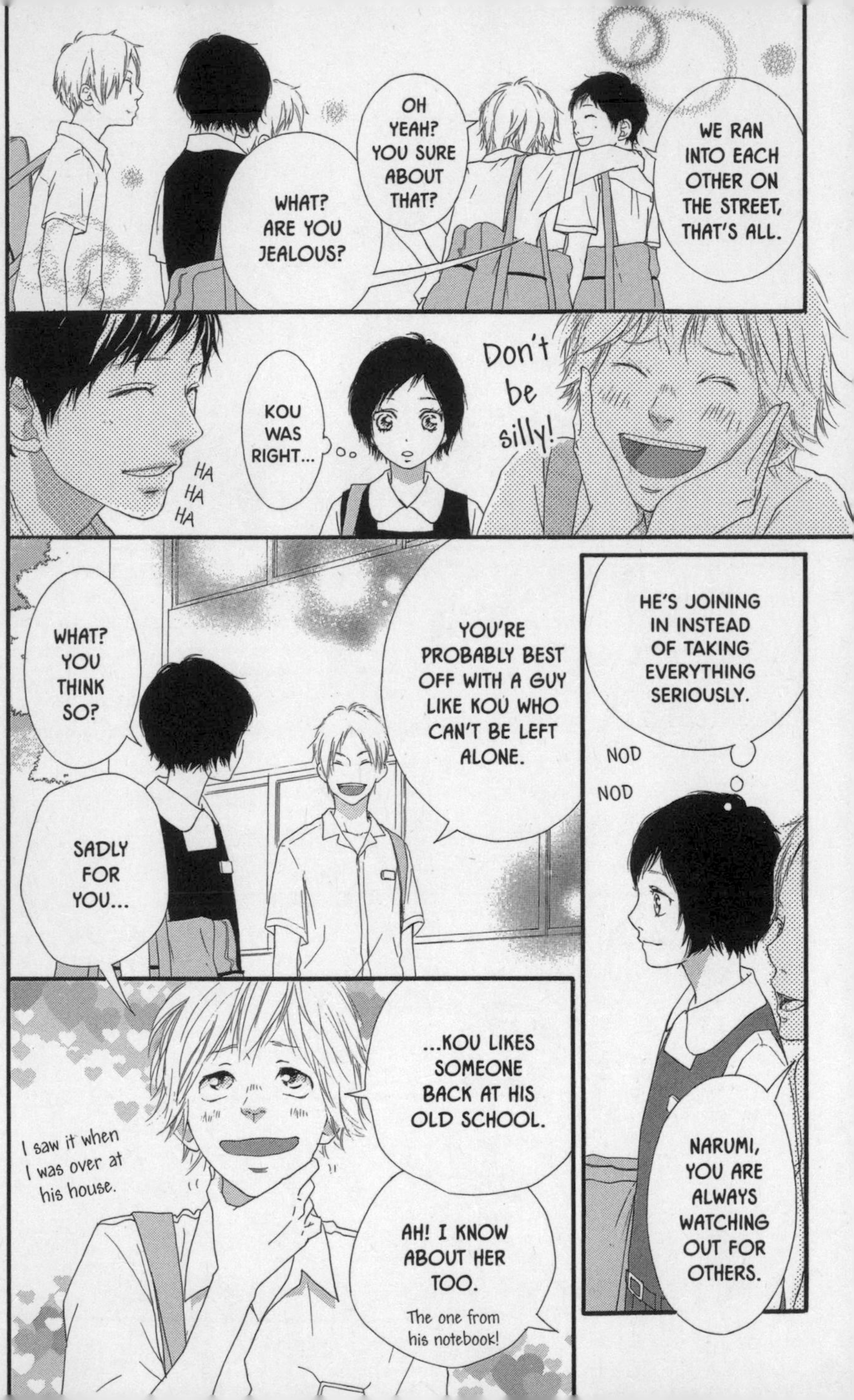
WE RAN INTO EACH OTHER ON THE STREET, THAT'S ALL.
OH YEAH? YOU SURE ABOUT THAT?
WHAT? ARE YOU JEALOUS?
Don't be silly!
KOU WAS RIGHT...
HA HA HA
HE'S JOINING IN INSTEAD OF TAKING EVERYTHING SERIOUSLY.
NOD NOD
NARUMI, YOU ARE ALWAYS WATCHING OUT FOR OTHERS.
YOU'RE PROBABLY BEST OFF WITH A GUY LIKE KOU WHO CAN'T BE LEFT ALONE.
WHAT? YOU THINK SO?
SADLY FOR YOU...
...KOU LIKES SOMEONE BACK AT HIS OLD SCHOOL.
I saw it when I was over at his house.
AH! I KNOW ABOUT HER TOO.
The one from his notebook!

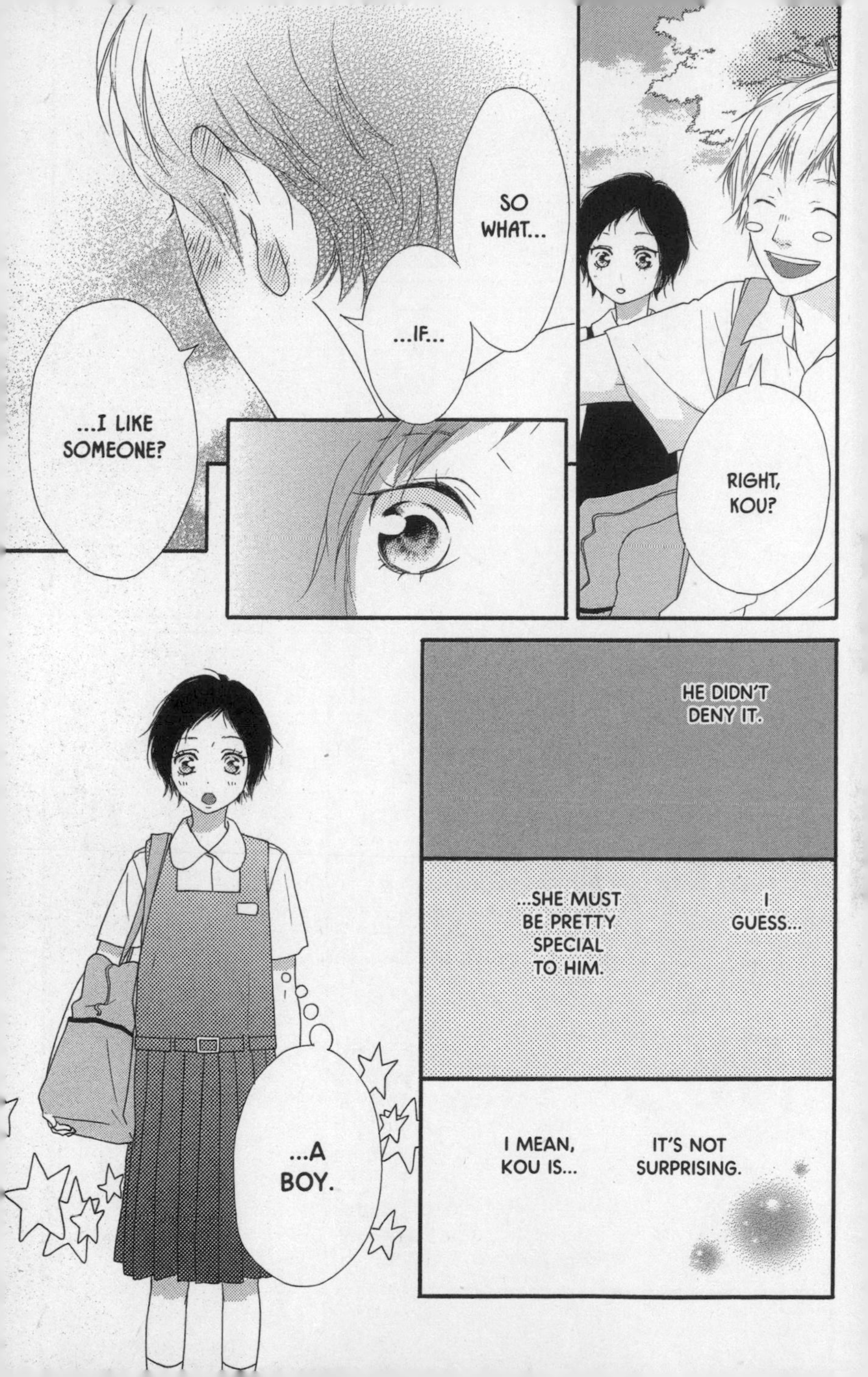
RIGHT, KOU?
SO WHAT...
...IF...
...I LIKE SOMEONE?
HE DIDN'T DENY IT.
I GUESS...
...SHE MUST BE PRETTY SPECIAL TO HIM.
IT'S NOT SURPRISING.
I MEAN, KOU IS...
...A BOY.

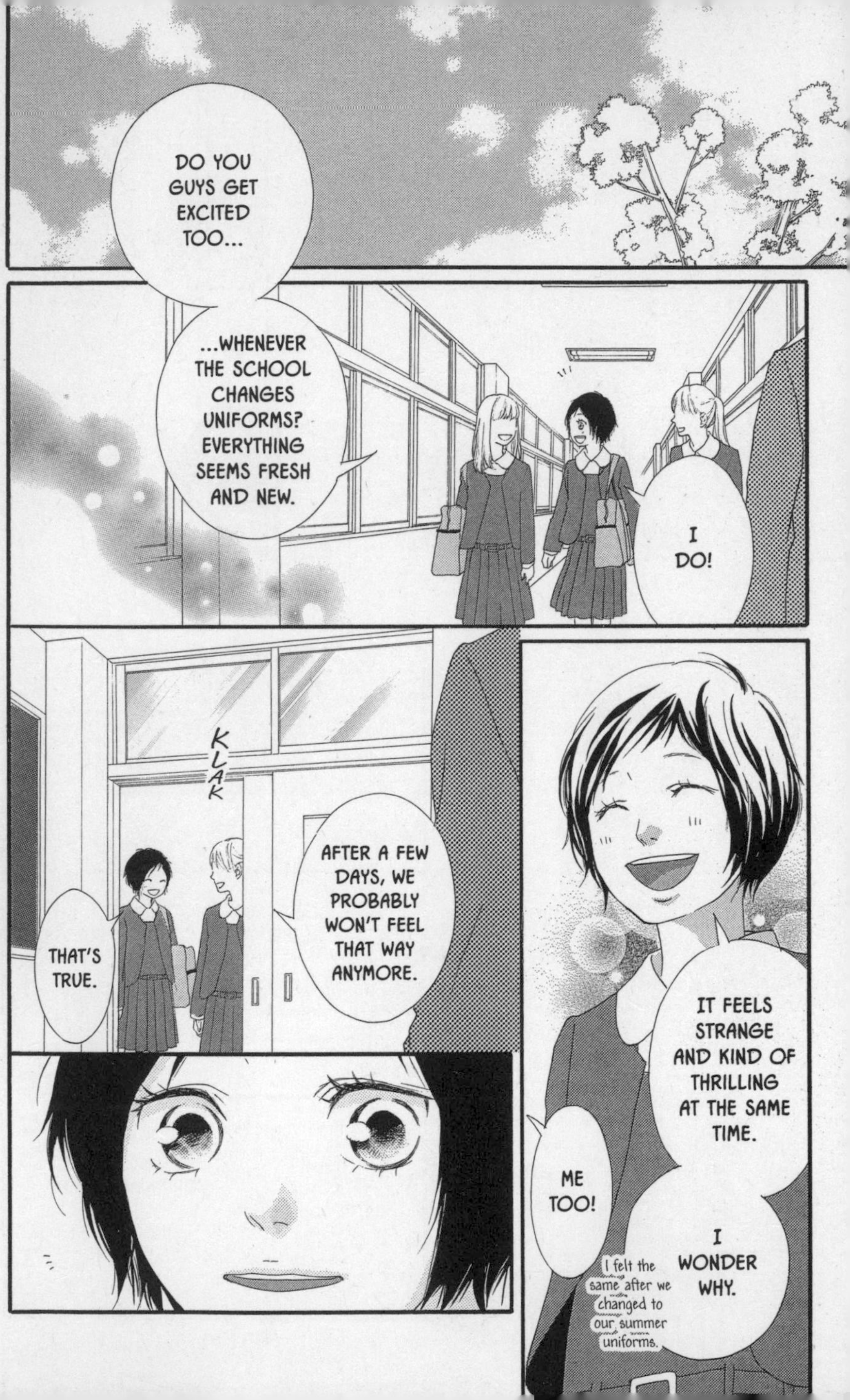
DO YOU GUYS GET EXCITED TOO...
...WHENEVER THE SCHOOL CHANGES UNIFORMS? EVERYTHING SEEMS FRESH AND NEW.
I DO!
IT FEELS STRANGE AND KIND OF THRILLING AT THE SAME TIME.
ME TOO!
I WONDER WHY.
I felt the same after we changed to our summer uniforms.
KLAK
AFTER A FEW DAYS, WE PROBABLY WON'T FEEL THAT WAY ANYMORE.
THAT'S TRUE.

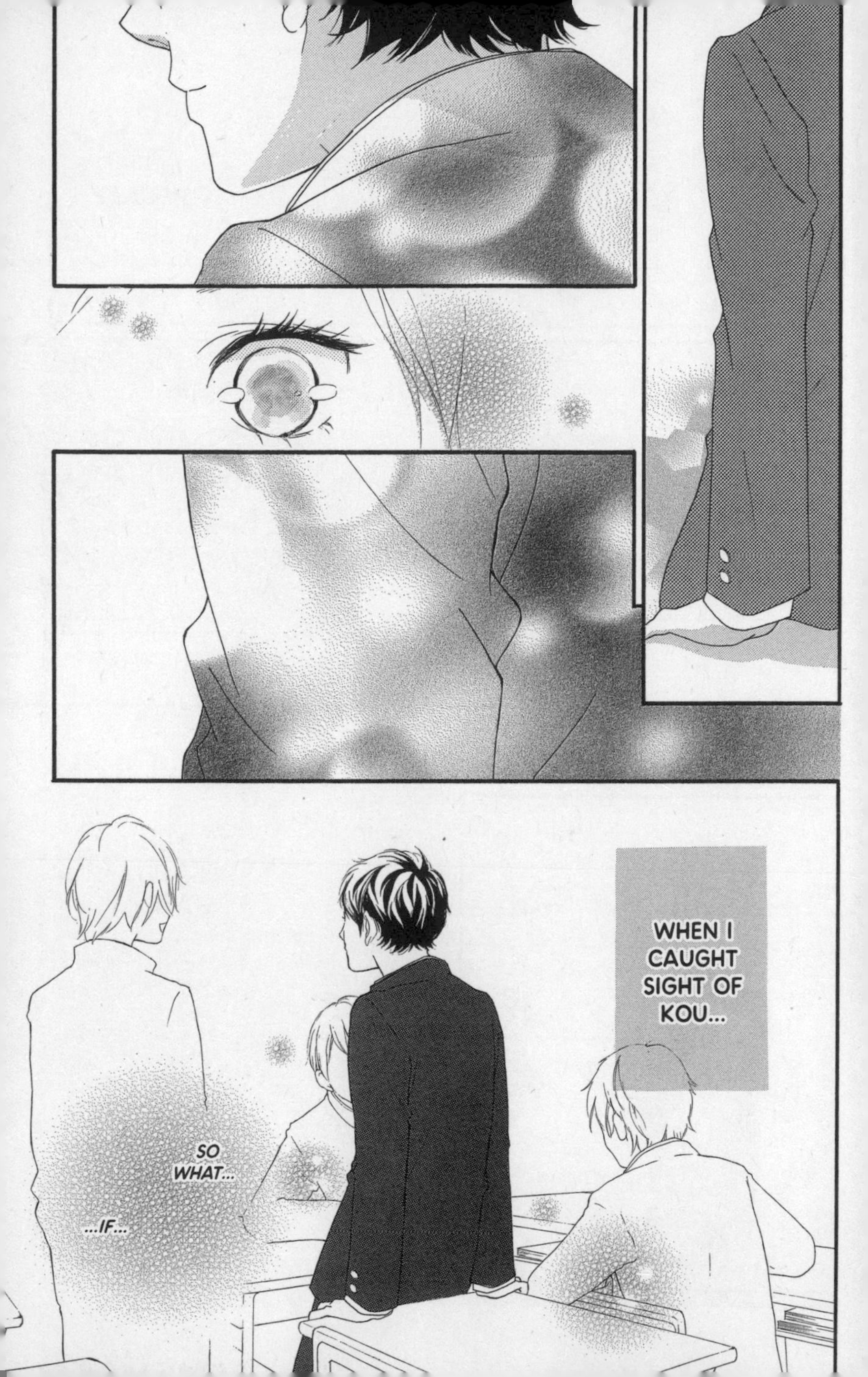
WHEN I CAUGHT SIGHT OF KOU...
SO WHAT...
...IF...

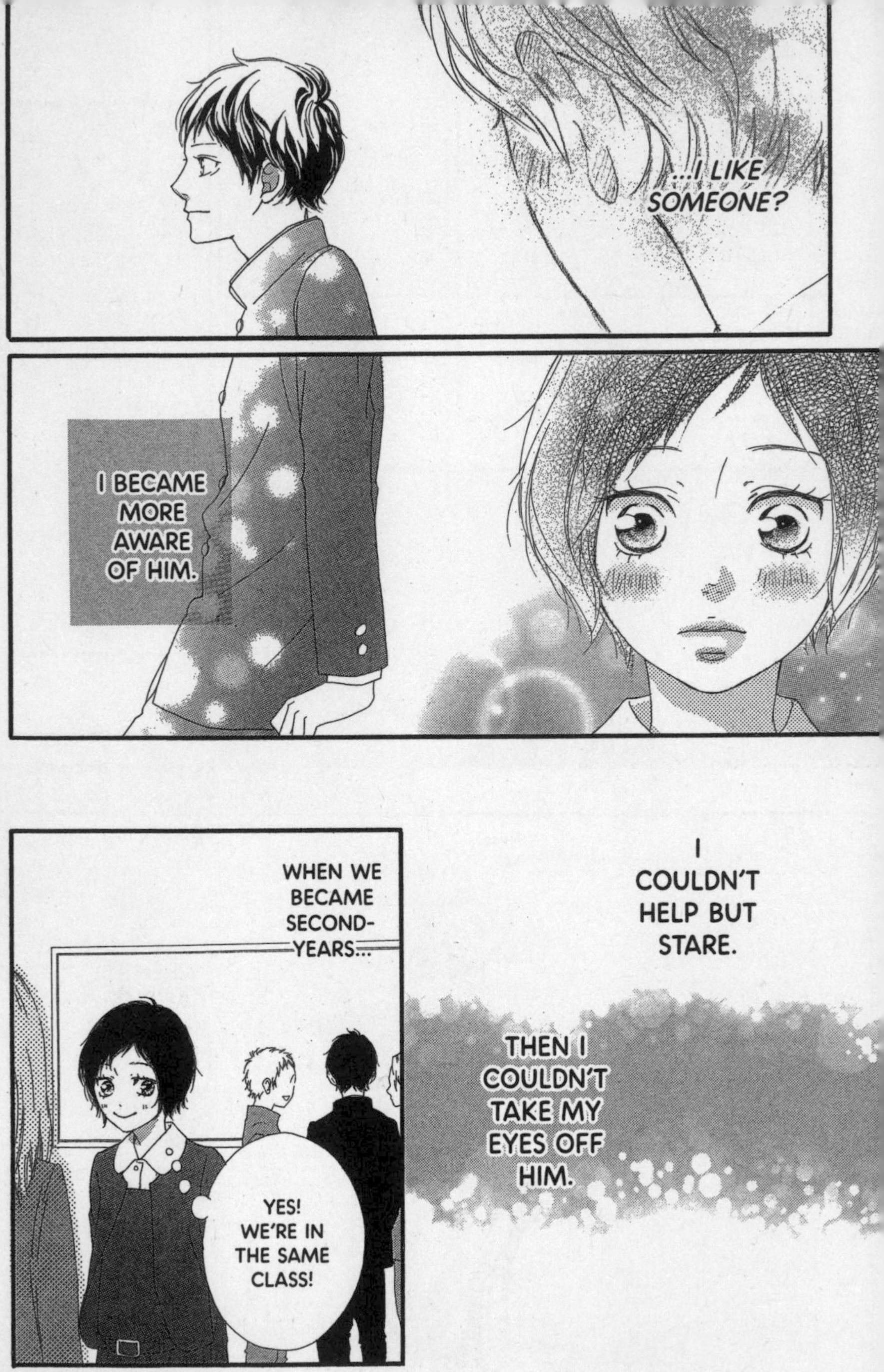
...I LIKE SOMEONE?
I BECAME MORE AWARE OF HIM.
I COULDN'T HELP BUT STARE.
THEN I COULDN'T TAKE MY EYES OFF HIM.
WHEN WE BECAME SECOND-YEARS...
YES! WE'RE IN THE SAME CLASS!

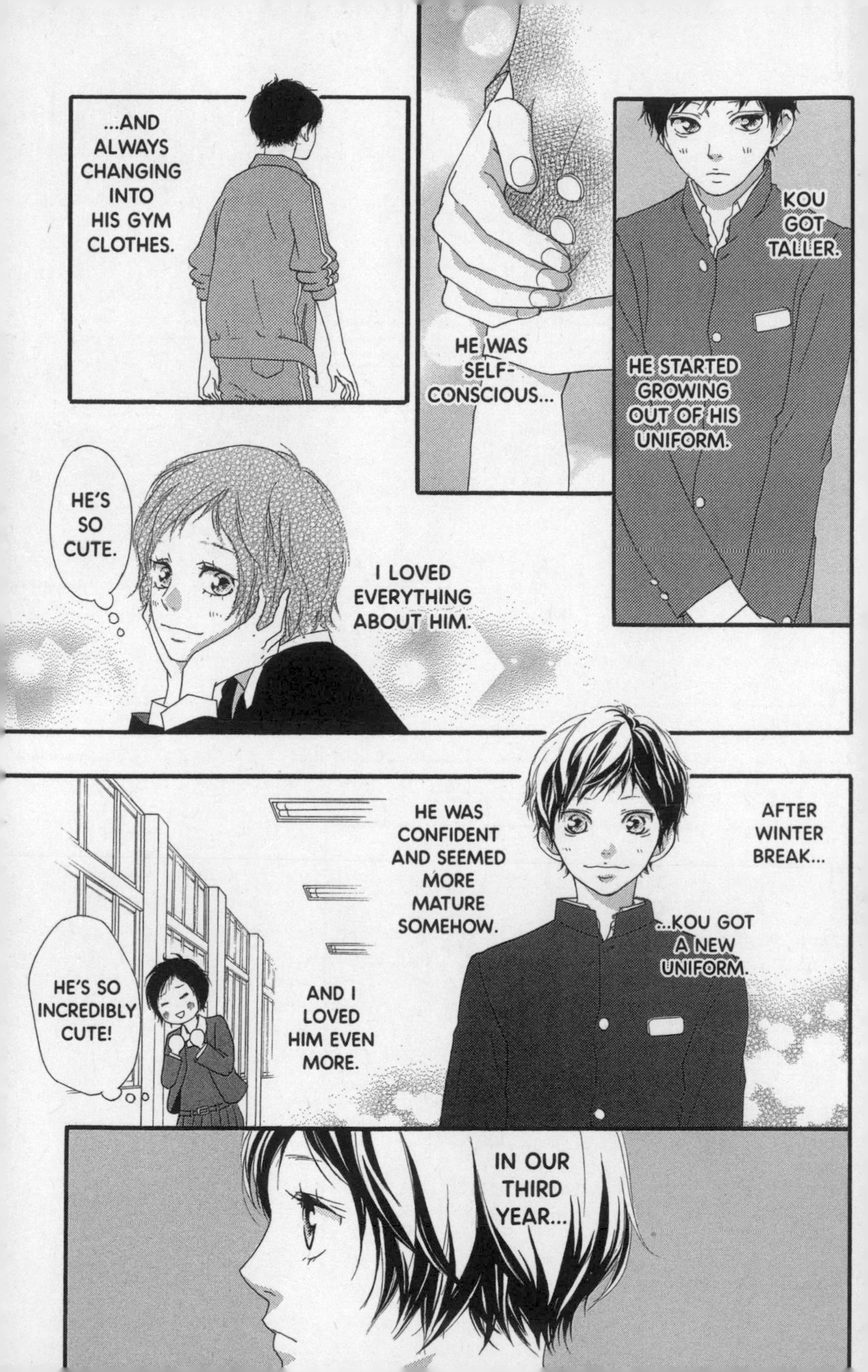
KOU GOT TALLER.
HE STARTED GROWING OUT OF HIS UNIFORM.
HE WAS SELF-CONSCIOUS...
...AND ALWAYS CHANGING INTO HIS GYM CLOTHES.
I LOVED EVERYTHING ABOUT HIM.
HE'S SO CUTE.
AFTER WINTER BREAK...
...KOU GOT A NEW UNIFORM.
HE WAS CONFIDENT AND SEEMED MORE MATURE SOMEHOW.
AND I LOVED HIM EVEN MORE.
HE'S SO INCREDIBLY CUTE!
IN OUR THIRD YEAR...

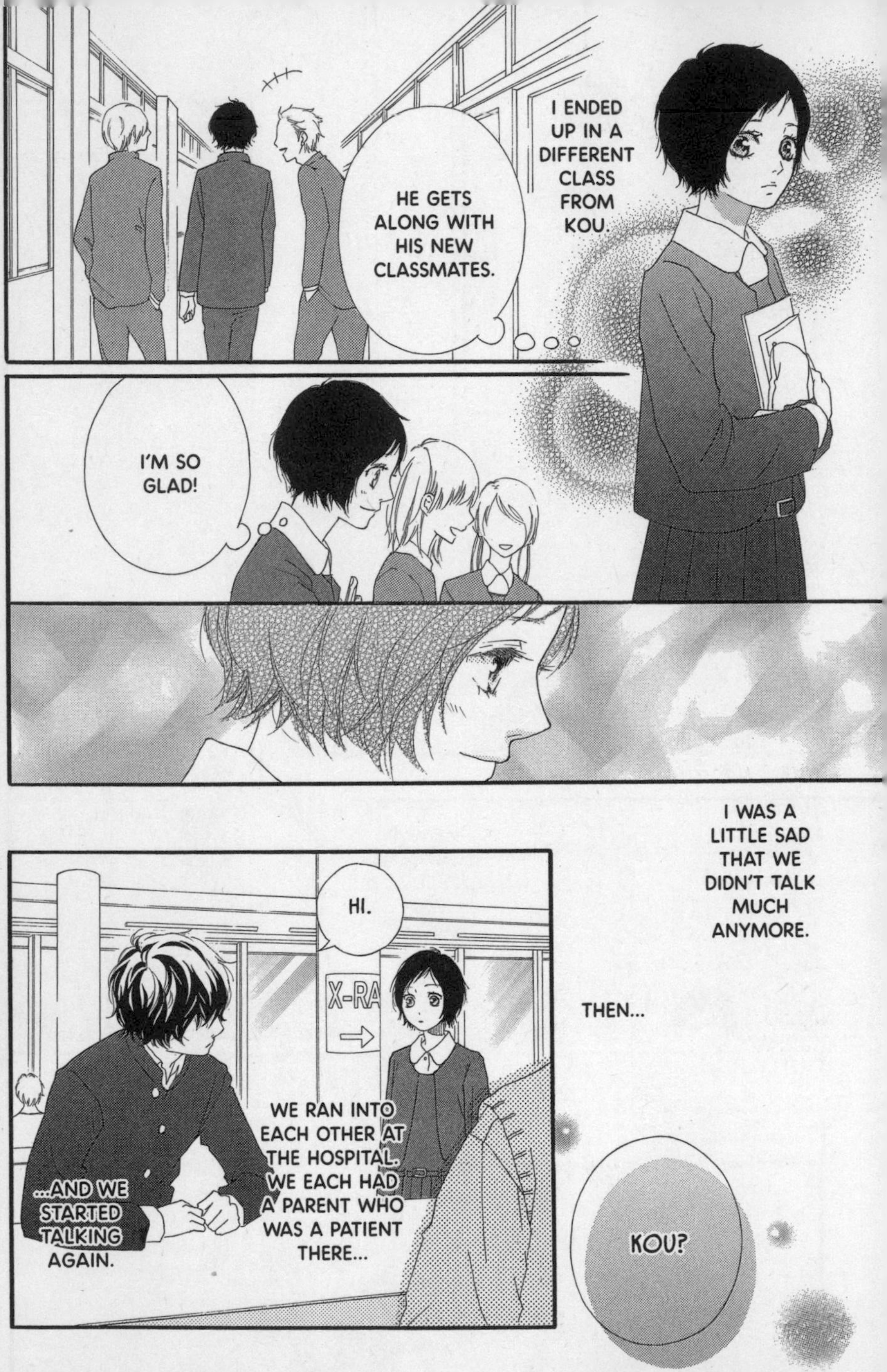
I ENDED UP IN A DIFFERENT CLASS FROM KOU.
HE GETS ALONG WITH HIS NEW CLASSMATES.
I'M SO GLAD!
I WAS A LITTLE SAD THAT WE DIDN'T TALK MUCH ANYMORE.
THEN...
KOU?
HI.
WE RAN INTO EACH OTHER AT THE HOSPITAL. WE EACH HAD A PARENT WHO WAS A PATIENT THERE...
...AND WE STARTED TALKING AGAIN.

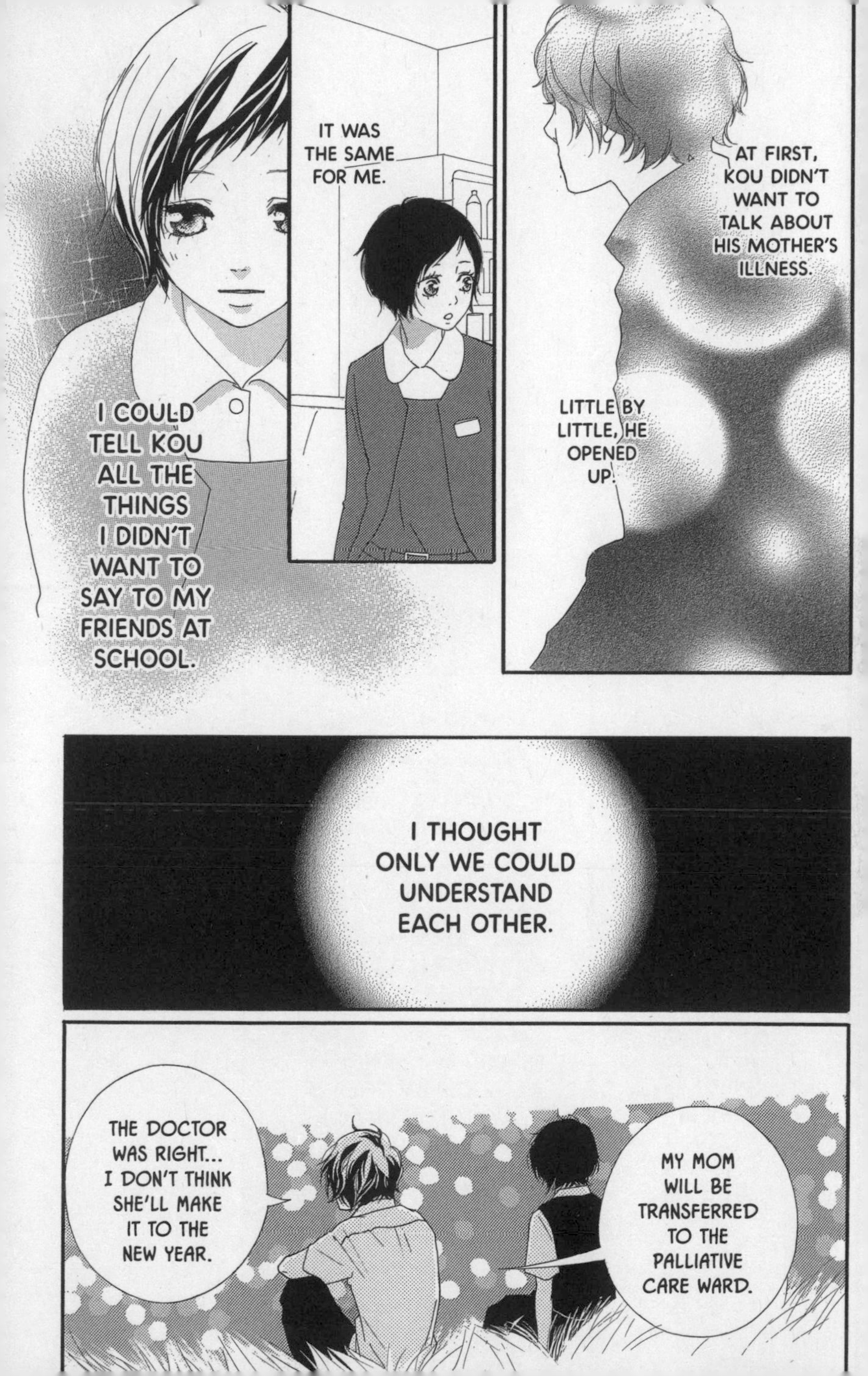
AT FIRST, KOU DIDN'T WANT TO TALK ABOUT HIS MOTHER'S ILLNESS.
LITTLE BY LITTLE, HE OPENED UP.
IT WAS THE SAME FOR ME.
I COULD TELL KOU ALL THE THINGS I DIDN'T WANT TO SAY TO MY FRIENDS AT SCHOOL.
I THOUGHT ONLY WE COULD UNDERSTAND EACH OTHER.
MY MOM WILL BE TRANSFERRED TO THE PALLIATIVE CARE WARD.
THE DOCTOR WAS RIGHT... I DON'T THINK SHE'LL MAKE IT TO THE NEW YEAR.

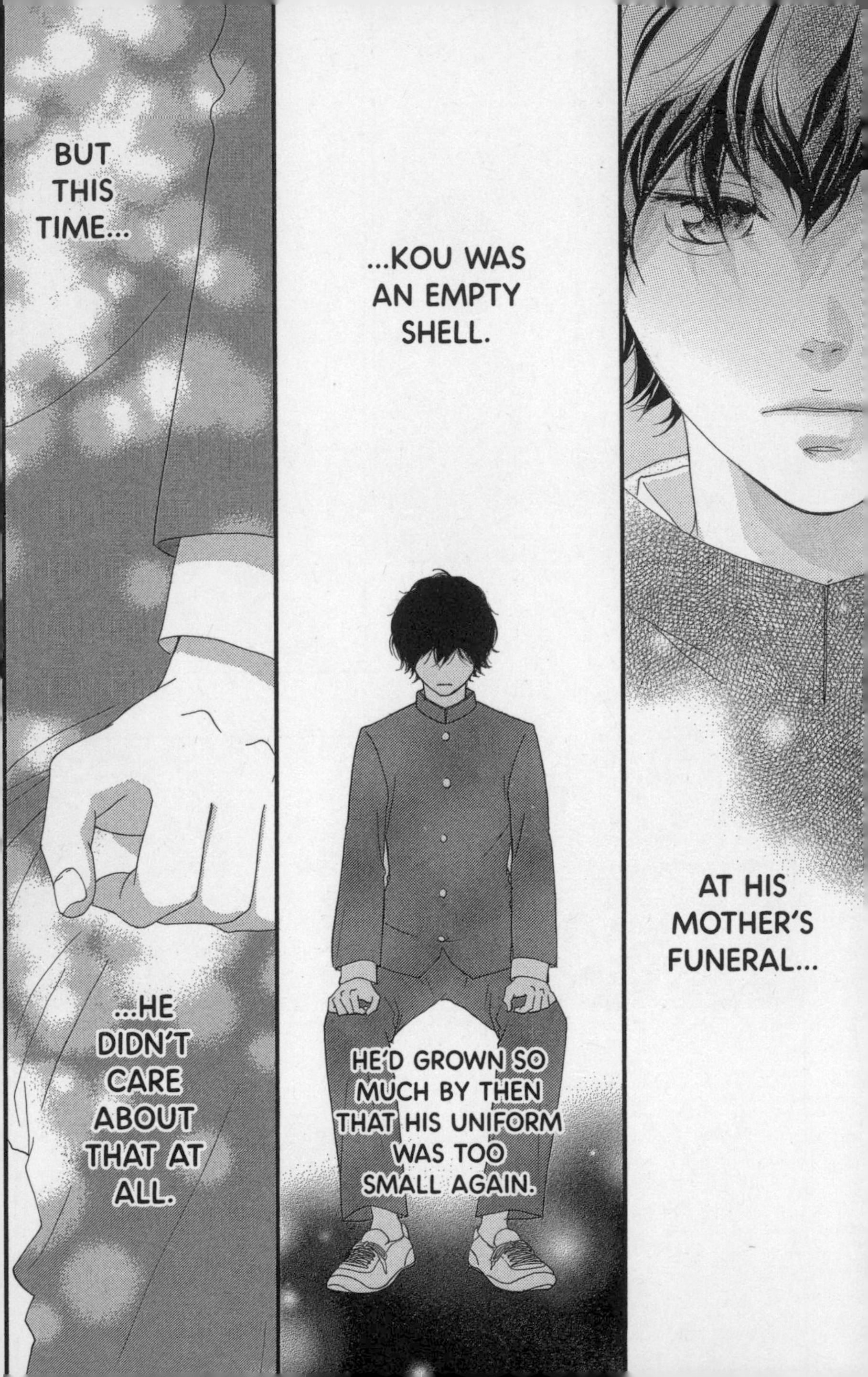
AT HIS MOTHER'S FUNERAL...
...KOU WAS AN EMPTY SHELL.
HE'D GROWN SO MUCH BY THEN THAT HIS UNIFORM WAS TOO SMALL AGAIN.
BUT THIS TIME...
...HE DIDN'T CARE ABOUT THAT AT ALL.

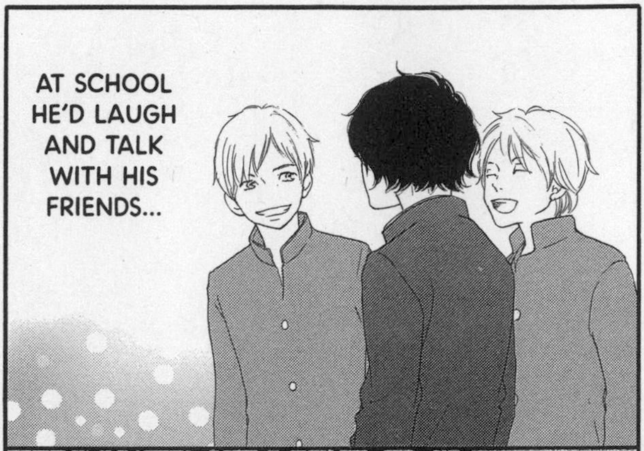
AT SCHOOL HE'D LAUGH AND TALK WITH HIS FRIENDS...

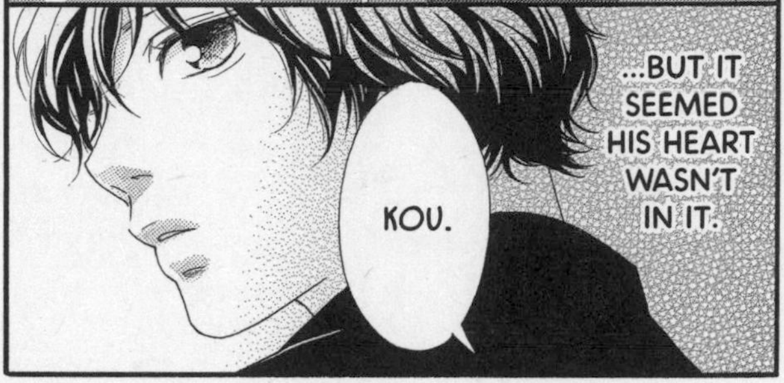
...BUT IT SEEMED HIS HEART WASN'T IN IT.
KOU.

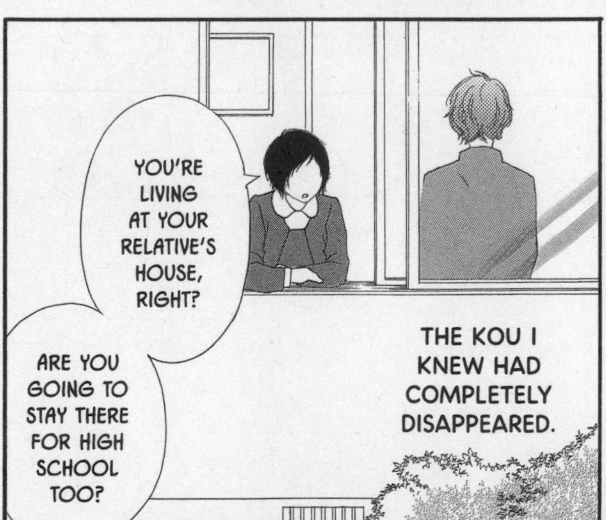
YOU'RE LIVING AT YOUR RELATIVE'S HOUSE, RIGHT?
ARE YOU GOING TO STAY THERE FOR HIGH SCHOOL TOO?
THE KOU I KNEW HAD COMPLETELY DISAPPEARED.

I love coffee. I drink it constantly while I work. Apparently drinking too much can chill your body. (I learned this from CAPSULE's Toshiko Koshijima's Twitter. ♡ She says you should limit yourself to 3 cups per day!) I try to be careful, but I have to say I really do enjoy the taste. I like my coffee black or as an au lait. Occasionally, when I want to enjoy both flavors at once, I will put them on my desk next to each other. Someone gave me an espresso machine the other day, and as a coffee lover, my excitement has been through the roof. I'm sooo happy! It reminds me of that feeling you get after receiving a Christmas present from Santa—a nostalgic "hooray" sensation. I haven't felt this way in ages!! And the coffee it makes is delicious. I'm excited to try all the different drinks. My espresso machine is my most beloved possession in my office right now.

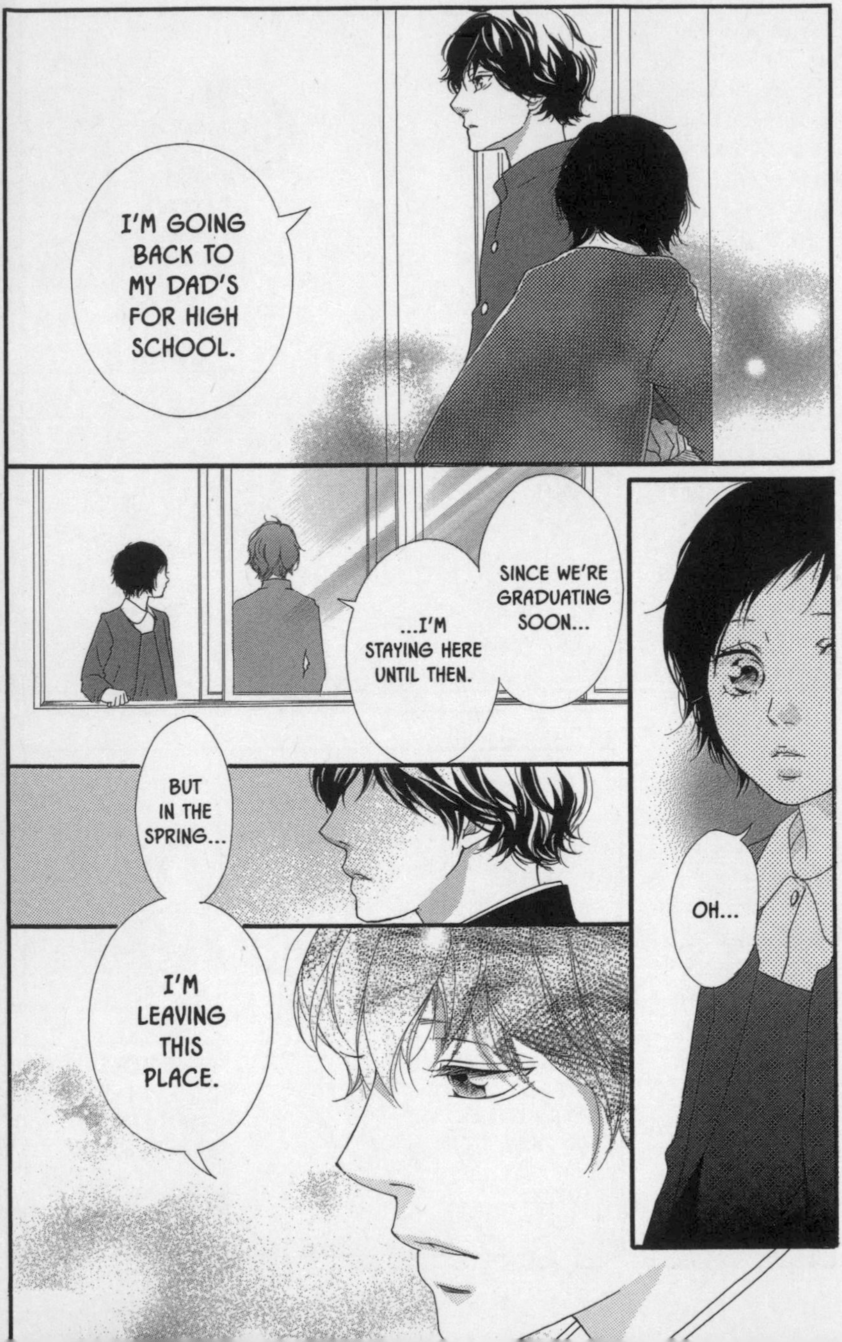
I'M GOING BACK TO MY DAD'S FOR HIGH SCHOOL.
OH...
SINCE WE'RE GRADUATING SOON...
...I'M STAYING HERE UNTIL THEN.
BUT IN THE SPRING...
I'M LEAVING THIS PLACE.

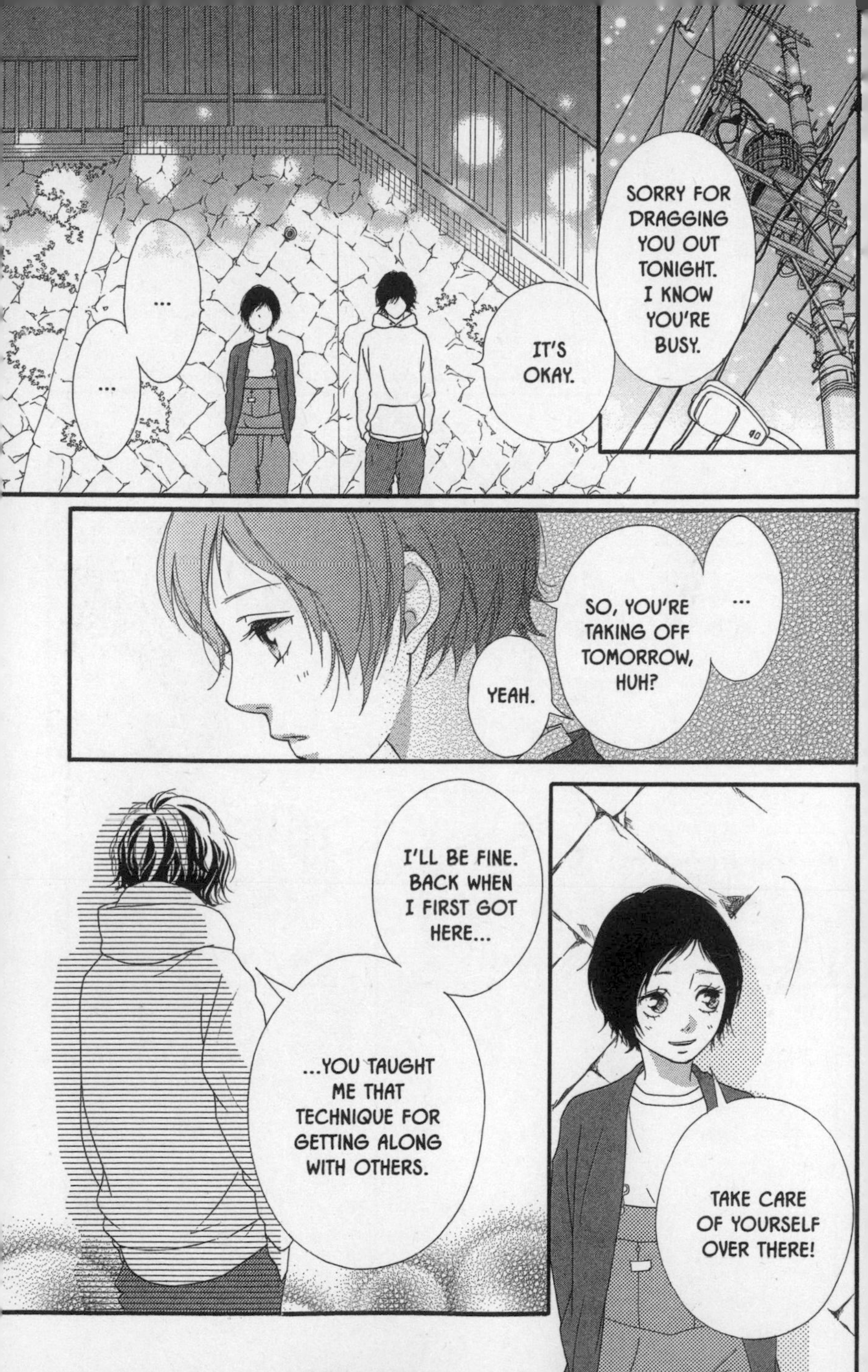
SORRY FOR DRAGGING YOU OUT TONIGHT. I KNOW YOU'RE BUSY.
IT'S OKAY.
...
...
...
SO, YOU'RE TAKING OFF TOMORROW, HUH?
YEAH.
TAKE CARE OF YOURSELF OVER THERE!
I'LL BE FINE. BACK WHEN I FIRST GOT HERE...
...YOU TAUGHT ME THAT TECHNIQUE FOR GETTING ALONG WITH OTHERS.

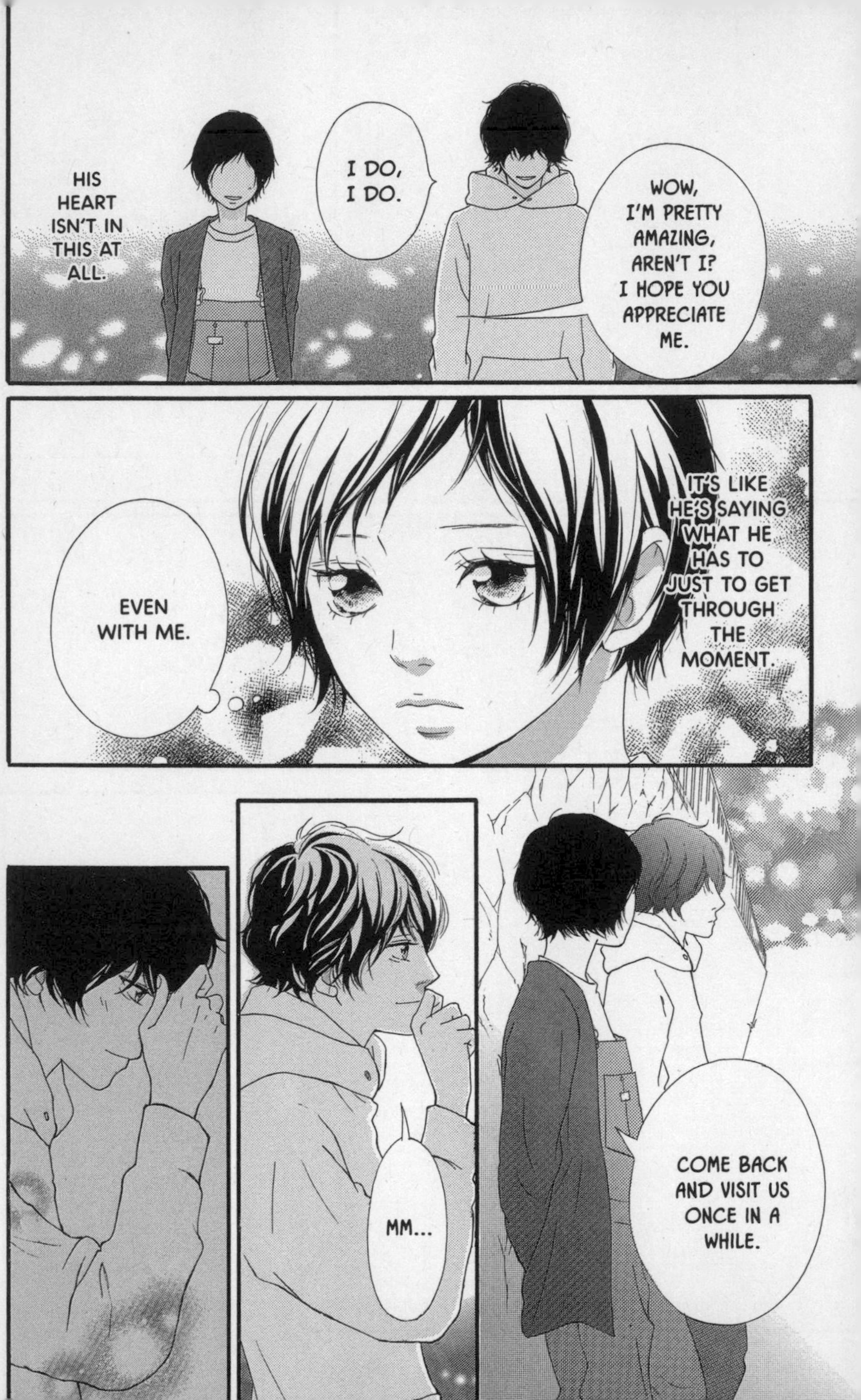
WOW, I'M PRETTY AMAZING, AREN'T I? I HOPE YOU APPRECIATE ME.
I DO, I DO.
HIS HEART ISN'T IN THIS AT ALL.
IT'S LIKE HE'S SAYING WHAT HE HAS TO JUST TO GET THROUGH THE MOMENT.
EVEN WITH ME.
COME BACK AND VISIT US ONCE IN A WHILE.
MM...

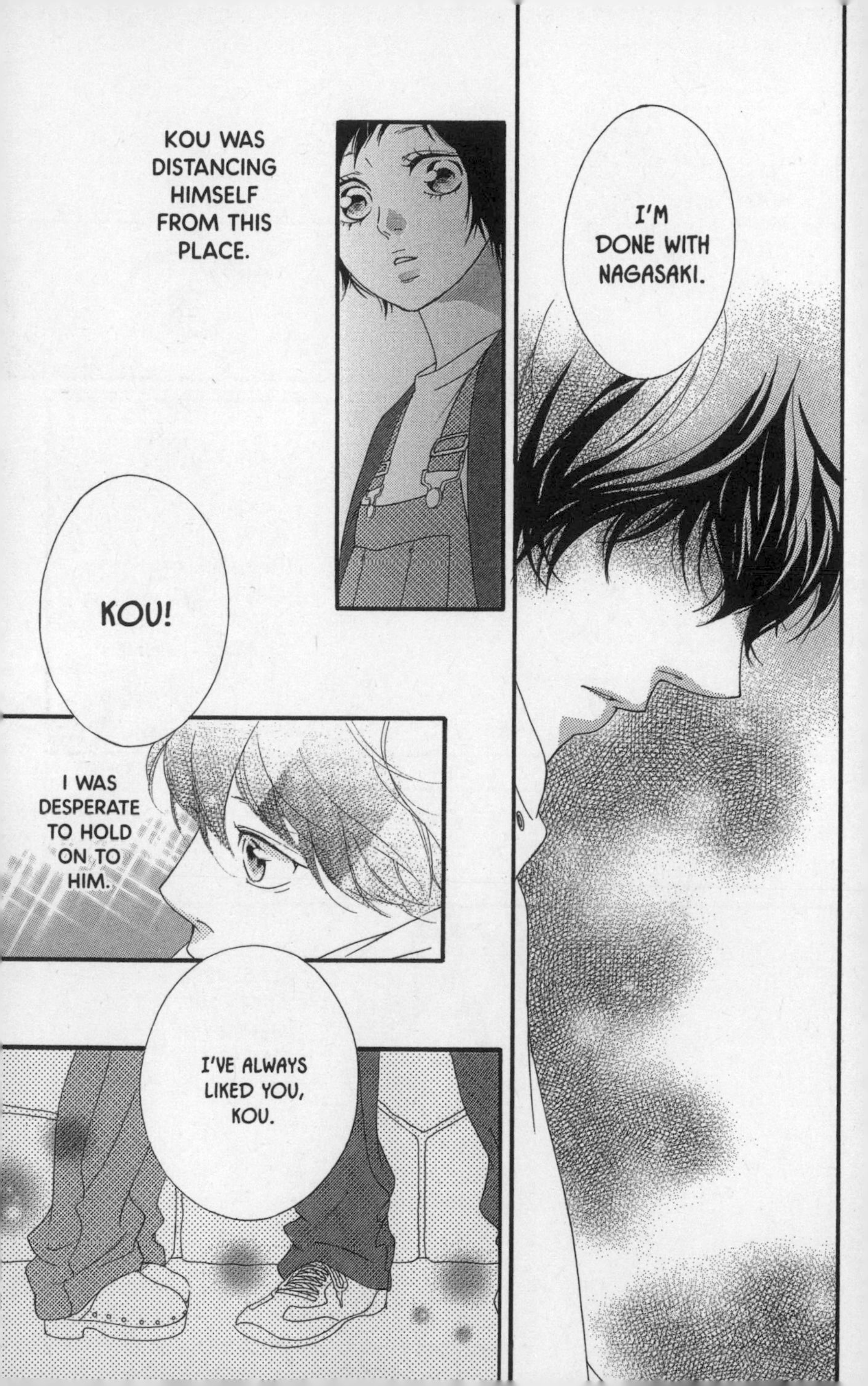
I'M DONE WITH NAGASAKI.
KOU WAS DISTANCING HIMSELF FROM THIS PLACE.
KOU!
I WAS DESPERATE TO HOLD ON TO HIM.
I'VE ALWAYS LIKED YOU, KOU.

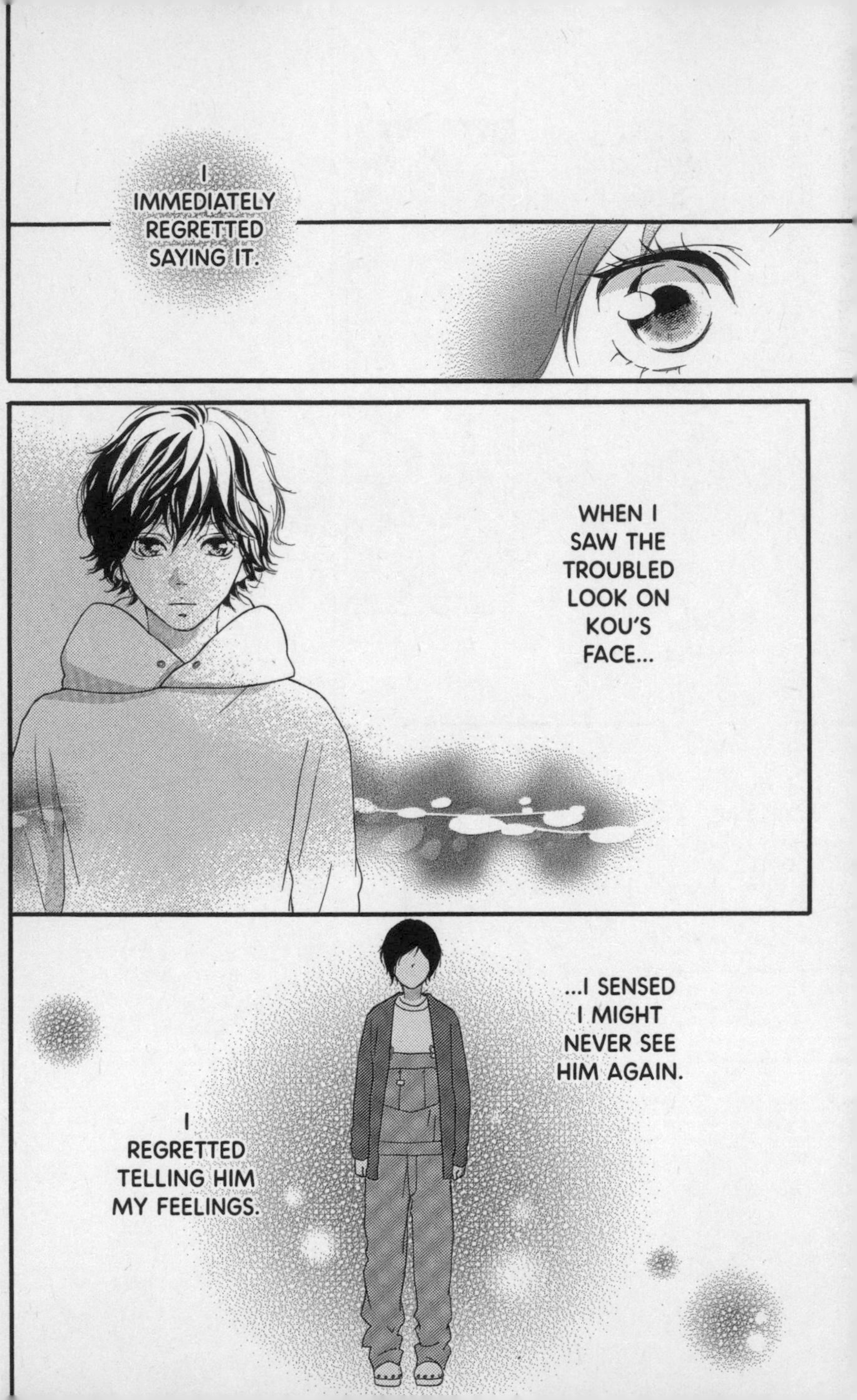
I IMMEDIATELY REGRETTED SAYING IT.
WHEN I SAW THE TROUBLED LOOK ON KOU'S FACE...
...I SENSED I MIGHT NEVER SEE HIM AGAIN.
I REGRETTED TELLING HIM MY FEELINGS.

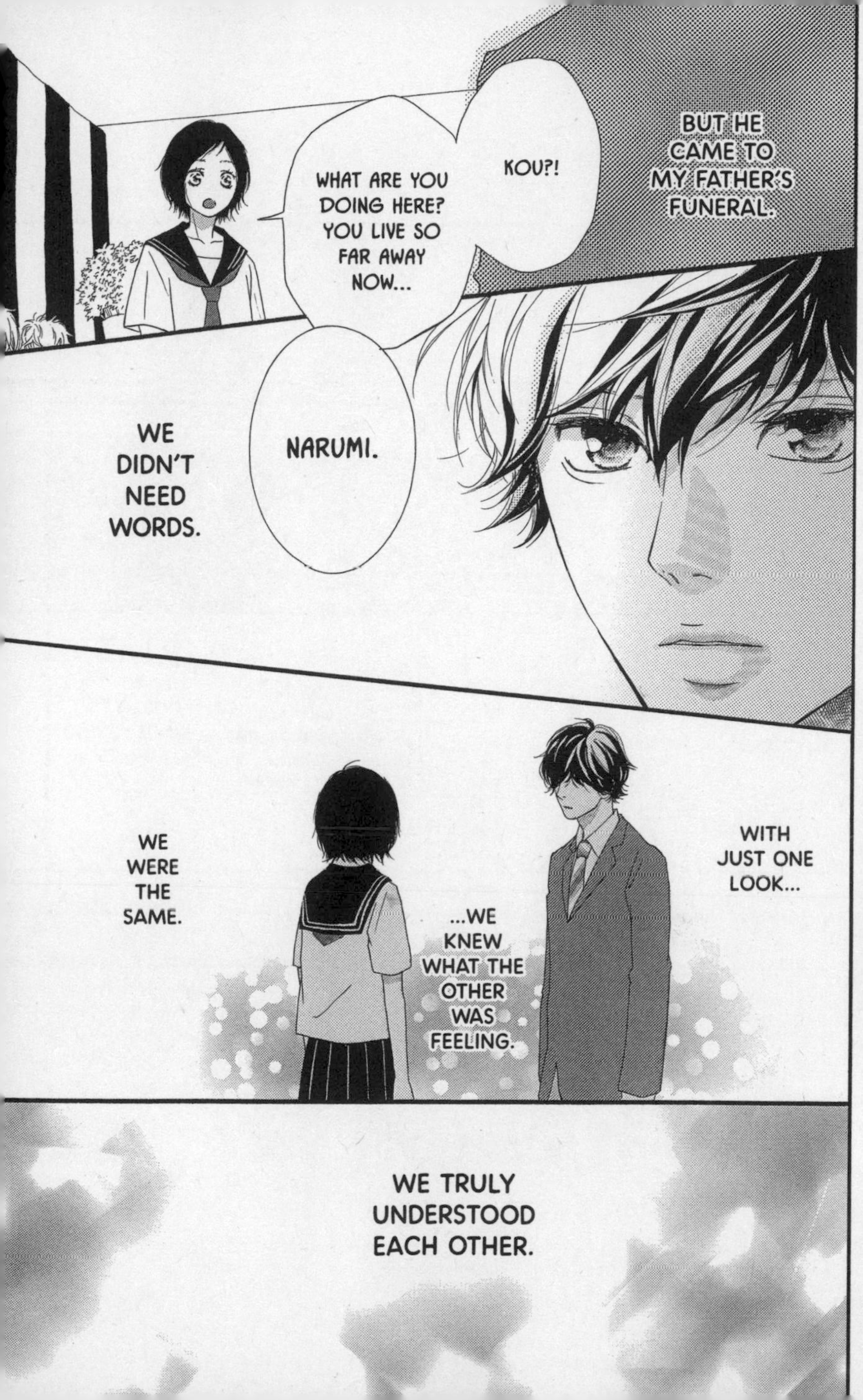
BUT HE CAME TO MY FATHER'S FUNERAL.
KOU?!
WHAT ARE YOU DOING HERE? YOU LIVE SO FAR AWAY NOW...
NARUMI.
WE DIDN'T NEED WORDS.
WITH JUST ONE LOOK...
...WE KNEW WHAT THE OTHER WAS FEELING.
WE WERE THE SAME.
WE TRULY UNDERSTOOD EACH OTHER.

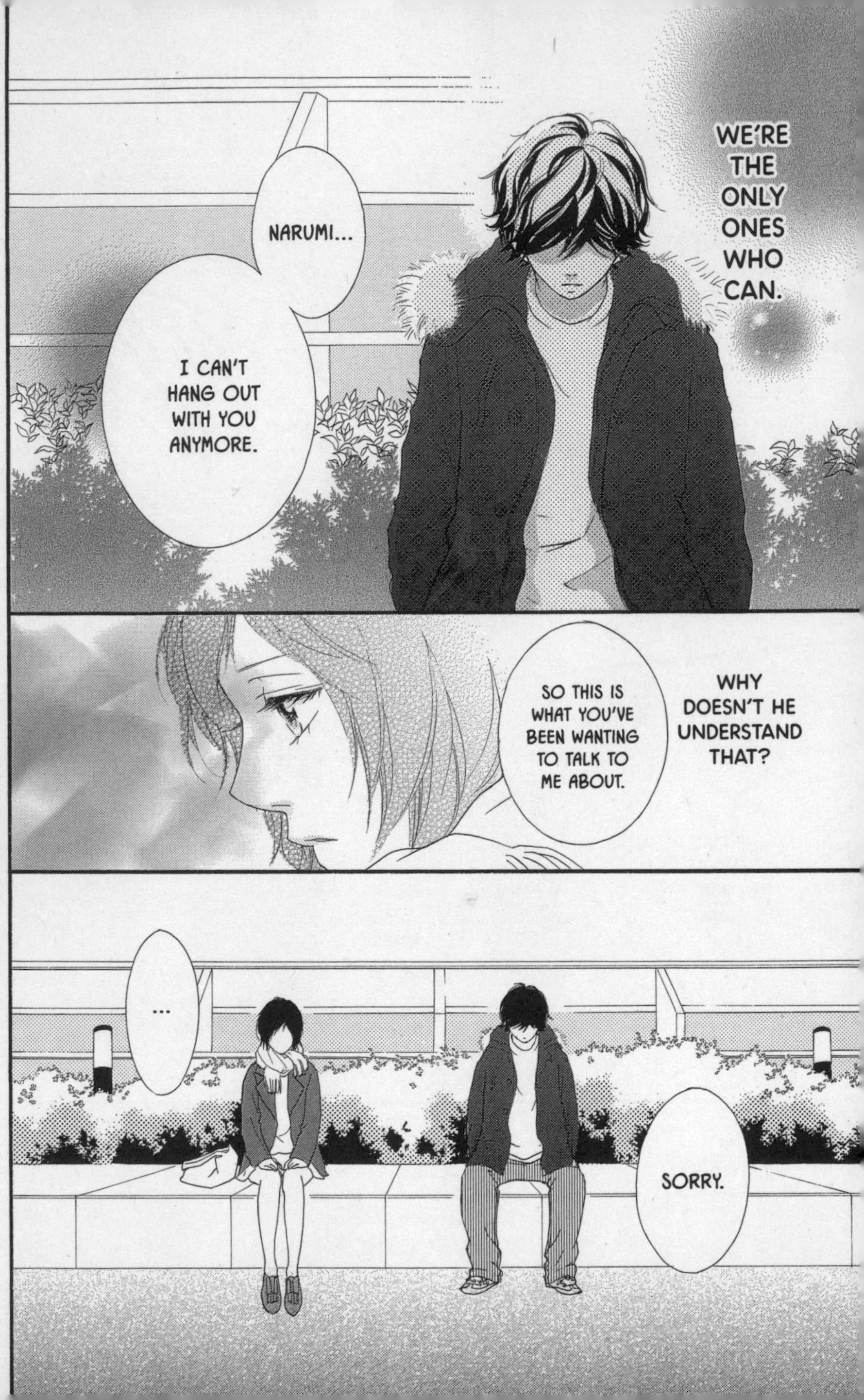
WE'RE THE ONLY ONES WHO CAN.
NARUMI...
I CAN'T HANG OUT WITH YOU ANYMORE.
WHY DOESN'T HE UNDERSTAND THAT?
SO THIS IS WHAT YOU'VE BEEN WANTING TO TALK TO ME ABOUT.
SORRY.
...

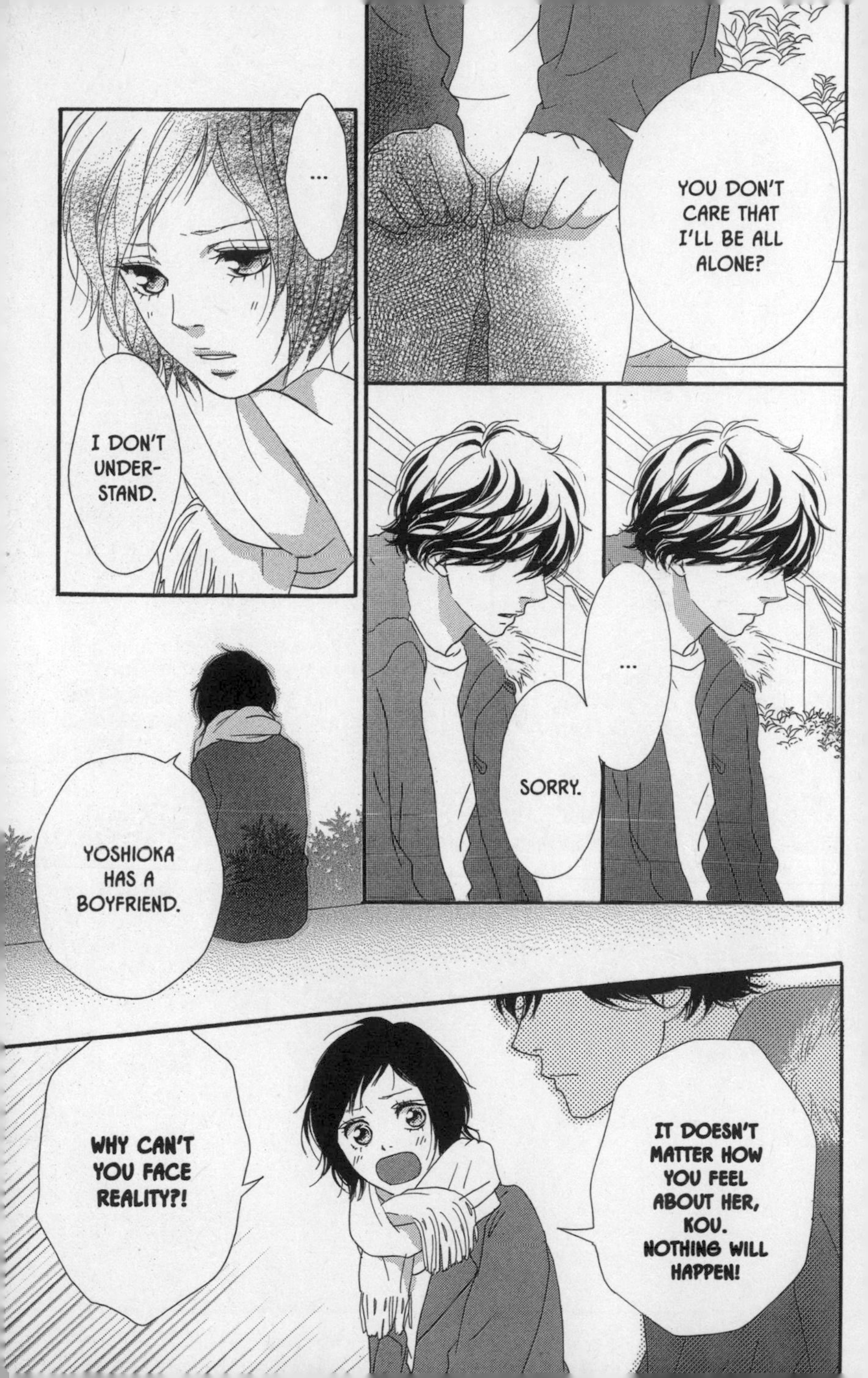
YOU DON'T CARE THAT I'LL BE ALL ALONE?
...
I DON'T UNDER-STAND.
...
SORRY.
YOSHIOKA HAS A BOYFRIEND.
IT DOESN'T MATTER HOW YOU FEEL ABOUT HER, KOU. NOTHING WILL HAPPEN!
WHY CAN'T YOU FACE REALITY?!

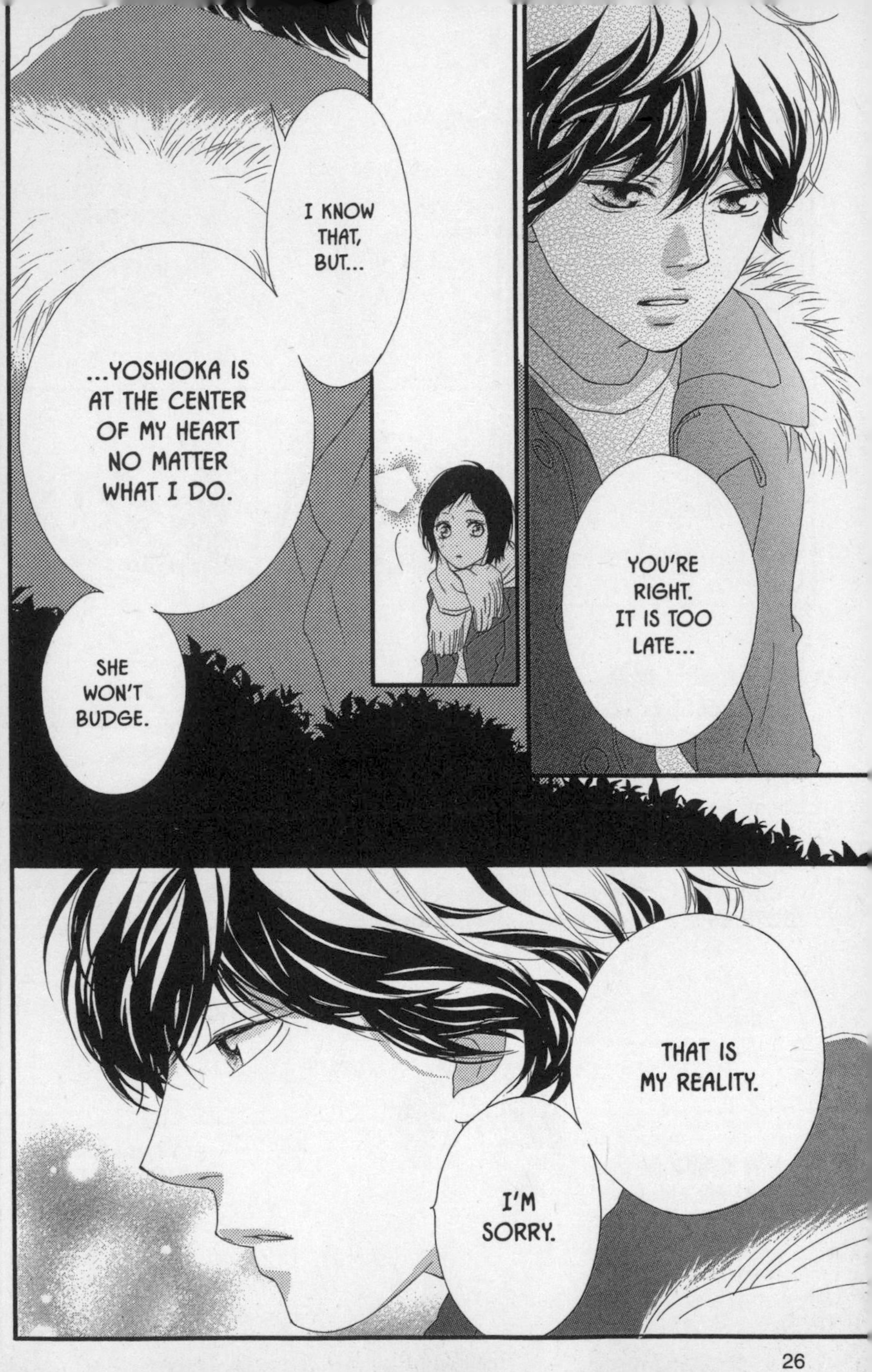
YOU'RE RIGHT. IT IS TOO LATE...
I KNOW THAT, BUT...
...YOSHIOKA IS AT THE CENTER OF MY HEART NO MATTER WHAT I DO.
SHE WON'T BUDGE.
THAT IS MY REALITY.
I'M SORRY.

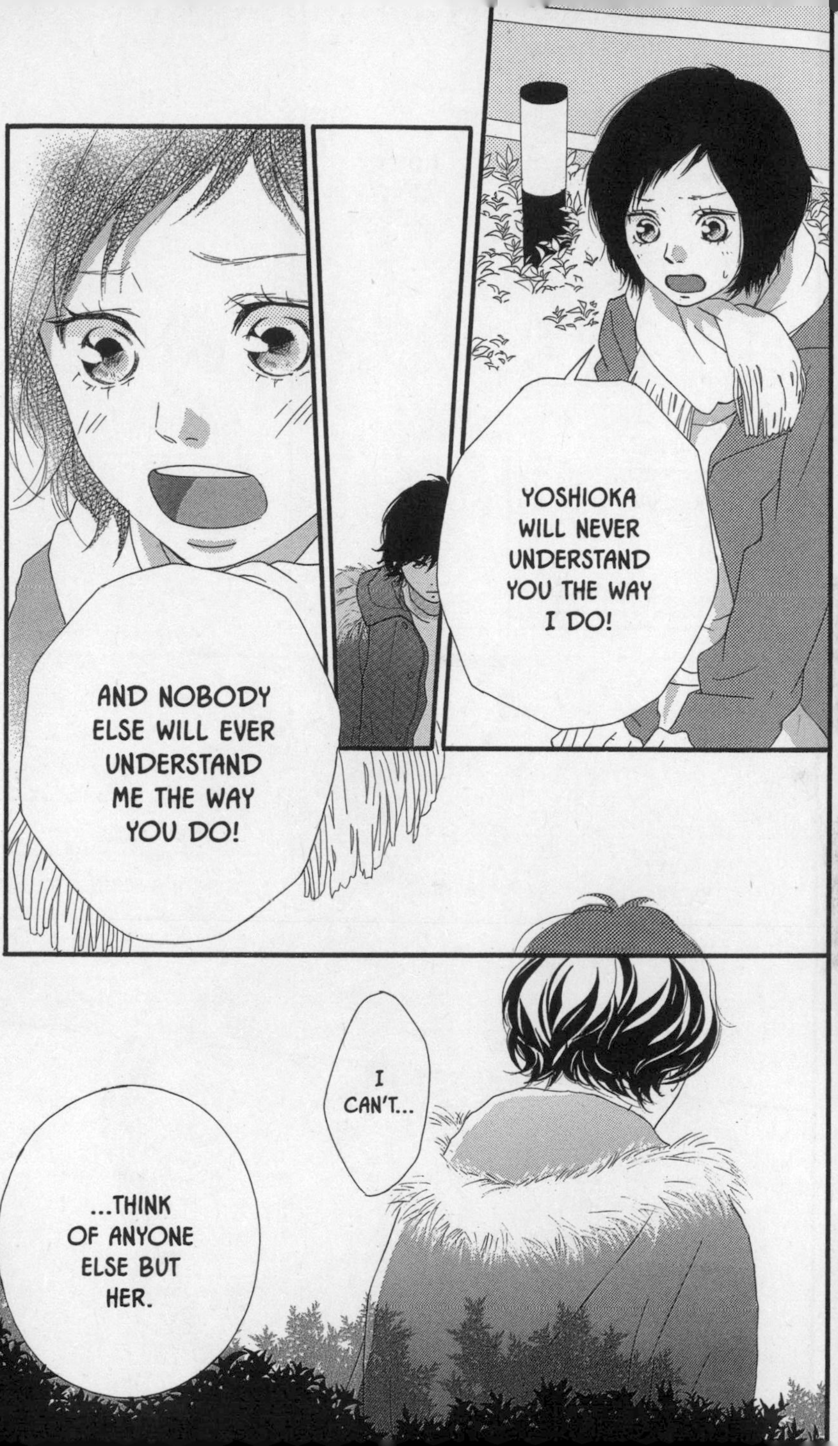
YOSHIOKA WILL NEVER UNDERSTAND YOU THE WAY I DO!
AND NOBODY ELSE WILL EVER UNDERSTAND ME THE WAY YOU DO!
I CAN'T...
...THINK OF ANYONE ELSE BUT HER.

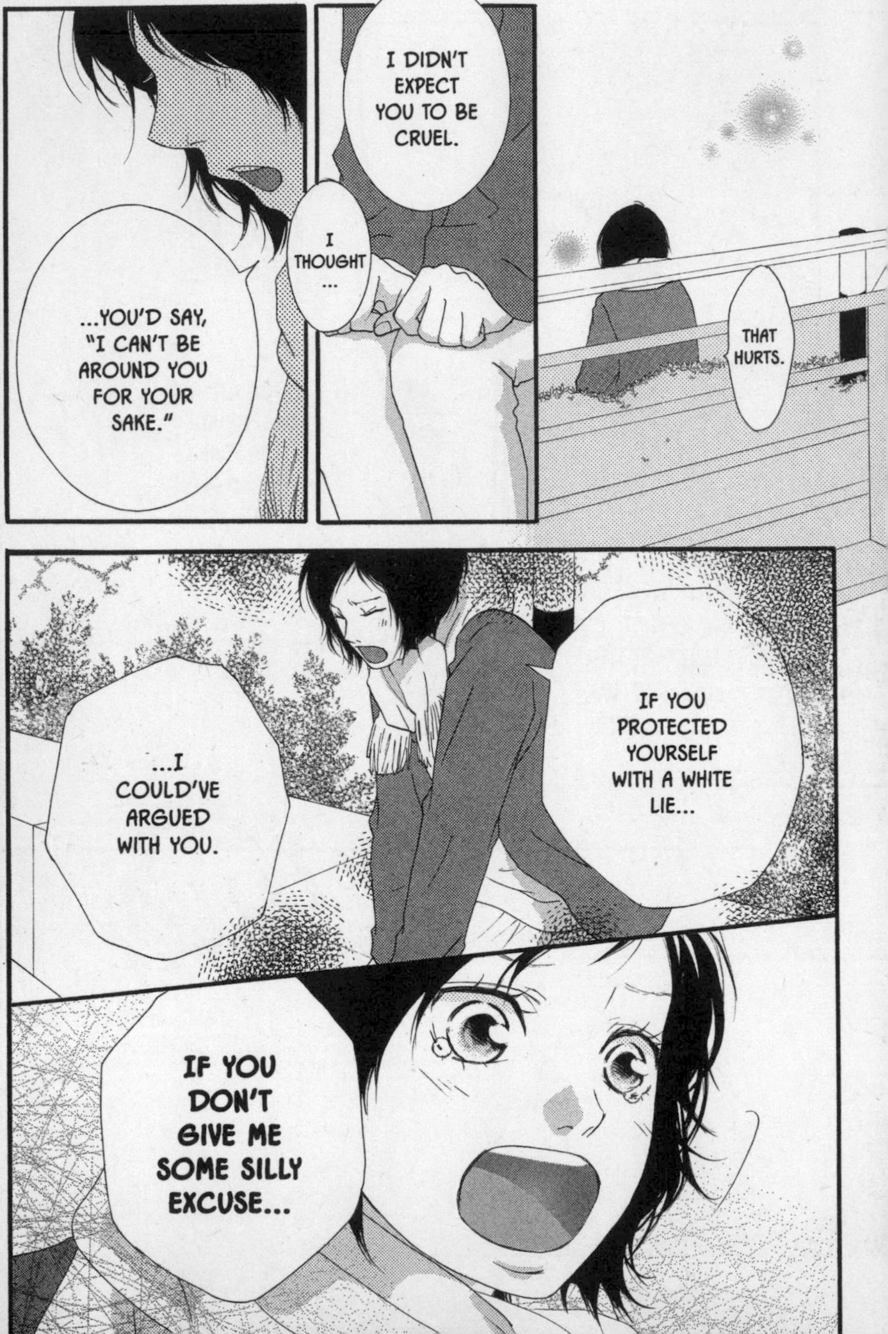
THAT HURTS.
I DIDN'T EXPECT YOU TO BE CRUEL.
I THOUGHT...
...YOU'D SAY, "I CAN'T BE AROUND YOU FOR YOUR SAKE."
IF YOU PROTECTED YOURSELF WITH A WHITE LIE...
...I COULD'VE ARGUED WITH YOU.
IF YOU DON'T GIVE ME SOME SILLY EXCUSE...

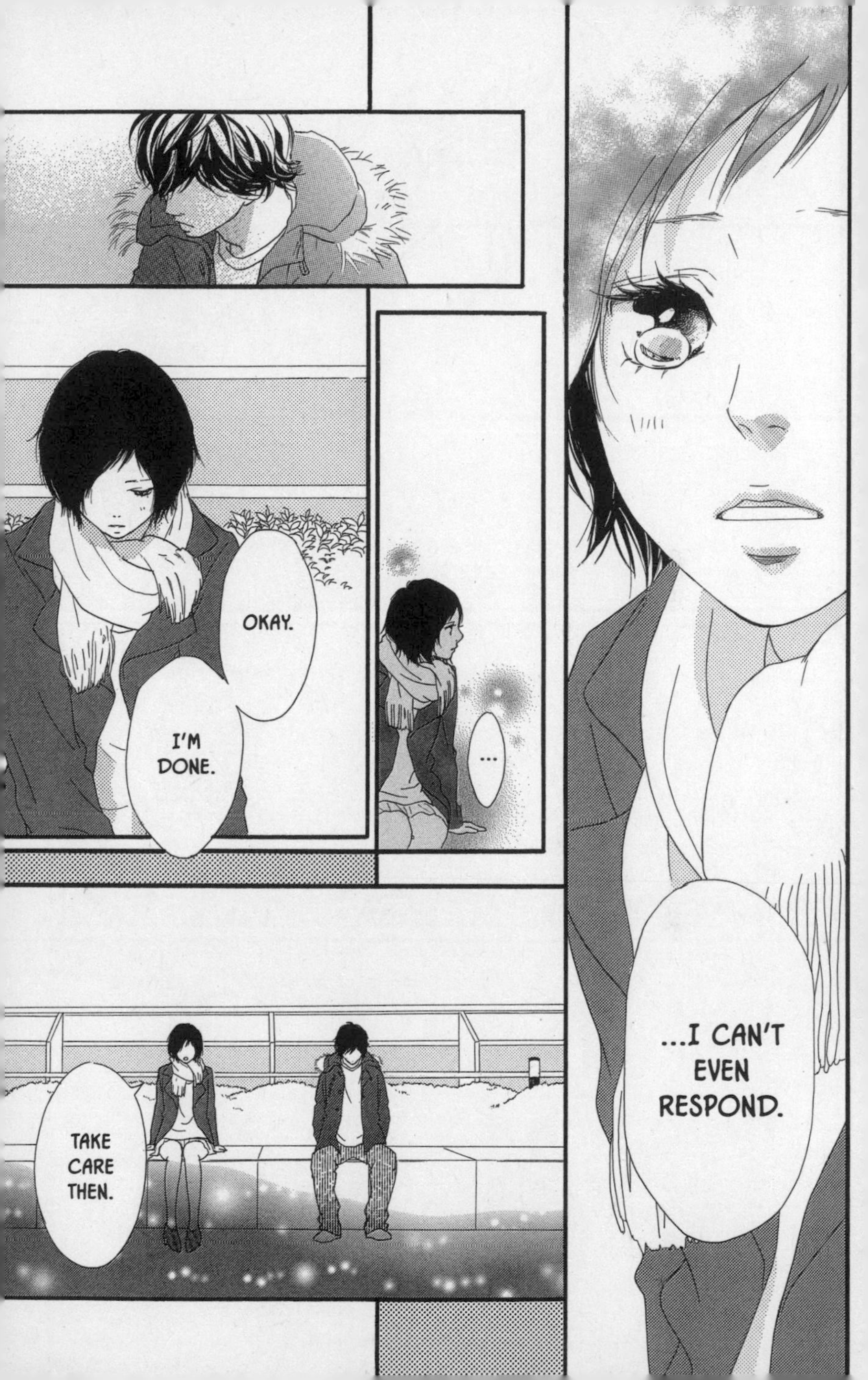
...I CAN'T EVEN RESPOND.
OKAY.
I'M DONE.
...
TAKE CARE THEN.

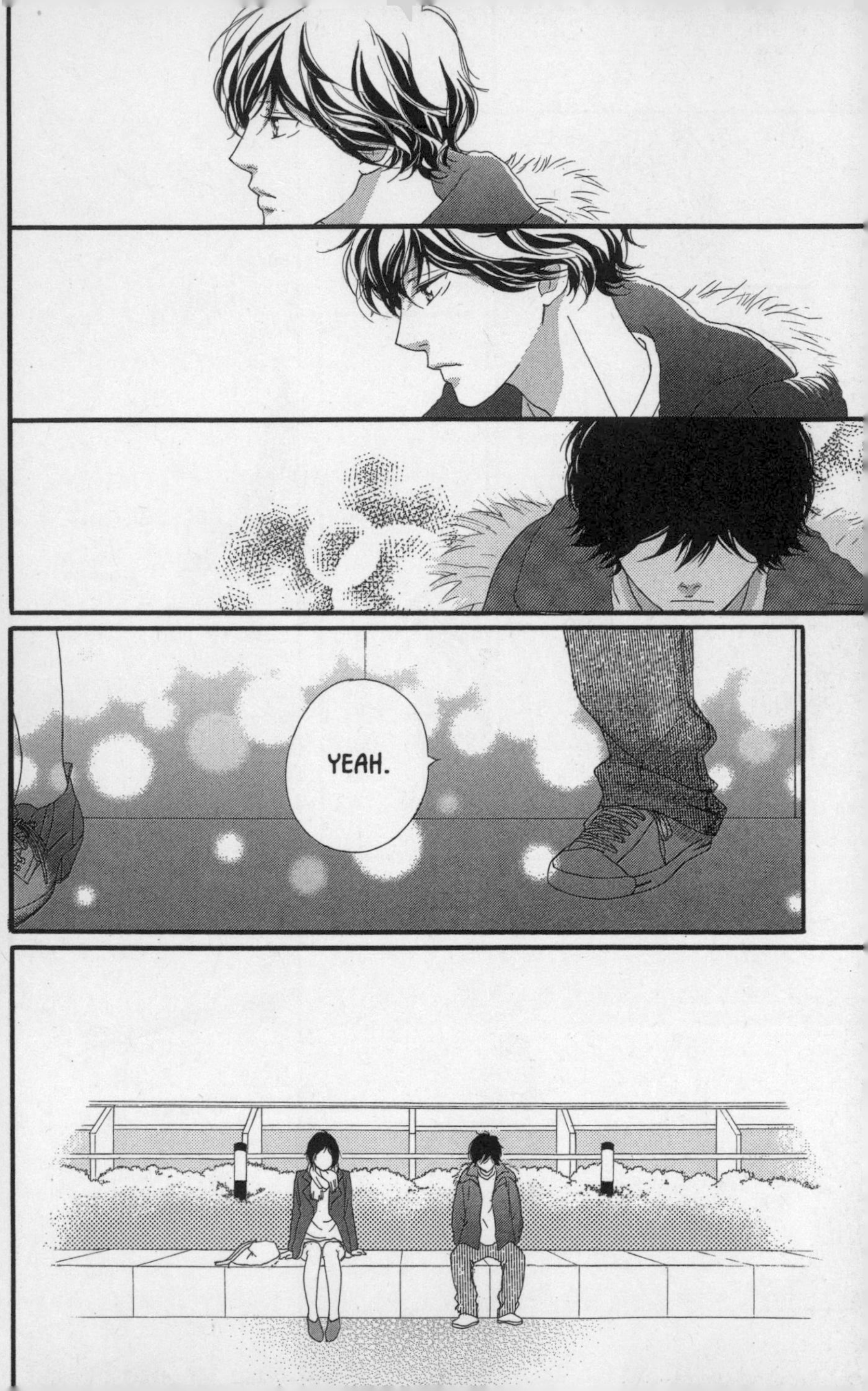
YEAH.

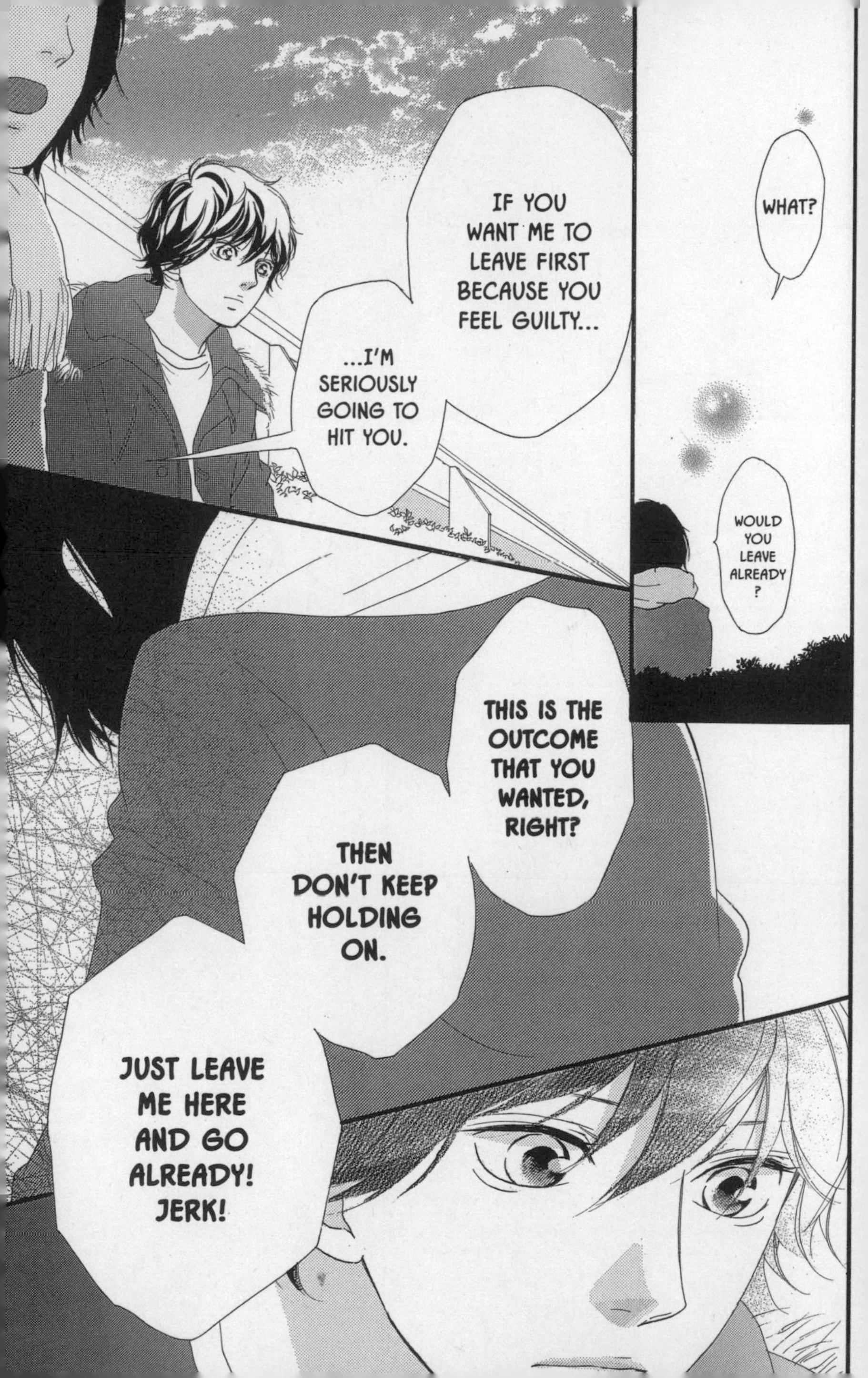
WHAT?
WOULD YOU LEAVE ALREADY?
IF YOU WANT ME TO LEAVE FIRST BECAUSE YOU FEEL GUILTY...
...I'M SERIOUSLY GOING TO HIT YOU.
THIS IS THE OUTCOME THAT YOU WANTED, RIGHT?
THEN DON'T KEEP HOLDING ON.
JUST LEAVE ME HERE AND GO ALREADY! JERK!

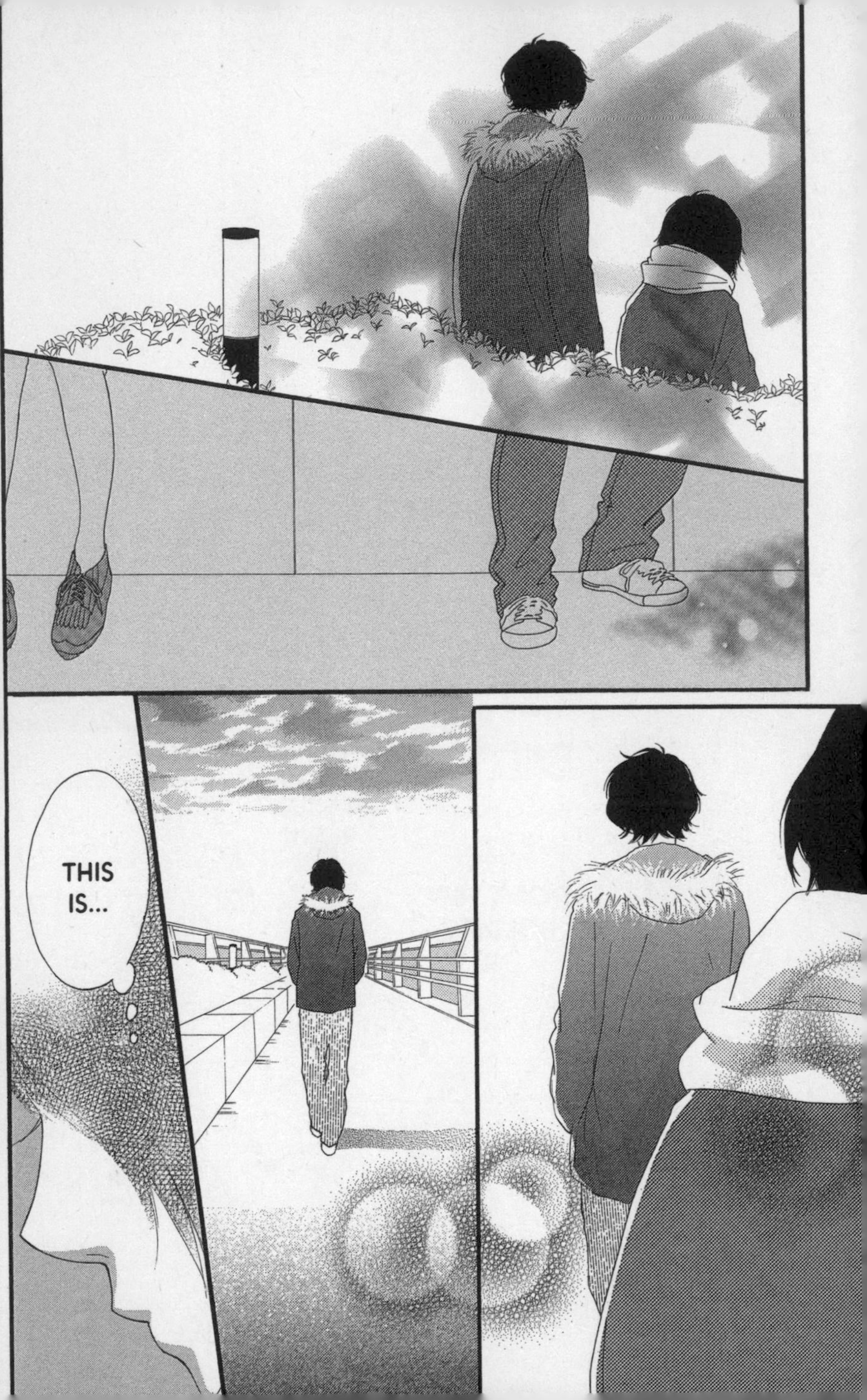
THIS IS...

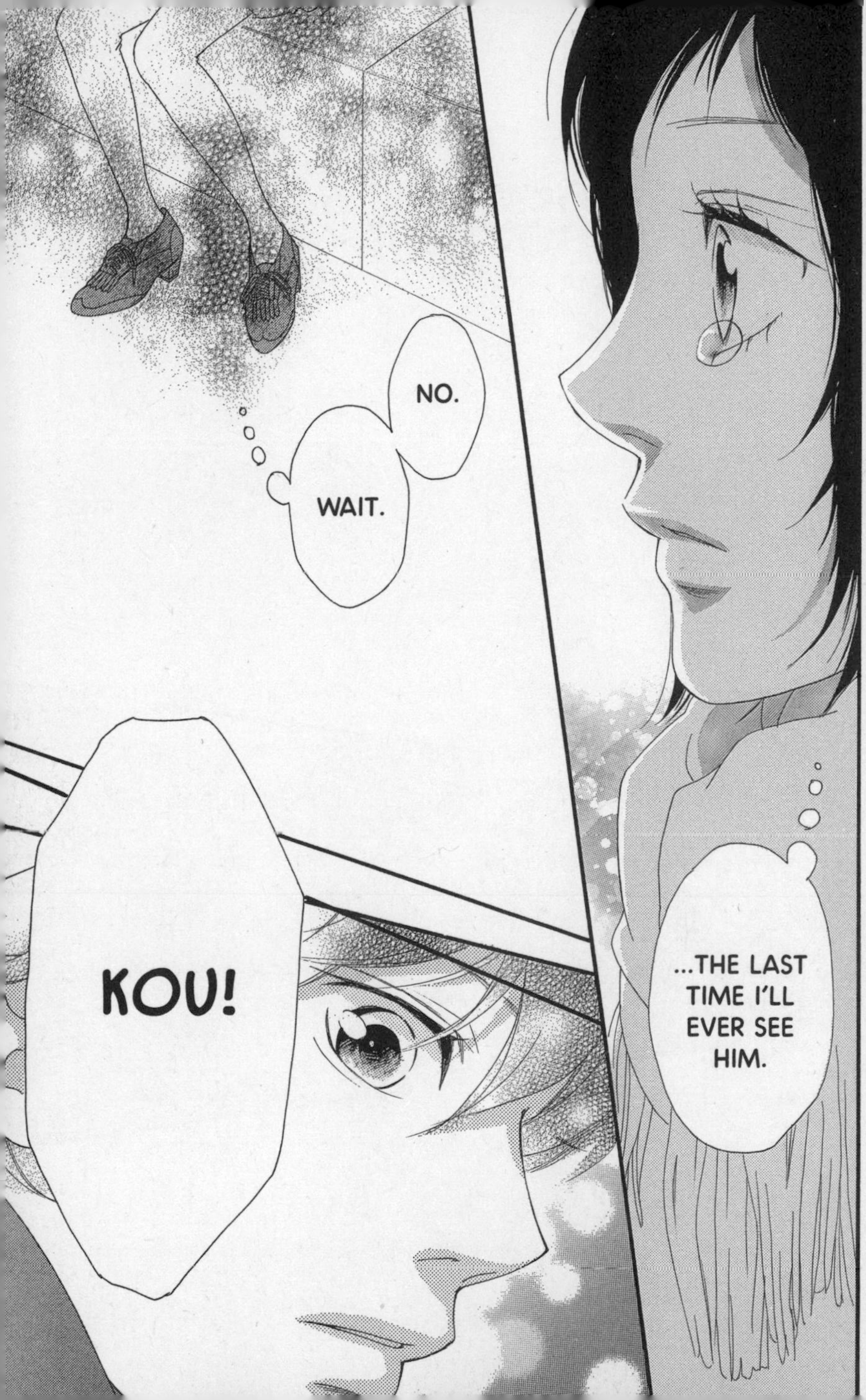
...THE LAST TIME I'LL EVER SEE HIM.
NO.
WAIT.
KOU!

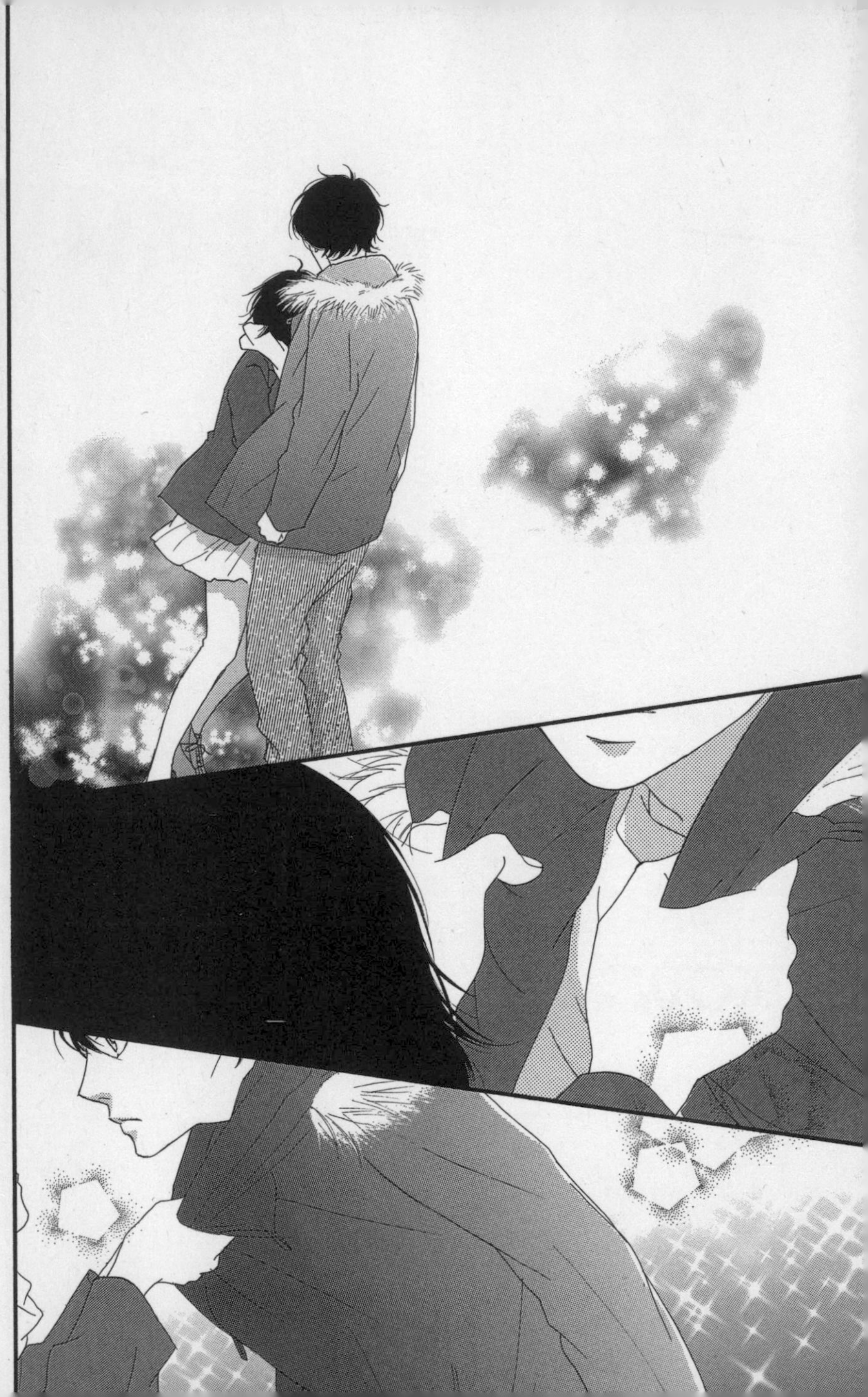

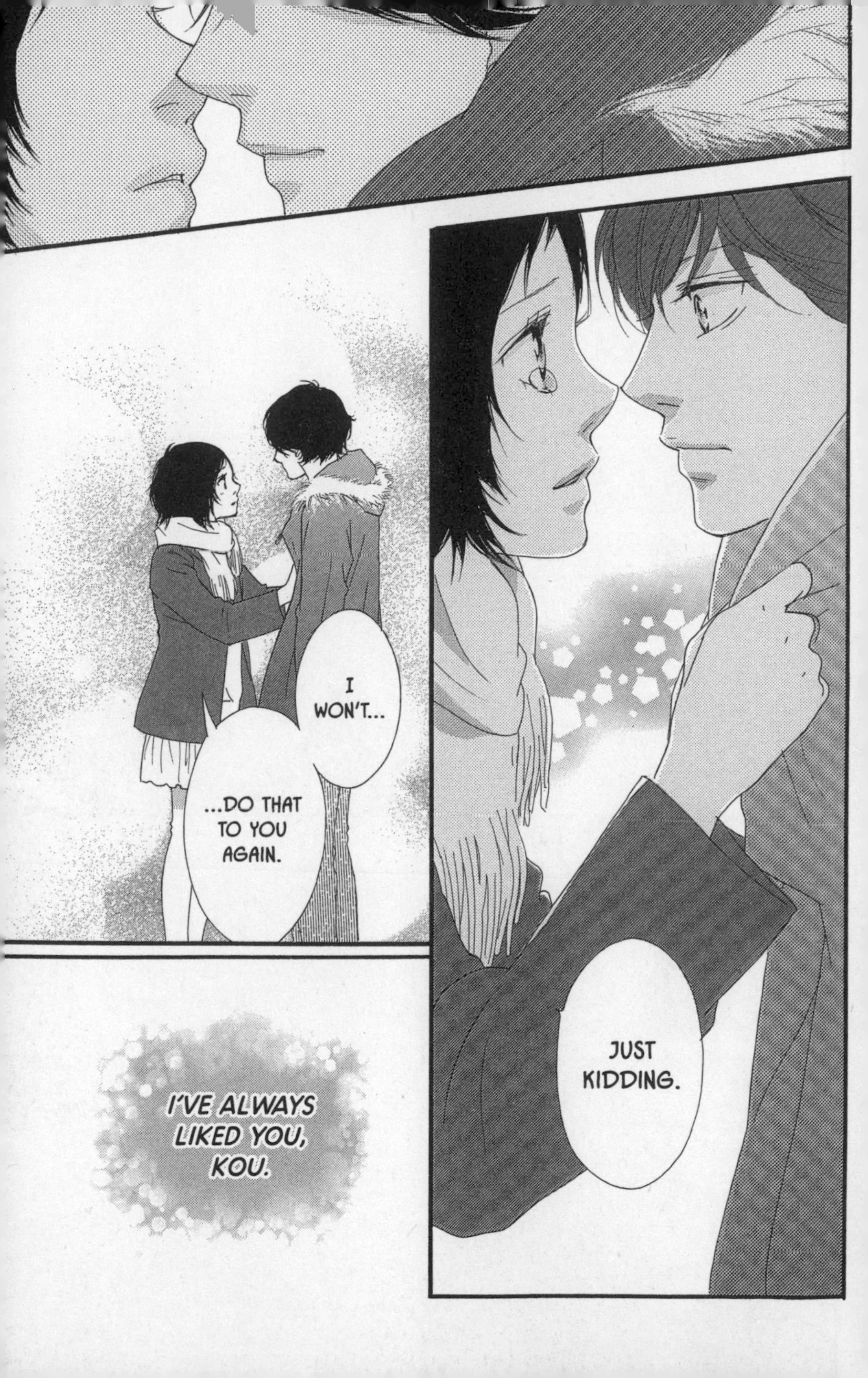
JUST KIDDING.
I WON'T...
...DO THAT TO YOU AGAIN.
I'VE ALWAYS LIKED YOU, KOU.

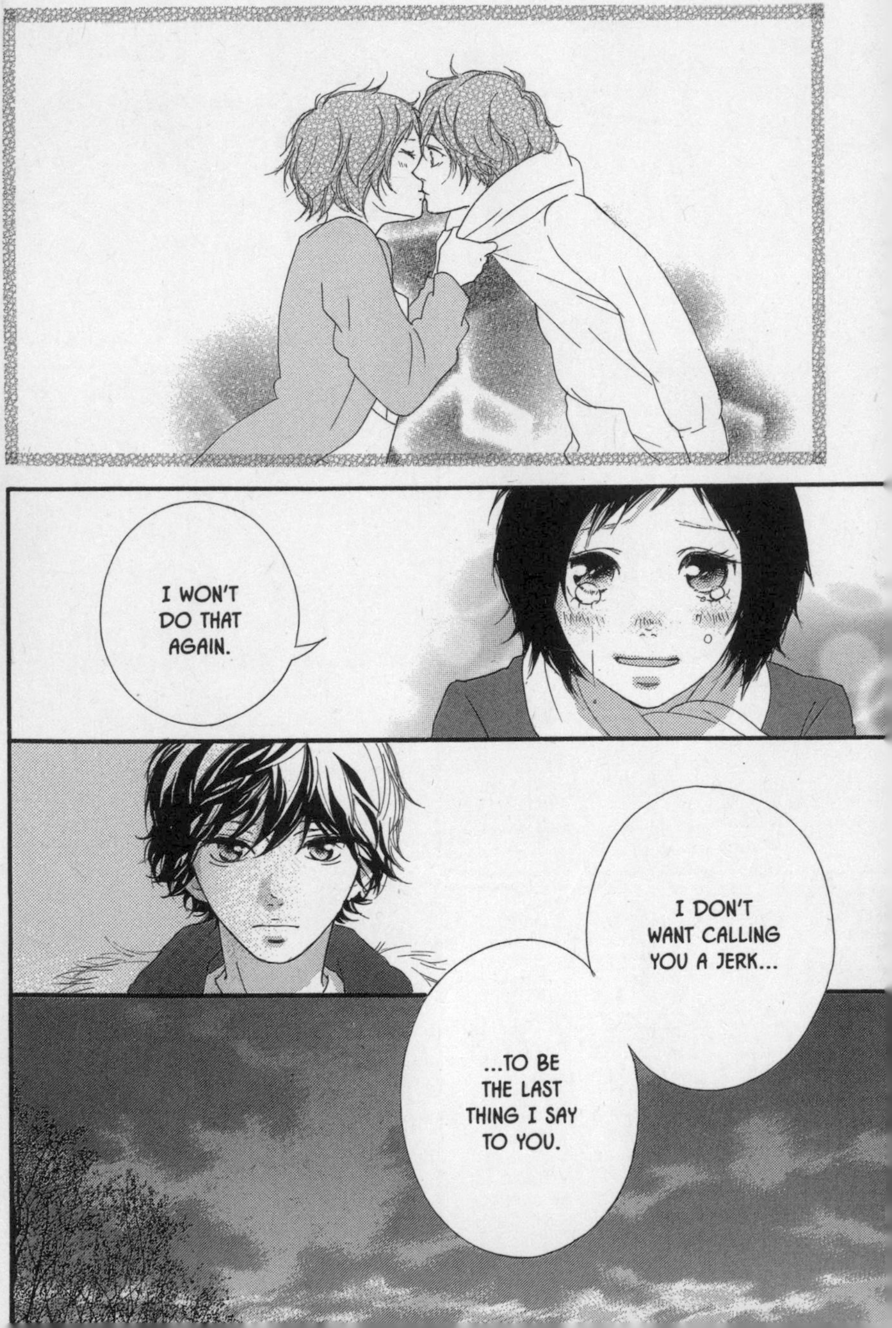
I WON'T DO THAT AGAIN.
I DON'T WANT CALLING YOU A JERK...
...TO BE THE LAST THING I SAY TO YOU.

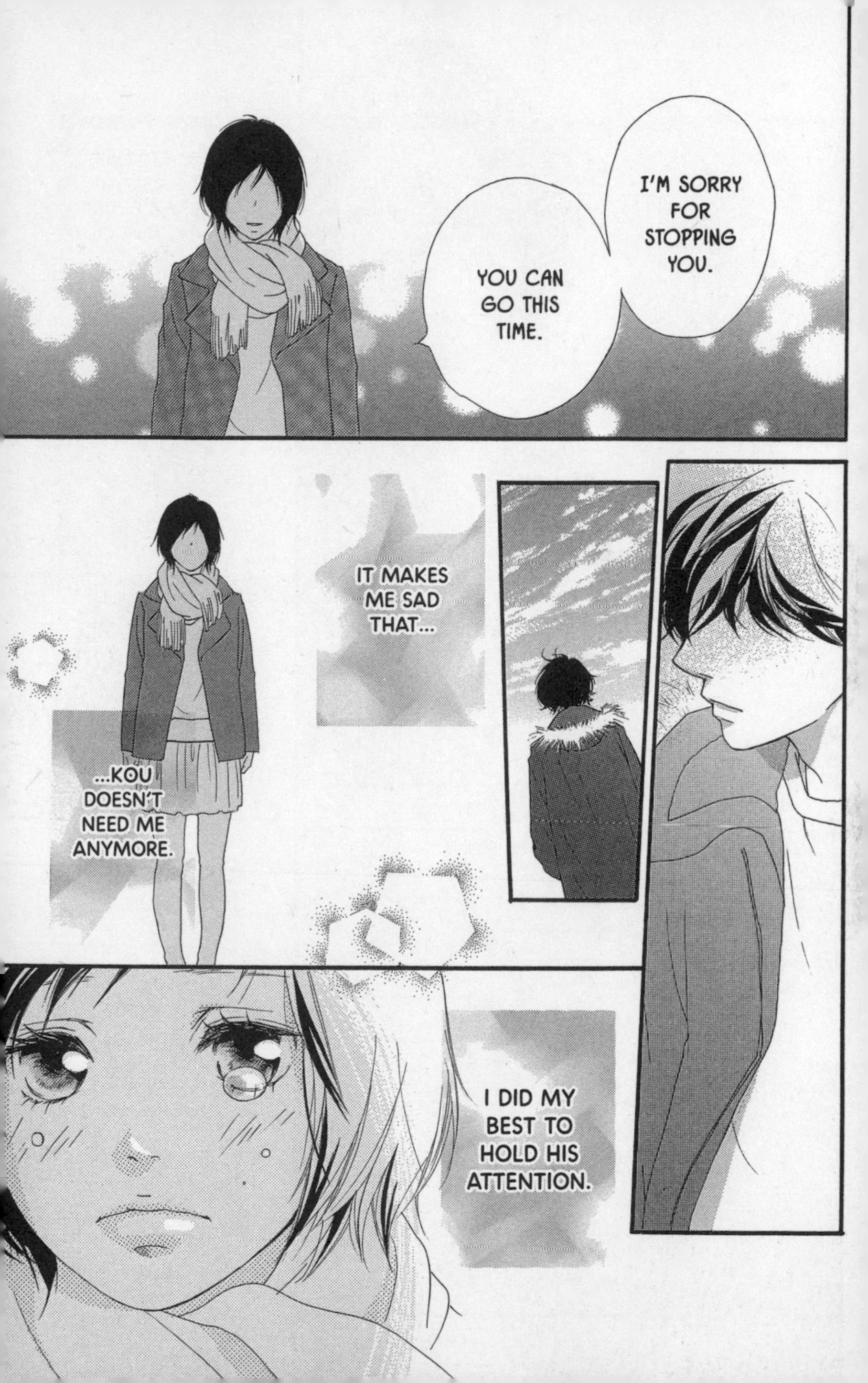
I'M SORRY FOR STOPPING YOU.
YOU CAN GO THIS TIME.
IT MAKES ME SAD THAT...
...KOU DOESN'T NEED ME ANYMORE.
I DID MY BEST TO HOLD HIS ATTENTION.

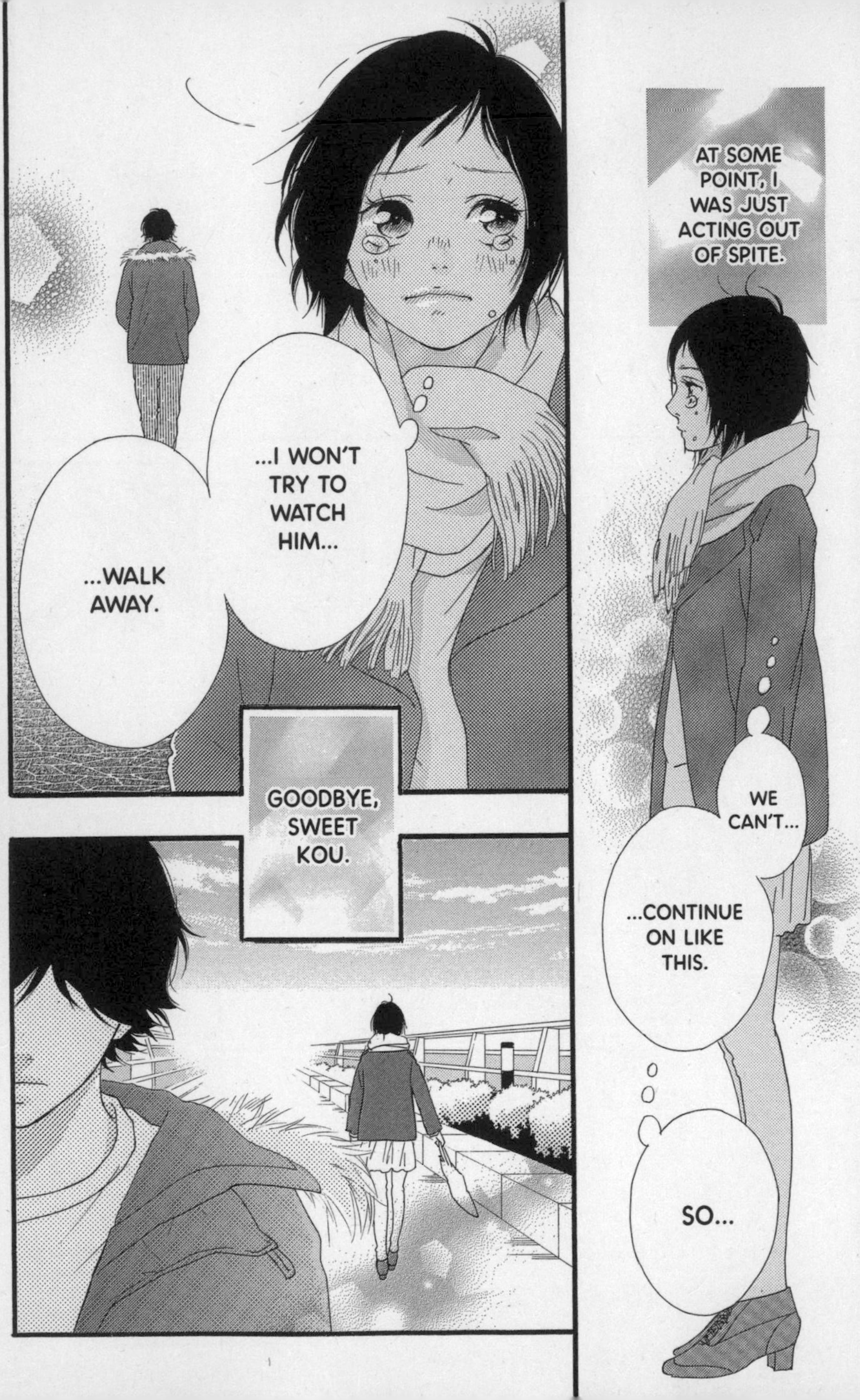
AT SOME POINT, I WAS JUST ACTING OUT OF SPITE.
WE CAN'T...
...CONTINUE ON LIKE THIS.
SO...
...I WON'T TRY TO WATCH HIM...
...WALK AWAY.
GOODBYE, SWEET KOU.

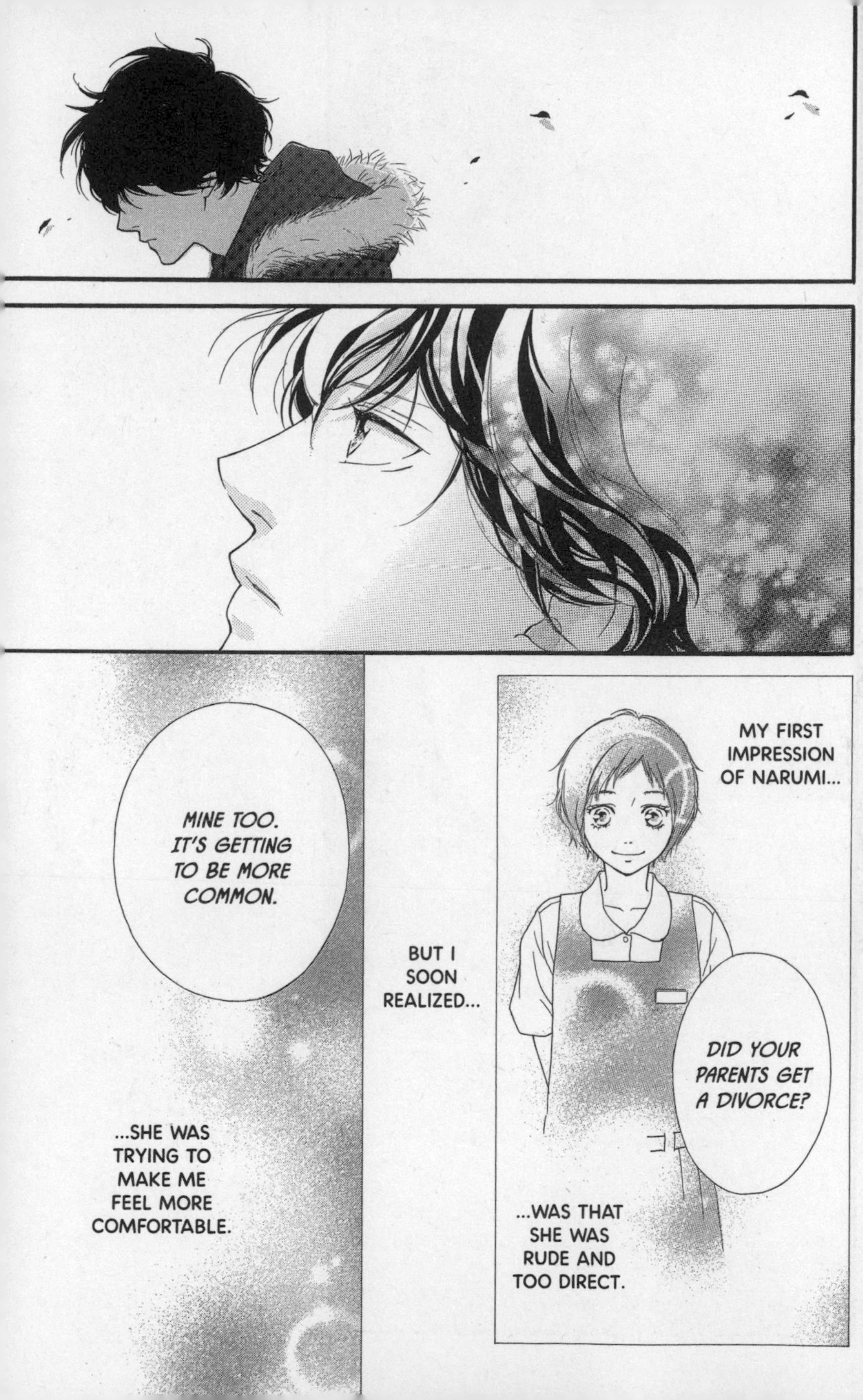
MY FIRST IMPRESSION OF NARUMI...
DID YOUR PARENTS GET A DIVORCE?
...WAS THAT SHE WAS RUDE AND TOO DIRECT.
BUT I SOON REALIZED...
MINE TOO. IT'S GETTING TO BE MORE COMMON.
...SHE WAS TRYING TO MAKE ME FEEL MORE COMFORTABLE.

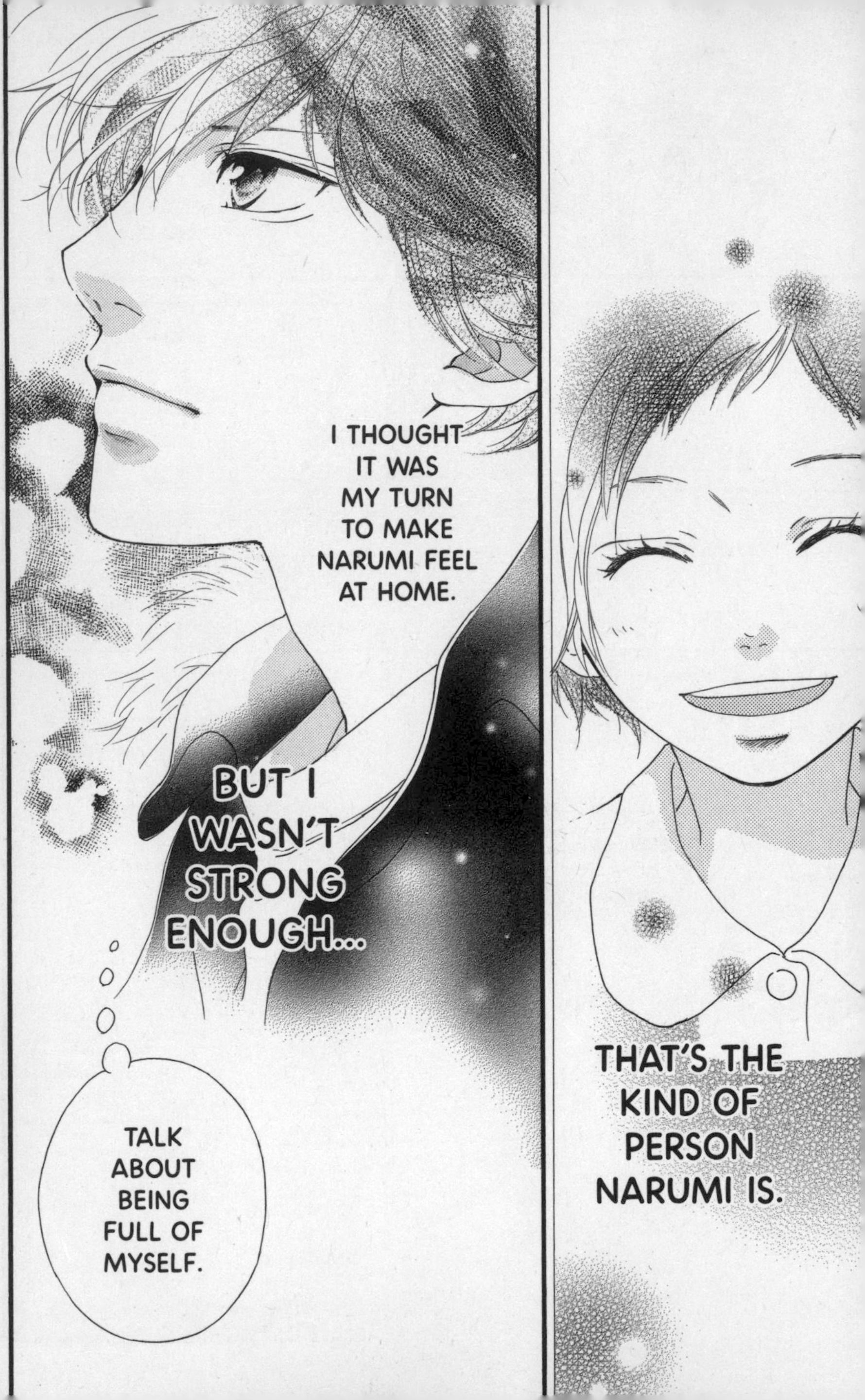
THAT'S THE KIND OF PERSON NARUMI IS.
I THOUGHT IT WAS MY TURN TO MAKE NARUMI FEEL AT HOME.
BUT I WASN'T STRONG ENOUGH...
TALK ABOUT BEING FULL OF MYSELF.

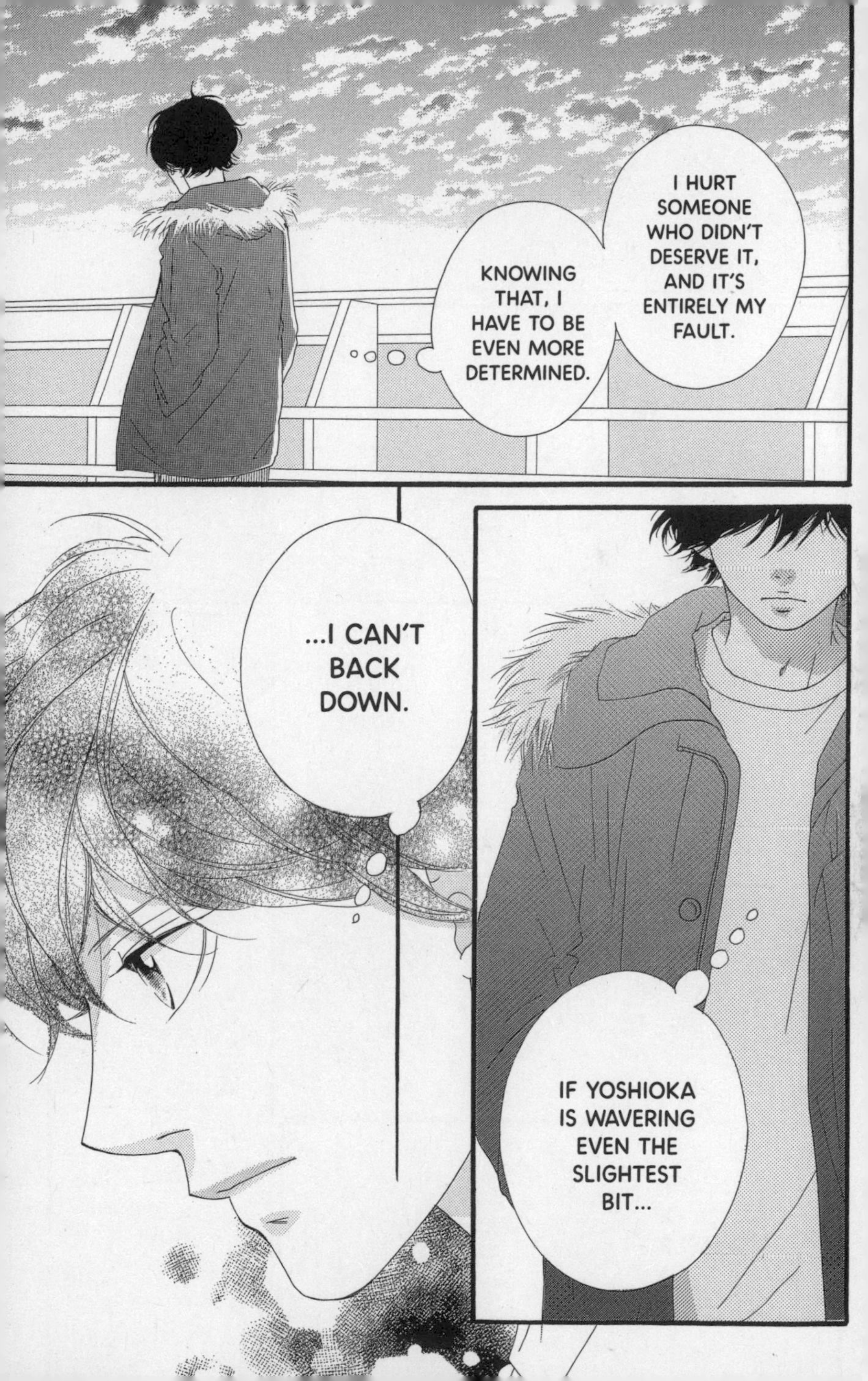
I HURT SOMEONE WHO DIDN'T DESERVE IT, AND IT'S ENTIRELY MY FAULT.
KNOWING THAT, I HAVE TO BE EVEN MORE DETERMINED.
IF YOSHIOKA IS WAVERING EVEN THE SLIGHTEST BIT...
...I CAN'T BACK DOWN.

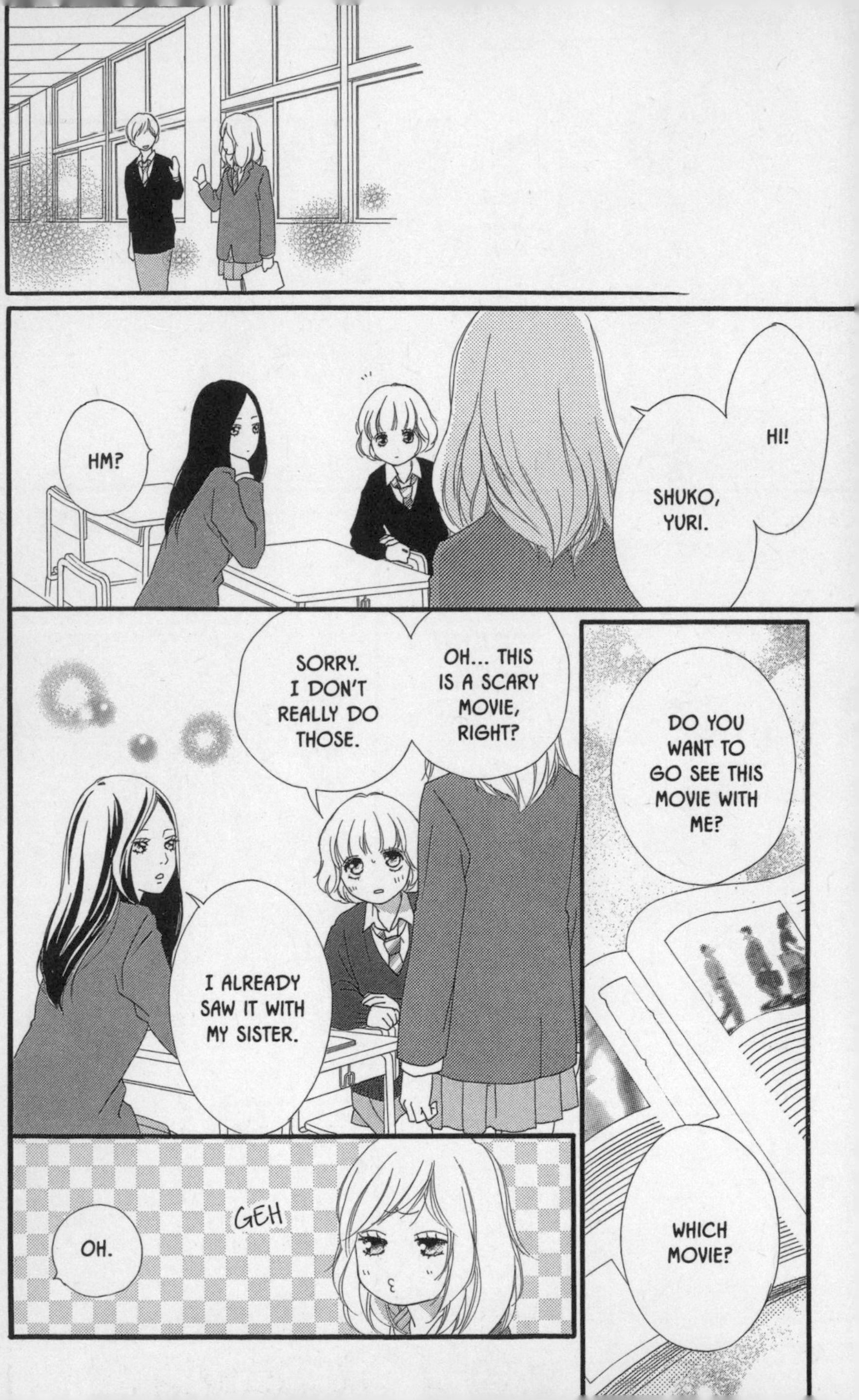
HI!
SHUKO, YURI.
HM?
DO YOU WANT TO GO SEE THIS MOVIE WITH ME?
WHICH MOVIE?
OH... THIS IS A SCARY MOVIE, RIGHT?
SORRY. I DON'T REALLY DO THOSE.
I ALREADY SAW IT WITH MY SISTER.
GEH
OH.

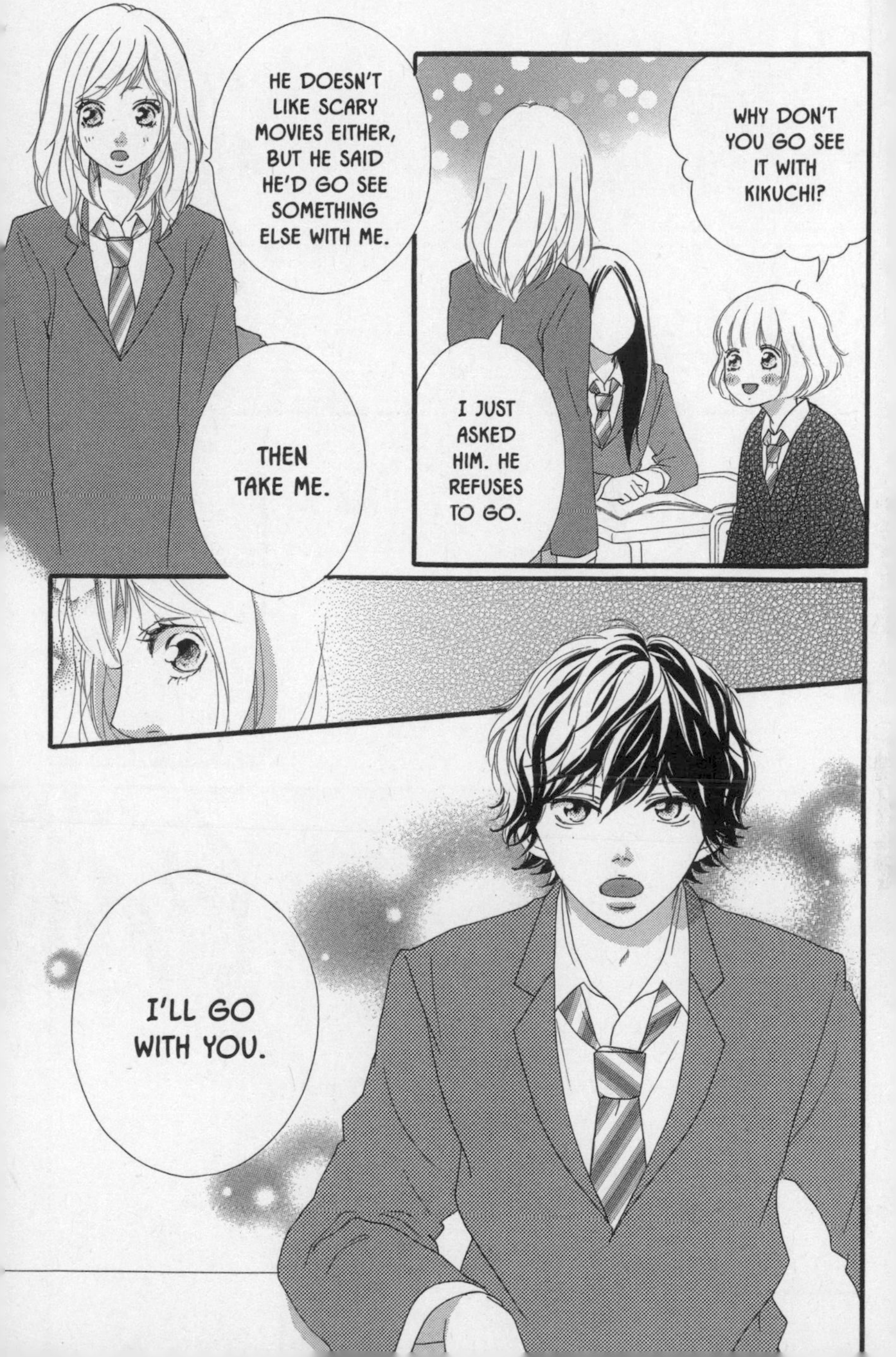
WHY DON'T YOU GO SEE IT WITH KIKUCHI?
I JUST ASKED HIM. HE REFUSES TO GO.
HE DOESN'T LIKE SCARY MOVIES EITHER, BUT HE SAID HE'D GO SEE SOMETHING ELSE WITH ME.
THEN TAKE ME.
I'LL GO WITH YOU.

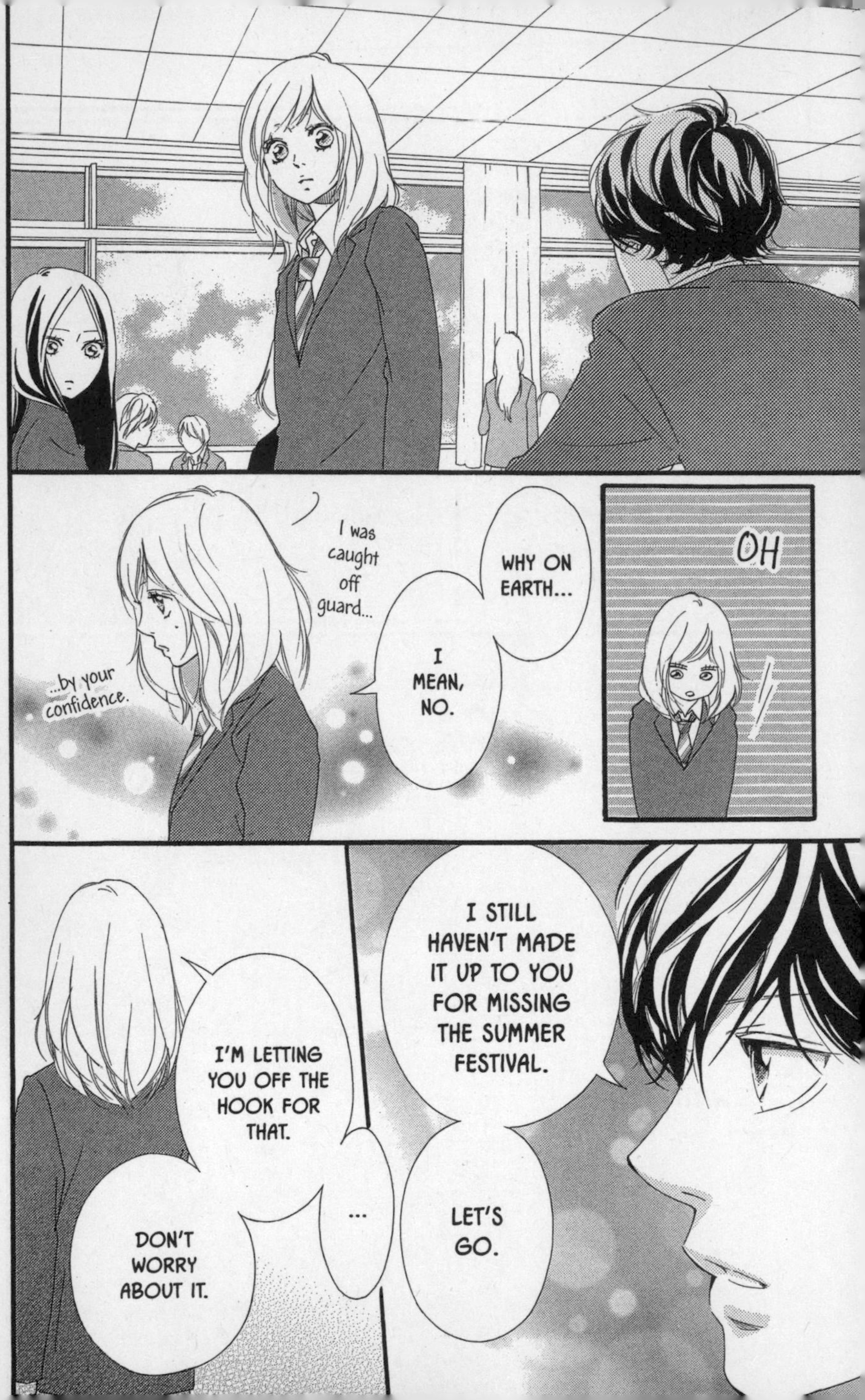
OH
WHY ON EARTH...
I MEAN, NO.
I was caught off guard...
...by your confidence.
I STILL HAVEN'T MADE IT UP TO YOU FOR MISSING THE SUMMER FESTIVAL.
LET'S GO.
...
I'M LETTING YOU OFF THE HOOK FOR THAT.
DON'T WORRY ABOUT IT.

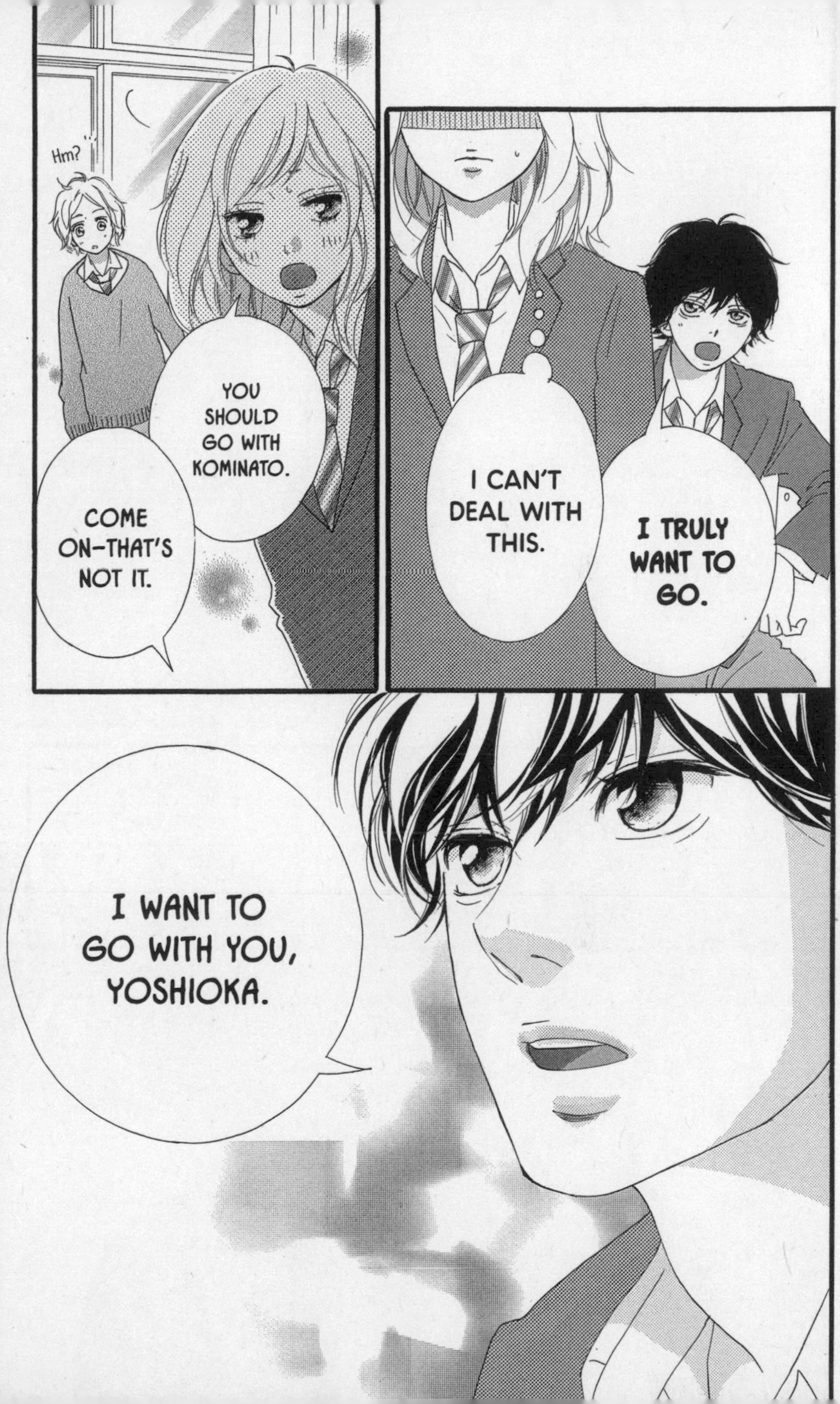
I TRULY WANT TO GO.
I CAN'T DEAL WITH THIS.
Hm?
YOU SHOULD GO WITH KOMINATO.
COME ON—THAT'S NOT IT.
I WANT TO GO WITH YOU, YOSHIOKA.

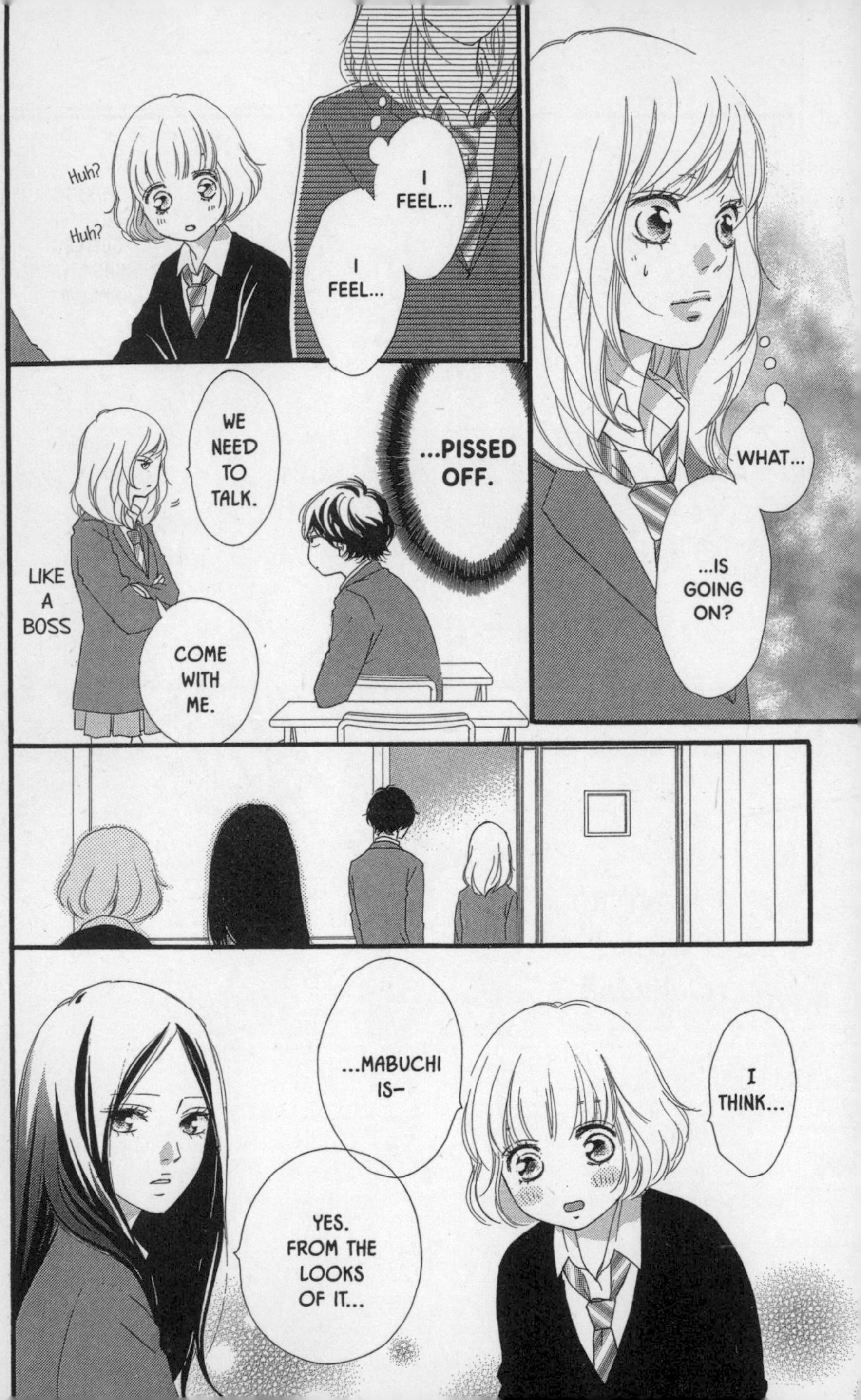
WHAT...
...IS GOING ON?
I FEEL...
I FEEL...
Huh?
Huh?
...PISSED OFF.
WE NEED TO TALK.
LIKE A BOSS
COME WITH ME.
I THINK...
...MABUCHI IS–
YES. FROM THE LOOKS OF IT...

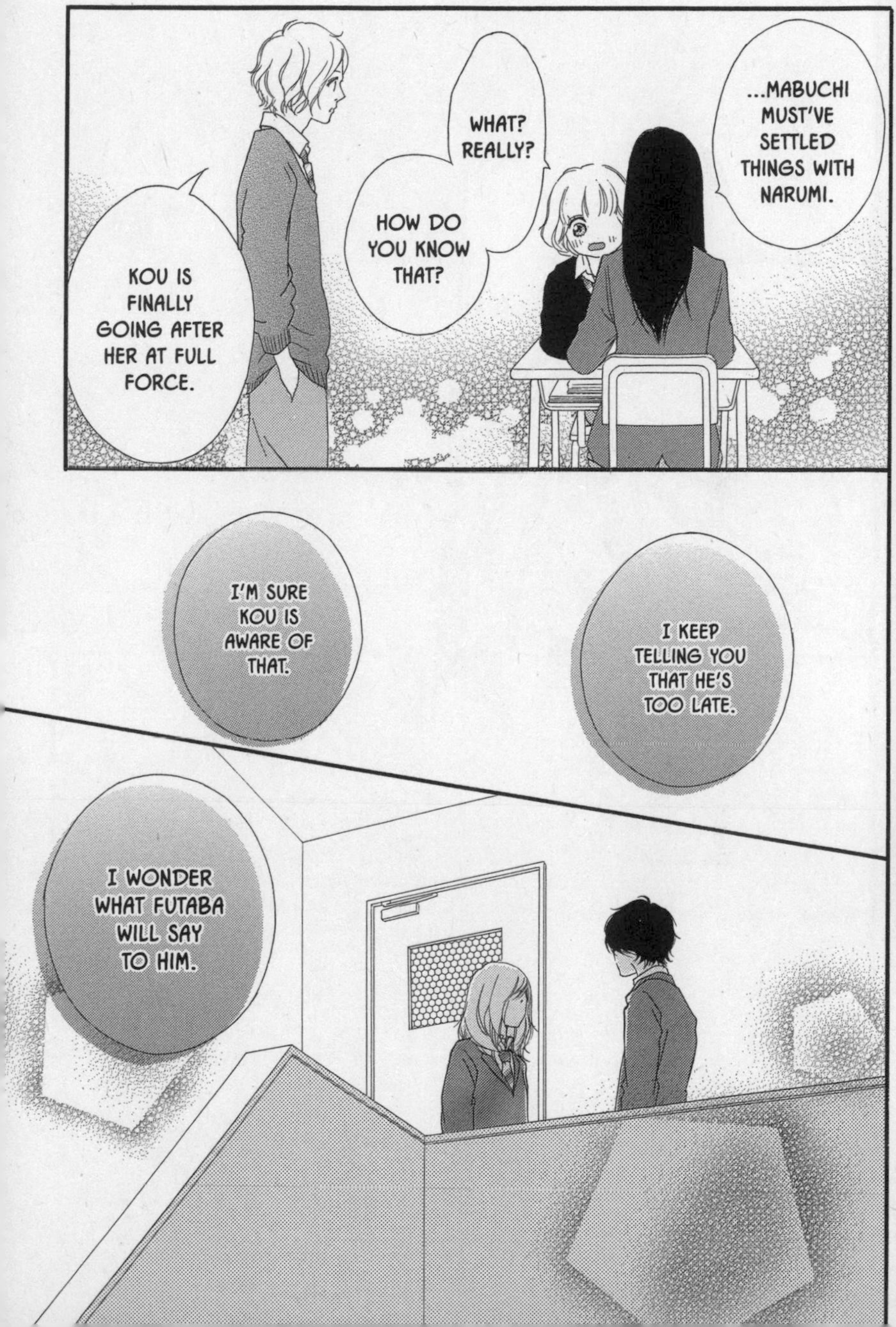
...MABUCHI MUST'VE SETTLED THINGS WITH NARUMI.
WHAT? REALLY?
HOW DO YOU KNOW THAT?
KOU IS FINALLY GOING AFTER HER AT FULL FORCE.
I KEEP TELLING YOU THAT HE'S TOO LATE.
I'M SURE KOU IS AWARE OF THAT.
I WONDER WHAT FUTABA WILL SAY TO HIM.

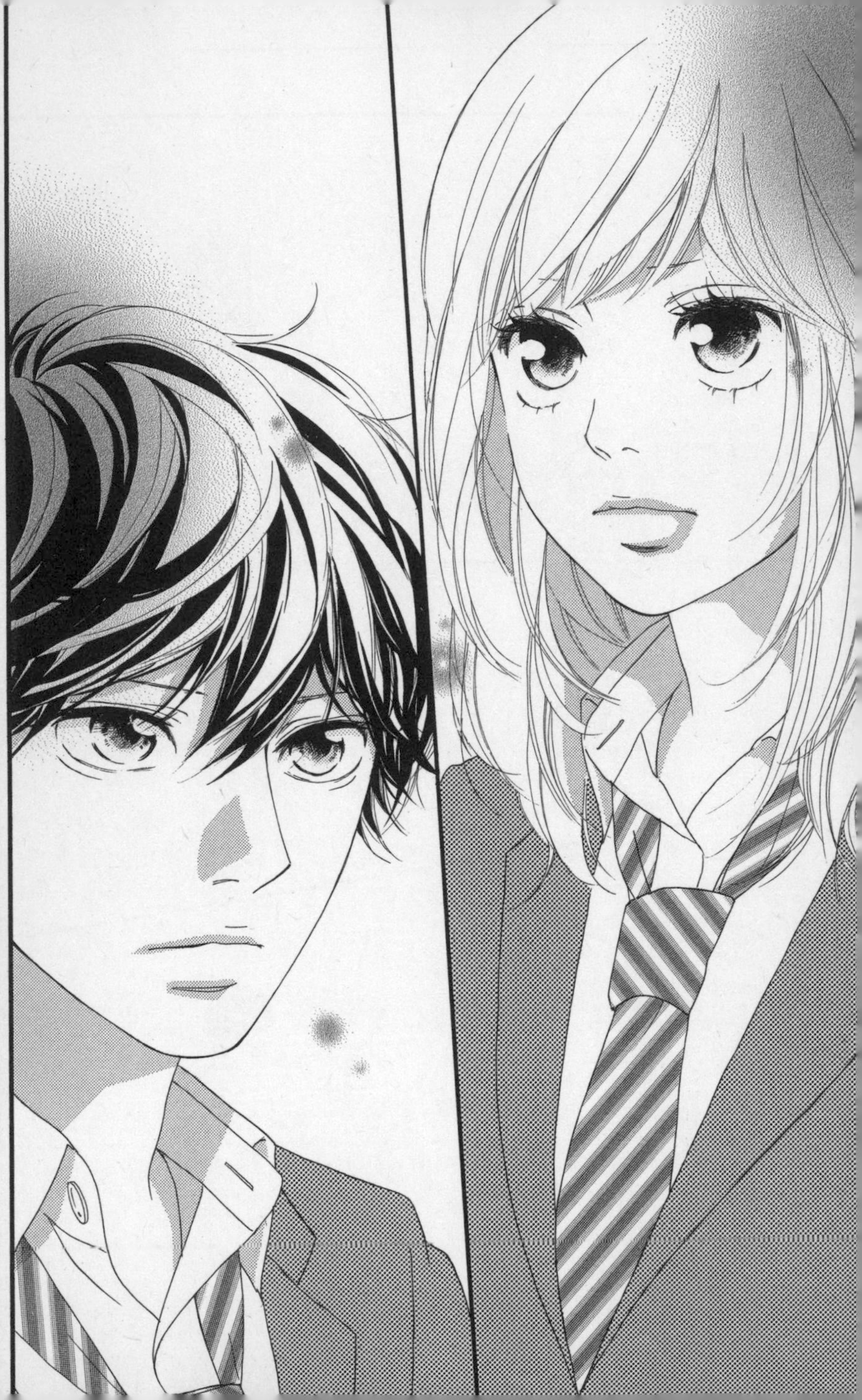

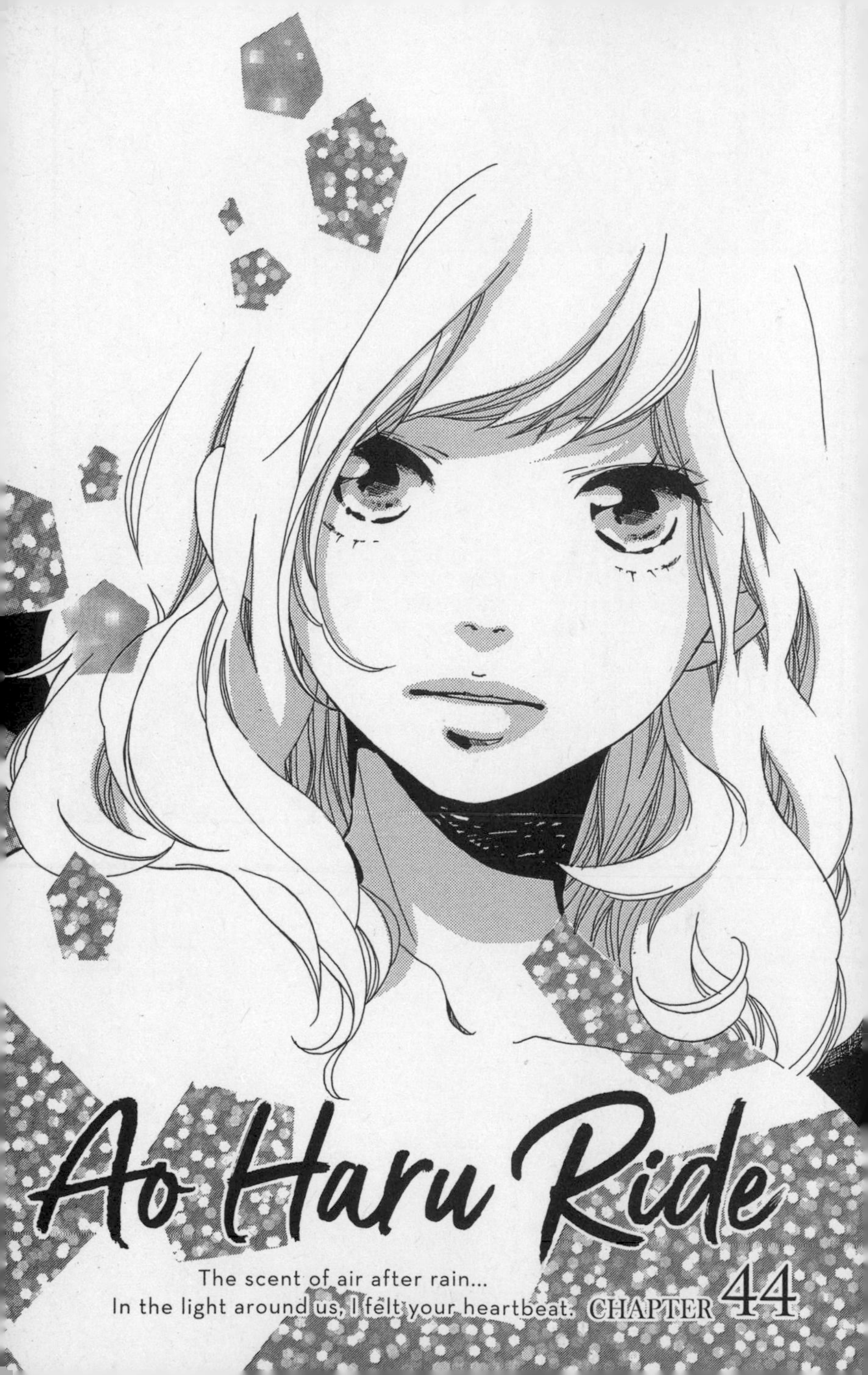
Ao Haru Ride
The scent of air after rain...
In the light around us, I felt your heartbeat.
CHAPTER 44

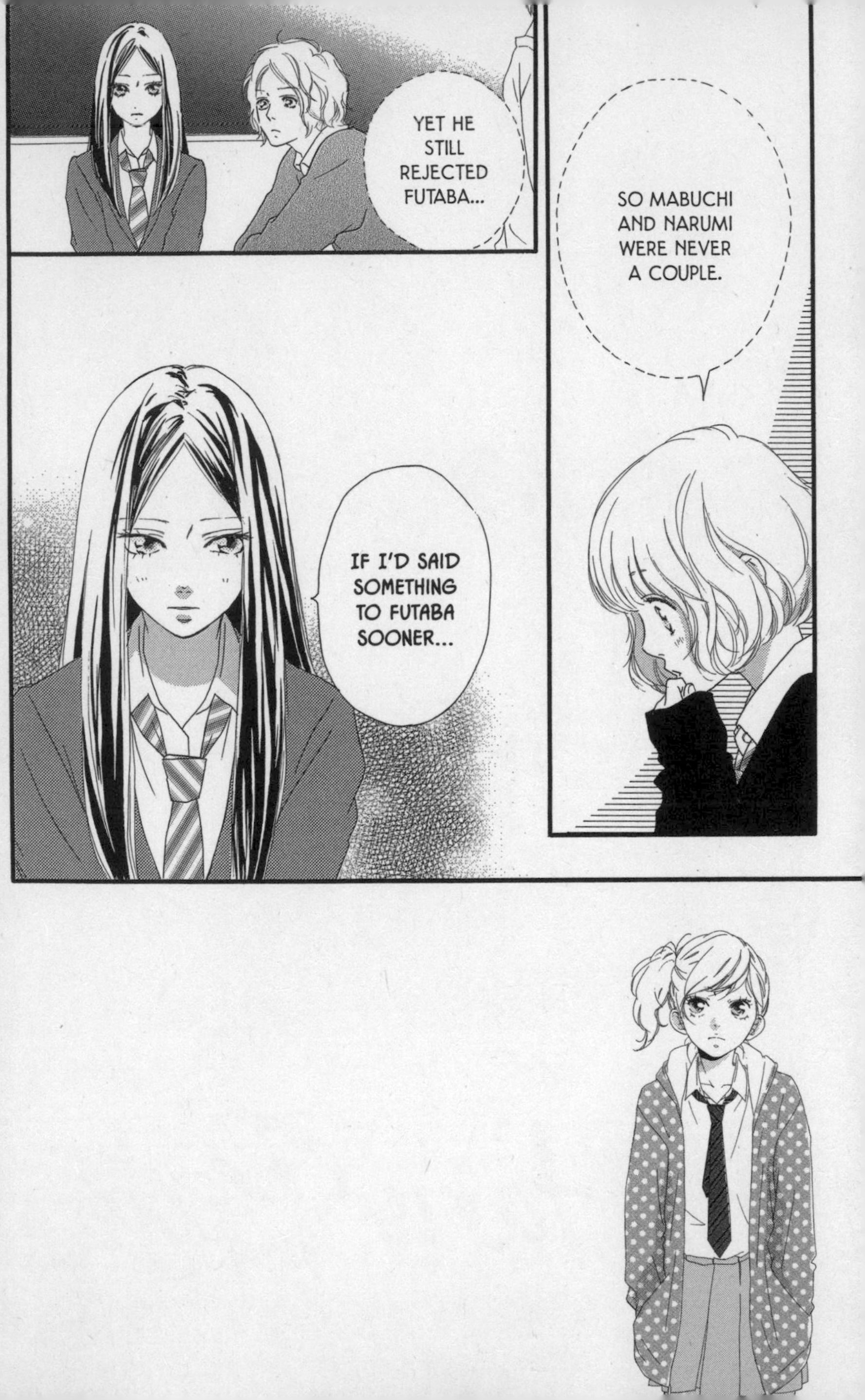
SO MABUCHI AND NARUMI WERE NEVER A COUPLE.
YET HE STILL REJECTED FUTABA...
IF I'D SAID SOMETHING TO FUTABA SOONER...

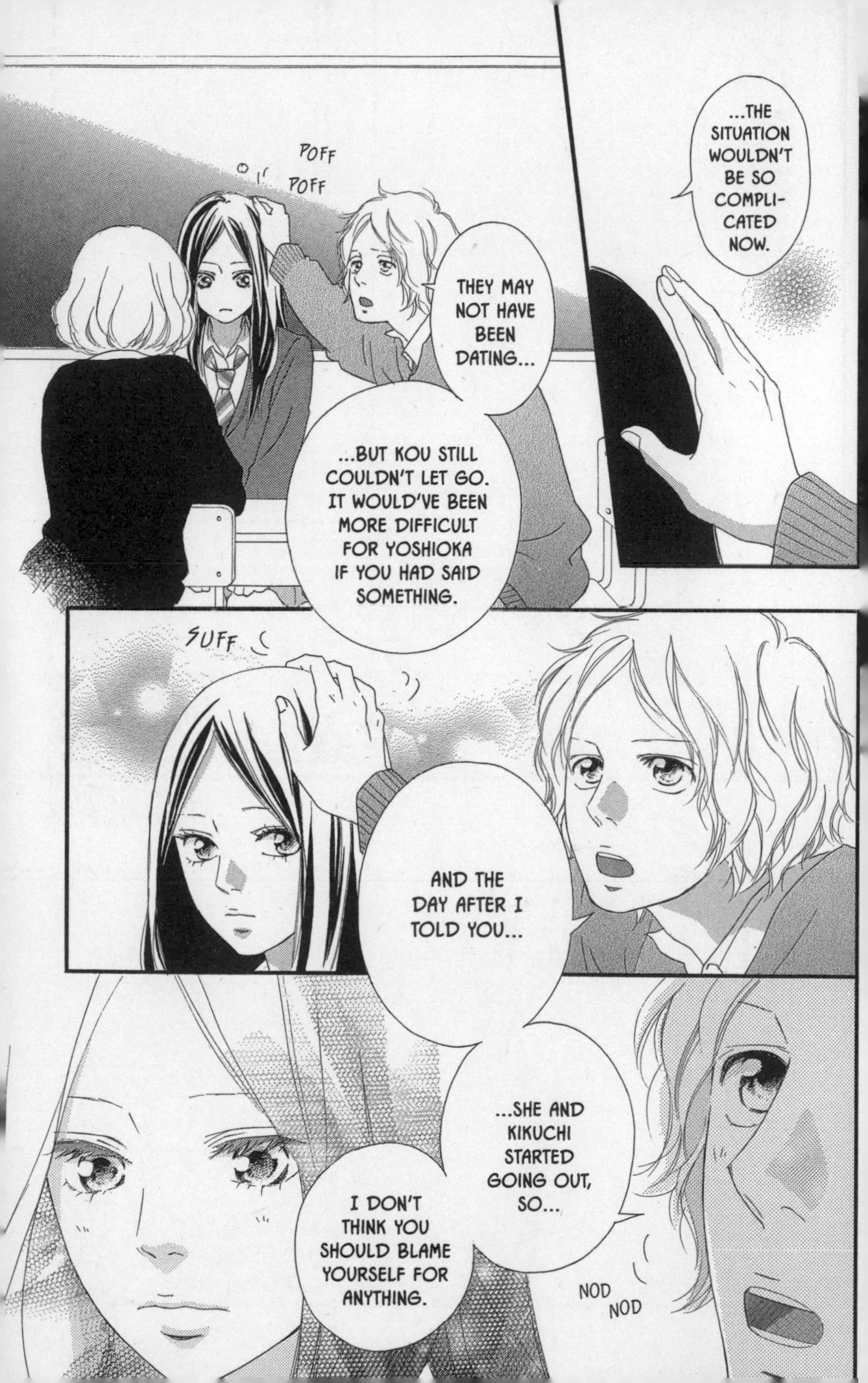
...THE SITUATION WOULDN'T BE SO COMPLICATED NOW.
POFF
POFF
THEY MAY NOT HAVE BEEN DATING...
...BUT KOU STILL COULDN'T LET GO. IT WOULD'VE BEEN MORE DIFFICULT FOR YOSHIOKA IF YOU HAD SAID SOMETHING.
SUFF
AND THE DAY AFTER I TOLD YOU...
...SHE AND KIKUCHI STARTED GOING OUT, SO...
NOD NOD
I DON'T THINK YOU SHOULD BLAME YOURSELF FOR ANYTHING.

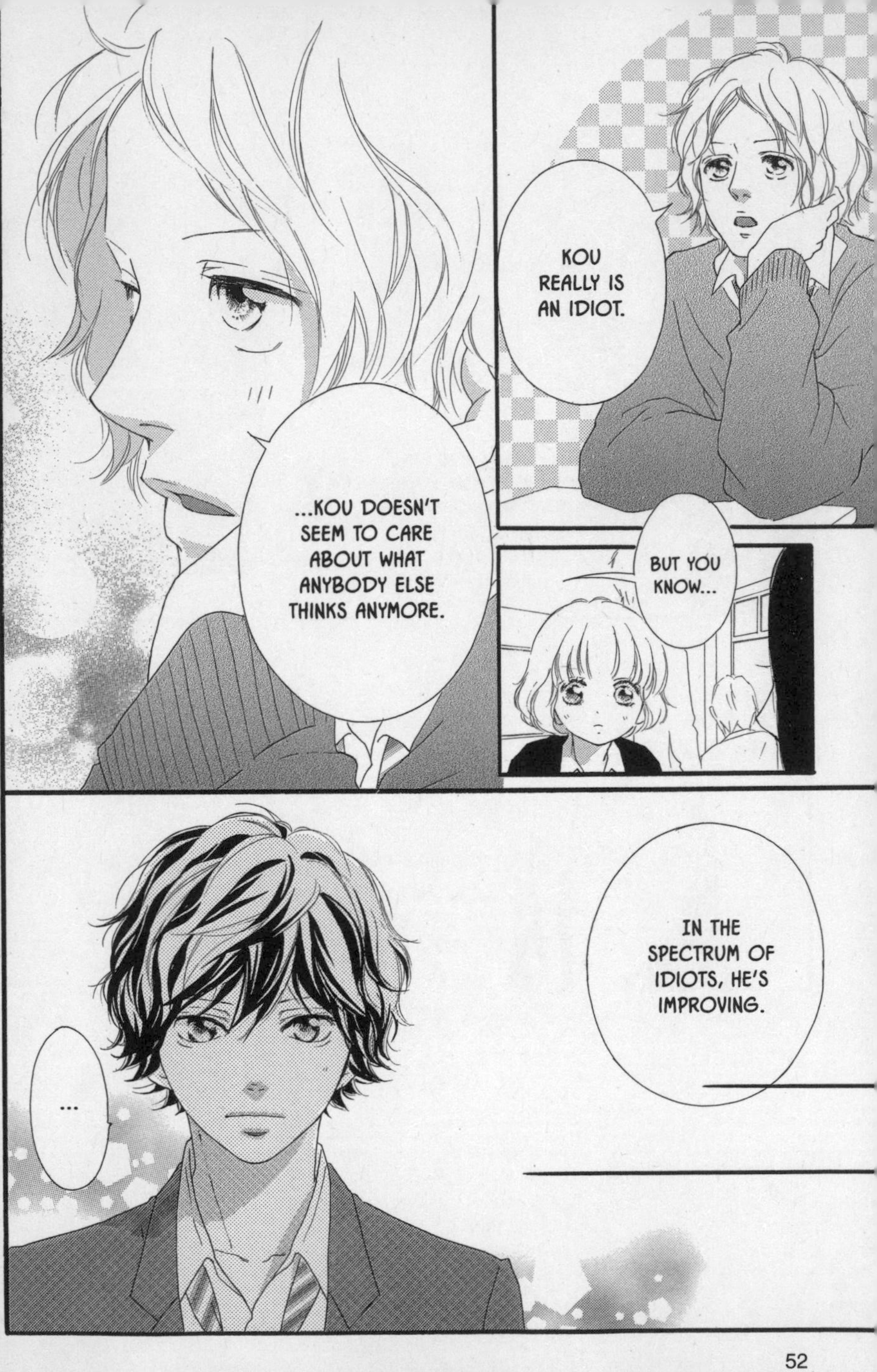
KOU REALLY IS AN IDIOT.
BUT YOU KNOW...
...KOU DOESN'T SEEM TO CARE ABOUT WHAT ANYBODY ELSE THINKS ANYMORE.
IN THE SPECTRUM OF IDIOTS, HE'S IMPROVING.
...

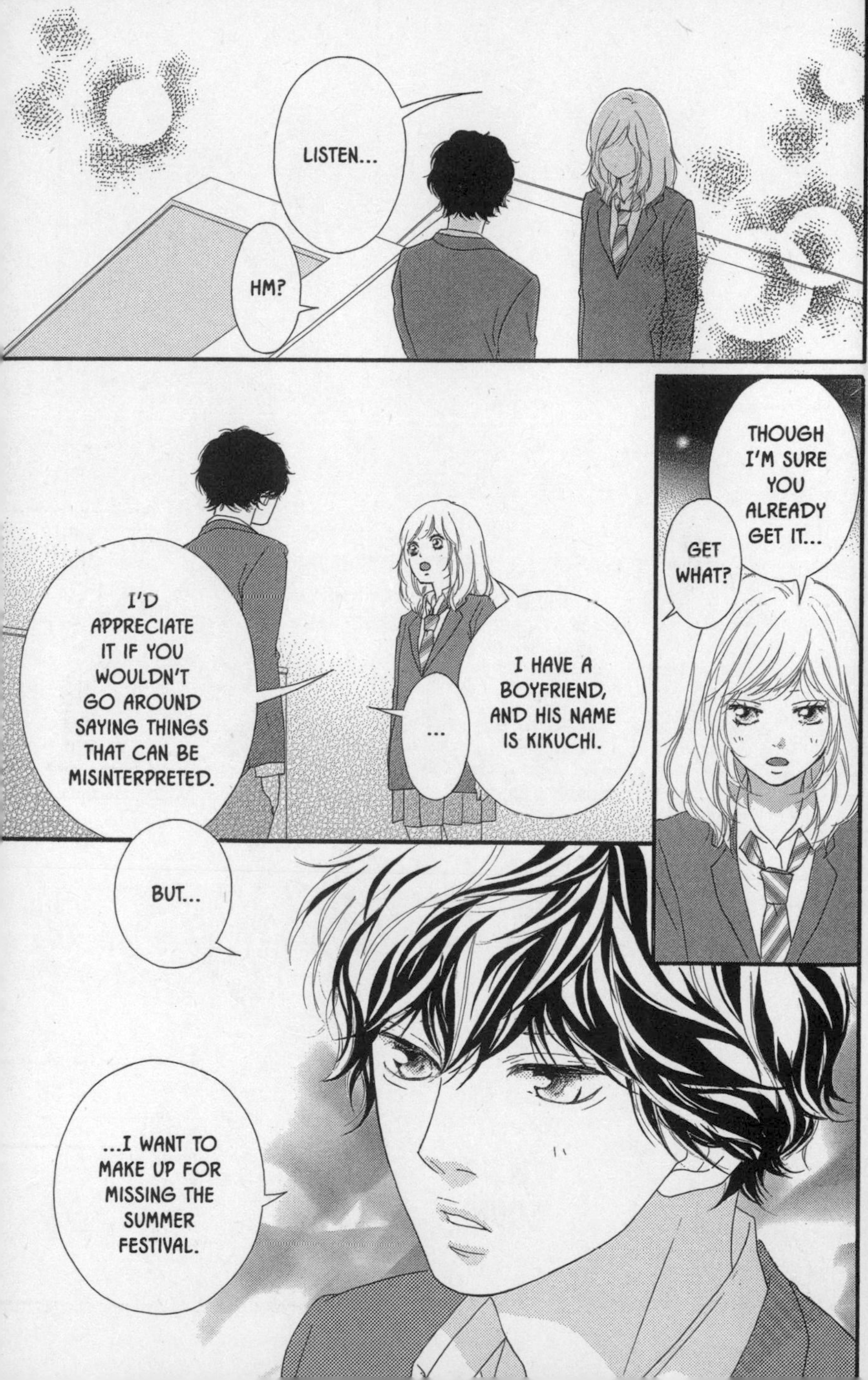
LISTEN...
HM?
THOUGH I'M SURE YOU ALREADY GET IT...
GET WHAT?
I HAVE A BOYFRIEND, AND HIS NAME IS KIKUCHI.
...
I'D APPRECIATE IT IF YOU WOULDN'T GO AROUND SAYING THINGS THAT CAN BE MISINTERPRETED.
BUT...
...I WANT TO MAKE UP FOR MISSING THE SUMMER FESTIVAL.

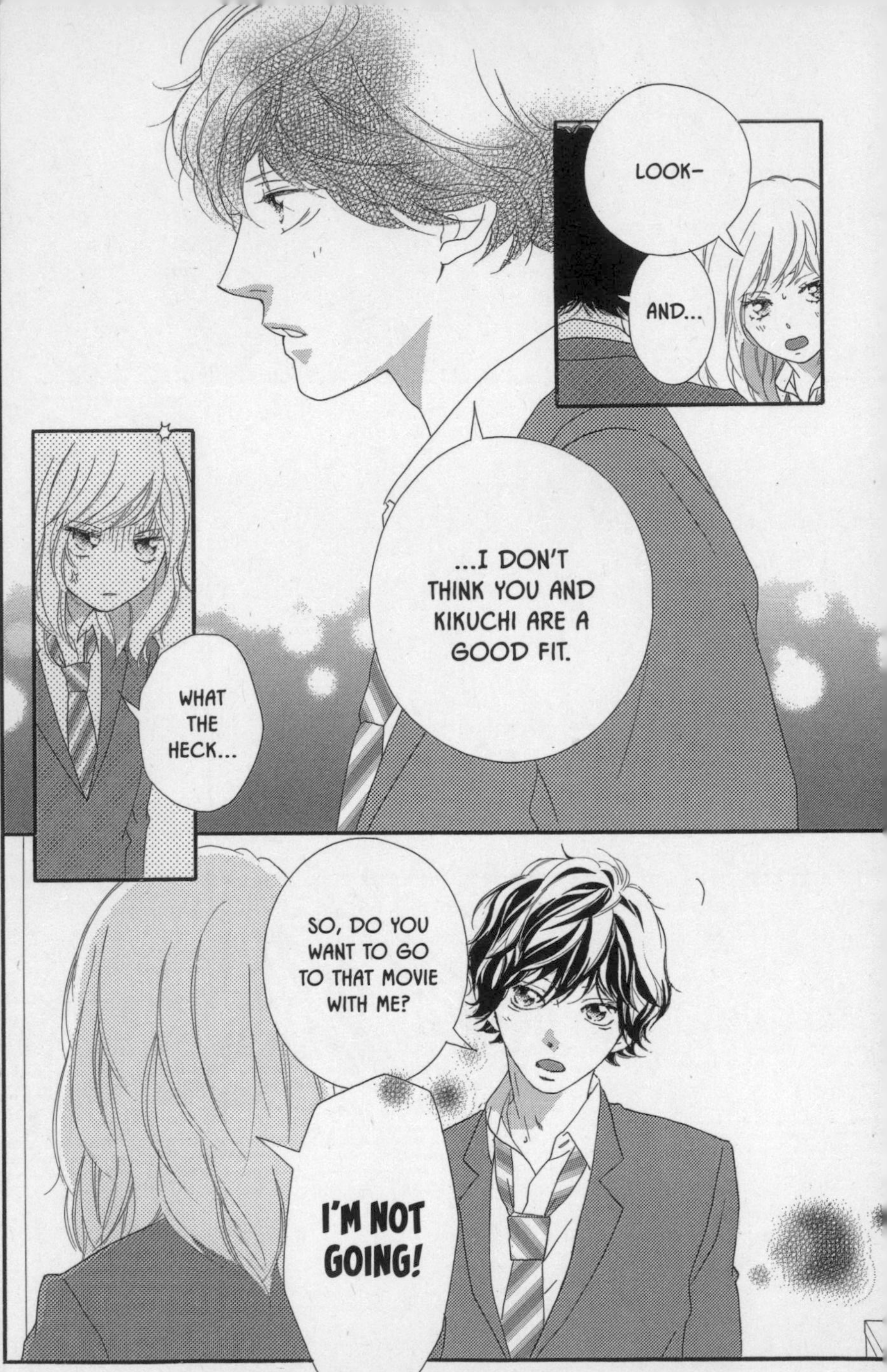
LOOK–
AND...
...I DON'T THINK YOU AND KIKUCHI ARE A GOOD FIT.
WHAT THE HECK...
SO, DO YOU WANT TO GO TO THAT MOVIE WITH ME?
I'M NOT GOING!

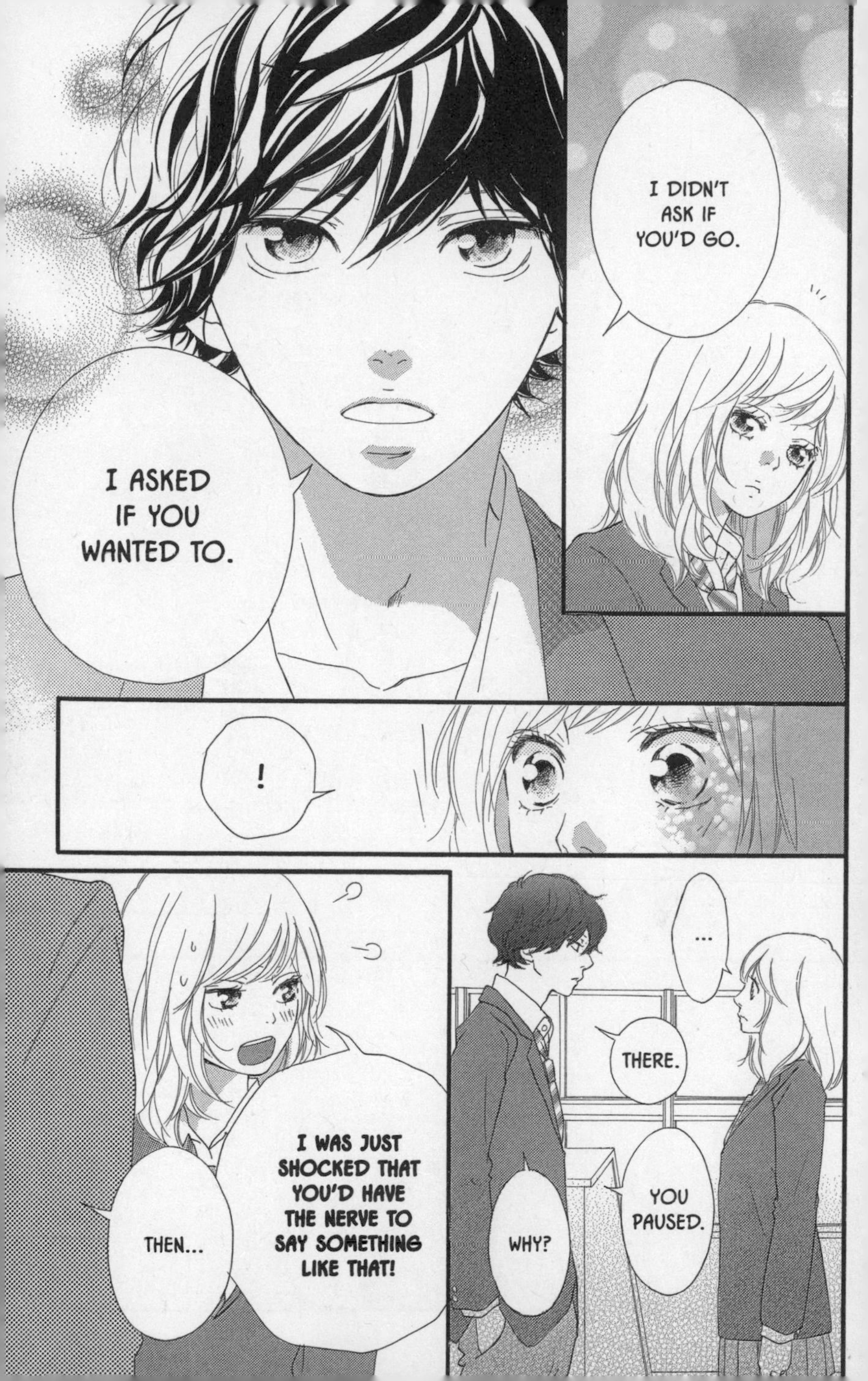
I DIDN'T ASK IF YOU'D GO.
I ASKED IF YOU WANTED TO.
!
...
THERE.
YOU PAUSED.
WHY?
I WAS JUST SHOCKED THAT YOU'D HAVE THE NERVE TO SAY SOMETHING LIKE THAT!
THEN...

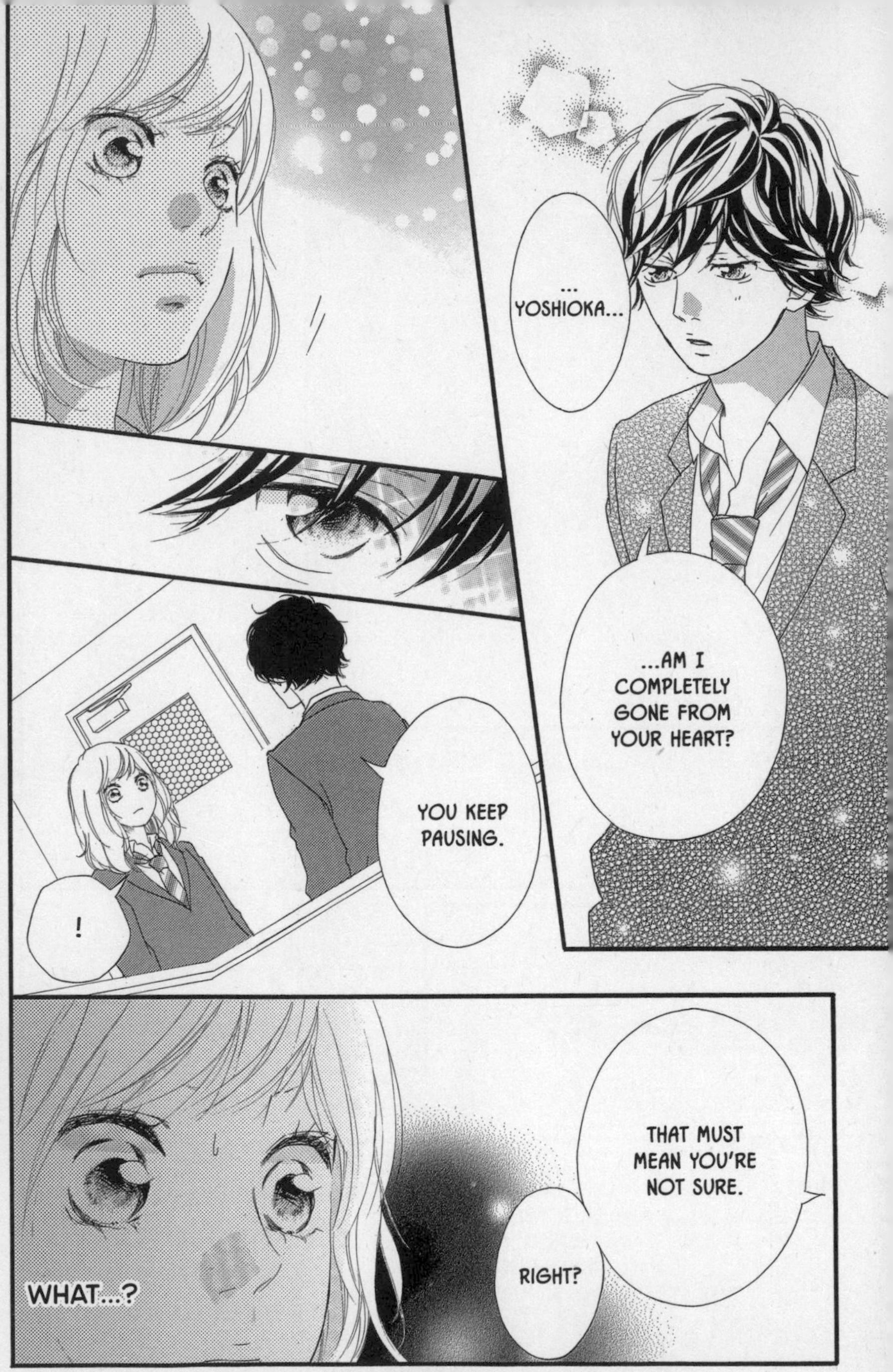
... YOSHIOKA...
...AM I COMPLETELY GONE FROM YOUR HEART?
YOU KEEP PAUSING.
!
THAT MUST MEAN YOU'RE NOT SURE.
RIGHT?
WHAT...?

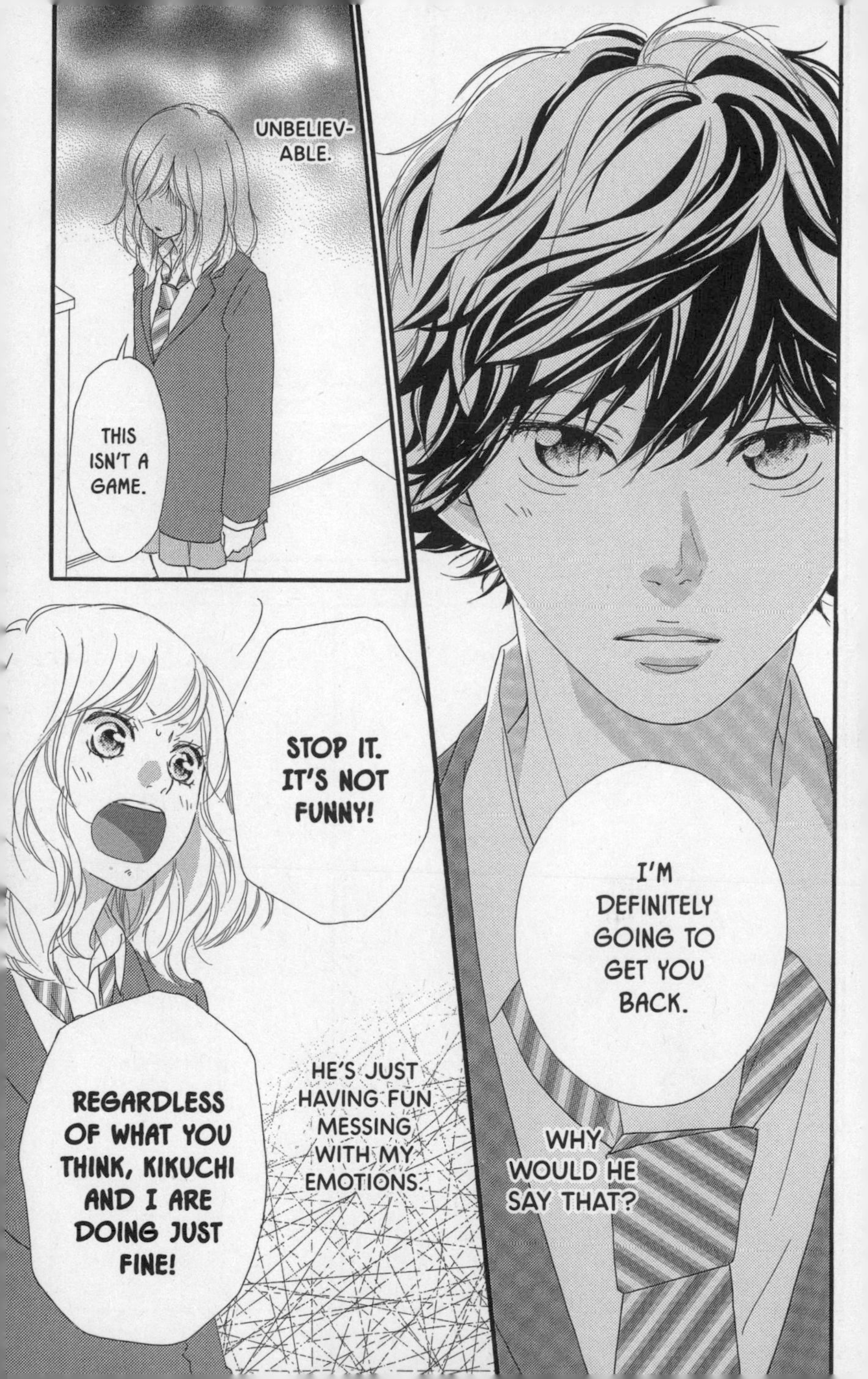
I'M DEFINITELY GOING TO GET YOU BACK.
WHY WOULD HE SAY THAT?
UNBELIEV-ABLE.
THIS ISN'T A GAME.
STOP IT. IT'S NOT FUNNY!
HE'S JUST HAVING FUN MESSING WITH MY EMOTIONS.
REGARDLESS OF WHAT YOU THINK, KIKUCHI AND I ARE DOING JUST FINE!

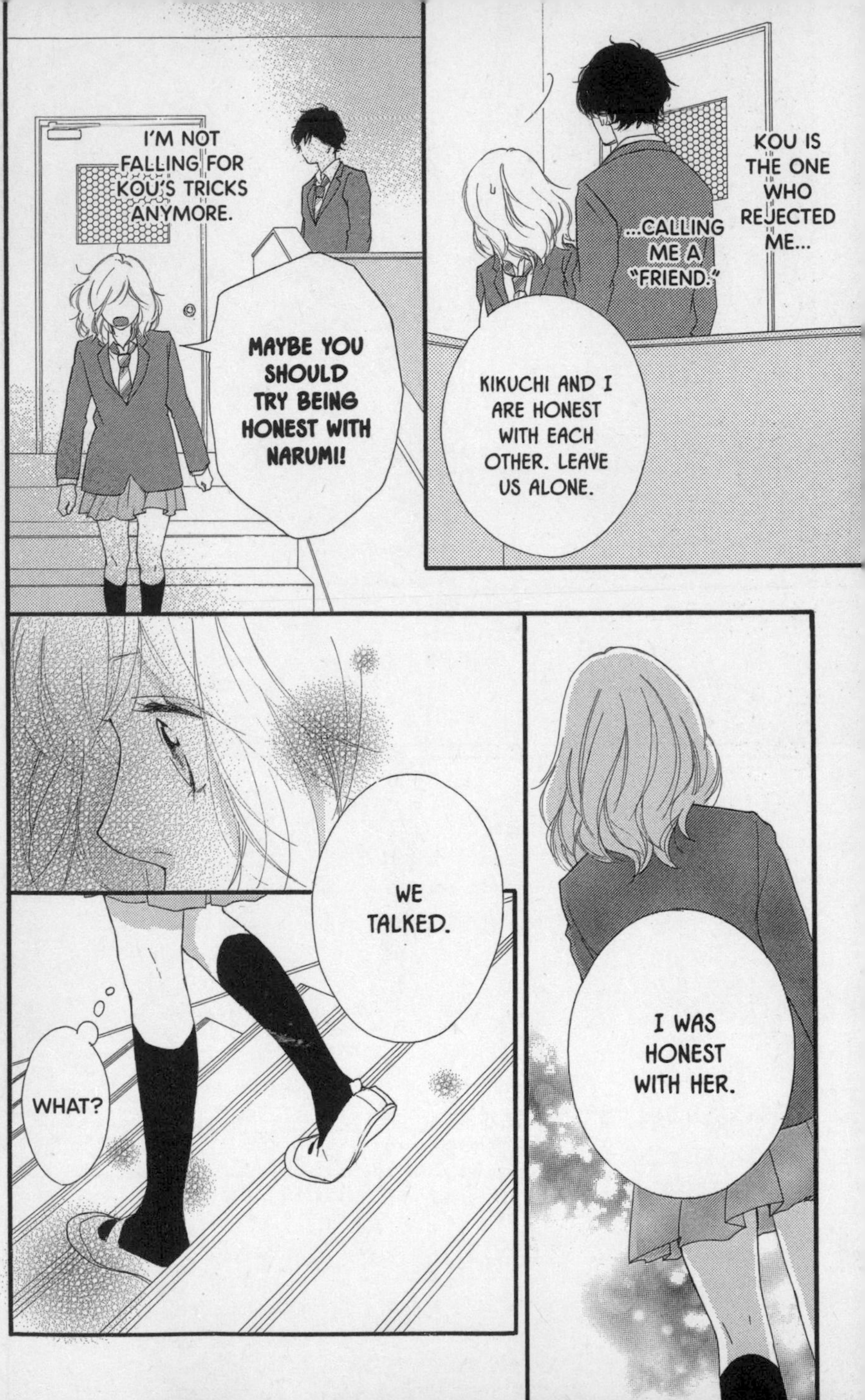
KOU IS THE ONE WHO REJECTED ME...
...CALLING ME A "FRIEND."
KIKUCHI AND I ARE HONEST WITH EACH OTHER. LEAVE US ALONE.
I'M NOT FALLING FOR KOU'S TRICKS ANYMORE.
MAYBE YOU SHOULD TRY BEING HONEST WITH NARUMI!
I WAS HONEST WITH HER.
WE TALKED.
WHAT?

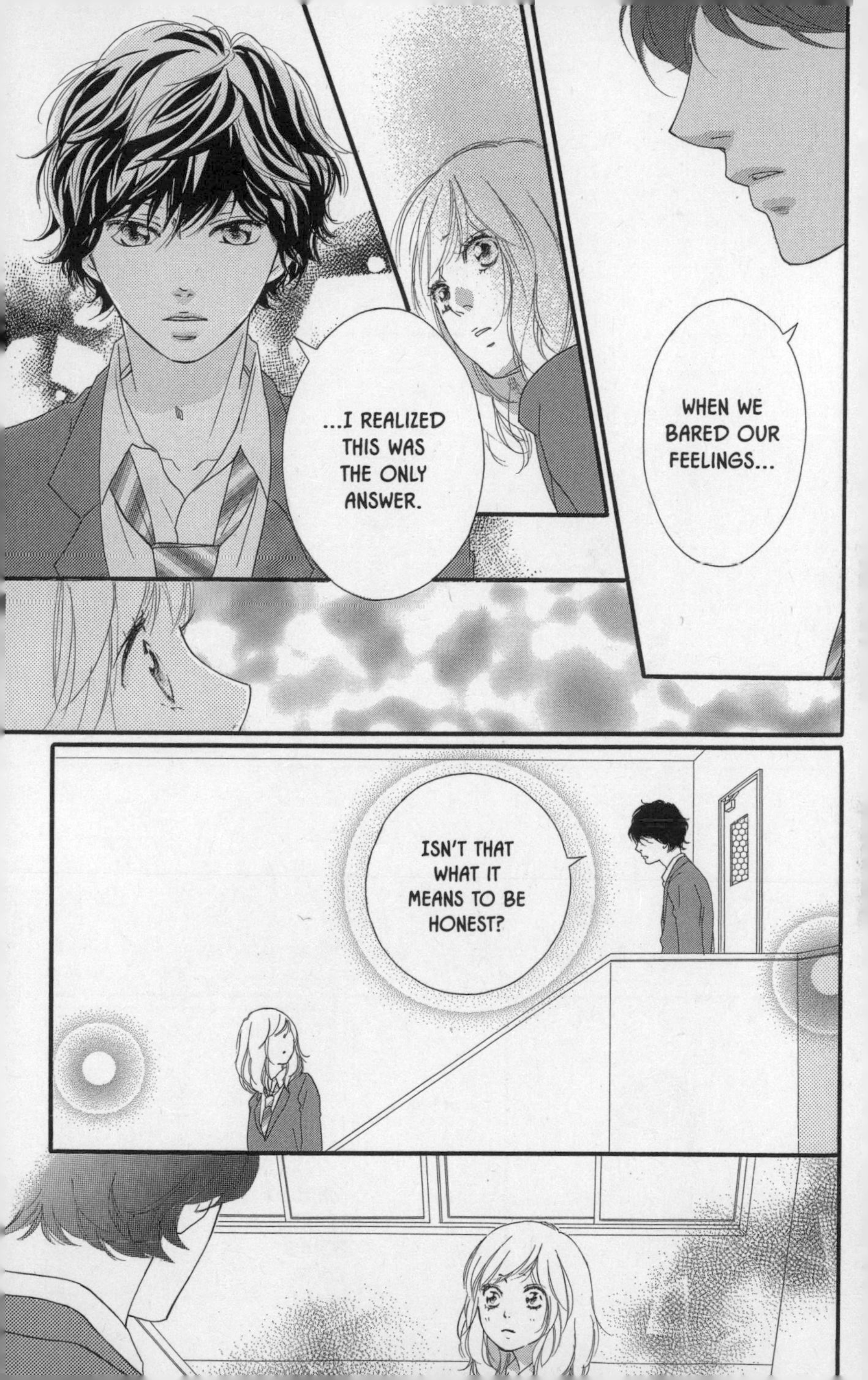
WHEN WE BARED OUR FEELINGS...
...I REALIZED THIS WAS THE ONLY ANSWER.
ISN'T THAT WHAT IT MEANS TO BE HONEST?

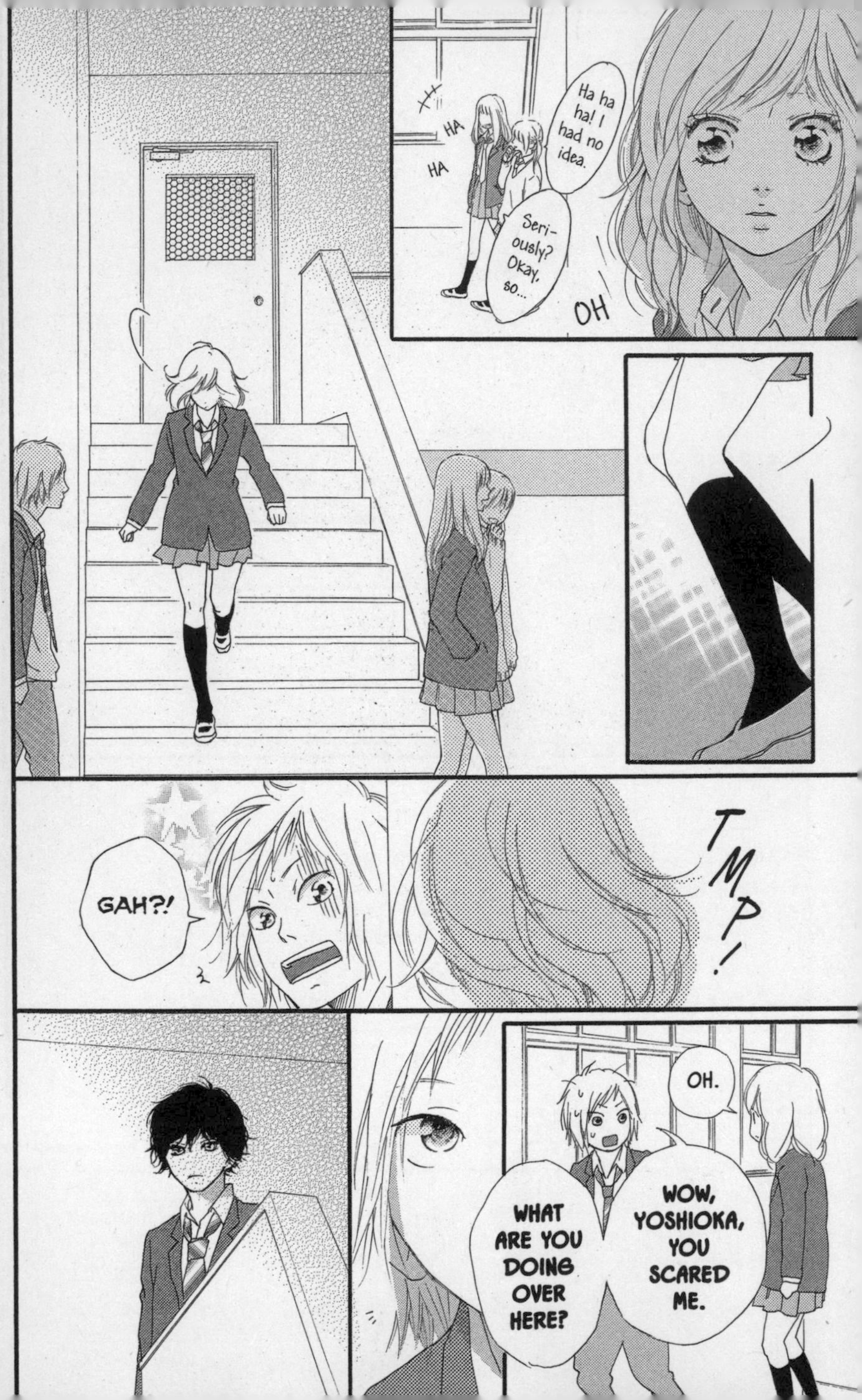
Ha ha ha! I had no idea.
Seri-ously? Okay, so...
HA
HA
OH
TMP!
GAH?!
OH.
WOW, YOSHIOKA, YOU SCARED ME.
WHAT ARE YOU DOING OVER HERE?

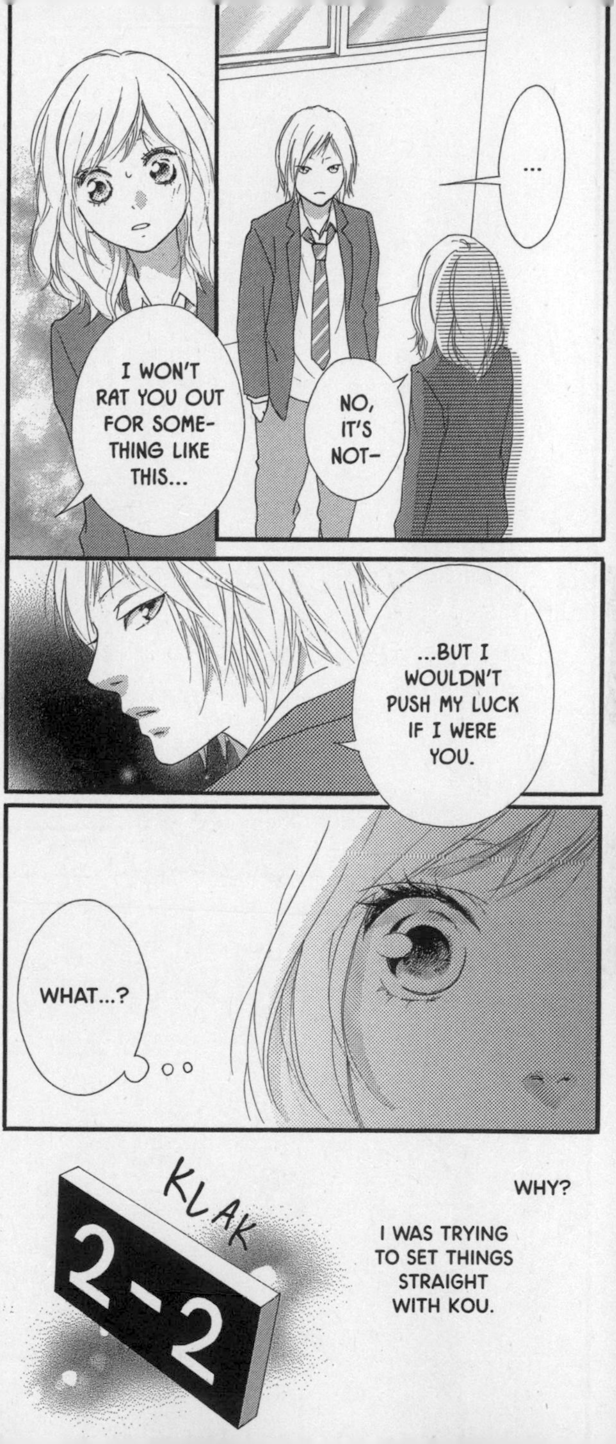
...
NO, IT'S NOT–
I WON'T RAT YOU OUT FOR SOMETHING LIKE THIS...
...BUT I WOULDN'T PUSH MY LUCK IF I WERE YOU.
WHAT...?
WHY?
I WAS TRYING TO SET THINGS STRAIGHT WITH KOU.
KLAK
2-2

For some reason, the other day I had this sudden desire to watch the *Romeo and the Black Brothers* anime. I bought the DVD box set on impulse. A fellow *Betsuma* artist, whom I will call Umi A., had passionately recommended the series to me a few years back, but I didn't think much of it at the time. A few years before that my sister had recommended it, but I just thought, "That's nice," and let it go. I don't know why, but I suddenly became curious about it, and I figured that because it was famous anyway I might as well get the box set! It was a pretty gutsy move in my opinion. Anyway, I watched it and after finishing the entire series, I fell so much in love with it that I wanted to apologize to Umi A. and my sister for not checking it out sooner. I loved it so much that I watched it three times in a row. My absolute favorite is episode 17—I watched that one over and over. It really is a wonderful and sweet episode. And now I want to watch it again...

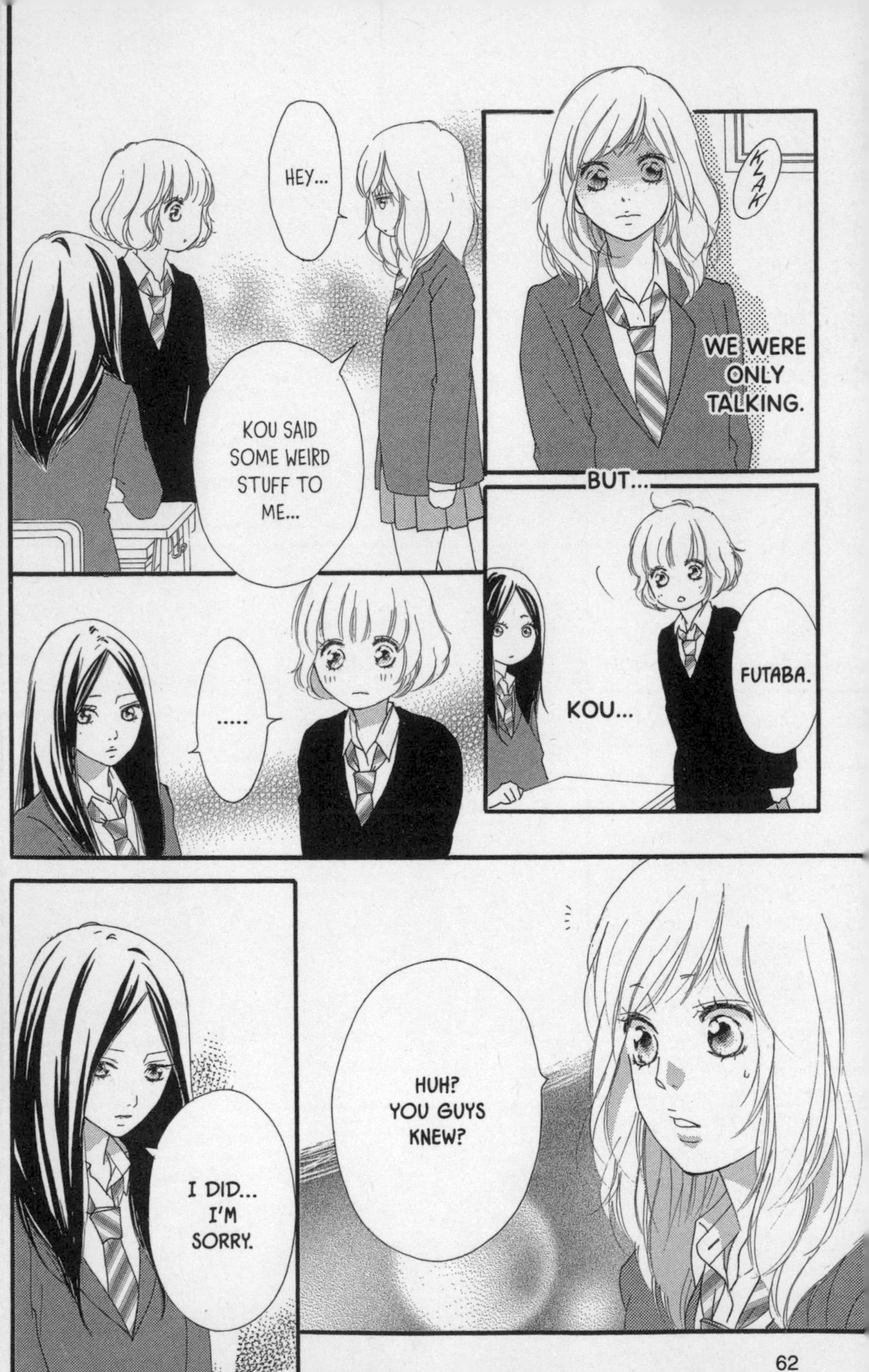
KLAK
WE WERE ONLY TALKING.
HEY...
KOU SAID SOME WEIRD STUFF TO ME...
BUT...
FUTABA.
KOU...
.....
HUH? YOU GUYS KNEW?
I DID... I'M SORRY.

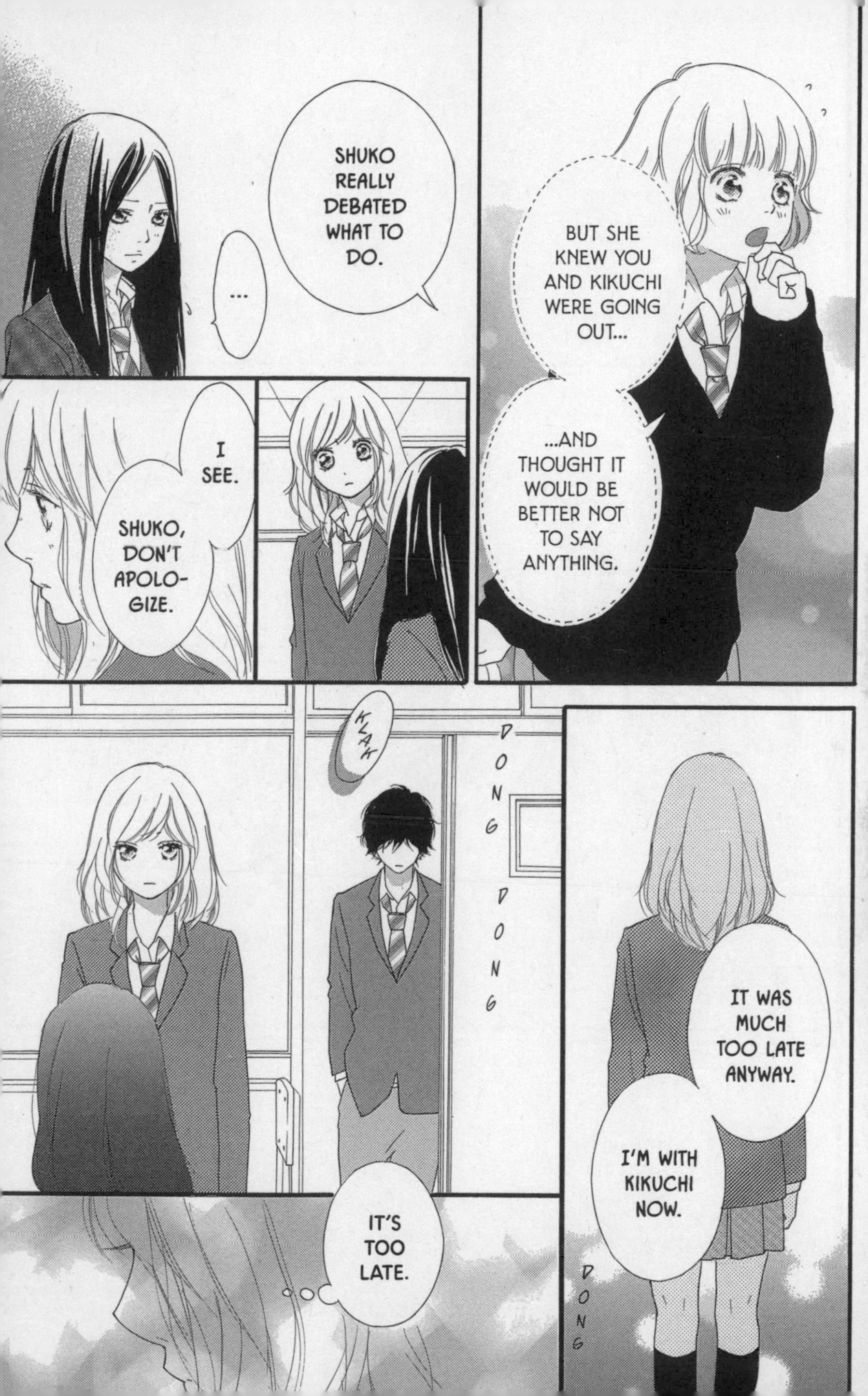
BUT SHE KNEW YOU AND KIKUCHI WERE GOING OUT...
...AND THOUGHT IT WOULD BE BETTER NOT TO SAY ANYTHING.
SHUKO REALLY DEBATED WHAT TO DO.
...
I SEE.
SHUKO, DON'T APOLOGIZE.
IT WAS MUCH TOO LATE ANYWAY.
I'M WITH KIKUCHI NOW.
DONG
DONG
DONG
KLAK
DONG
IT'S TOO LATE.

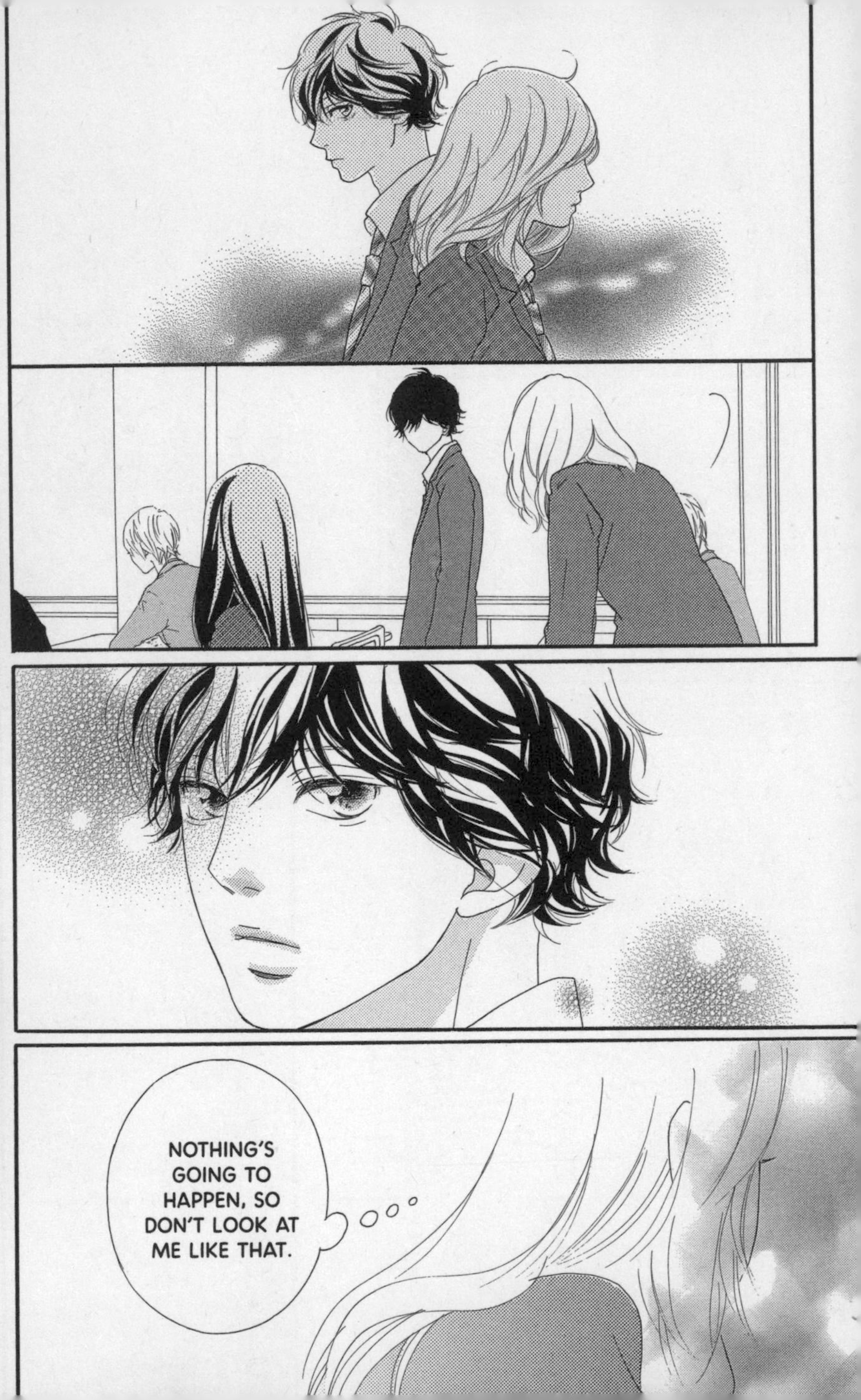
NOTHING'S GOING TO HAPPEN, SO DON'T LOOK AT ME LIKE THAT.

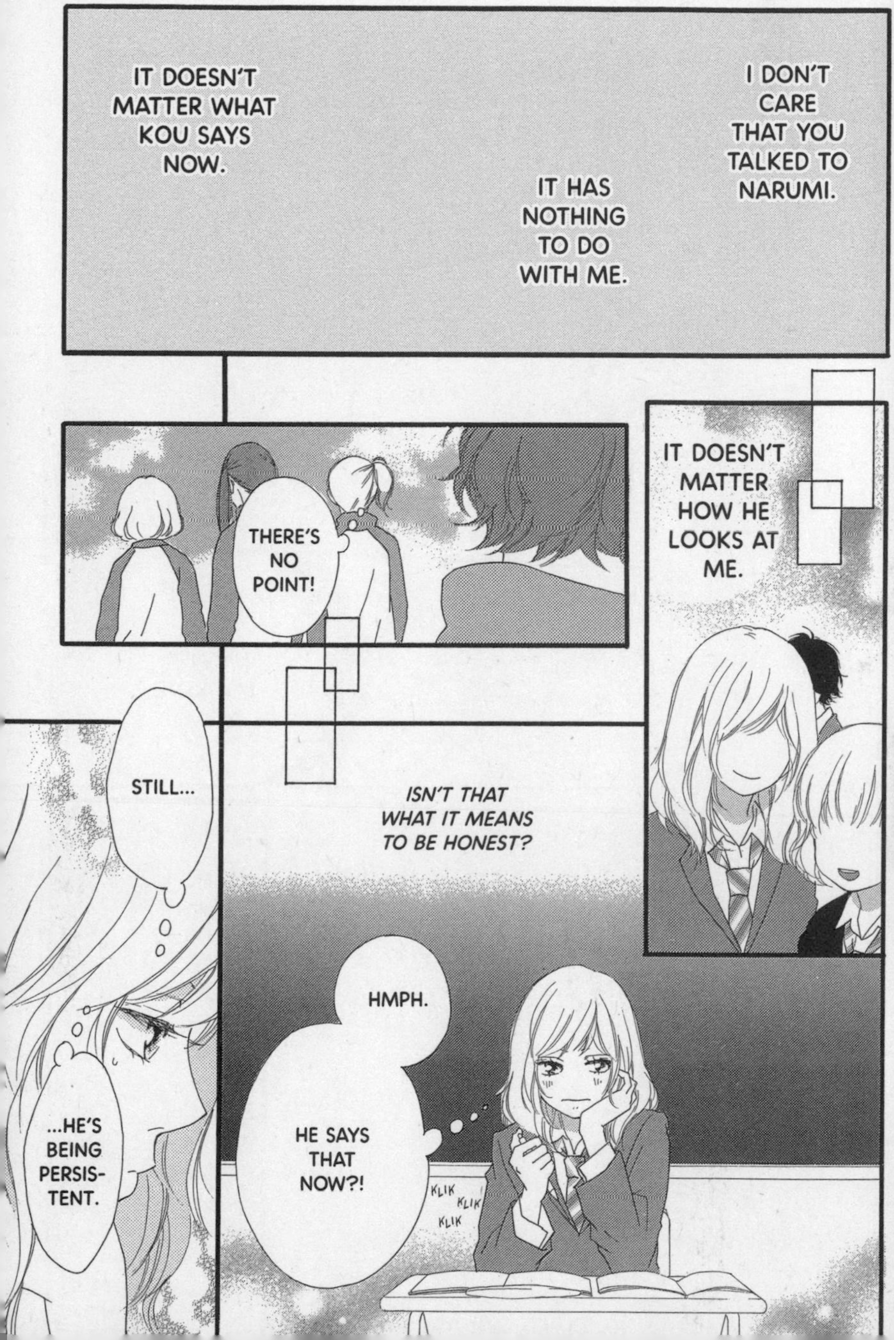
I DON'T CARE THAT YOU TALKED TO NARUMI.
IT HAS NOTHING TO DO WITH ME.
IT DOESN'T MATTER WHAT KOU SAYS NOW.
IT DOESN'T MATTER HOW HE LOOKS AT ME.
THERE'S NO POINT!
ISN'T THAT WHAT IT MEANS TO BE HONEST?
HMPH.
HE SAYS THAT NOW?!
KLIK KLIK KLIK
STILL...
...HE'S BEING PERSIS-TENT.

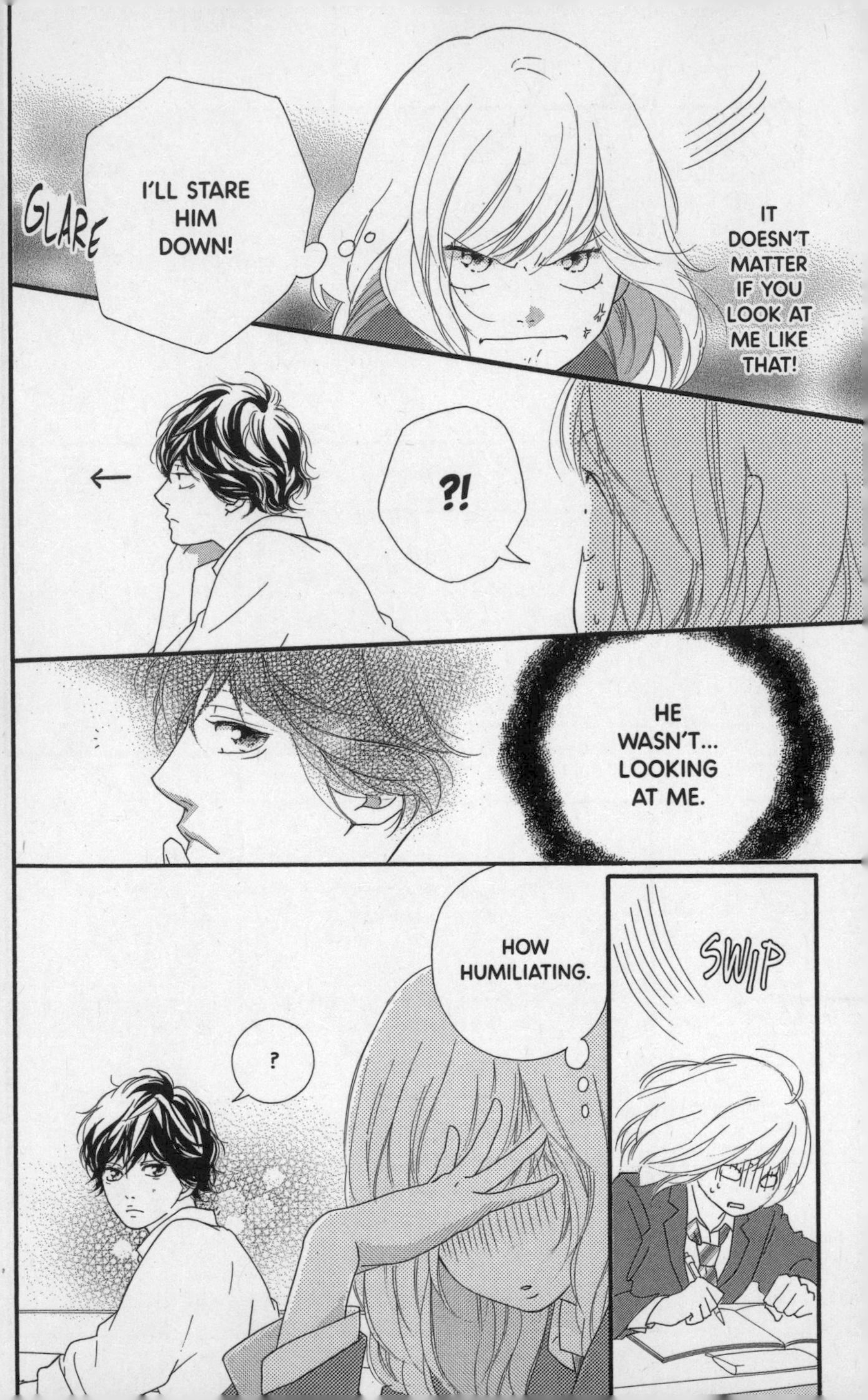

IT DOESN'T MATTER IF YOU LOOK AT ME LIKE THAT!
I'LL STARE HIM DOWN!
GLARE
?!
HE WASN'T... LOOKING AT ME.
SWIP
HOW HUMILIATING.
?

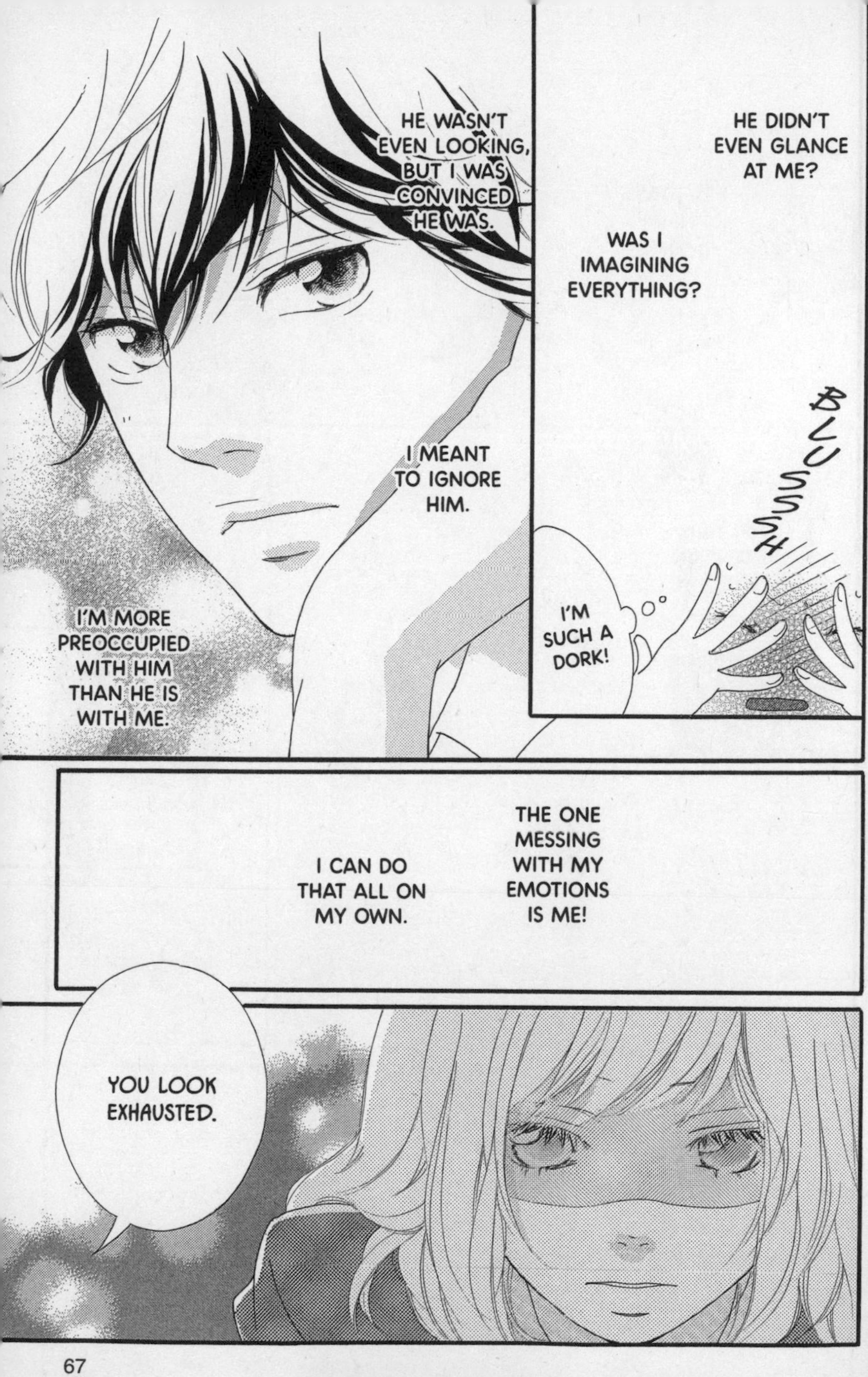
HE DIDN'T EVEN GLANCE AT ME?
WAS I IMAGINING EVERYTHING?
BLUSSSH
I'M SUCH A DORK!
HE WASN'T EVEN LOOKING, BUT I WAS CONVINCED HE WAS.
I MEANT TO IGNORE HIM.
I'M MORE PREOCCUPIED WITH HIM THAN HE IS WITH ME.
THE ONE MESSING WITH MY EMOTIONS IS ME!
I CAN DO THAT ALL ON MY OWN.
YOU LOOK EXHAUSTED.

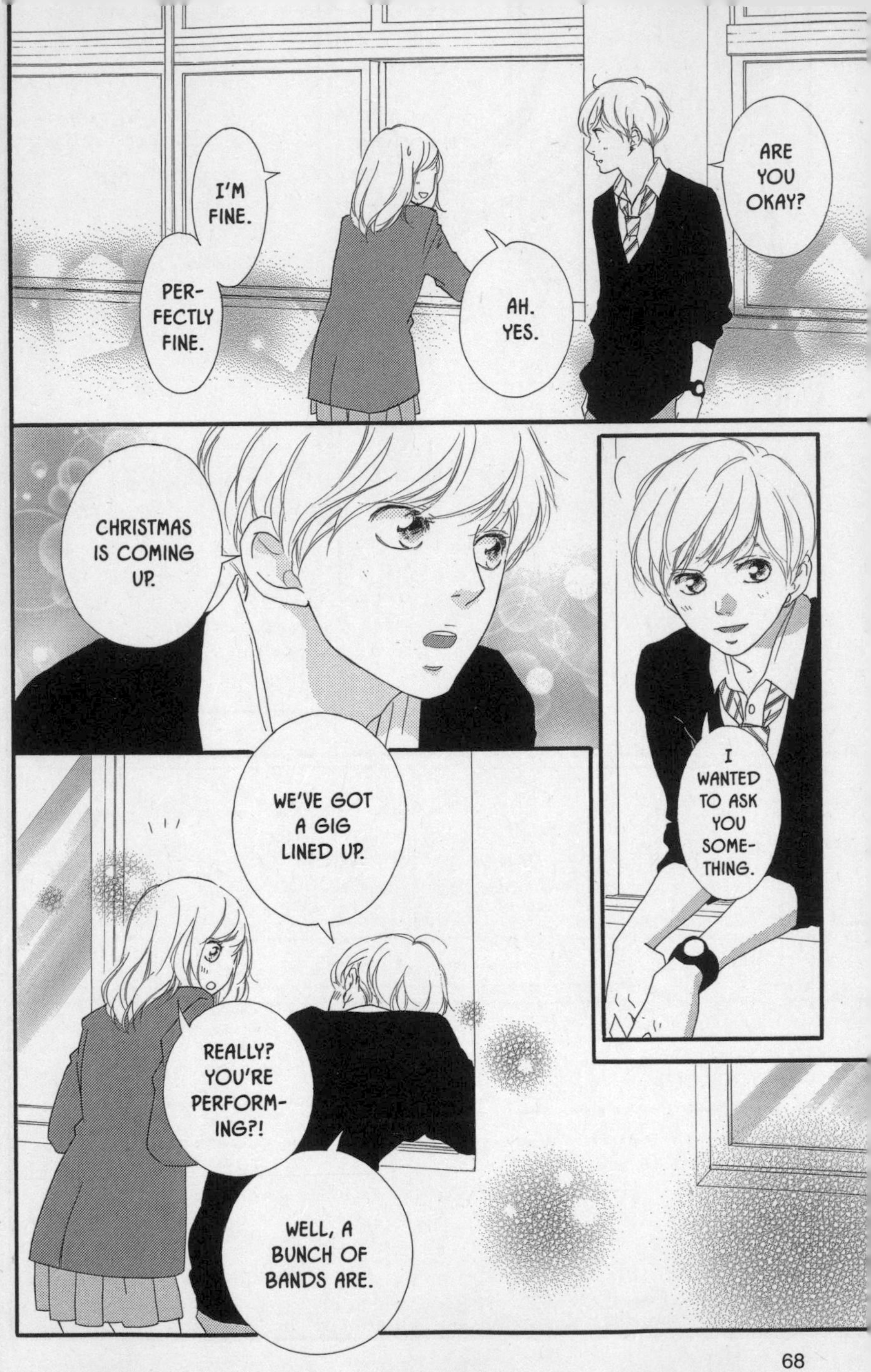
ARE YOU OKAY?
AH. YES.
I'M FINE.
PER-FECTLY FINE.
I WANTED TO ASK YOU SOME-THING.
CHRISTMAS IS COMING UP.
WE'VE GOT A GIG LINED UP.
REALLY? YOU'RE PERFORM-ING?!
WELL, A BUNCH OF BANDS ARE.

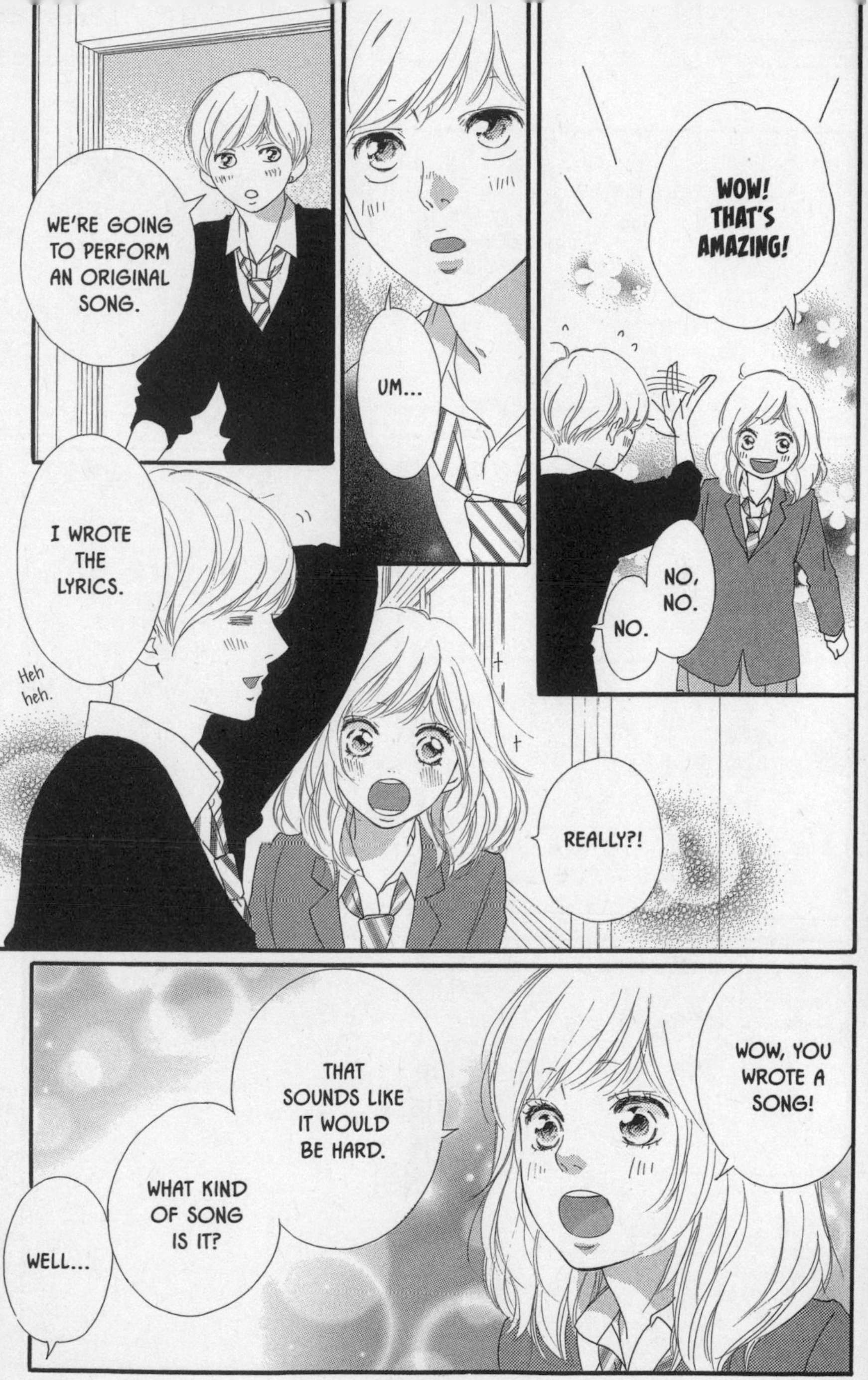
WOW! THAT'S AMAZING!
NO, NO.
NO.
UM...
WE'RE GOING TO PERFORM AN ORIGINAL SONG.
I WROTE THE LYRICS.
Heh heh.
REALLY?!
WOW, YOU WROTE A SONG!
THAT SOUNDS LIKE IT WOULD BE HARD.
WHAT KIND OF SONG IS IT?
WELL...

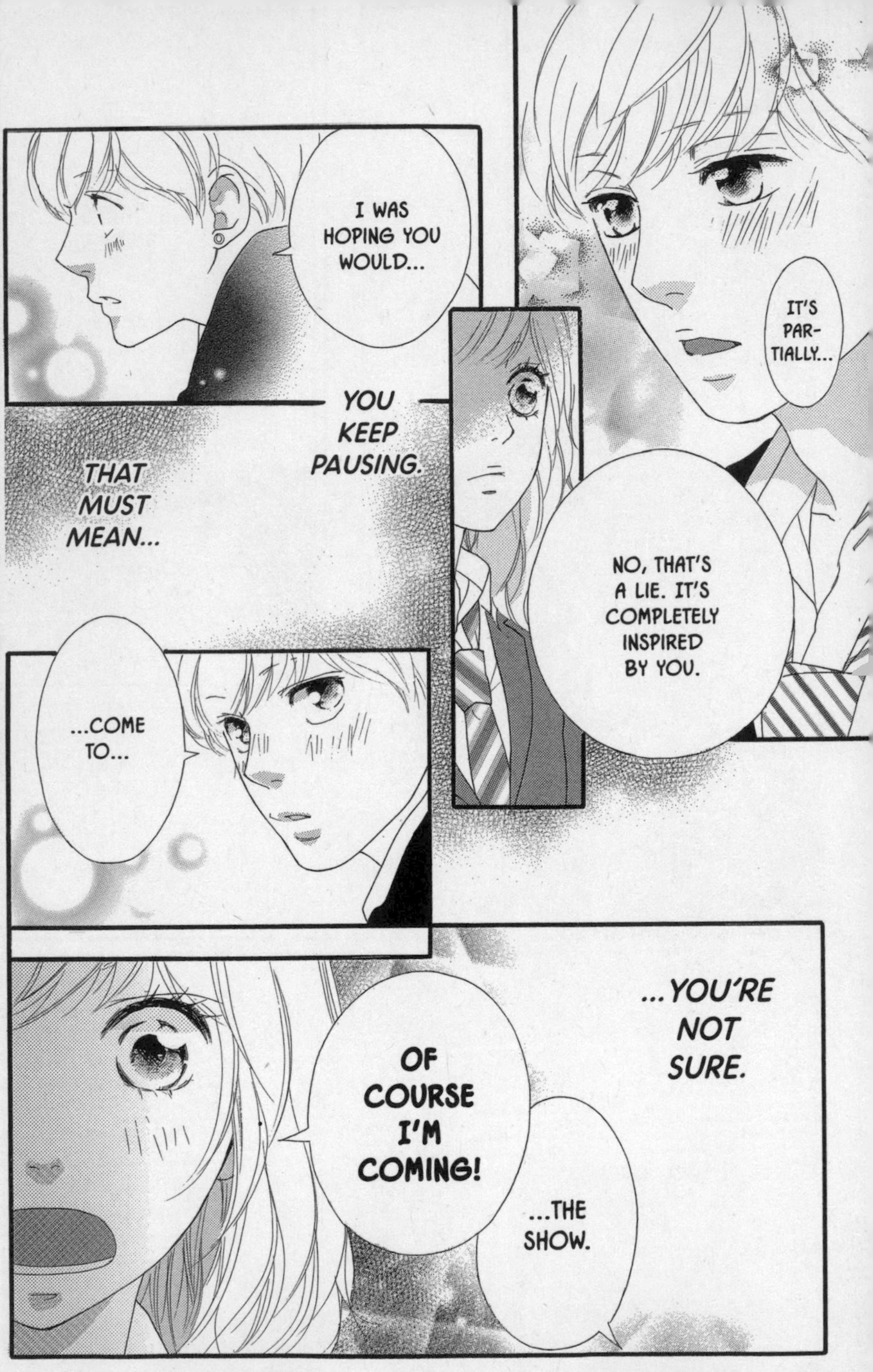
IT'S PARTIALLY...
NO, THAT'S A LIE. IT'S COMPLETELY INSPIRED BY YOU.
I WAS HOPING YOU WOULD...
YOU KEEP PAUSING.
THAT MUST MEAN...
...COME TO...
...YOU'RE NOT SURE.
...THE SHOW.
OF COURSE I'M COMING!

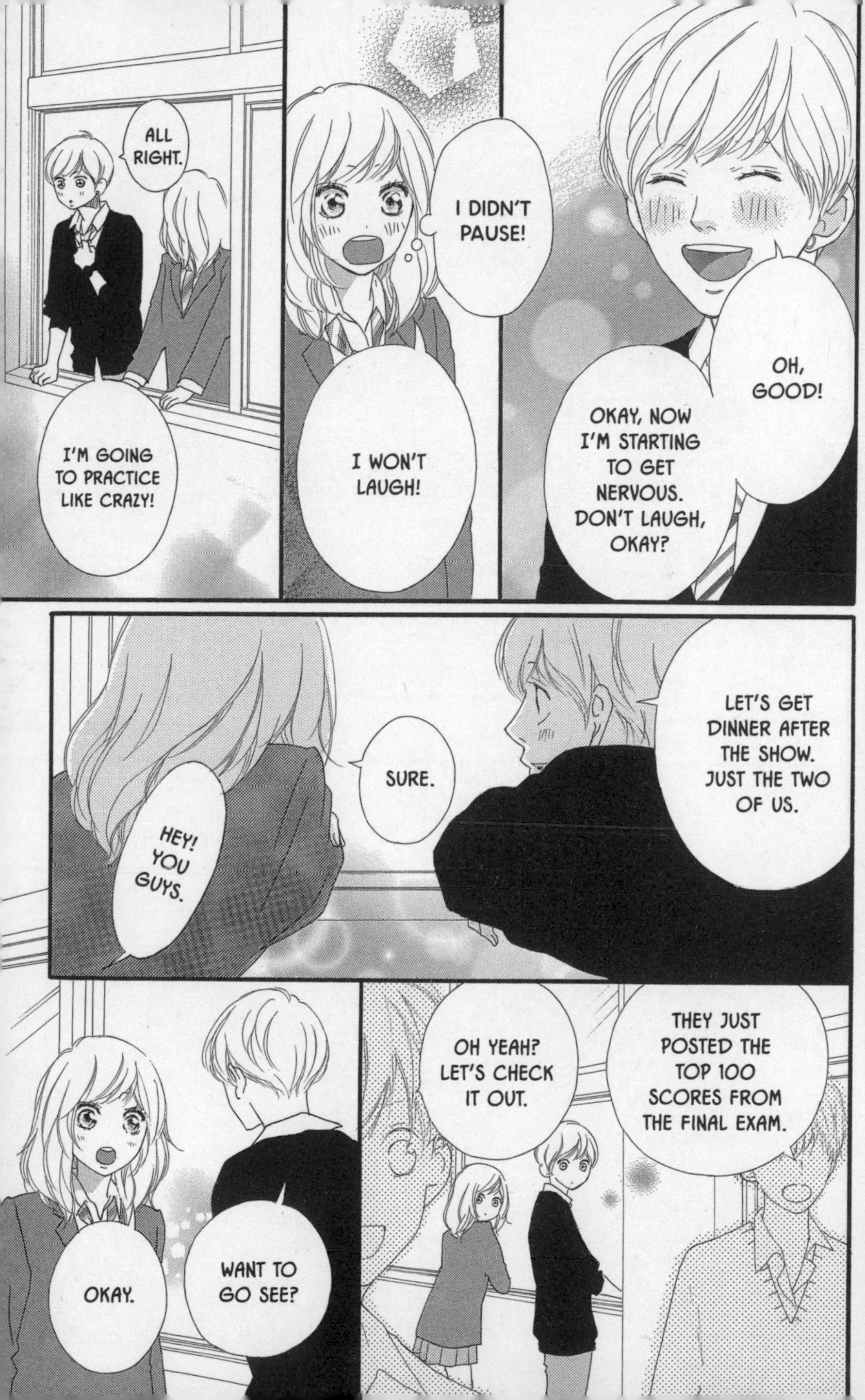
OH, GOOD!
OKAY, NOW I'M STARTING TO GET NERVOUS. DON'T LAUGH, OKAY?
I DIDN'T PAUSE!
I WON'T LAUGH!
ALL RIGHT.
I'M GOING TO PRACTICE LIKE CRAZY!
LET'S GET DINNER AFTER THE SHOW. JUST THE TWO OF US.
SURE.
HEY! YOU GUYS.
THEY JUST POSTED THE TOP 100 SCORES FROM THE FINAL EXAM.
OH YEAH? LET'S CHECK IT OUT.
WANT TO GO SEE?
OKAY.

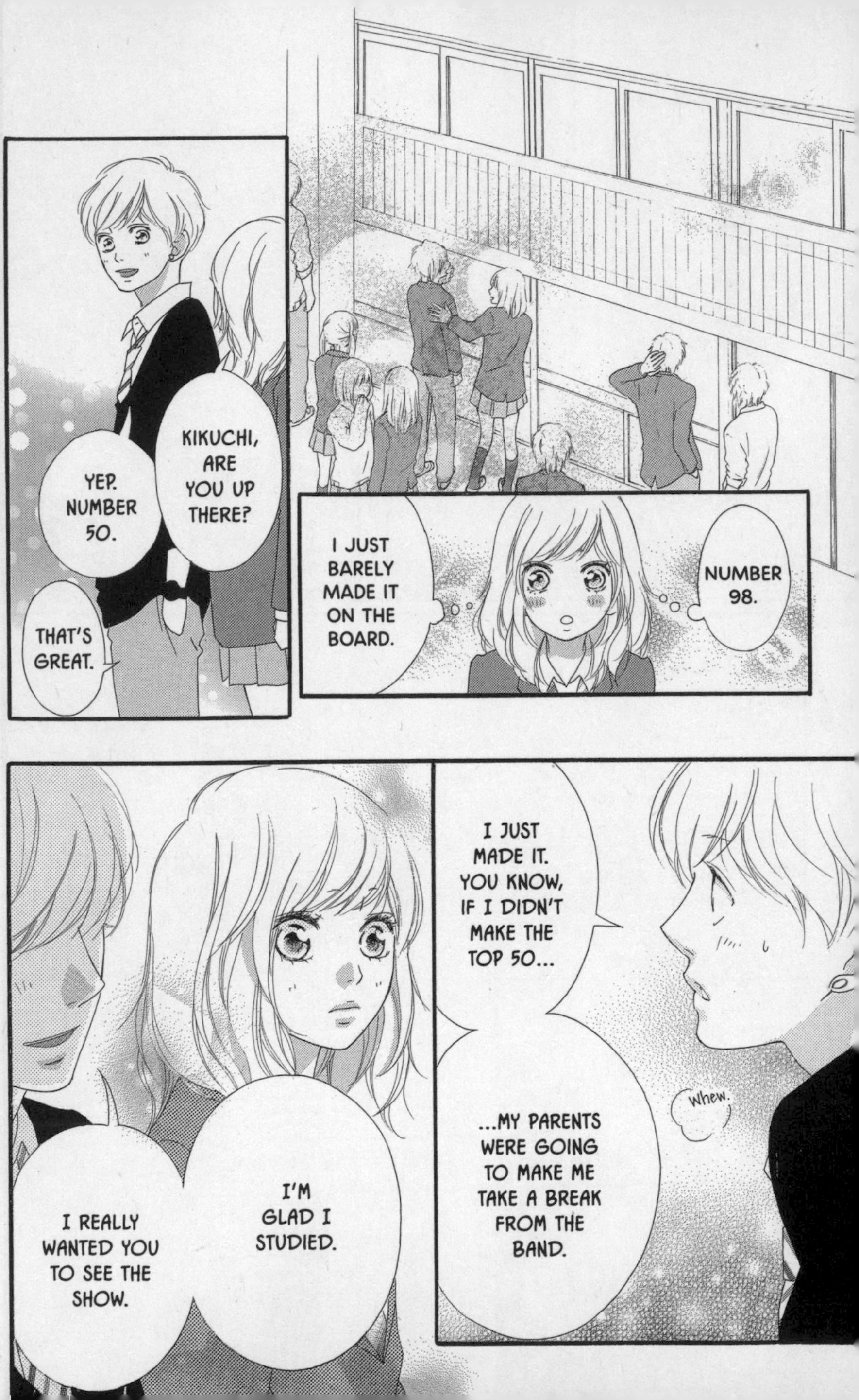
NUMBER 98.
I JUST BARELY MADE IT ON THE BOARD.
KIKUCHI, ARE YOU UP THERE?
YEP. NUMBER 50.
THAT'S GREAT.
I JUST MADE IT. YOU KNOW, IF I DIDN'T MAKE THE TOP 50...
Whew.
...MY PARENTS WERE GOING TO MAKE ME TAKE A BREAK FROM THE BAND.
I'M GLAD I STUDIED.
I REALLY WANTED YOU TO SEE THE SHOW.

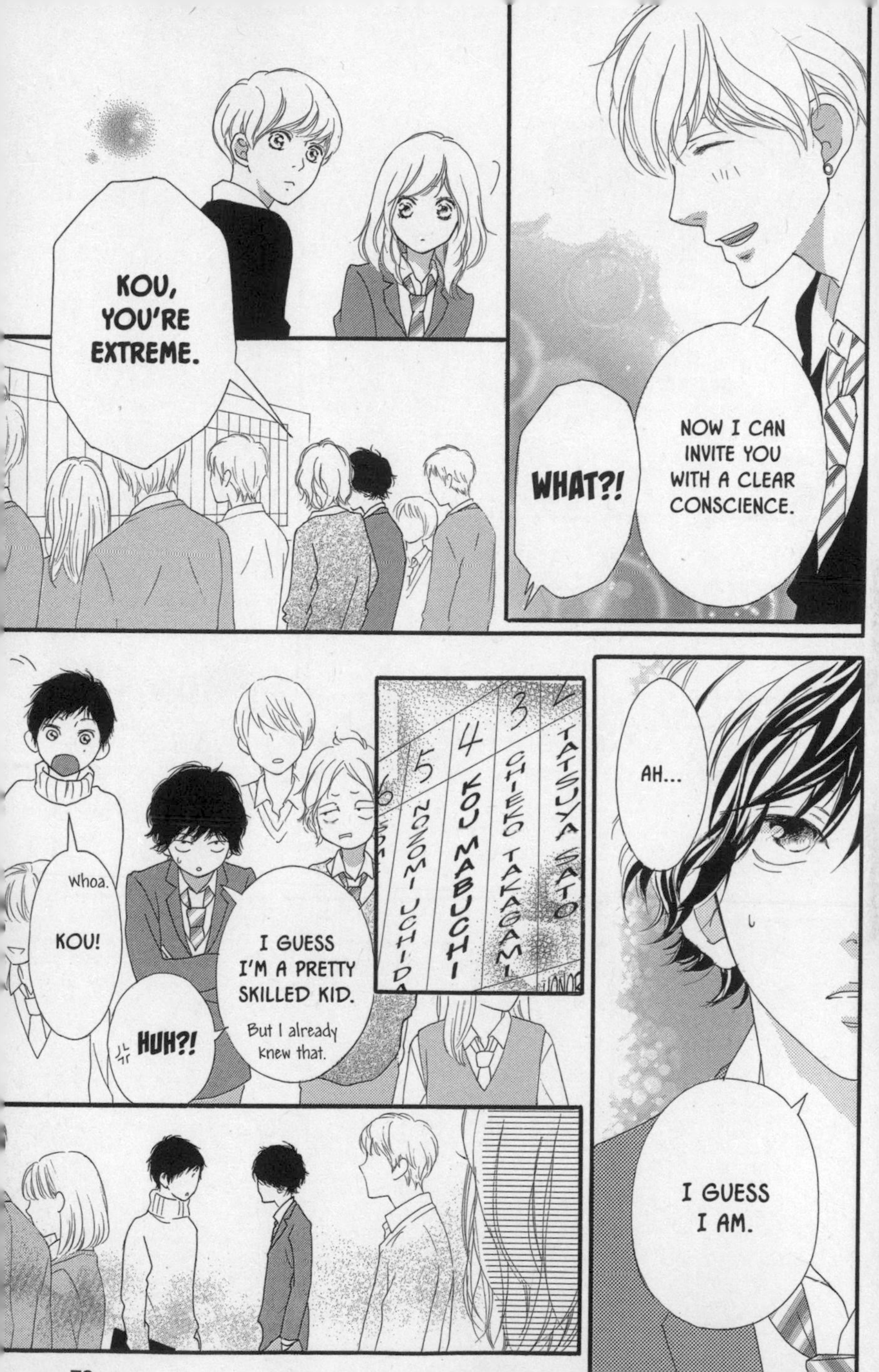
NOW I CAN INVITE YOU WITH A CLEAR CONSCIENCE.
WHAT?!
KOU, YOU'RE EXTREME.
AH...
I GUESS I AM.
2 TATSUYA SATO
3 CHIEKO TAKAGAMI
4 KOU MABUCHI
5 NOZOMI UCHIDA
6
I GUESS I'M A PRETTY SKILLED KID.
But I already knew that.
HUH?!
Whoa.
KOU!

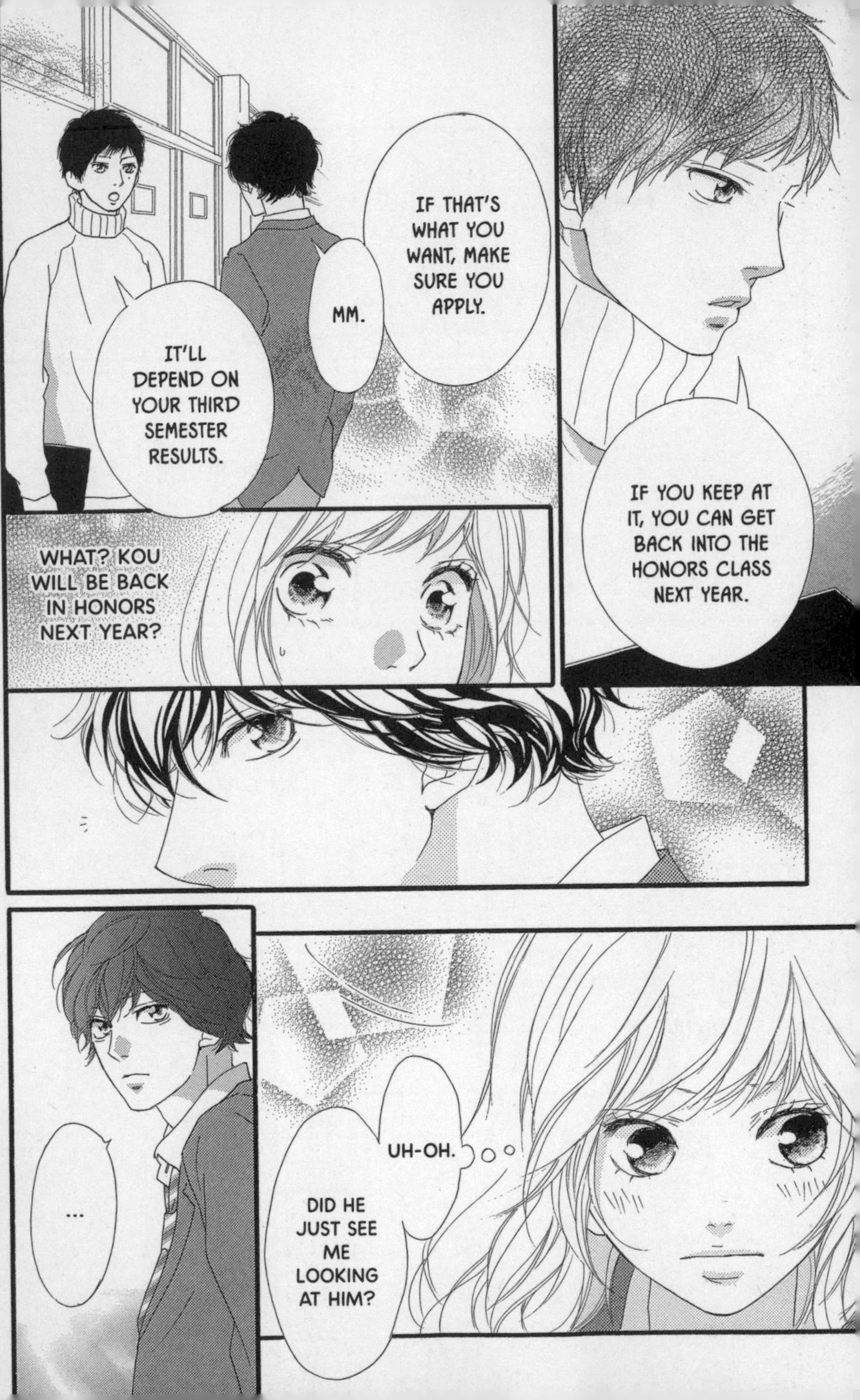
IF YOU KEEP AT IT, YOU CAN GET BACK INTO THE HONORS CLASS NEXT YEAR.
IF THAT'S WHAT YOU WANT, MAKE SURE YOU APPLY.
MM.
IT'LL DEPEND ON YOUR THIRD SEMESTER RESULTS.
WHAT? KOU WILL BE BACK IN HONORS NEXT YEAR?
UH-OH.
DID HE JUST SEE ME LOOKING AT HIM?
...

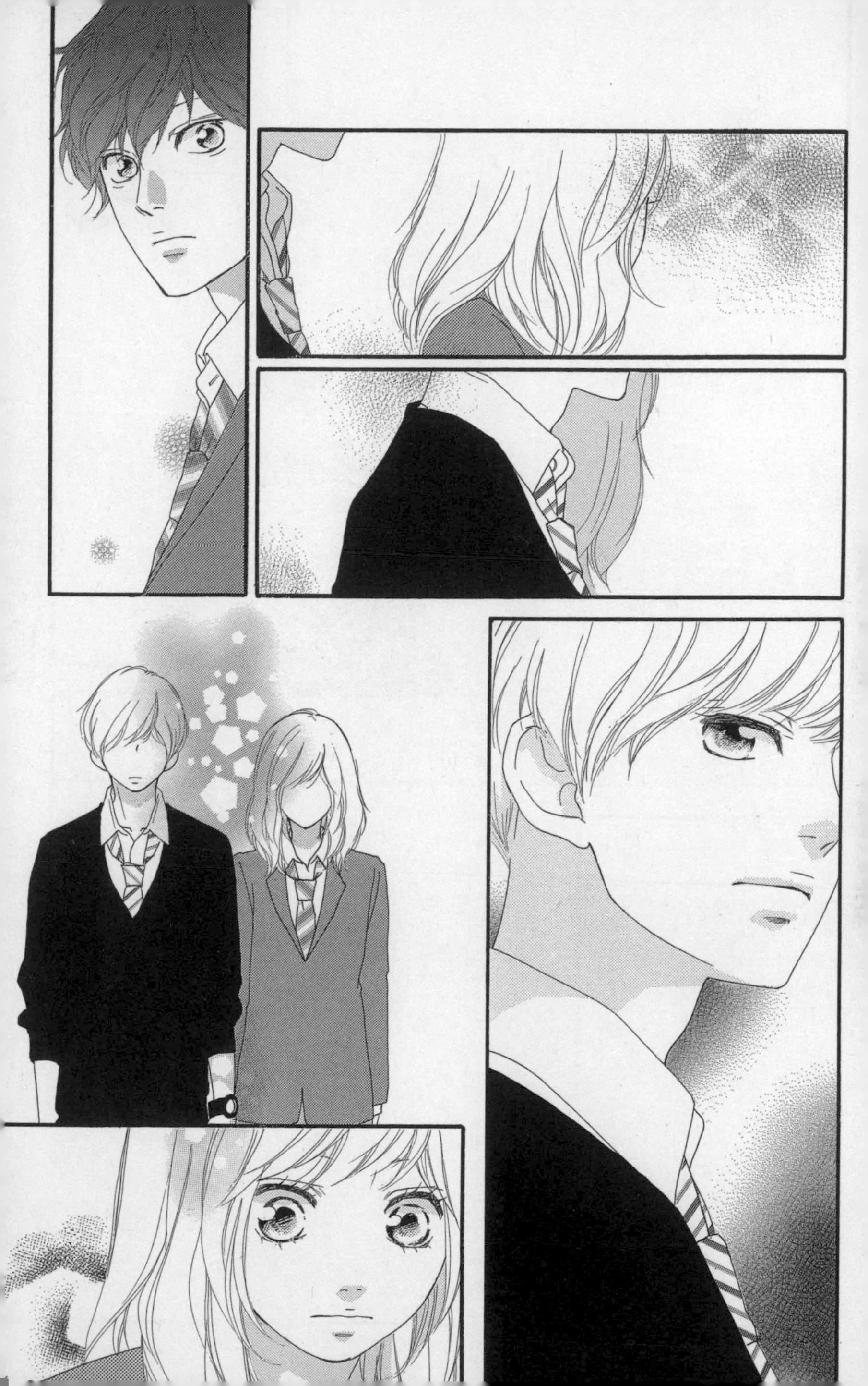

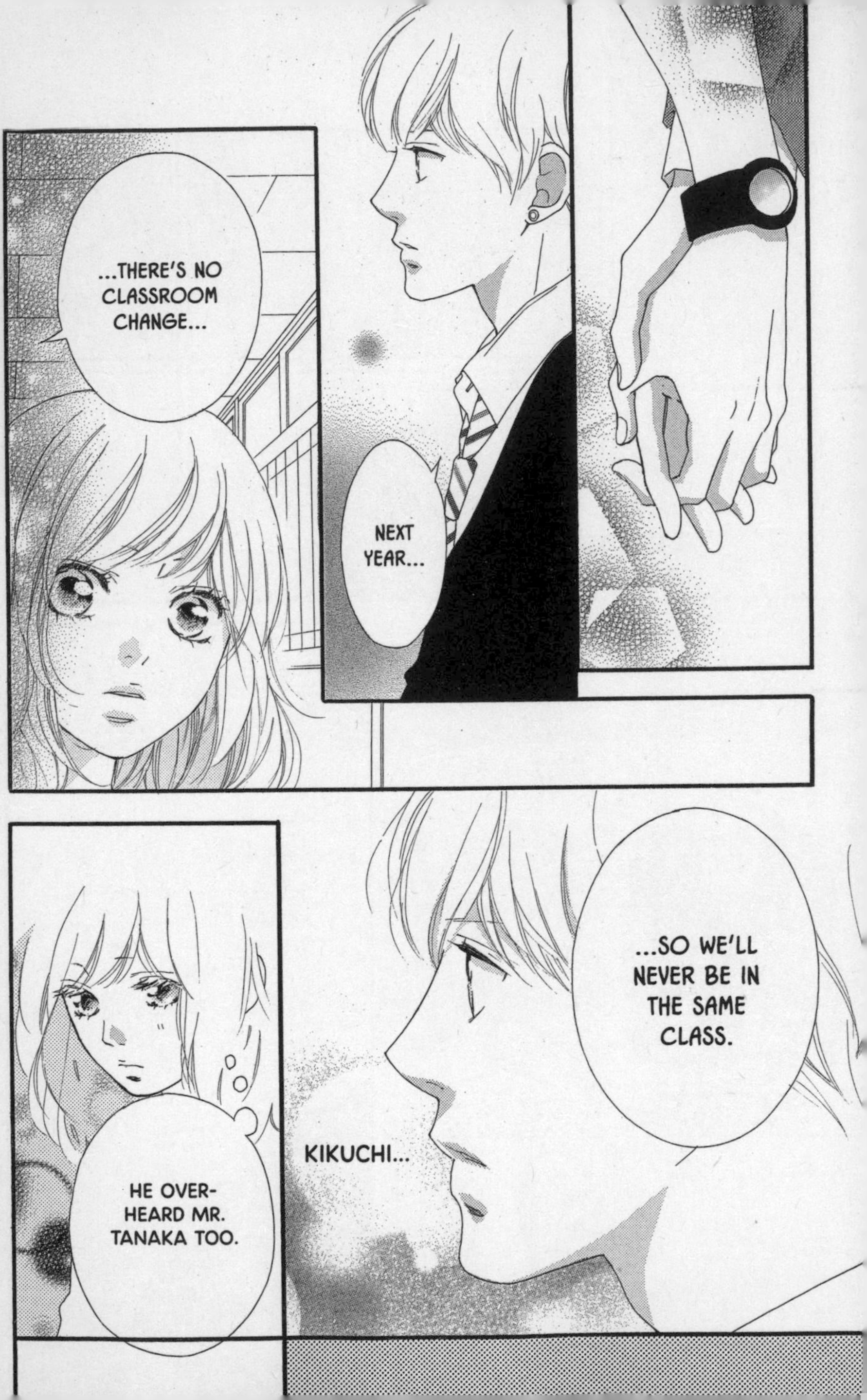
NEXT YEAR...
...THERE'S NO CLASSROOM CHANGE...
...SO WE'LL NEVER BE IN THE SAME CLASS.
KIKUCHI...
HE OVER-HEARD MR. TANAKA TOO.

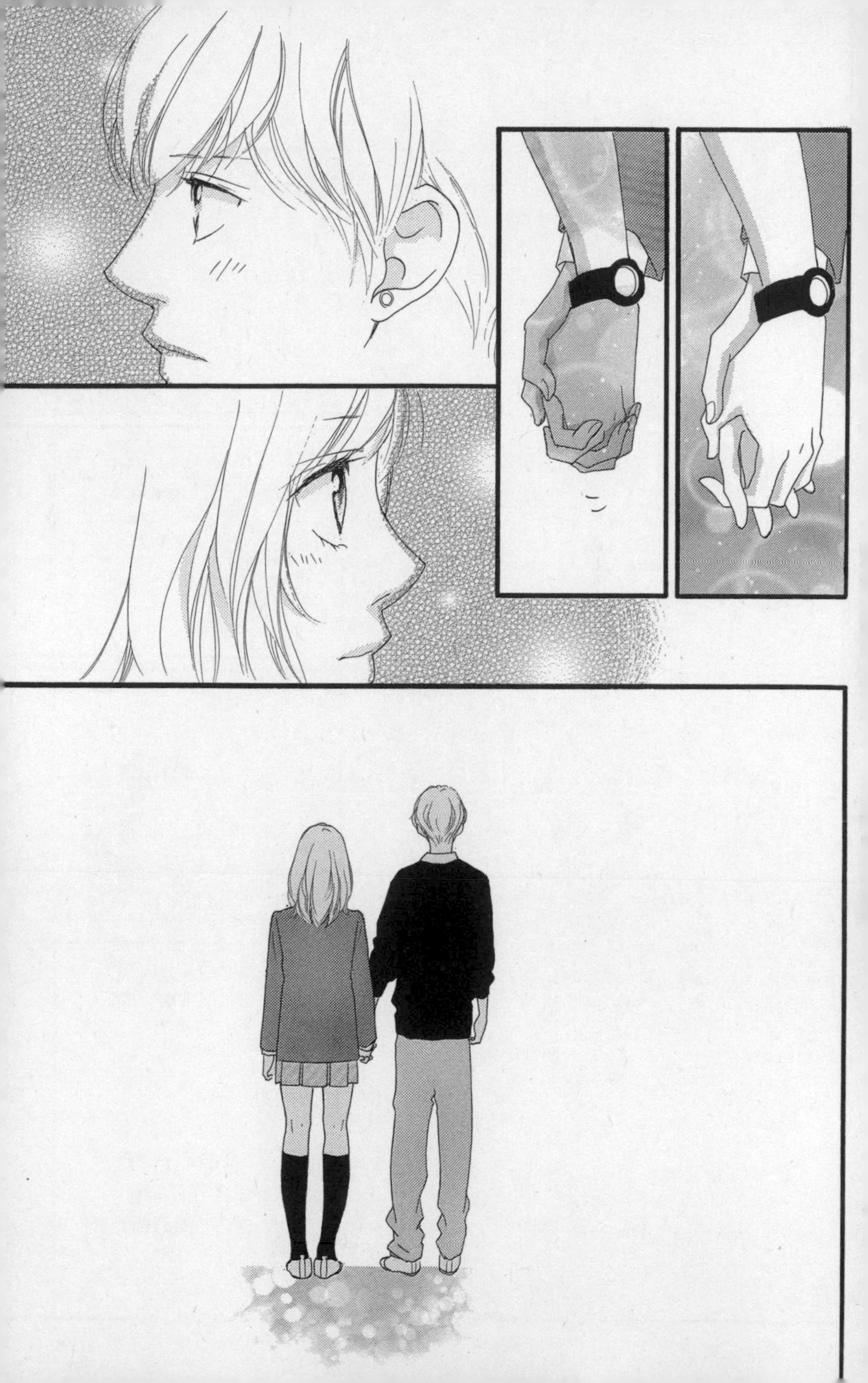

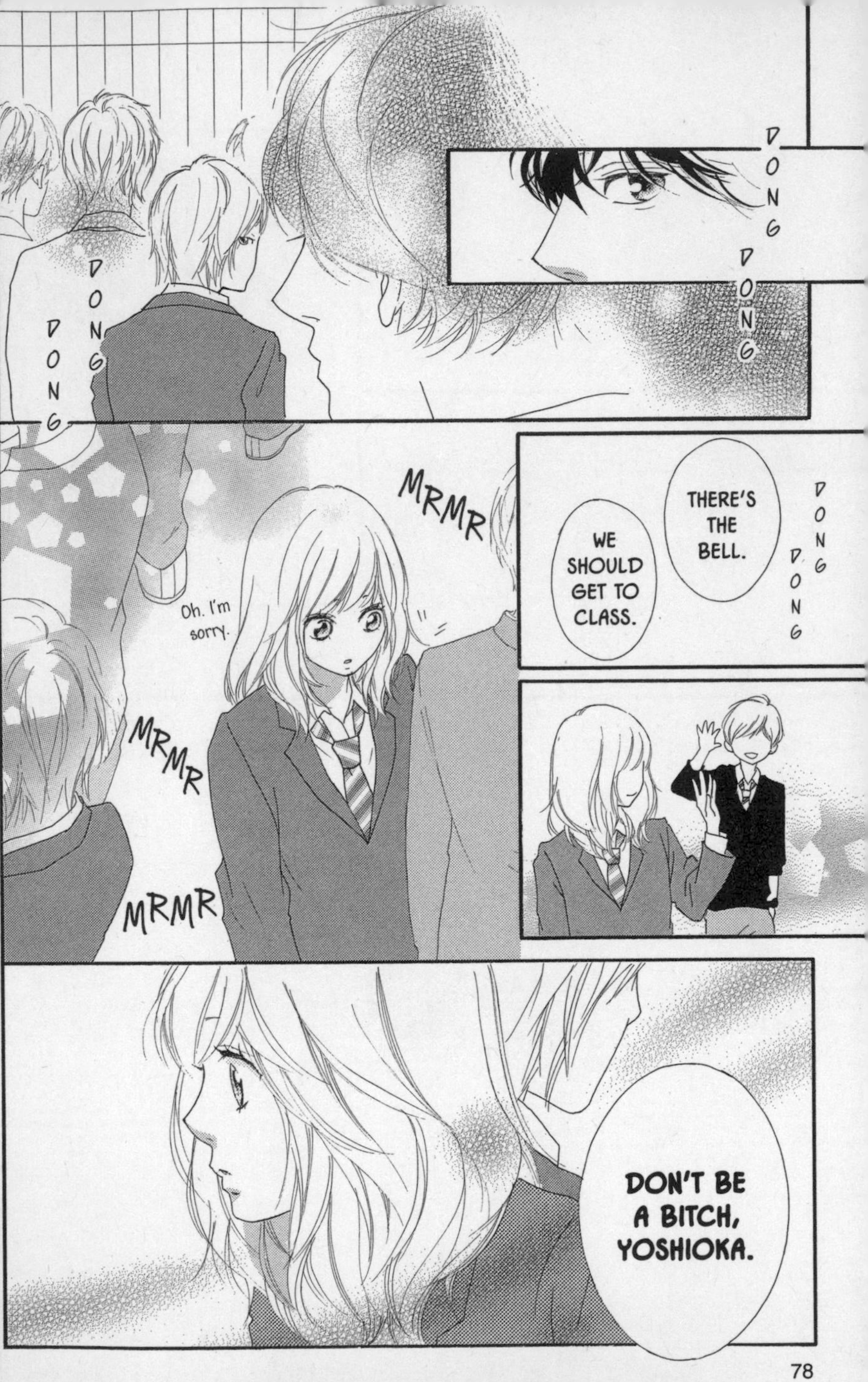
DONG DONG
DONG DONG
THERE'S THE BELL.
WE SHOULD GET TO CLASS.
DONG DONG
MRMR
Oh. I'm sorry.
MRMR
MRMR
DON'T BE A BITCH, YOSHIOKA.

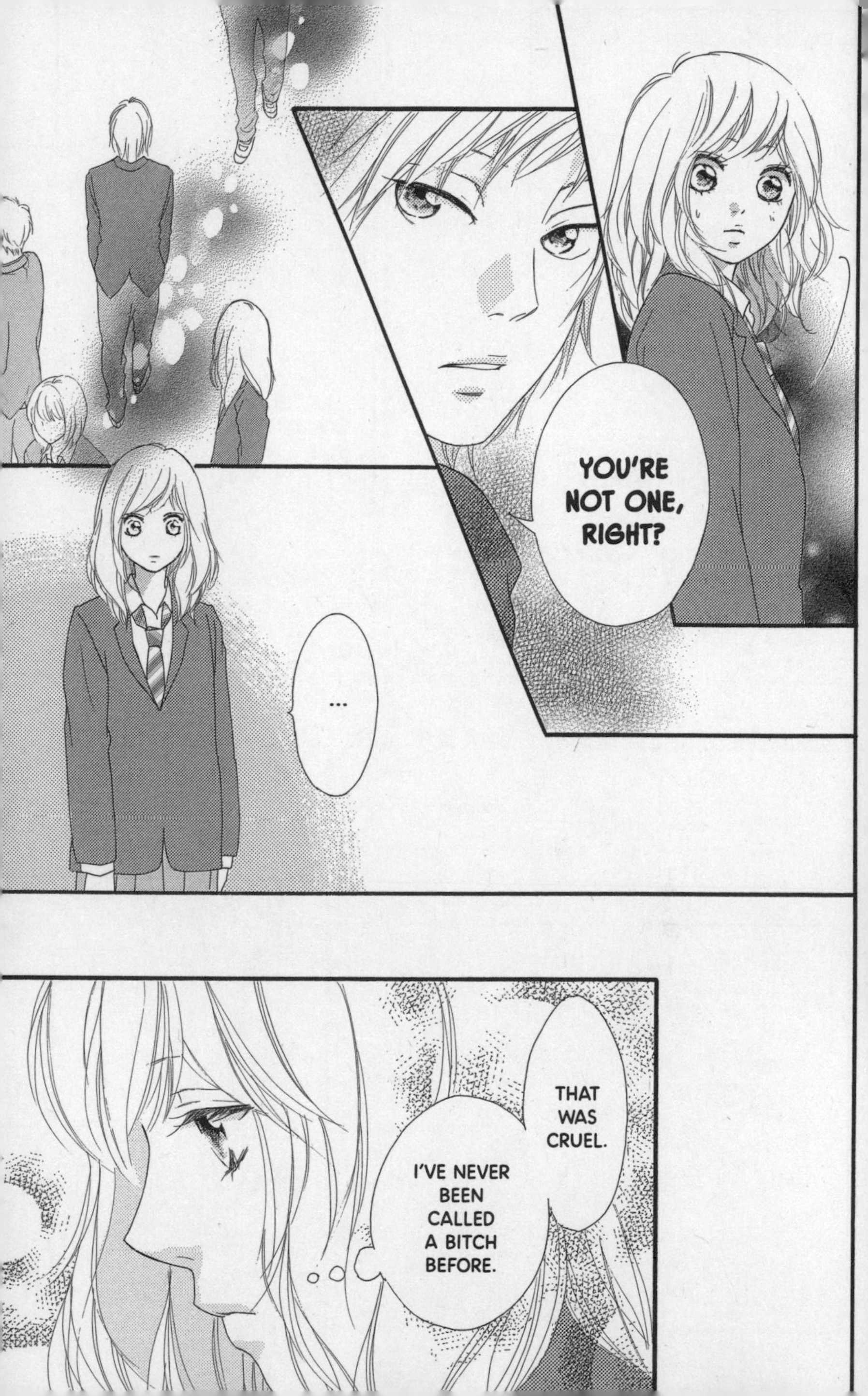
YOU'RE NOT ONE, RIGHT?
...
THAT WAS CRUEL.
I'VE NEVER BEEN CALLED A BITCH BEFORE.

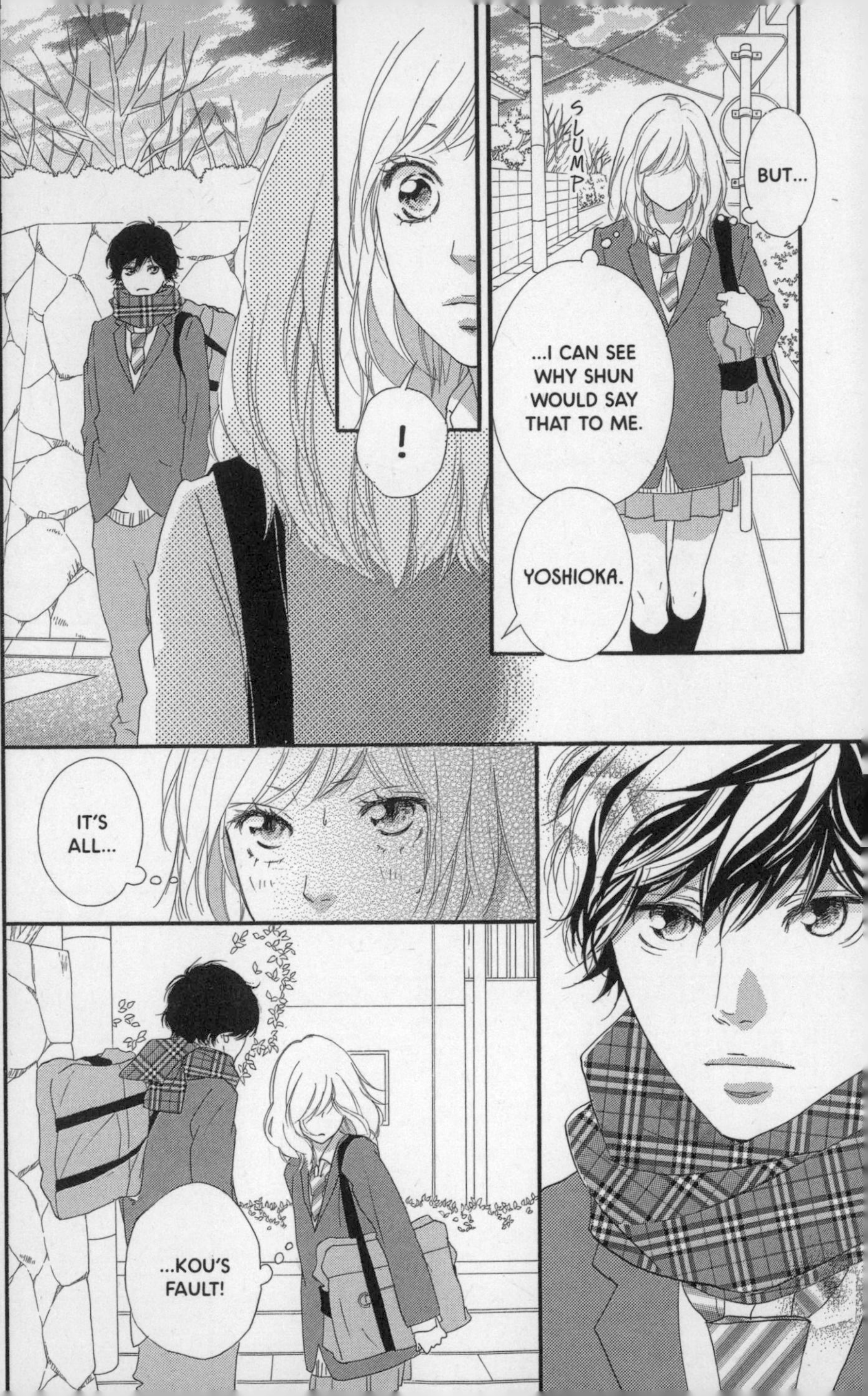

BUT...
SLUMP
...I CAN SEE WHY SHUN WOULD SAY THAT TO ME.
YOSHIOKA.
!
IT'S ALL...
...KOU'S FAULT!

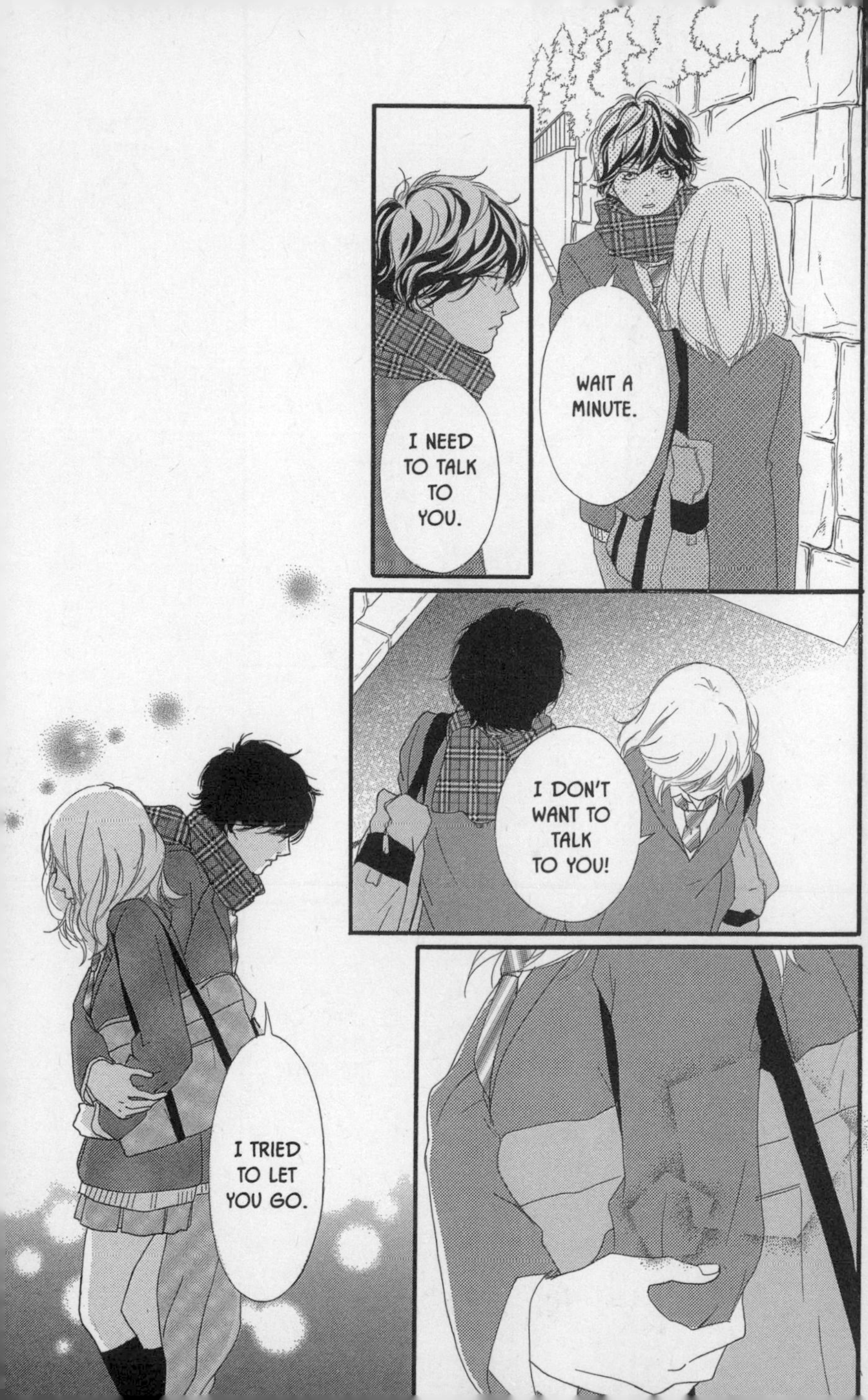
WAIT A MINUTE.
I NEED TO TALK TO YOU.
I DON'T WANT TO TALK TO YOU!
I TRIED TO LET YOU GO.

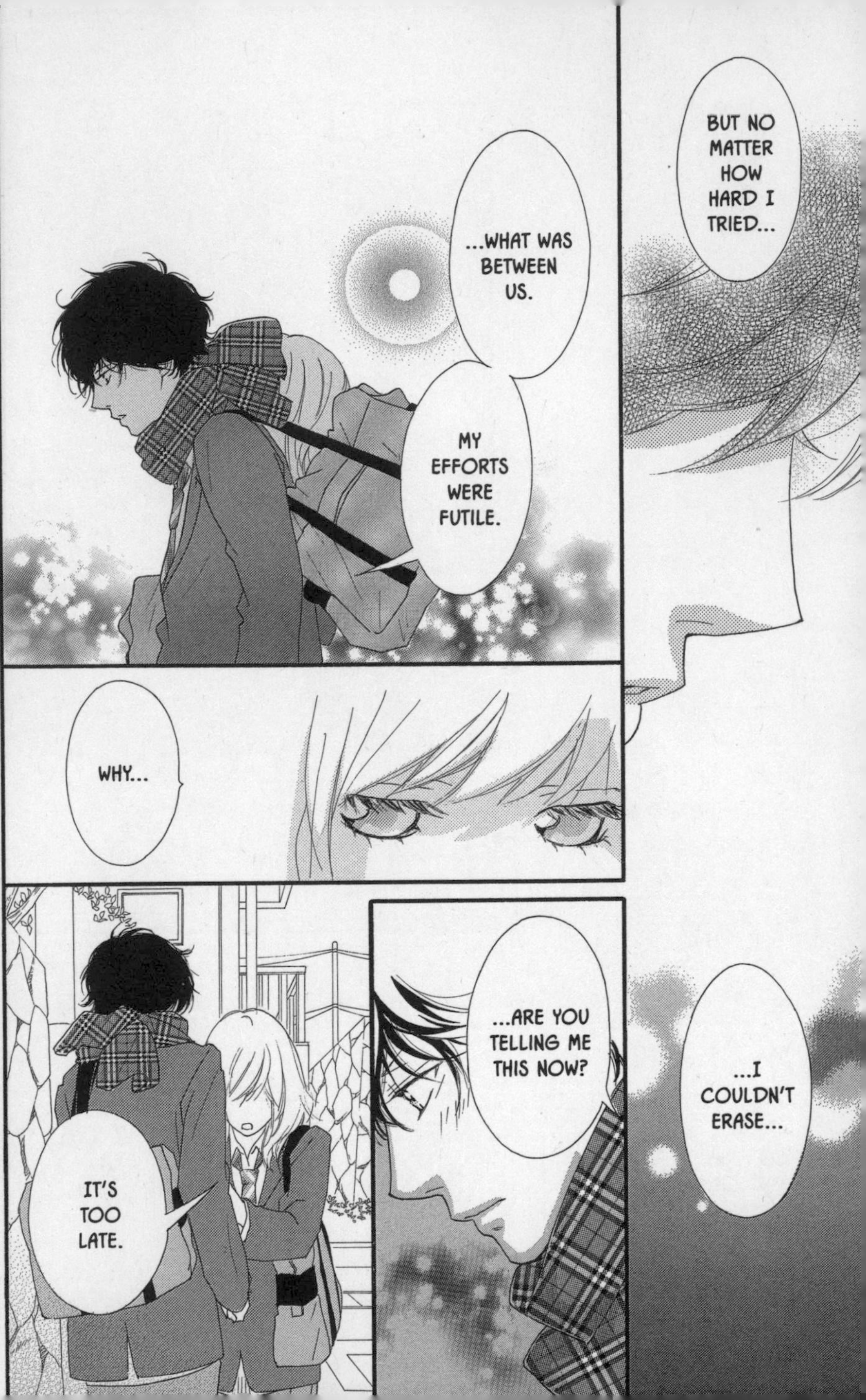
BUT NO MATTER HOW HARD I TRIED...
...I COULDN'T ERASE...
...WHAT WAS BETWEEN US.
MY EFFORTS WERE FUTILE.
WHY...
...ARE YOU TELLING ME THIS NOW?
IT'S TOO LATE.

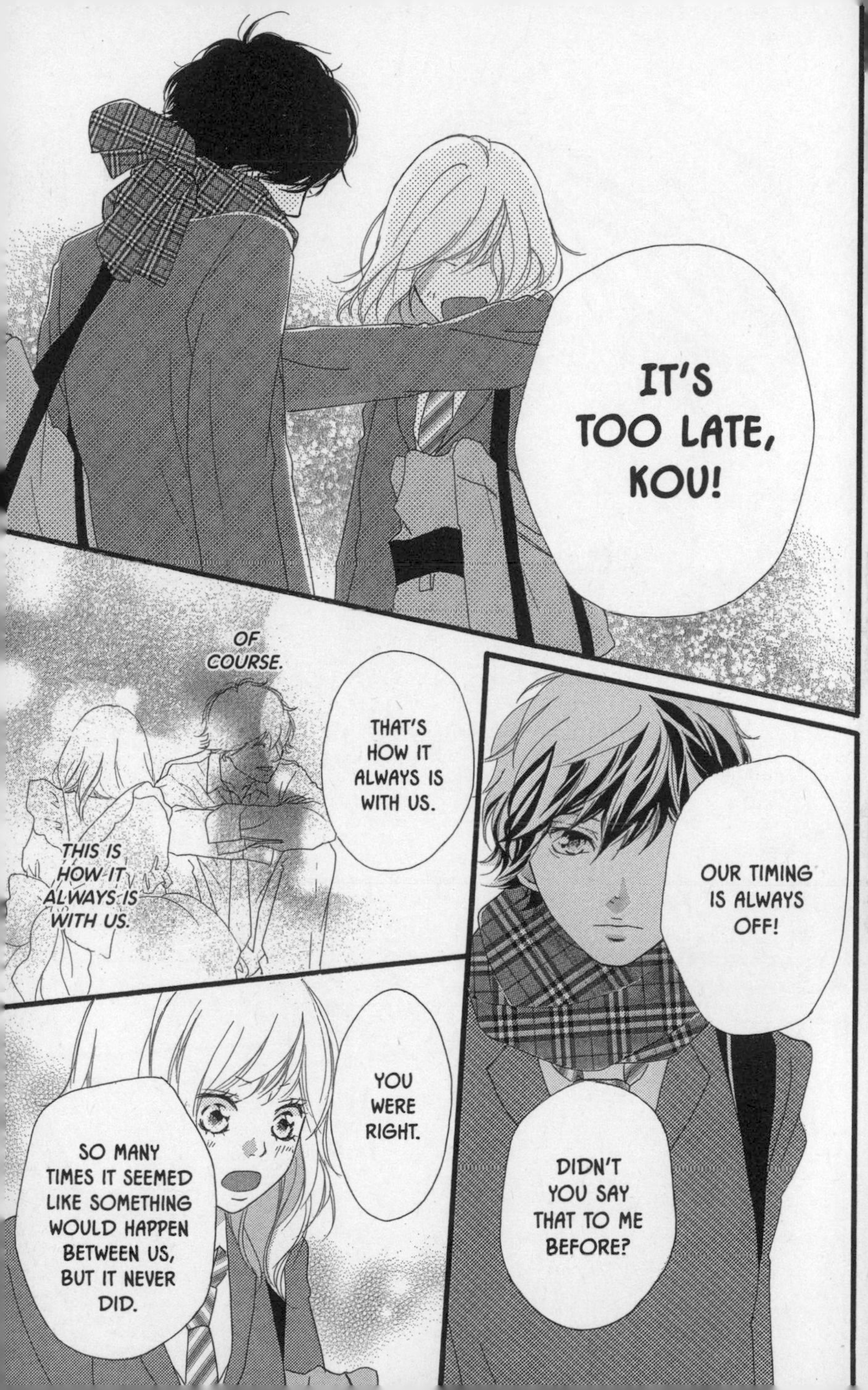
IT'S TOO LATE, KOU!
OUR TIMING IS ALWAYS OFF!
DIDN'T YOU SAY THAT TO ME BEFORE?
OF COURSE.
THAT'S HOW IT ALWAYS IS WITH US.
THIS IS HOW IT ALWAYS IS WITH US.
YOU WERE RIGHT.
SO MANY TIMES IT SEEMED LIKE SOMETHING WOULD HAPPEN BETWEEN US, BUT IT NEVER DID.

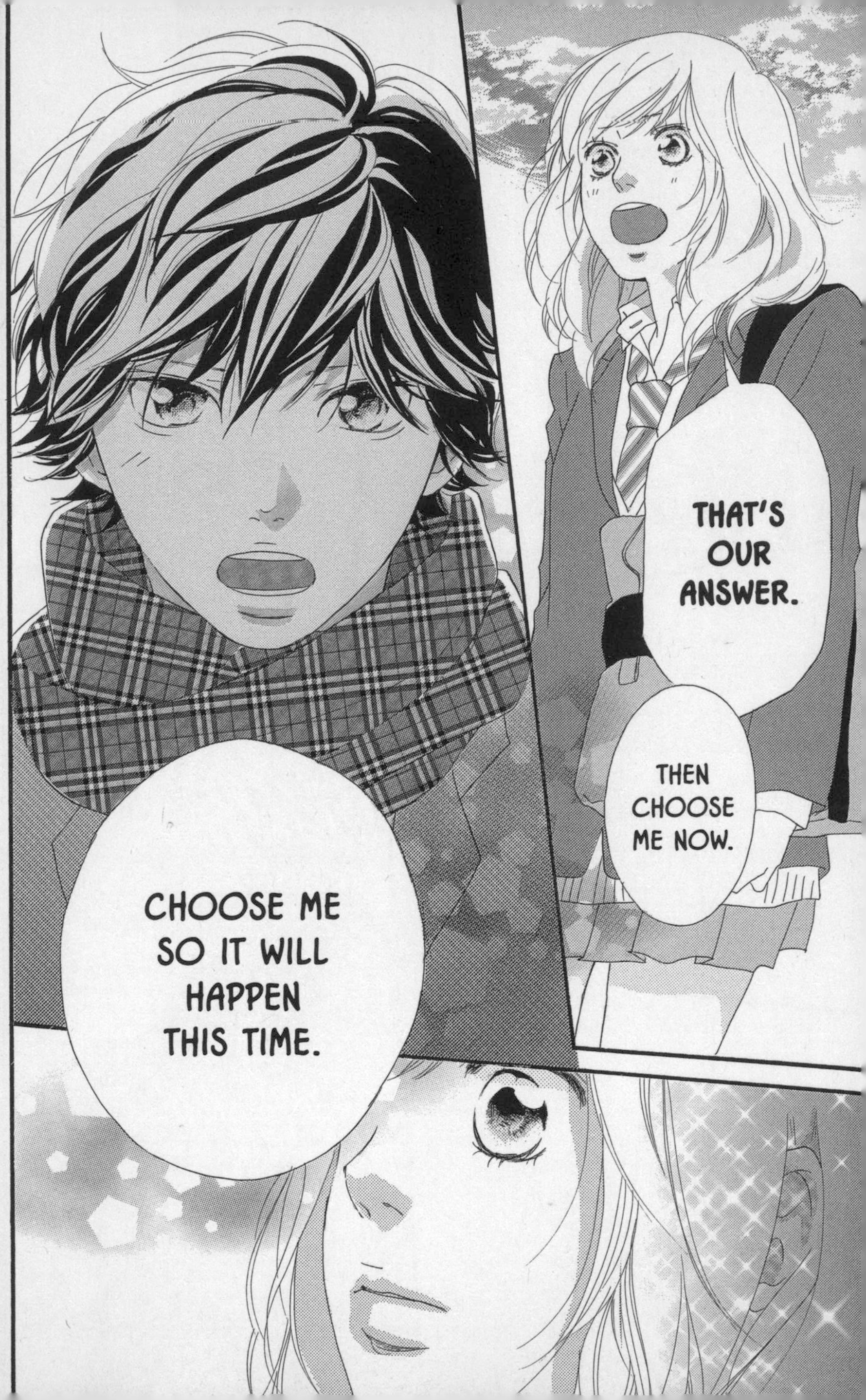
THAT'S OUR ANSWER.
THEN CHOOSE ME NOW.
CHOOSE ME SO IT WILL HAPPEN THIS TIME.

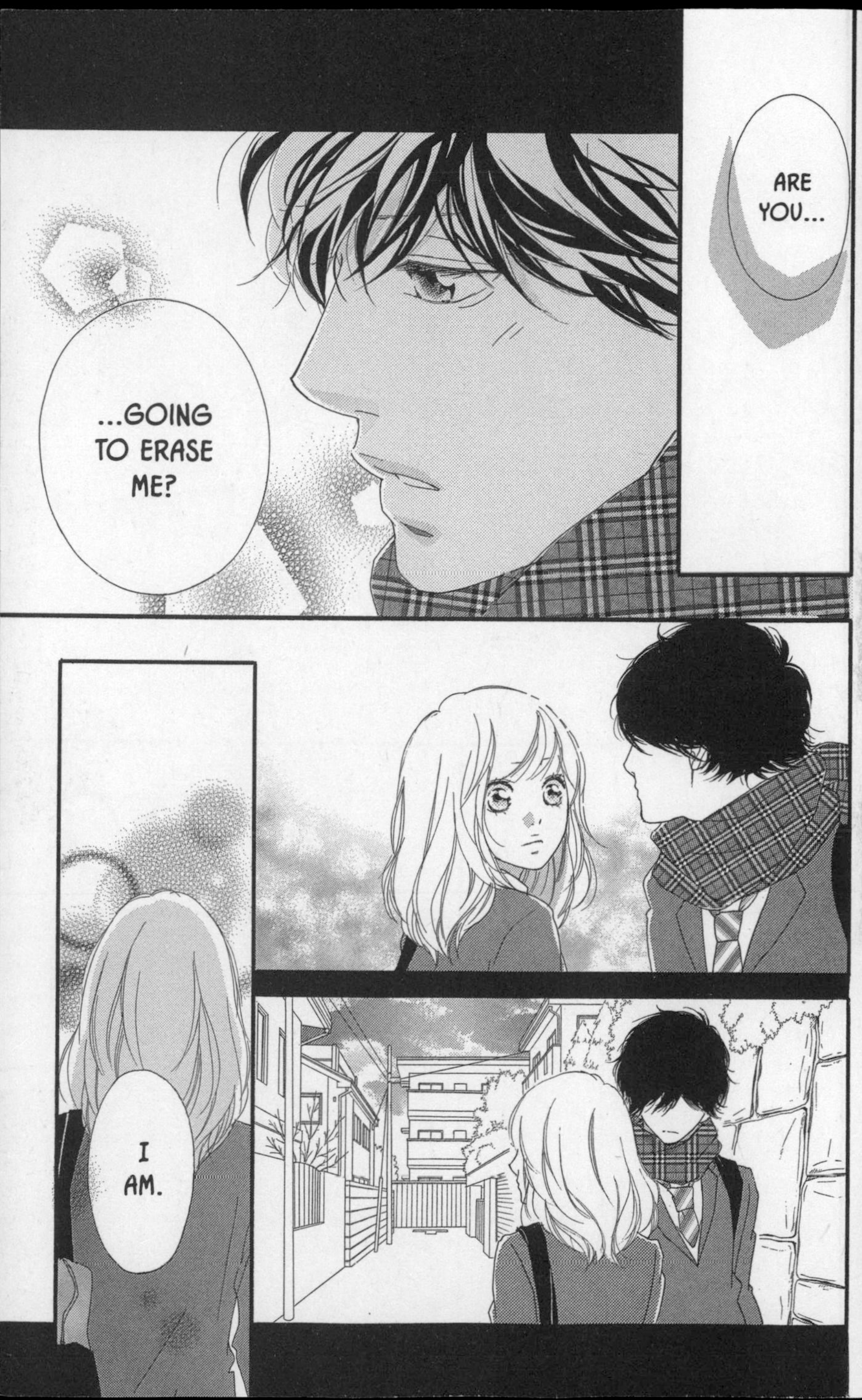
ARE YOU...
...GOING TO ERASE ME?
I AM.

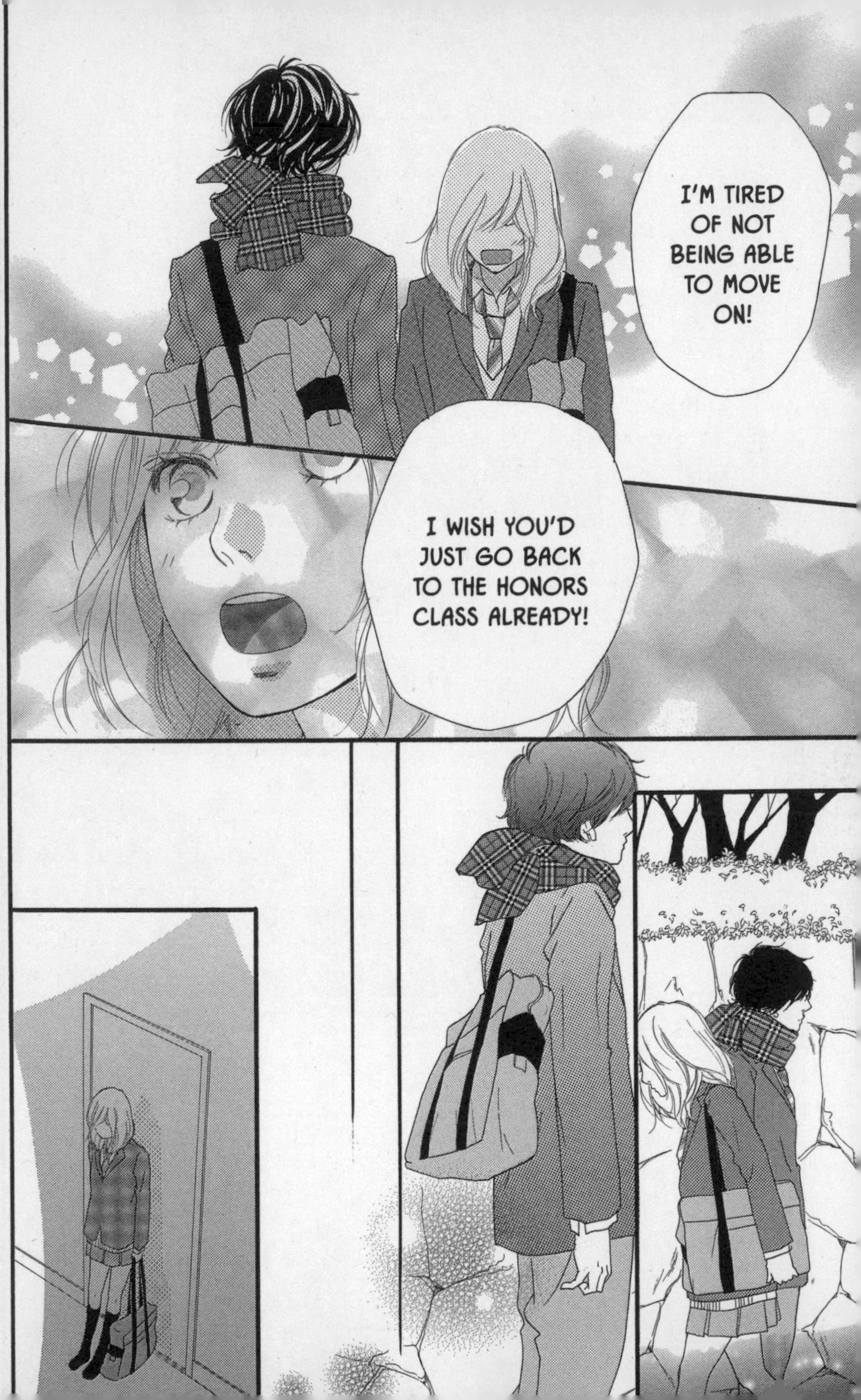
I'M TIRED OF NOT BEING ABLE TO MOVE ON!
I WISH YOU'D JUST GO BACK TO THE HONORS CLASS ALREADY!

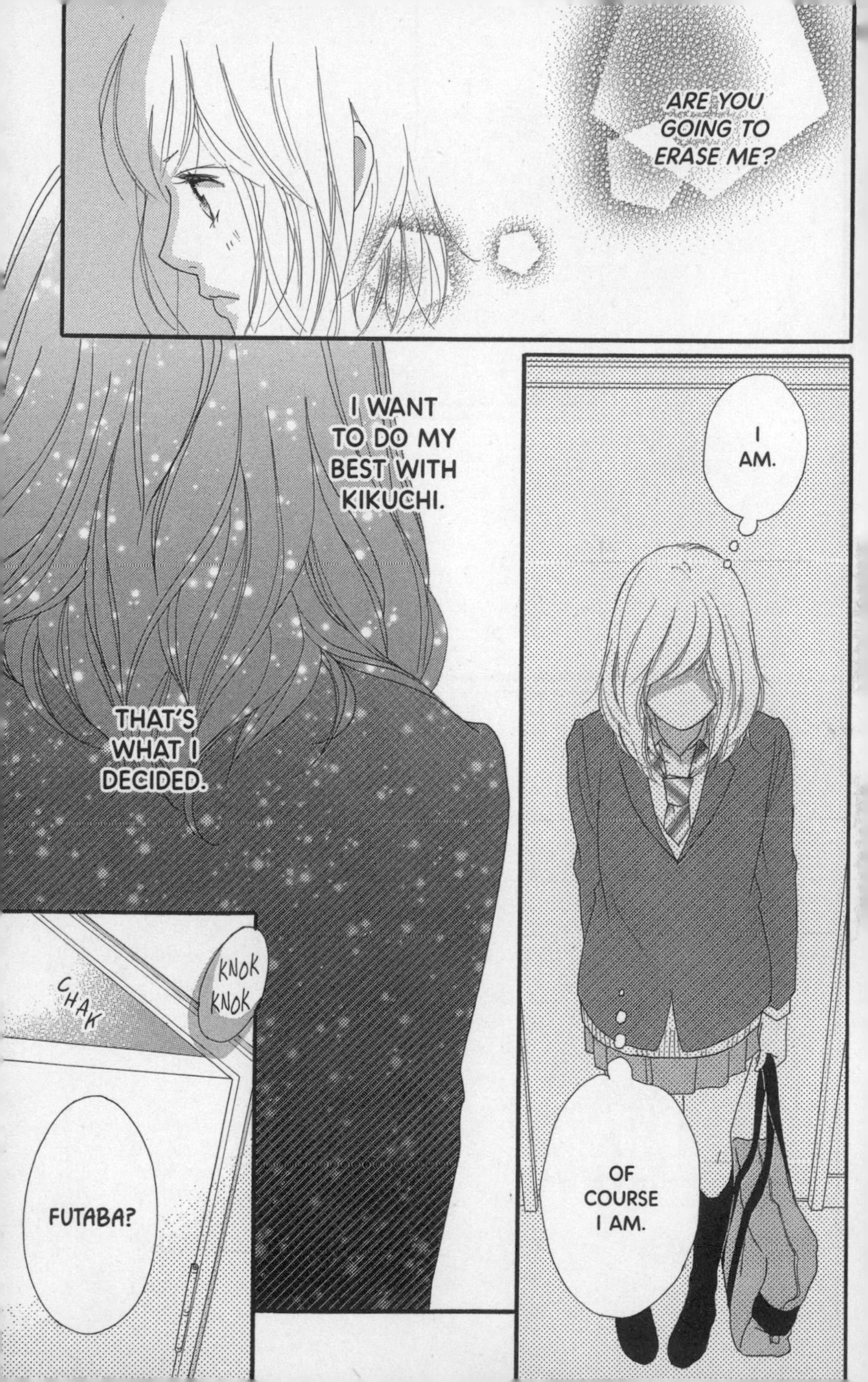
ARE YOU GOING TO ERASE ME?
I AM.
OF COURSE I AM.
I WANT TO DO MY BEST WITH KIKUCHI.
THAT'S WHAT I DECIDED.
KNOK KNOK
CHAK
FUTABA?

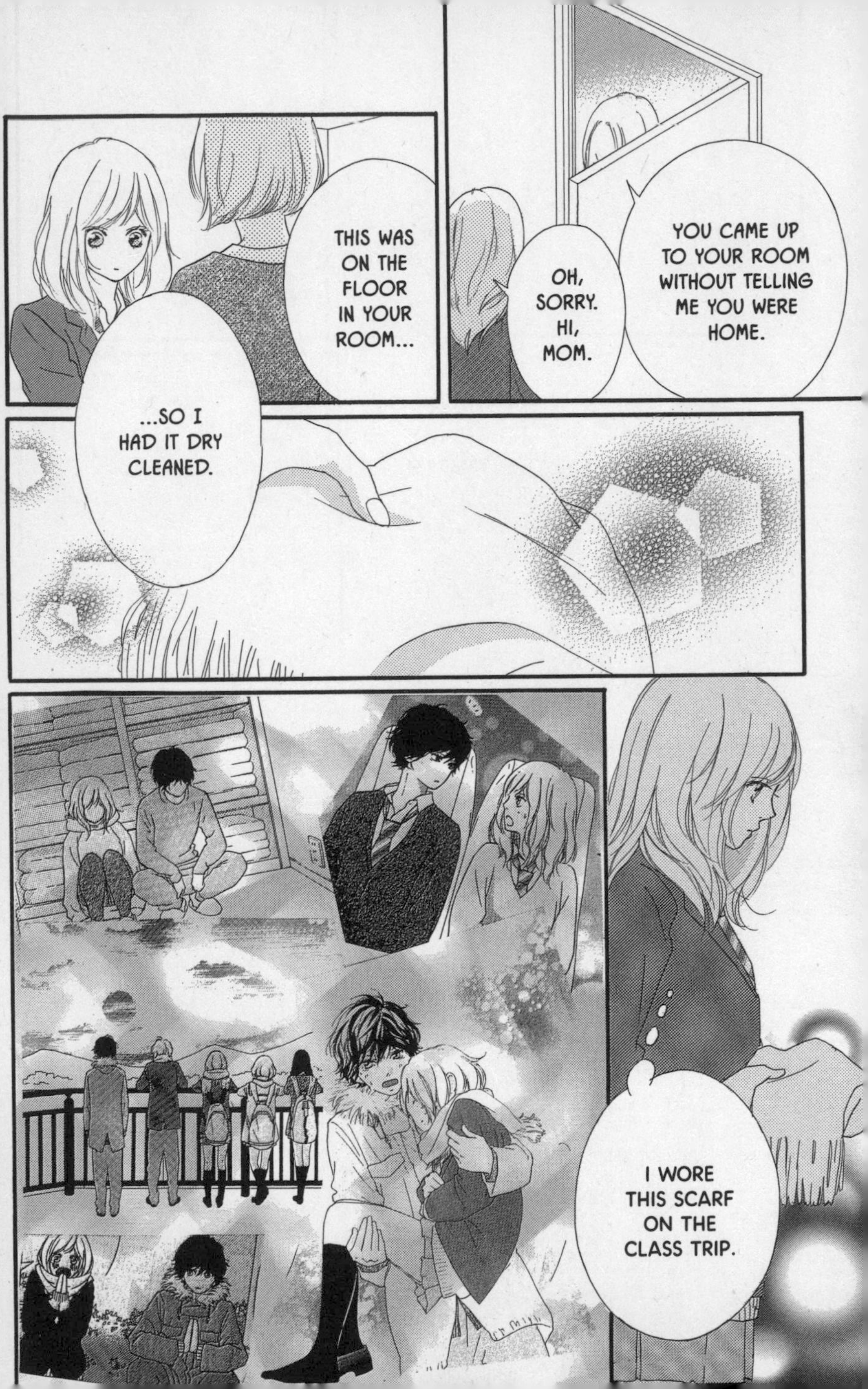
YOU CAME UP TO YOUR ROOM WITHOUT TELLING ME YOU WERE HOME.
OH, SORRY. HI, MOM.
THIS WAS ON THE FLOOR IN YOUR ROOM...
...SO I HAD IT DRY CLEANED.
I WORE THIS SCARF ON THE CLASS TRIP.

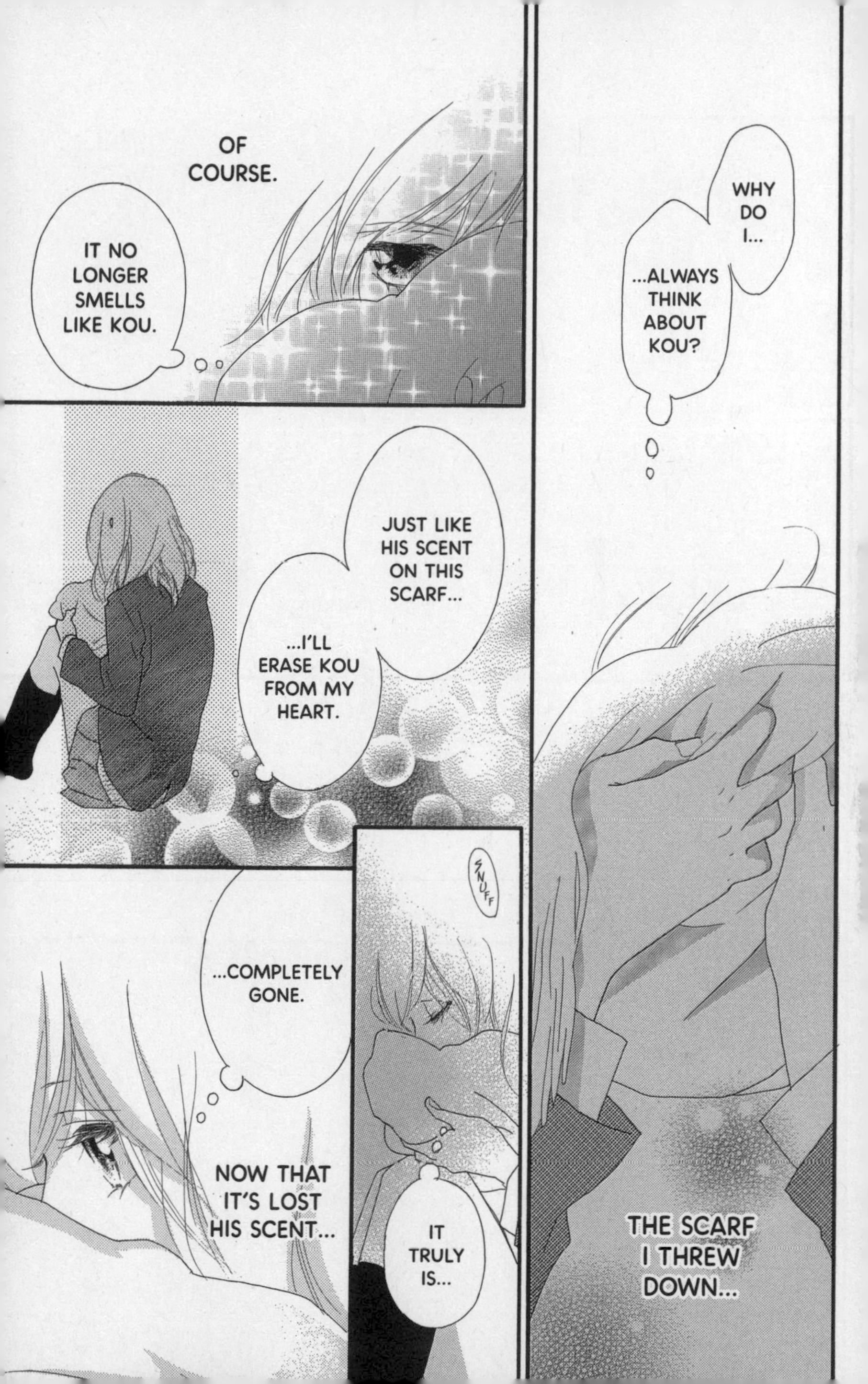
WHY DO I...
...ALWAYS THINK ABOUT KOU?
THE SCARF I THREW DOWN...
IT NO LONGER SMELLS LIKE KOU.
OF COURSE.
JUST LIKE HIS SCENT ON THIS SCARF...
...I'LL ERASE KOU FROM MY HEART.
SNUFF
IT TRULY IS...
...COMPLETELY GONE.
NOW THAT IT'S LOST HIS SCENT...

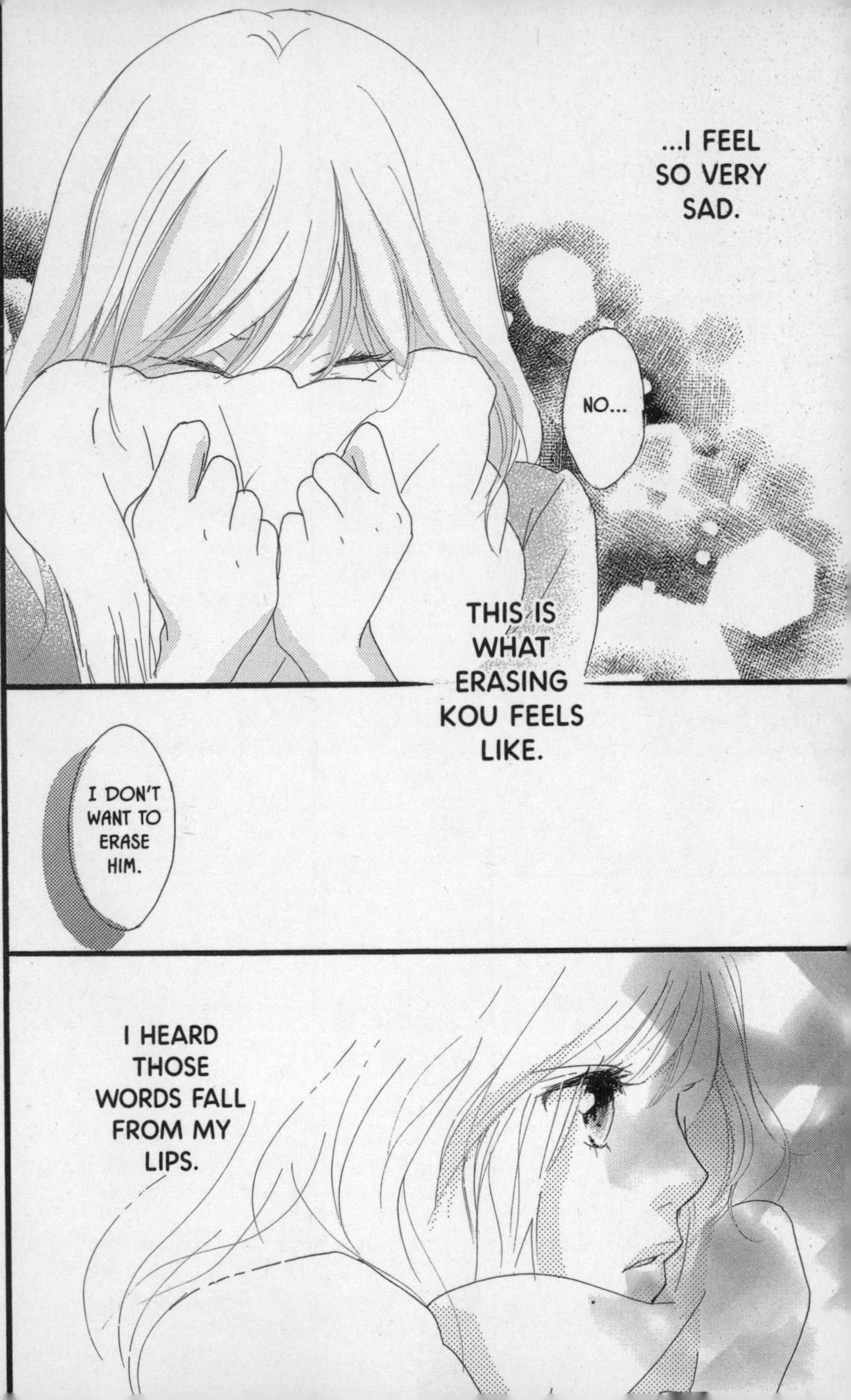
...I FEEL SO VERY SAD.
NO...
THIS IS WHAT ERASING KOU FEELS LIKE.
I DON'T WANT TO ERASE HIM.
I HEARD THOSE WORDS FALL FROM MY LIPS.

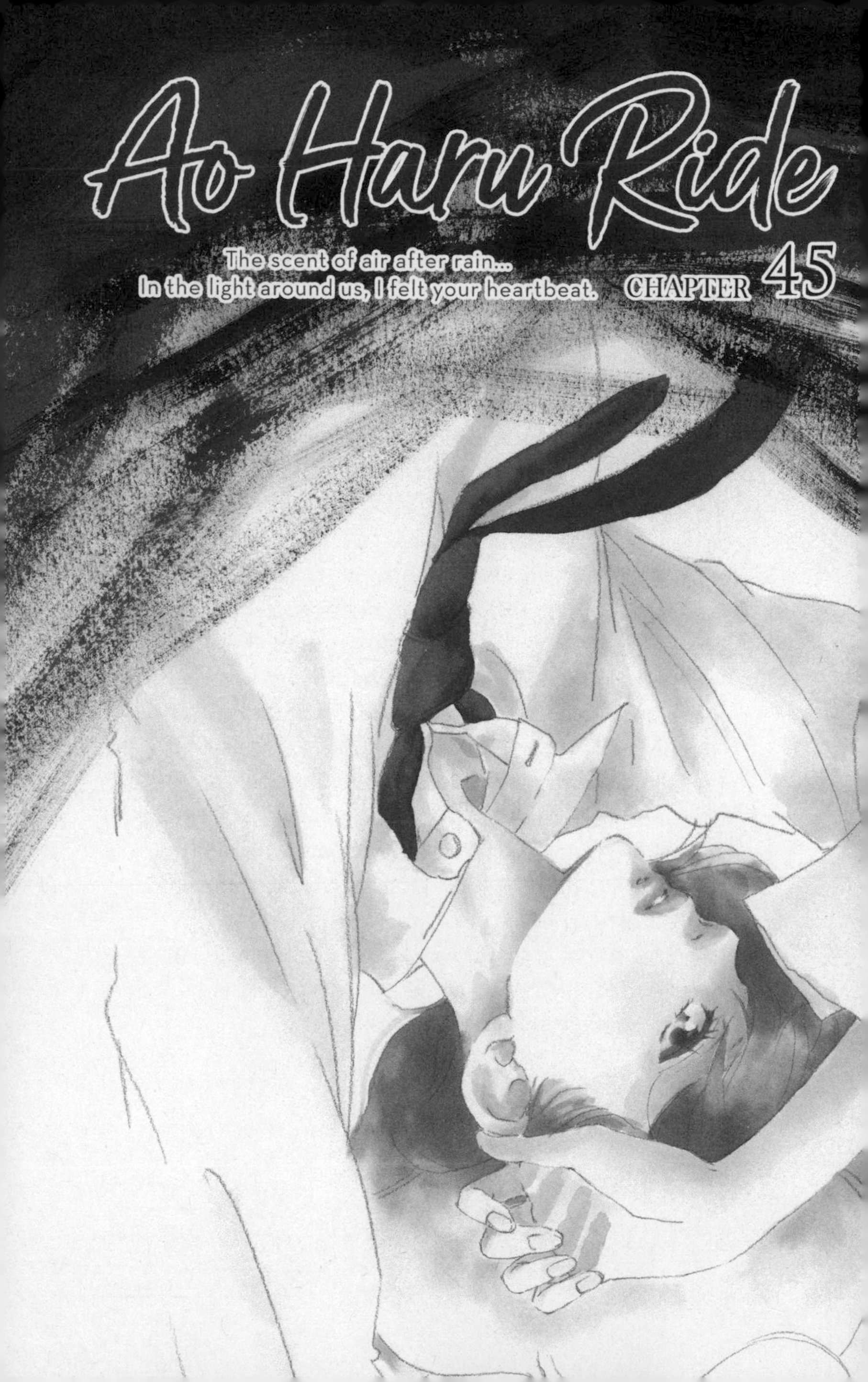

Ao Haru Ride
The scent of air after rain...
In the light around us, I felt your heartbeat.
CHAPTER 45

Speaking of Kou's home in Nagasaki... The station closest
to his house is Haiki Station, and a number of my Twitter
followers have let me know that the station has since been
changed. Apparently the old building was constructed during
the Meiji era and is made of wood. Its details are just
adorable. Now that the old building is no longer being used,
I am grateful to have had the opportunity to visit, photograph,
and incorporate it into this story. (Are they keeping the old
building as it is? I wonder...) Before I visited, I had never
heard of Haiki Station. While I was touring Nagasaki by taxi,
I asked my driver to take me to any nearby station, and
that was where he brought me. I ended up there by chance.
The station was amazingly adorable and so much fun to
photograph. When I got back home, I learned that the station
was right by Huis Ten Bosch, so that's when I came up with
having Kou and Futaba sneak out of there in volume 11.
I have a lot of memories of Haiki. When I think about how
Kou will never again be able to step out onto the same
station platform as he did with his mother back in junior
high, it makes my heart ache. But I think there's also
something special in that sadness. There's something about
it that reminds me that Kou is also changing. I'm glad to
have happened upon Haiki Station that day.

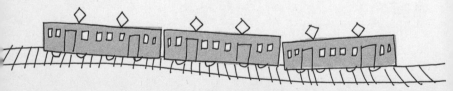

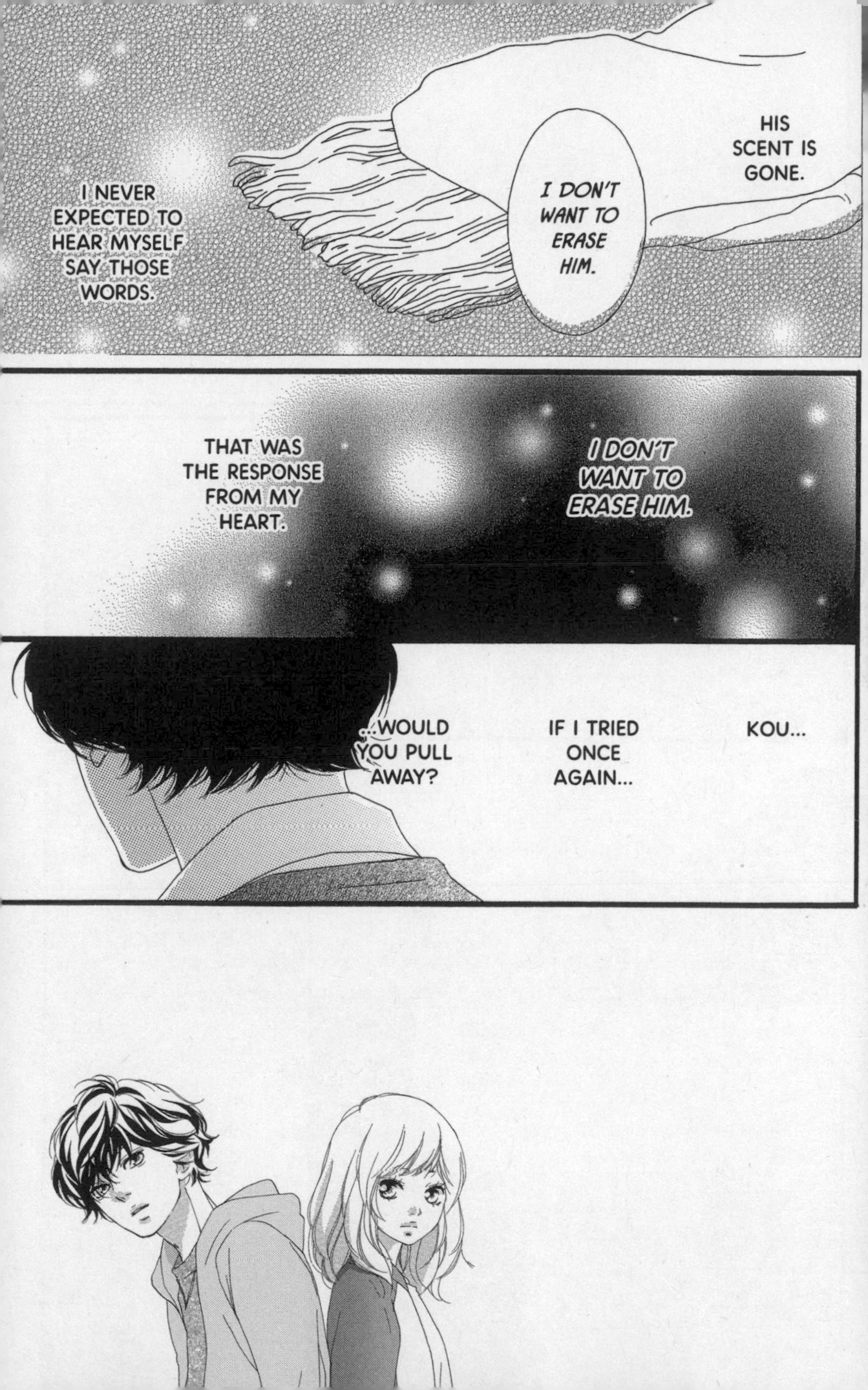
HIS SCENT IS GONE.
I DON'T WANT TO ERASE HIM.
I NEVER EXPECTED TO HEAR MYSELF SAY THOSE WORDS.
I DON'T WANT TO ERASE HIM.
THAT WAS THE RESPONSE FROM MY HEART.
KOU...
IF I TRIED ONCE AGAIN...
...WOULD YOU PULL AWAY?

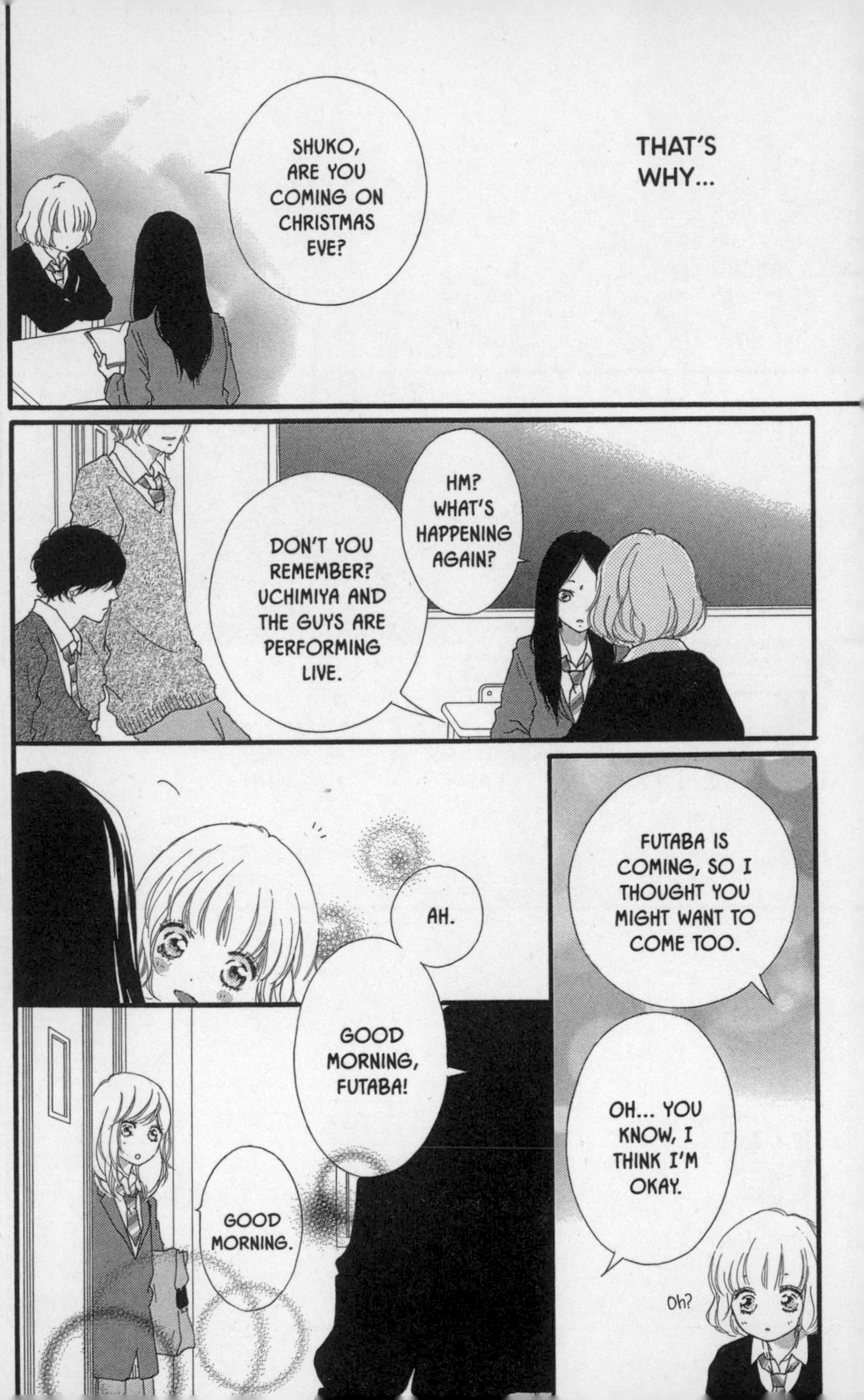
THAT'S WHY...
SHUKO, ARE YOU COMING ON CHRISTMAS EVE?
HM? WHAT'S HAPPENING AGAIN?
DON'T YOU REMEMBER? UCHIMIYA AND THE GUYS ARE PERFORMING LIVE.
FUTABA IS COMING, SO I THOUGHT YOU MIGHT WANT TO COME TOO.
OH... YOU KNOW, I THINK I'M OKAY.
Oh?
AH.
GOOD MORNING, FUTABA!
GOOD MORNING.

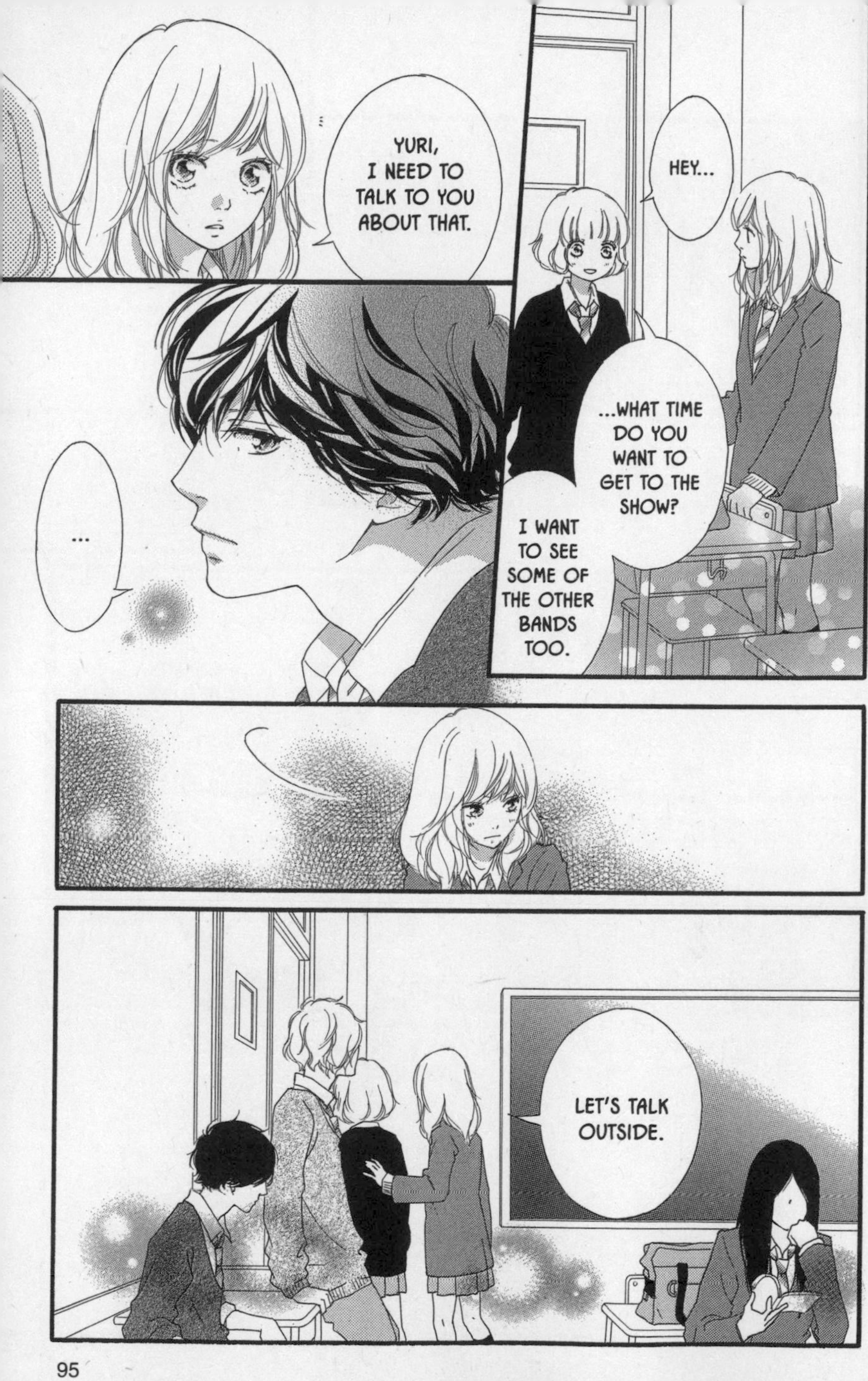
HEY...
...WHAT TIME DO YOU WANT TO GET TO THE SHOW?
I WANT TO SEE SOME OF THE OTHER BANDS TOO.
YURI, I NEED TO TALK TO YOU ABOUT THAT.
...
LET'S TALK OUTSIDE.

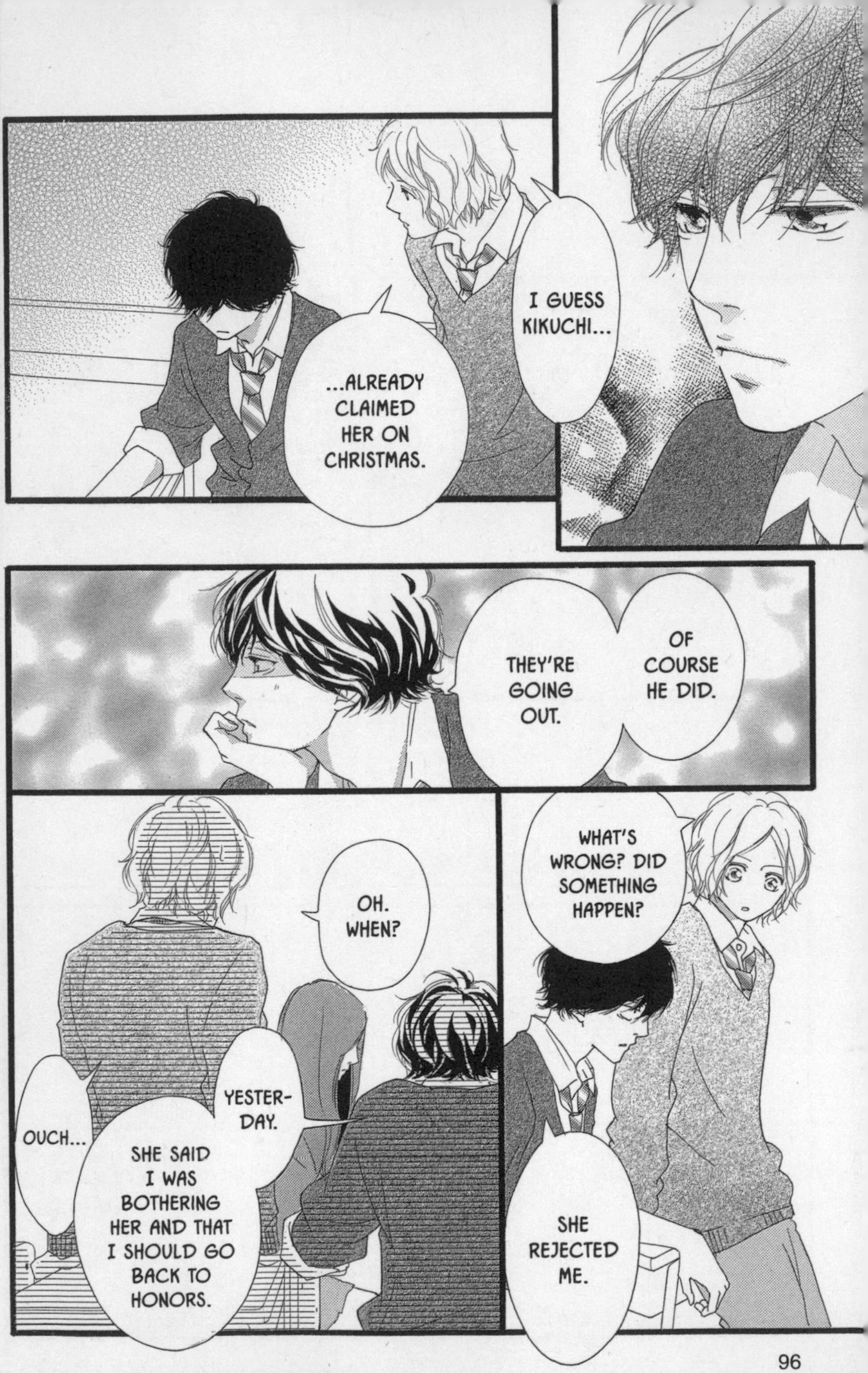
I GUESS KIKUCHI...
...ALREADY CLAIMED HER ON CHRISTMAS.
OF COURSE HE DID.
THEY'RE GOING OUT.
WHAT'S WRONG? DID SOMETHING HAPPEN?
SHE REJECTED ME.
OH. WHEN?
YESTER-DAY.
SHE SAID I WAS BOTHERING HER AND THAT I SHOULD GO BACK TO HONORS.
OUCH...

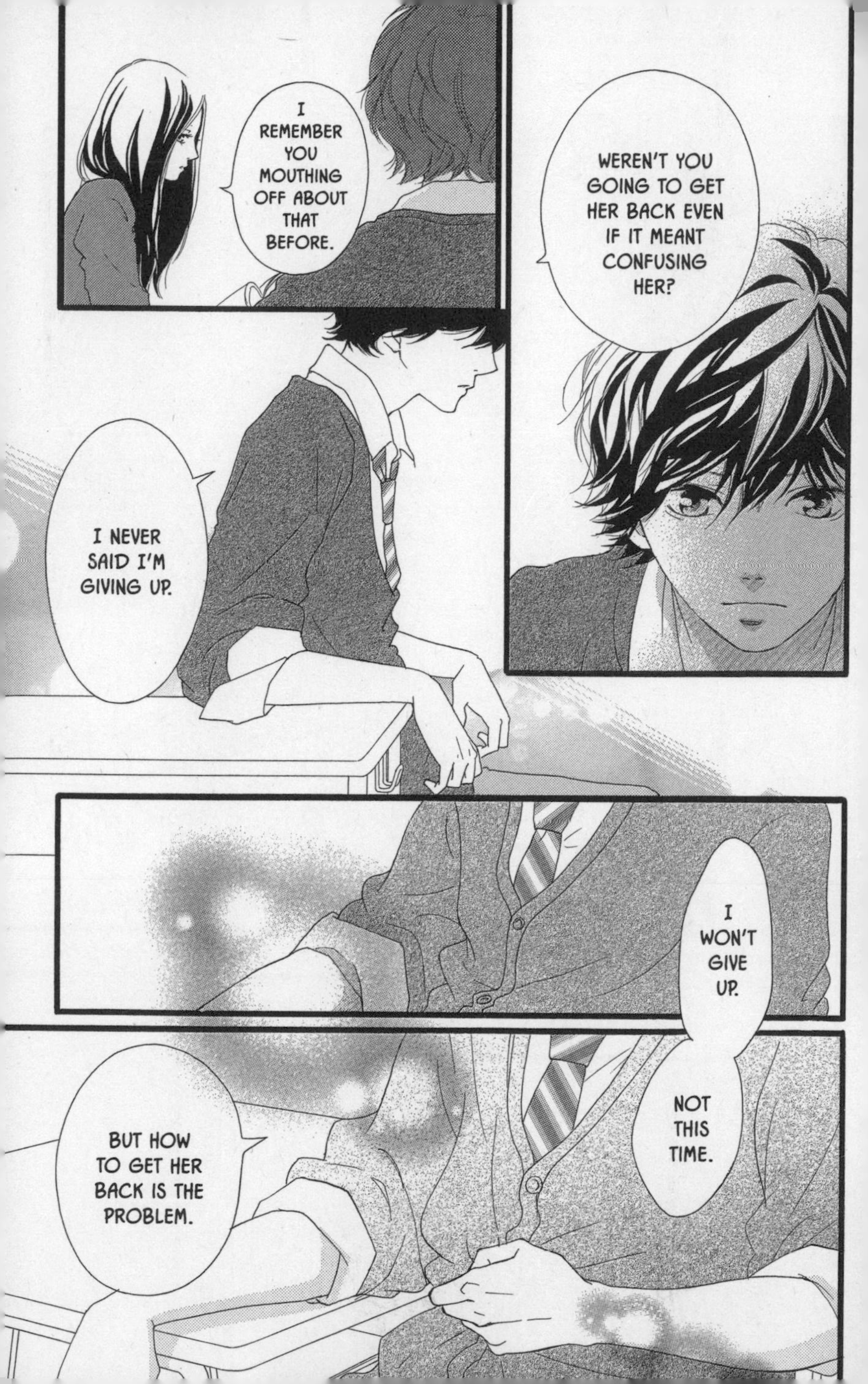
WEREN'T YOU GOING TO GET HER BACK EVEN IF IT MEANT CONFUSING HER?
I REMEMBER YOU MOUTHING OFF ABOUT THAT BEFORE.
I NEVER SAID I'M GIVING UP.
I WON'T GIVE UP.
NOT THIS TIME.
BUT HOW TO GET HER BACK IS THE PROBLEM.

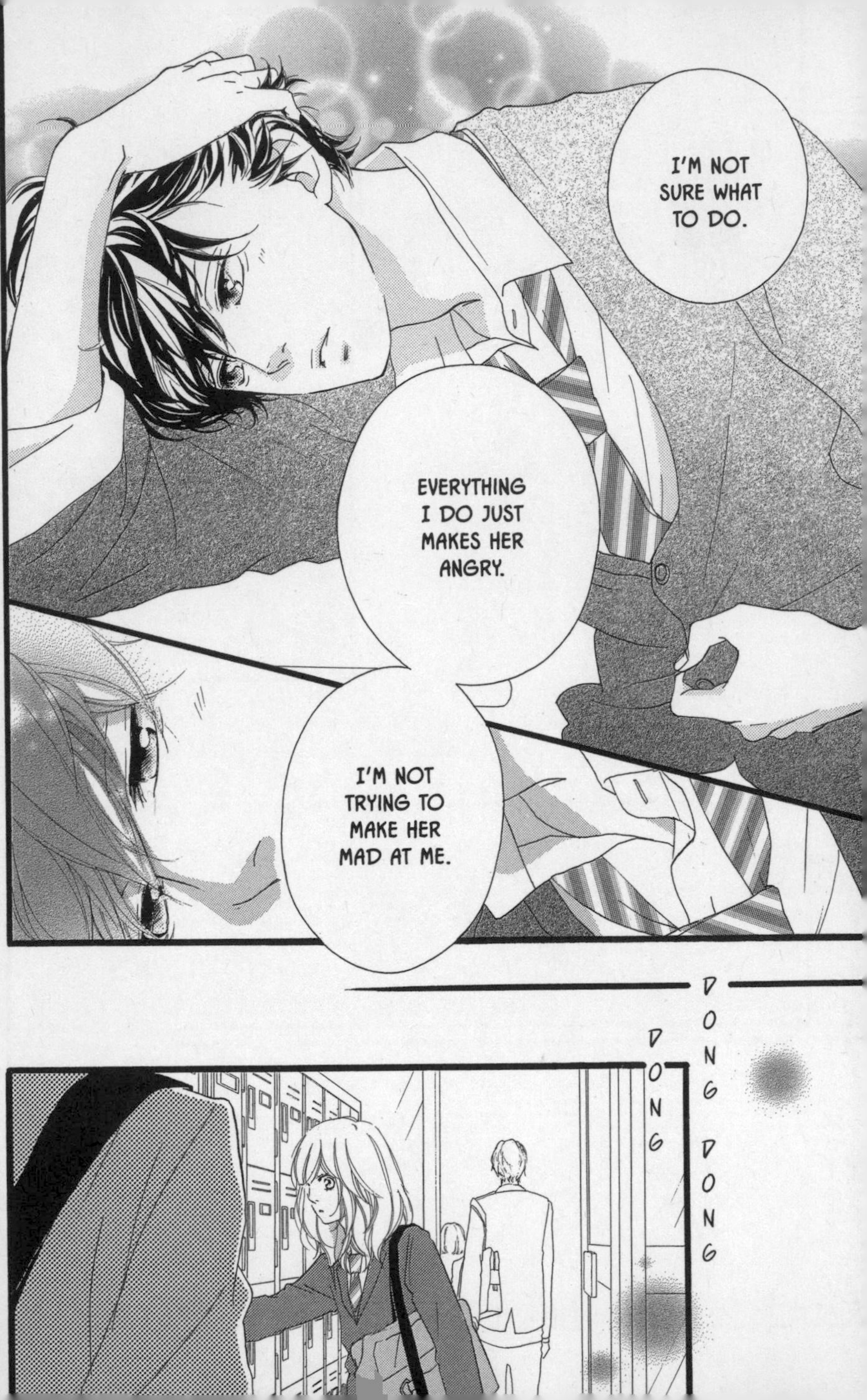
I'M NOT SURE WHAT TO DO.
EVERYTHING I DO JUST MAKES HER ANGRY.
I'M NOT TRYING TO MAKE HER MAD AT ME.
DONG DONG
DONG
DONG

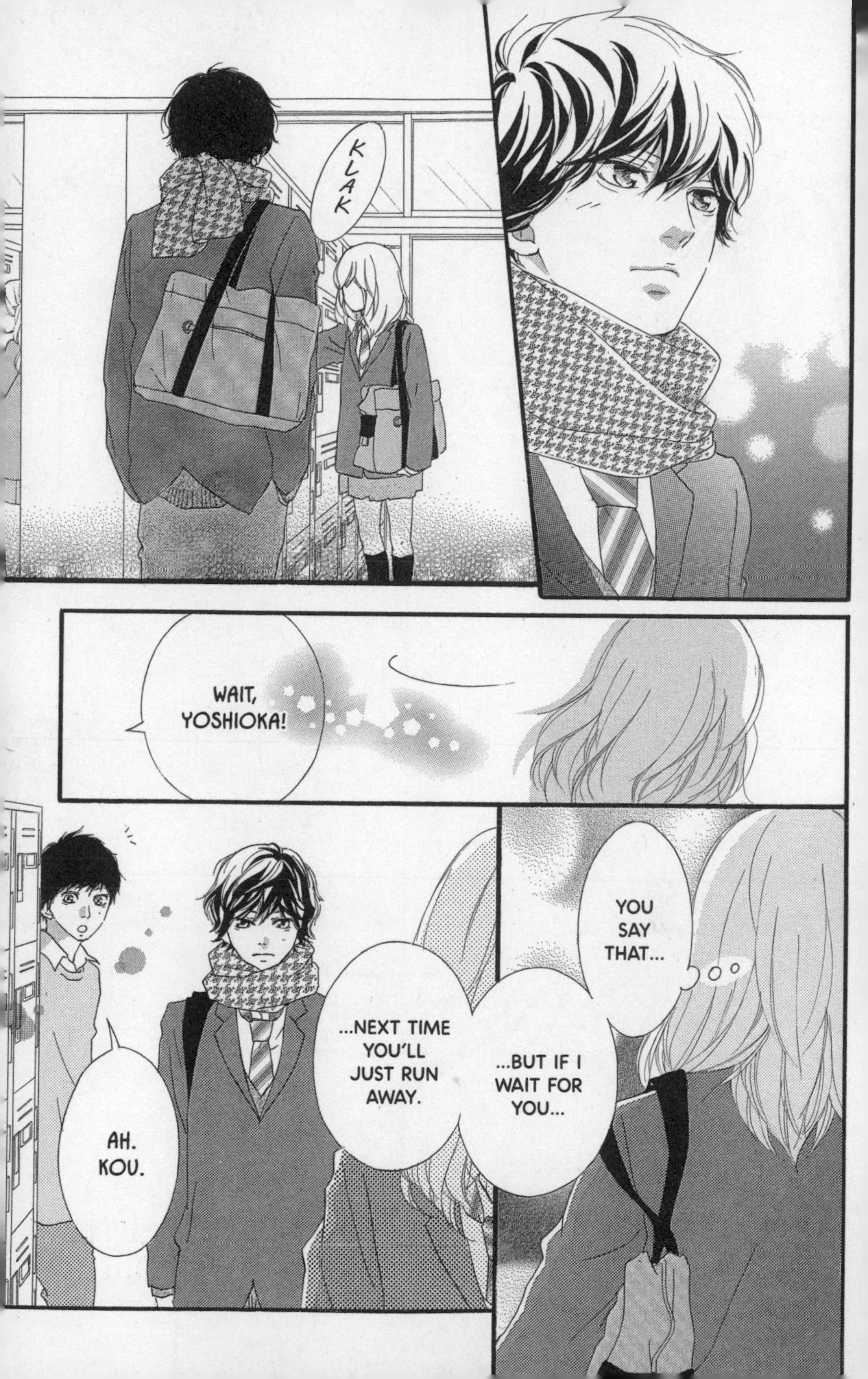
KLAK
WAIT, YOSHIOKA!
YOU SAY THAT...
...BUT IF I WAIT FOR YOU...
...NEXT TIME YOU'LL JUST RUN AWAY.
AH. KOU.

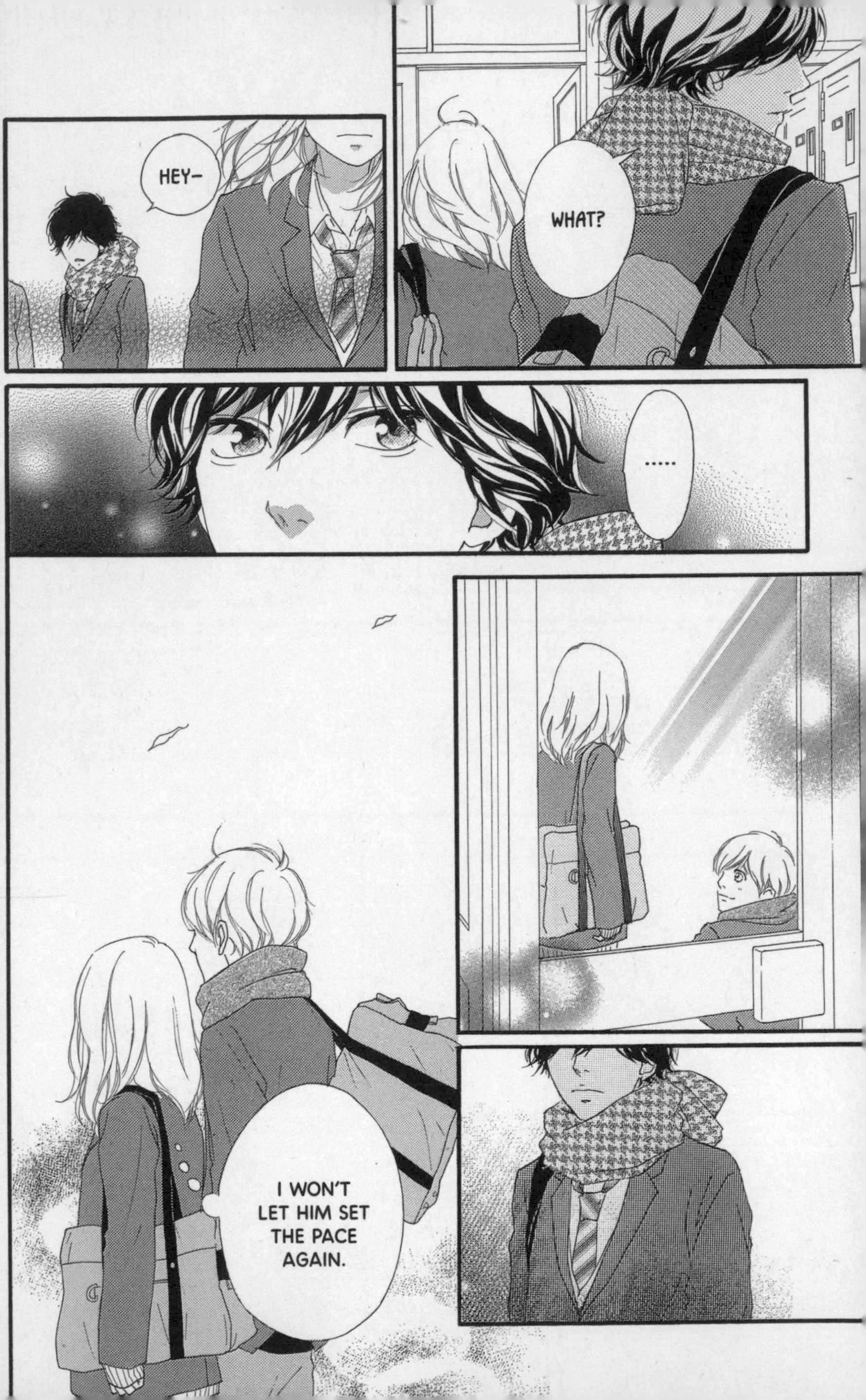
WHAT?
HEY–
......
I WON'T LET HIM SET THE PACE AGAIN.

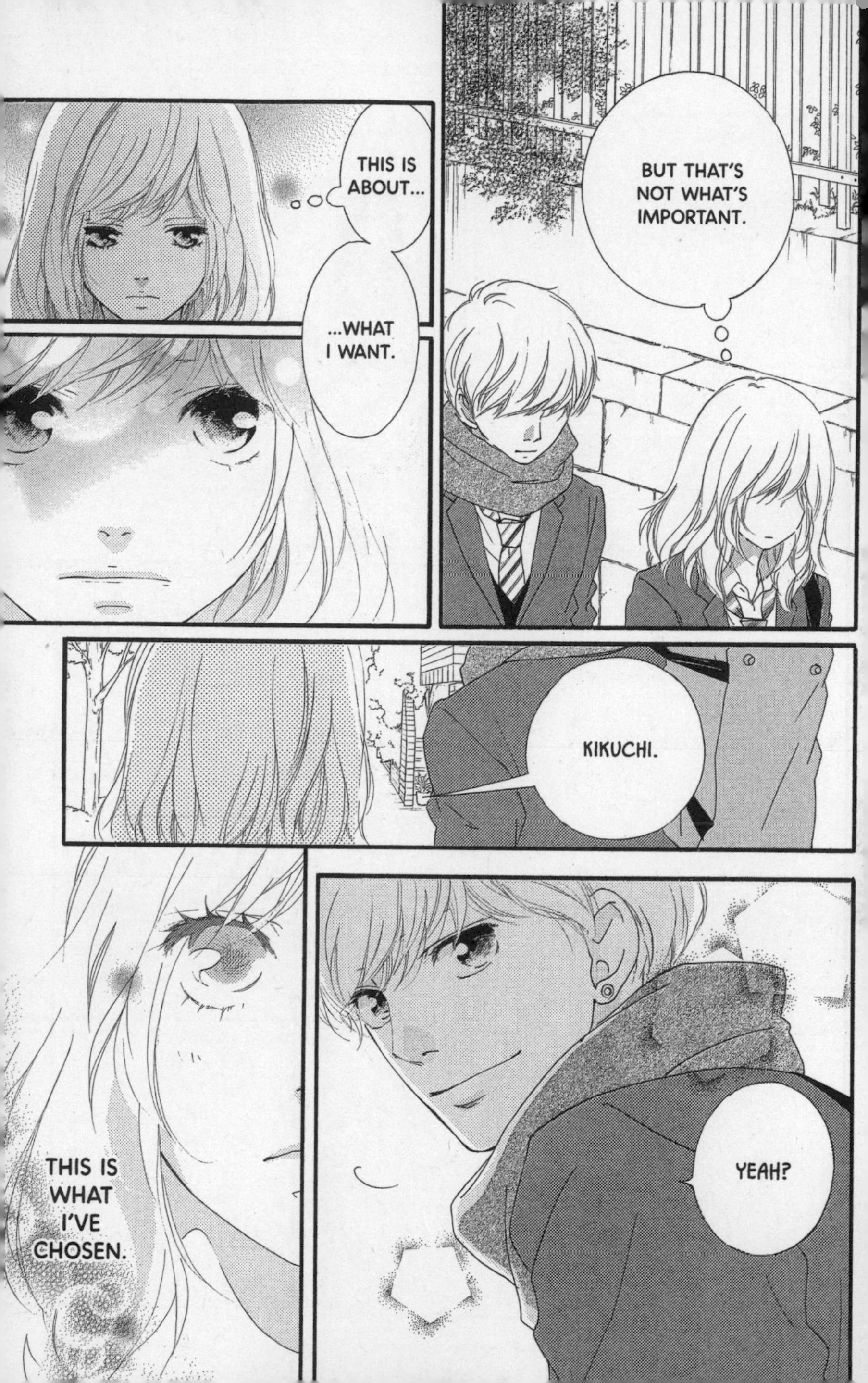
BUT THAT'S NOT WHAT'S IMPORTANT.
THIS IS ABOUT...
...WHAT I WANT.
KIKUCHI.
YEAH?
THIS IS WHAT I'VE CHOSEN.

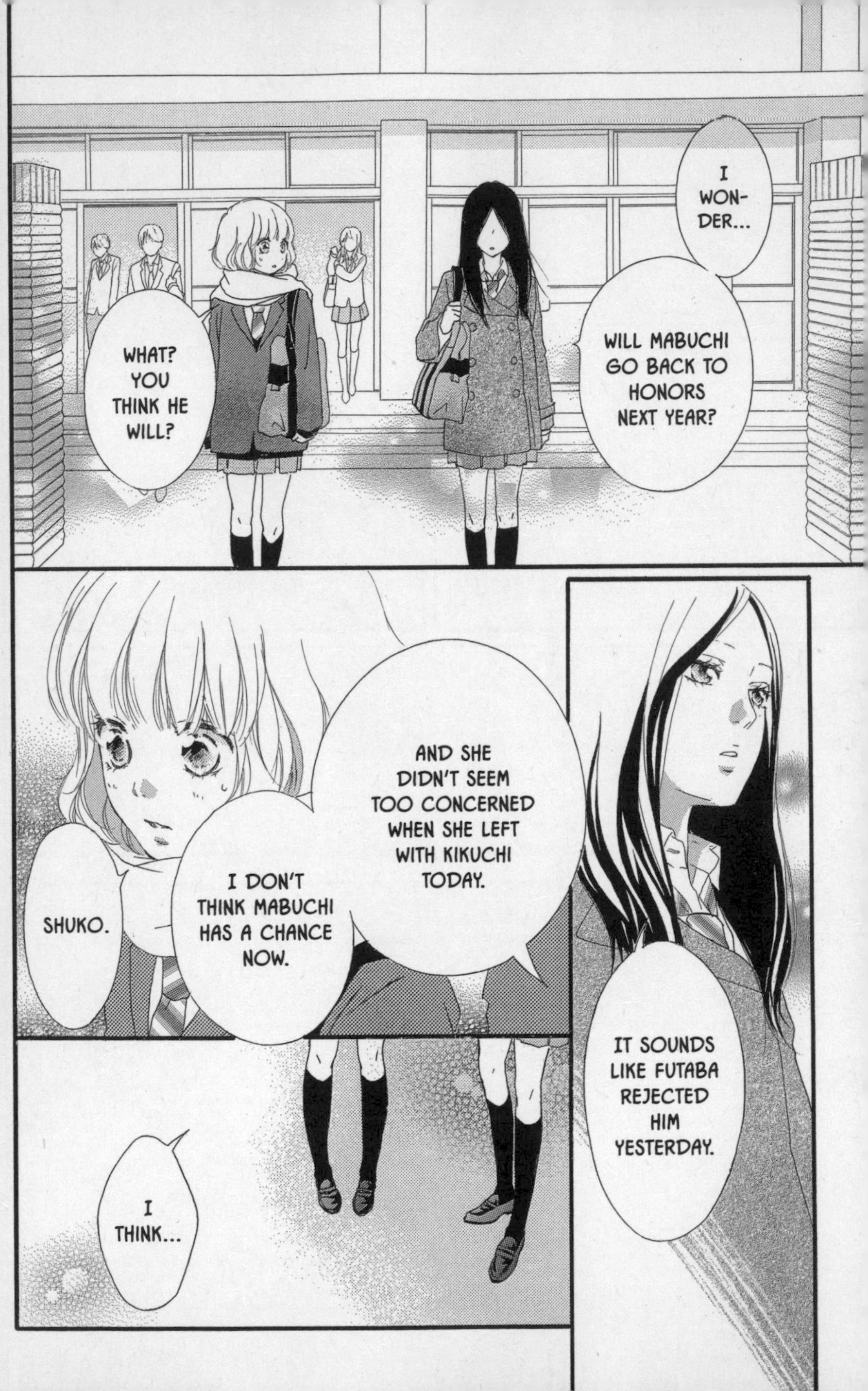
I WON-DER...
WILL MABUCHI GO BACK TO HONORS NEXT YEAR?
WHAT? YOU THINK HE WILL?
IT SOUNDS LIKE FUTABA REJECTED HIM YESTERDAY.
AND SHE DIDN'T SEEM TOO CONCERNED WHEN SHE LEFT WITH KIKUCHI TODAY.
I DON'T THINK MABUCHI HAS A CHANCE NOW.
SHUKO.
I THINK...

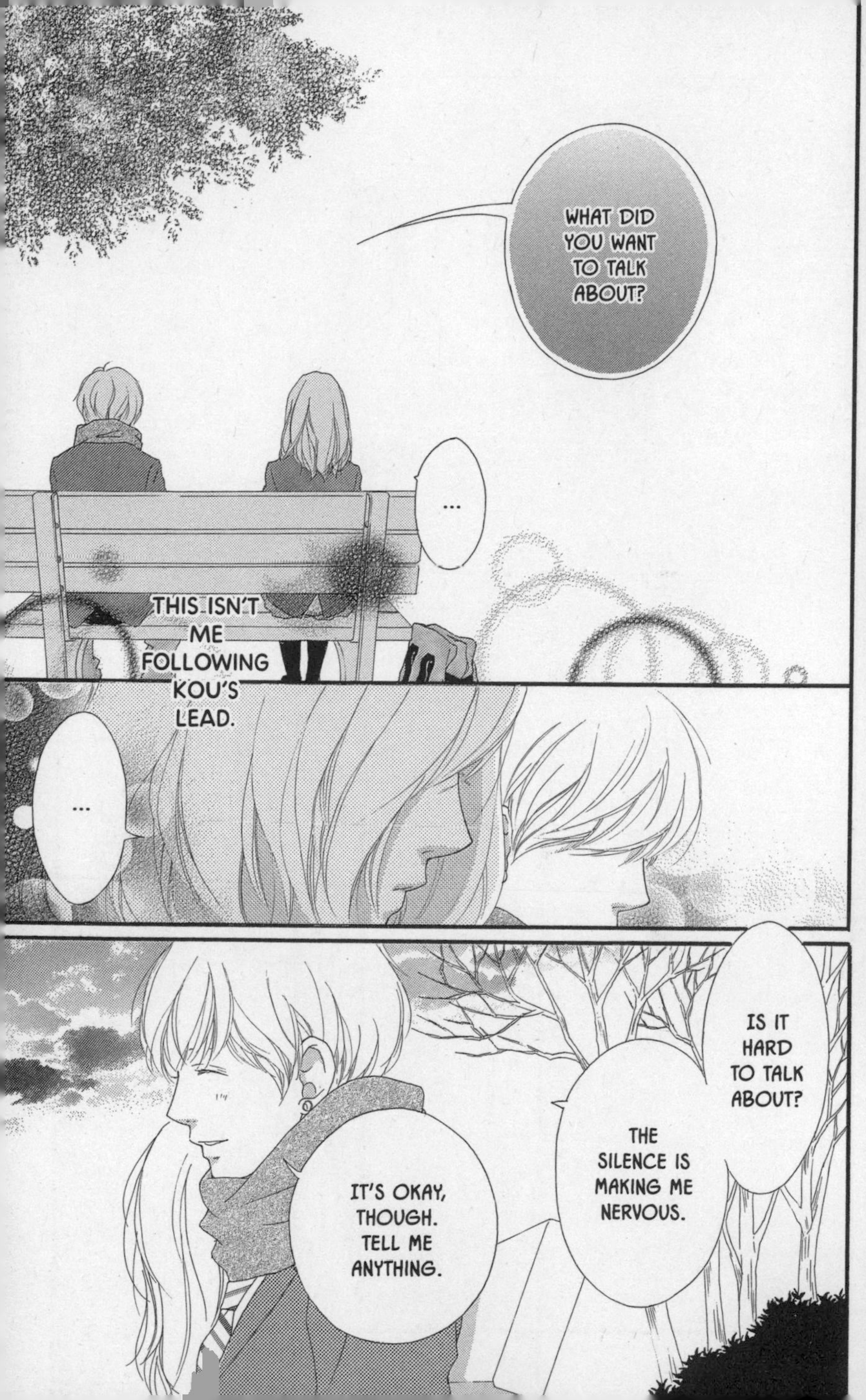
WHAT DID YOU WANT TO TALK ABOUT?
...
THIS ISN'T ME FOLLOWING KOU'S LEAD.
...
IS IT HARD TO TALK ABOUT?
THE SILENCE IS MAKING ME NERVOUS.
IT'S OKAY, THOUGH. TELL ME ANYTHING.

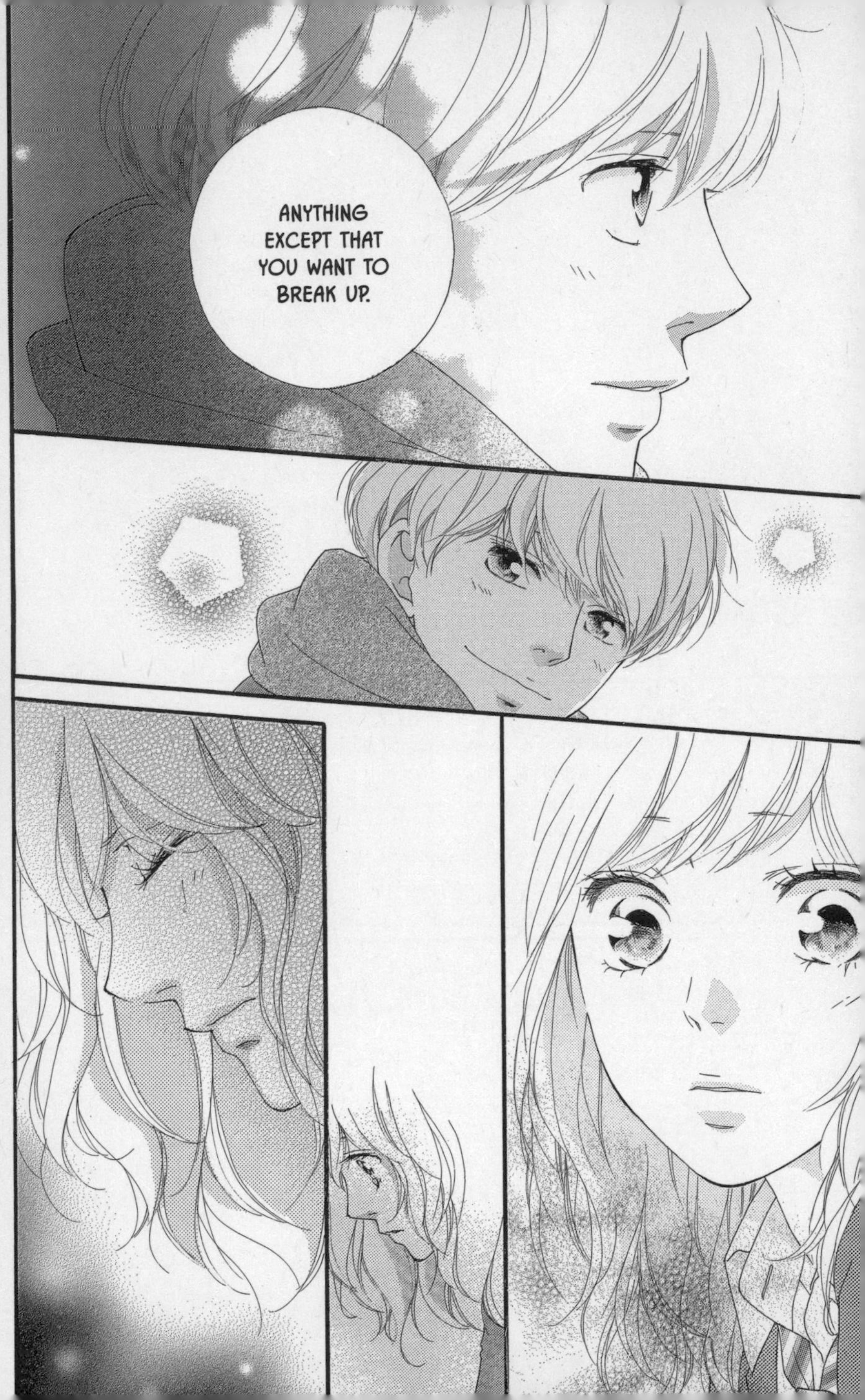
ANYTHING EXCEPT THAT YOU WANT TO BREAK UP.

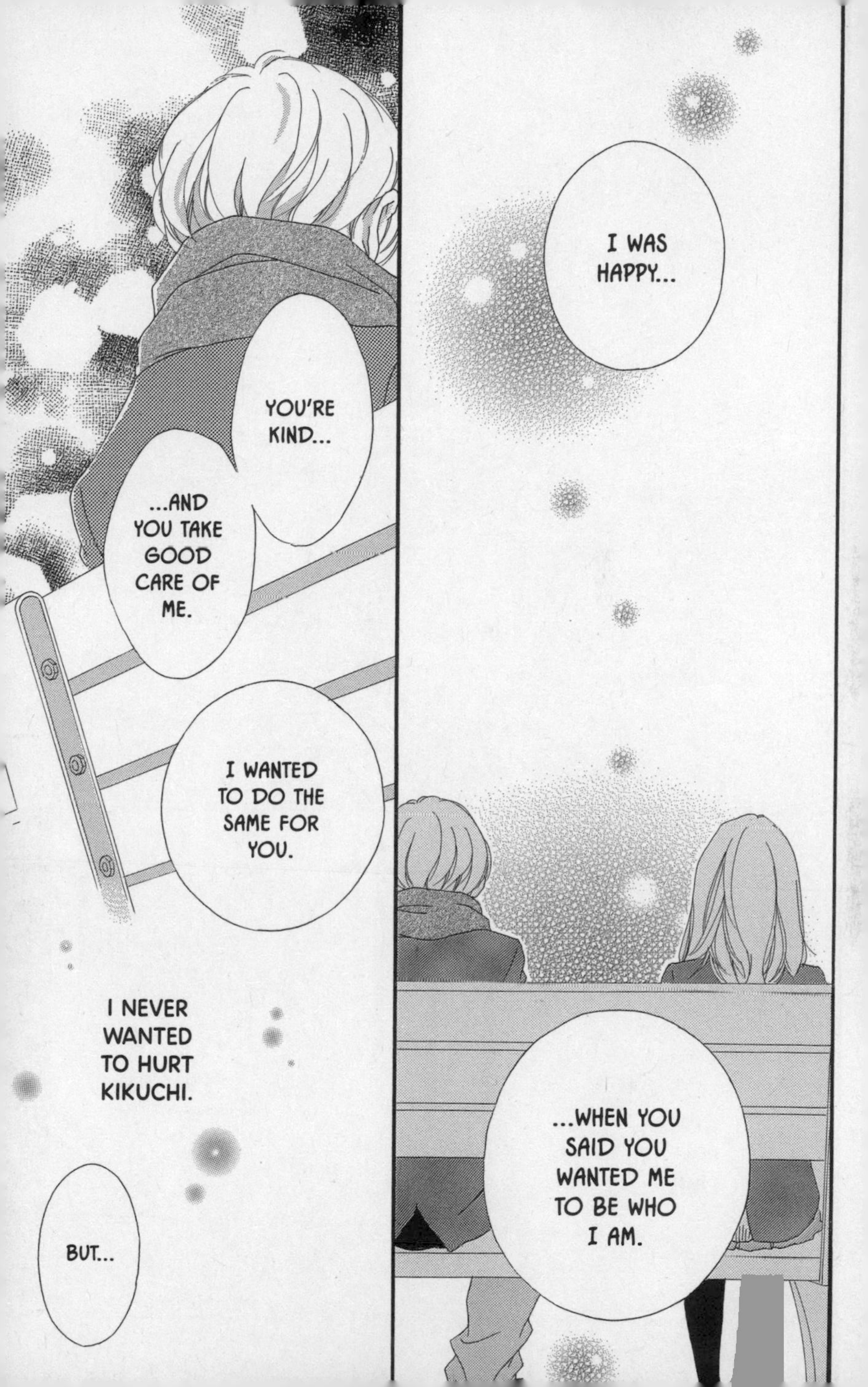
I WAS HAPPY...
...WHEN YOU SAID YOU WANTED ME TO BE WHO I AM.
YOU'RE KIND...
...AND YOU TAKE GOOD CARE OF ME.
I WANTED TO DO THE SAME FOR YOU.
I NEVER WANTED TO HURT KIKUCHI.
BUT...

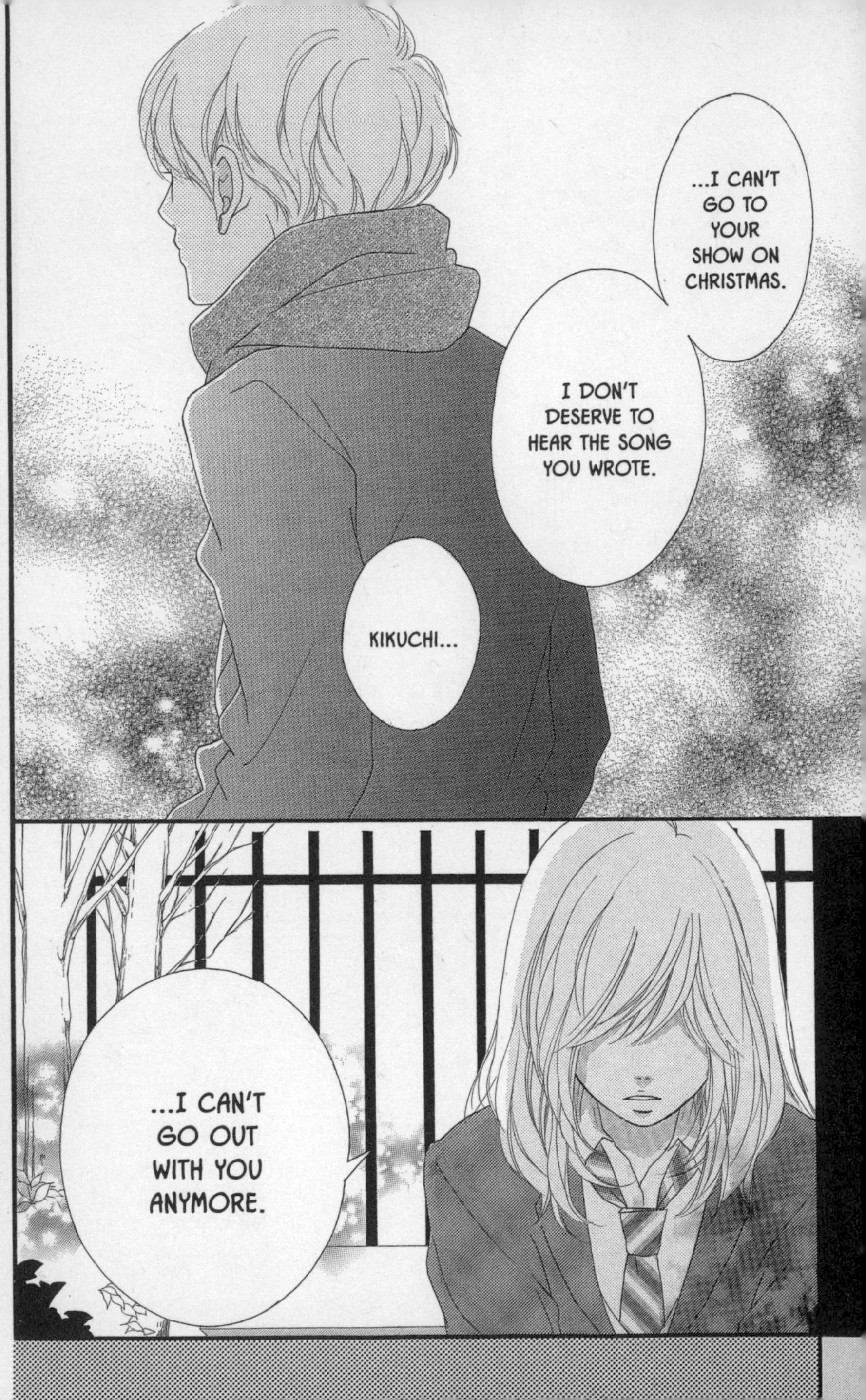
...I CAN'T GO TO YOUR SHOW ON CHRISTMAS.
I DON'T DESERVE TO HEAR THE SONG YOU WROTE.
KIKUCHI...
...I CAN'T GO OUT WITH YOU ANYMORE.

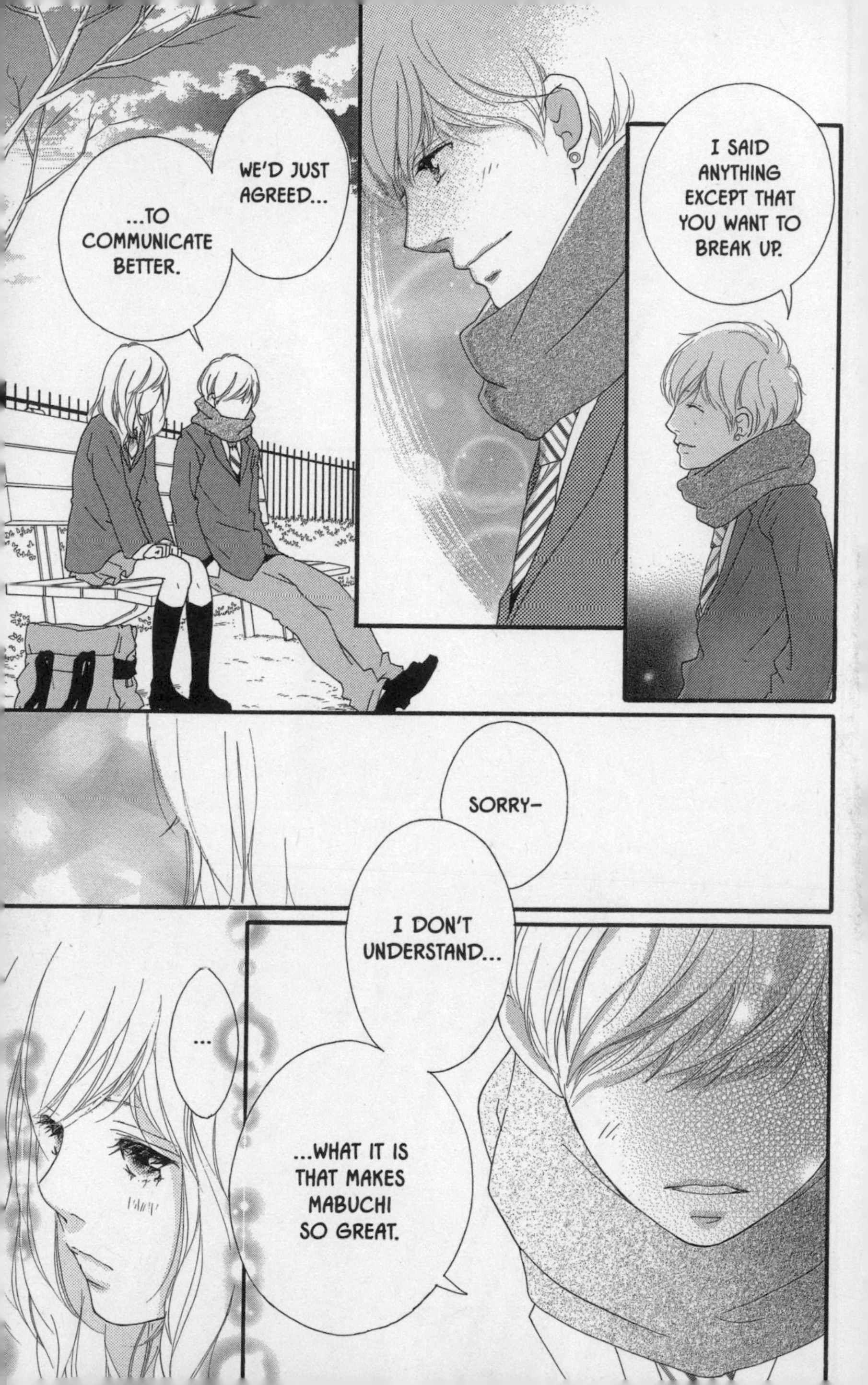
I SAID ANYTHING EXCEPT THAT YOU WANT TO BREAK UP.
WE'D JUST AGREED...
...TO COMMUNICATE BETTER.
SORRY-
I DON'T UNDERSTAND...
...WHAT IT IS THAT MAKES MABUCHI SO GREAT.
...

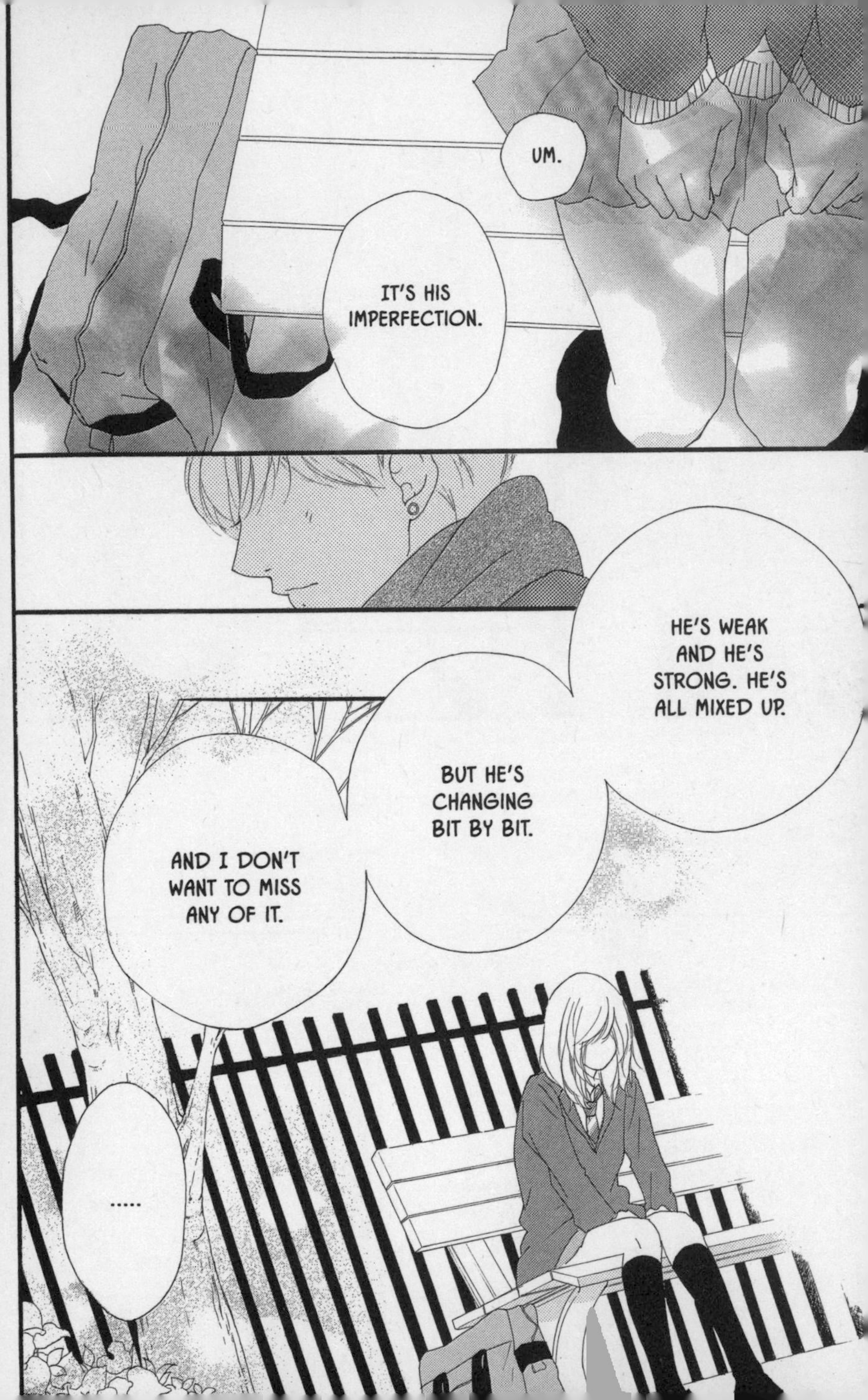
UM.
IT'S HIS IMPERFECTION.
HE'S WEAK AND HE'S STRONG. HE'S ALL MIXED UP.
BUT HE'S CHANGING BIT BY BIT.
AND I DON'T WANT TO MISS ANY OF IT.
.....

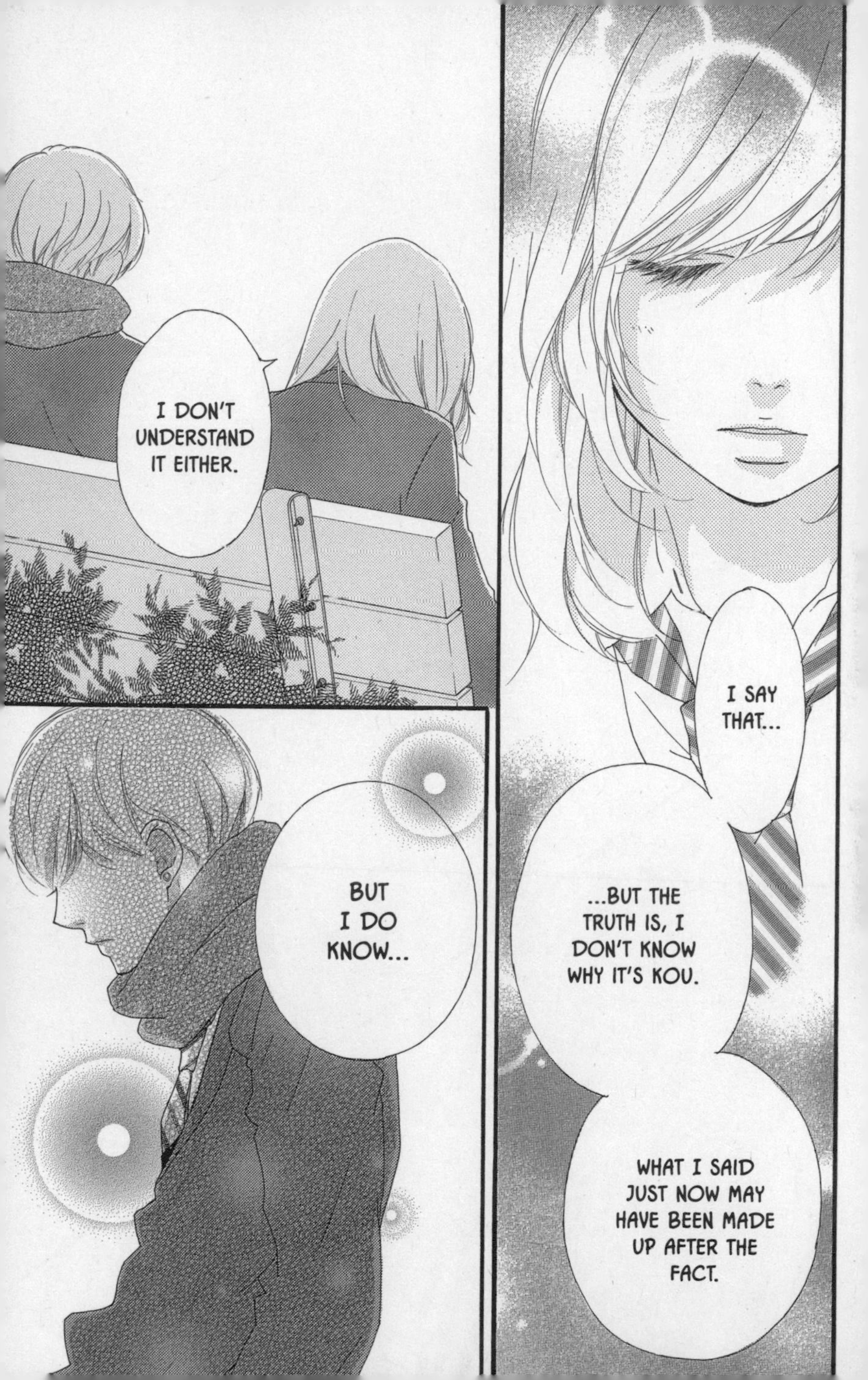
I SAY THAT...
...BUT THE TRUTH IS, I DON'T KNOW WHY IT'S KOU.
WHAT I SAID JUST NOW MAY HAVE BEEN MADE UP AFTER THE FACT.
I DON'T UNDERSTAND IT EITHER.
BUT I DO KNOW...

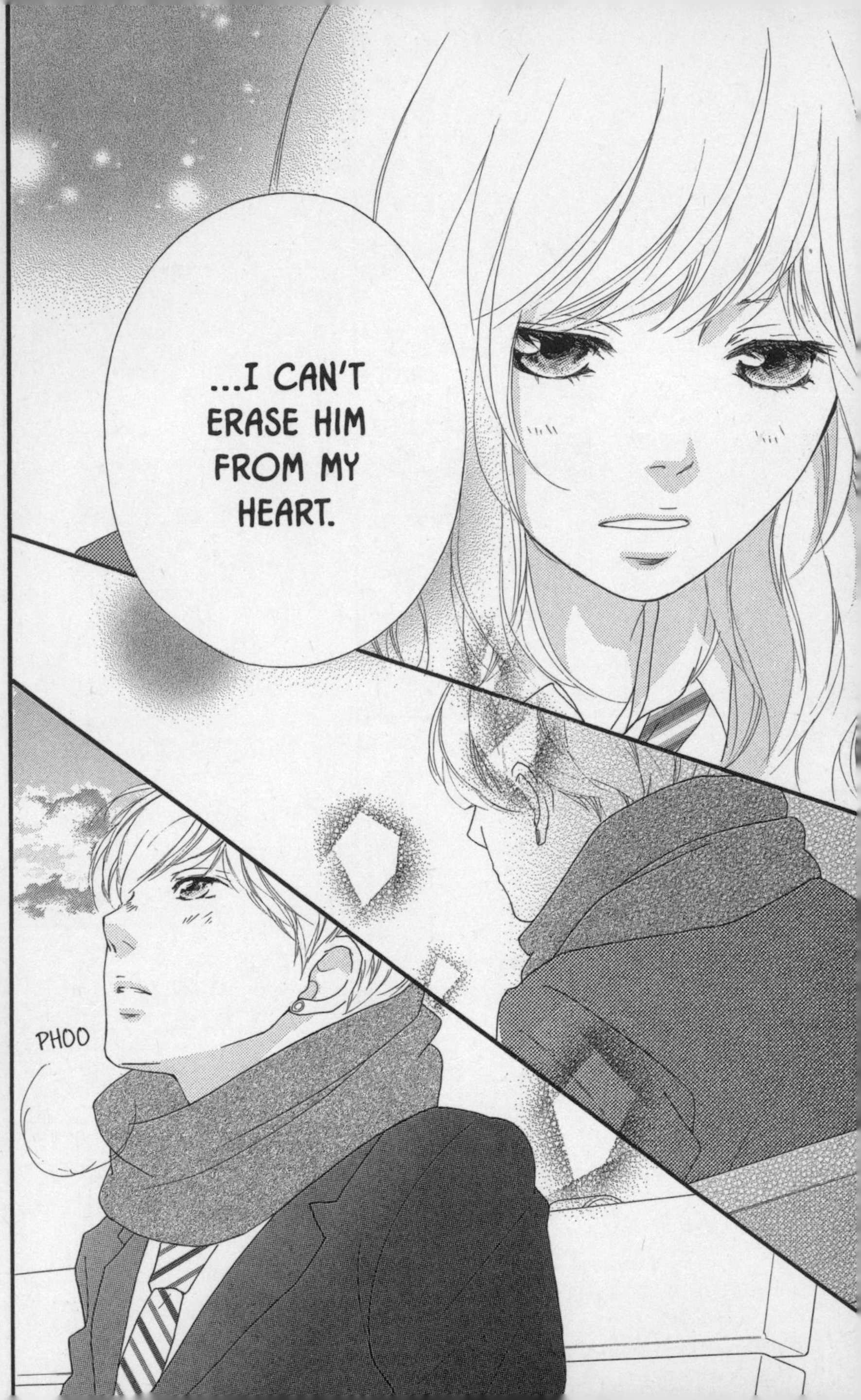
...I CAN'T ERASE HIM FROM MY HEART.
PHOO

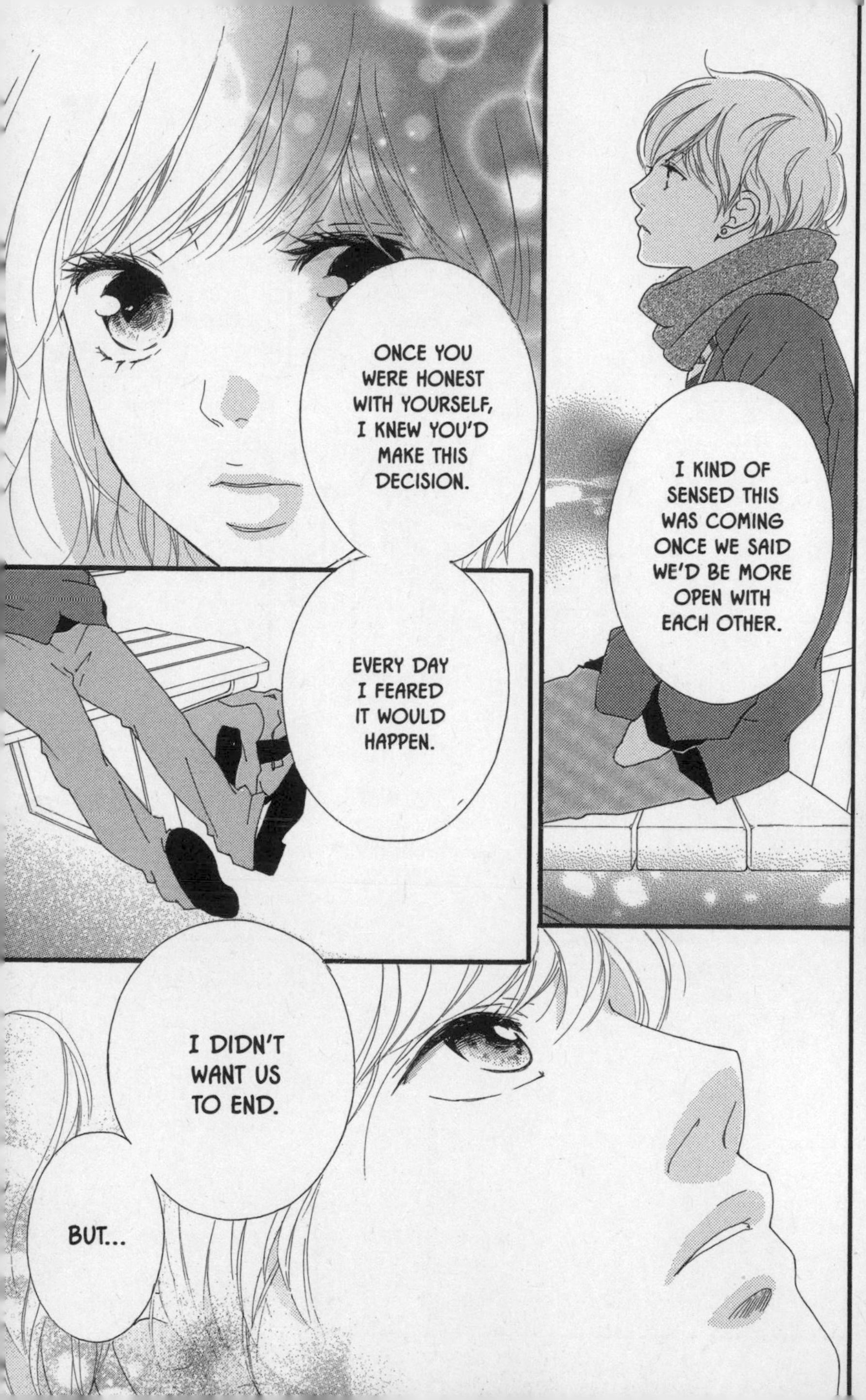
I KIND OF SENSED THIS WAS COMING ONCE WE SAID WE'D BE MORE OPEN WITH EACH OTHER.
ONCE YOU WERE HONEST WITH YOURSELF, I KNEW YOU'D MAKE THIS DECISION.
EVERY DAY I FEARED IT WOULD HAPPEN.
I DIDN'T WANT US TO END.
BUT...

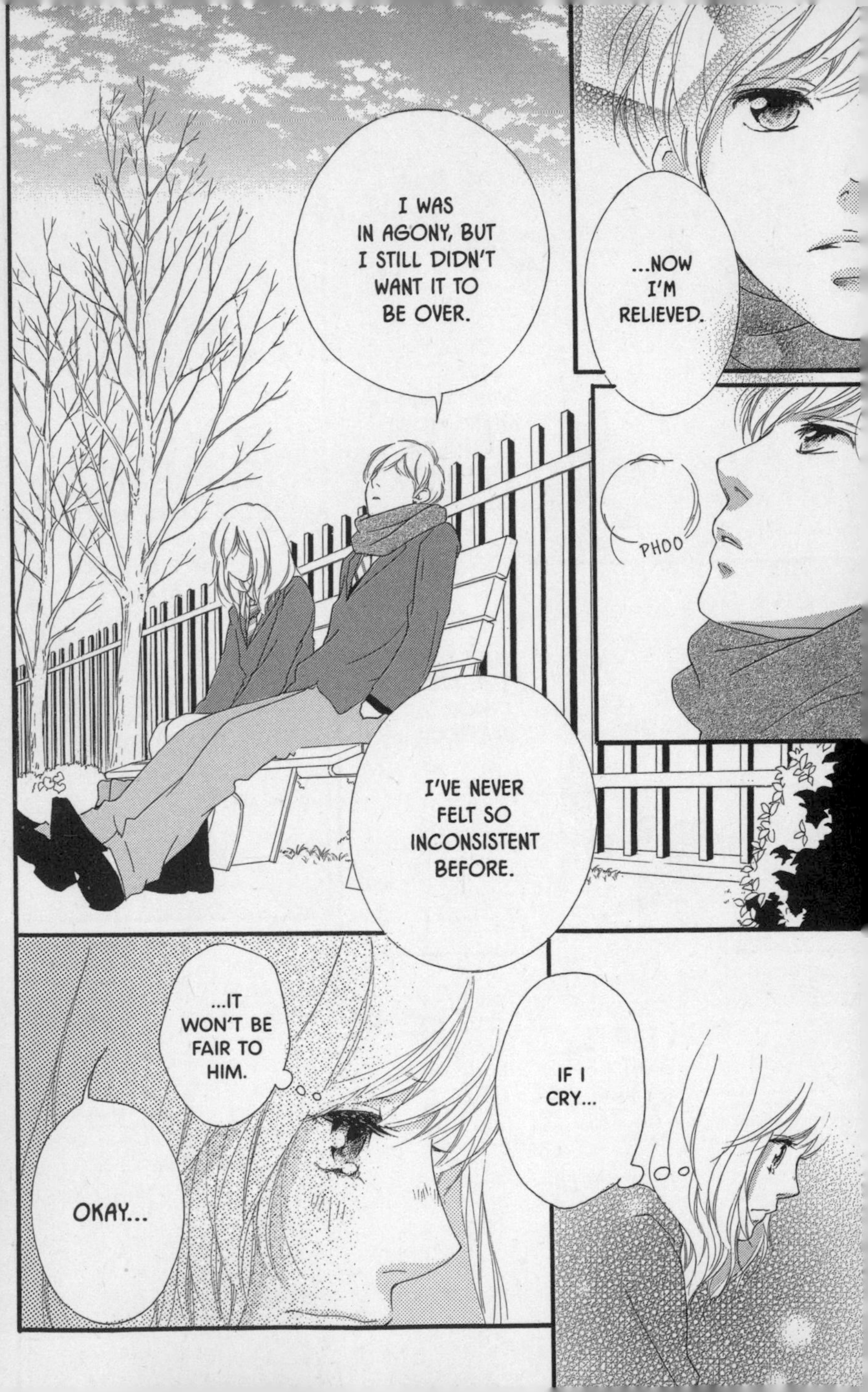
...NOW I'M RELIEVED.
PHOO
I'VE NEVER FELT SO INCONSISTENT BEFORE.
I WAS IN AGONY, BUT I STILL DIDN'T WANT IT TO BE OVER.
IF I CRY...
...IT WON'T BE FAIR TO HIM.
OKAY...

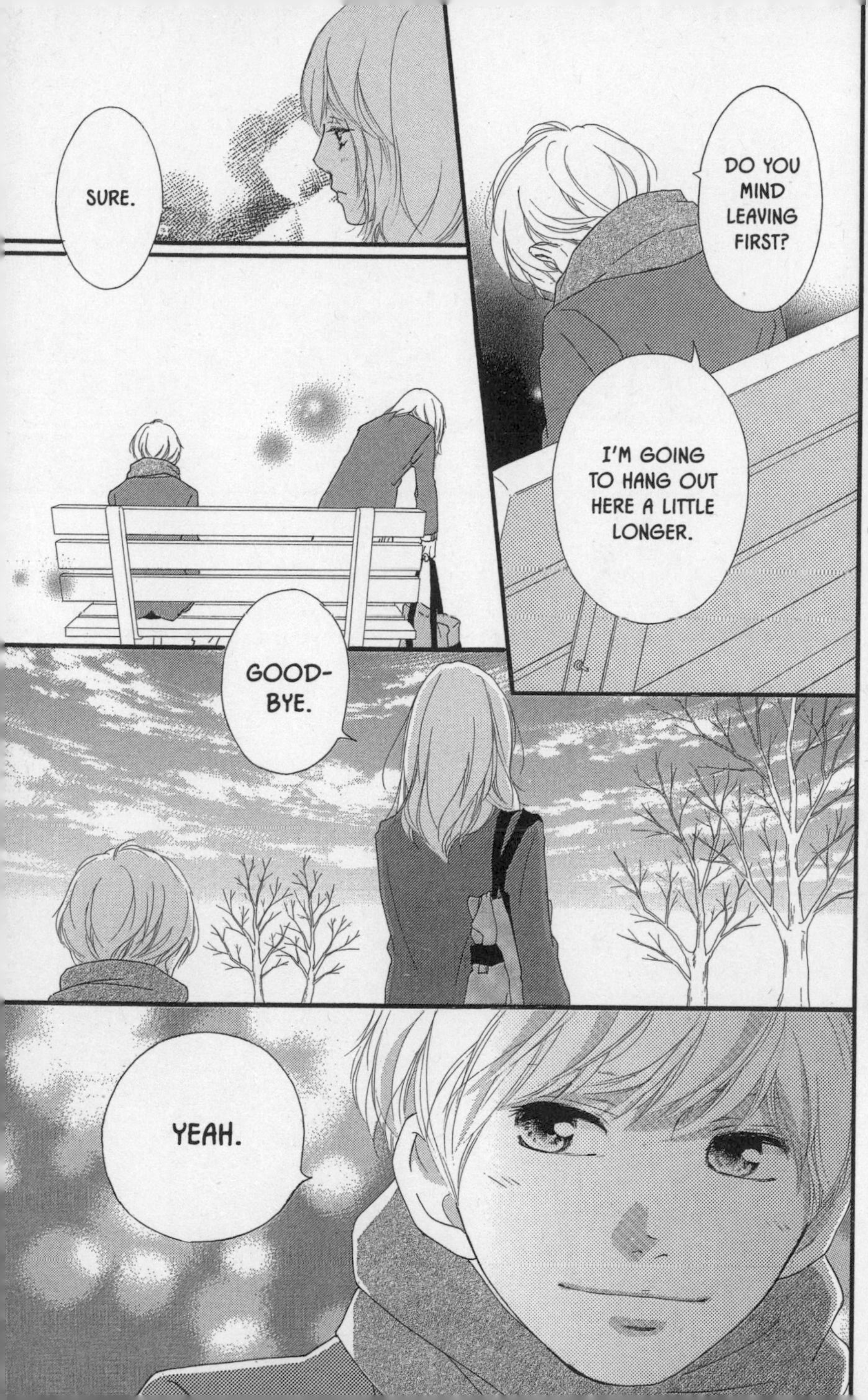
DO YOU MIND LEAVING FIRST?
I'M GOING TO HANG OUT HERE A LITTLE LONGER.
SURE.
GOOD-BYE.
YEAH.

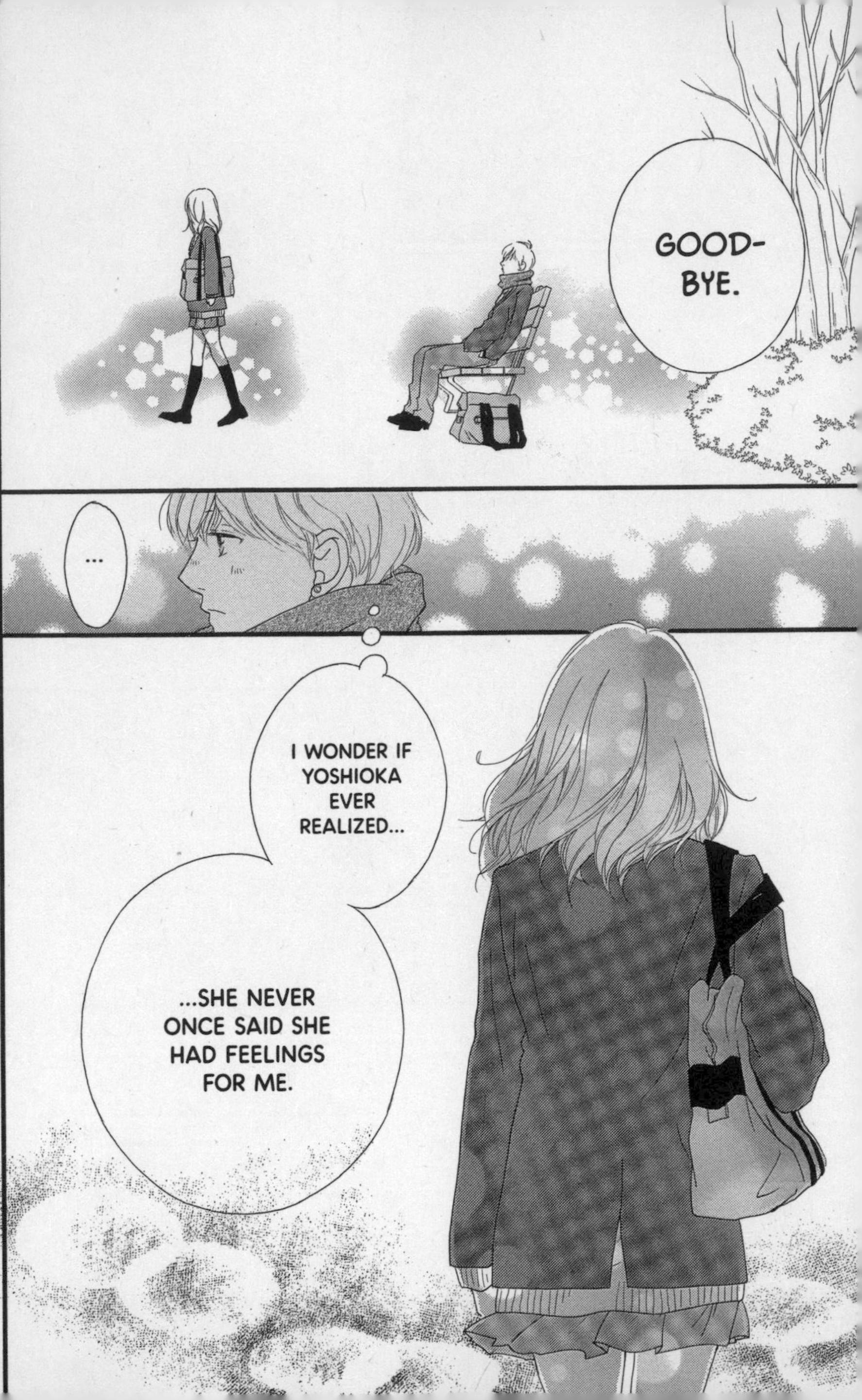
GOOD-BYE.
...
I WONDER IF YOSHIOKA EVER REALIZED...
...SHE NEVER ONCE SAID SHE HAD FEELINGS FOR ME.

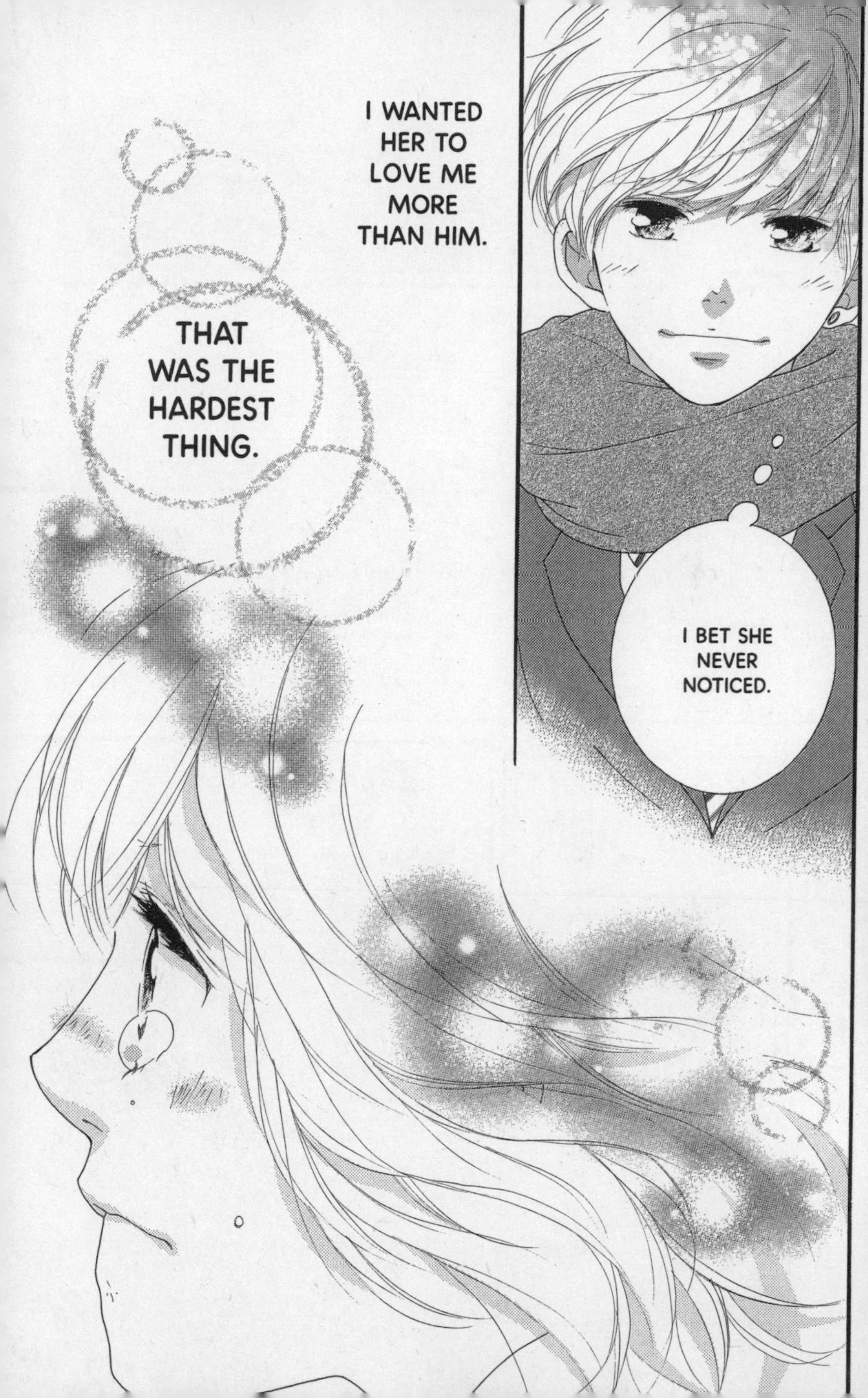
I BET SHE NEVER NOTICED.
I WANTED HER TO LOVE ME MORE THAN HIM.
THAT WAS THE HARDEST THING.

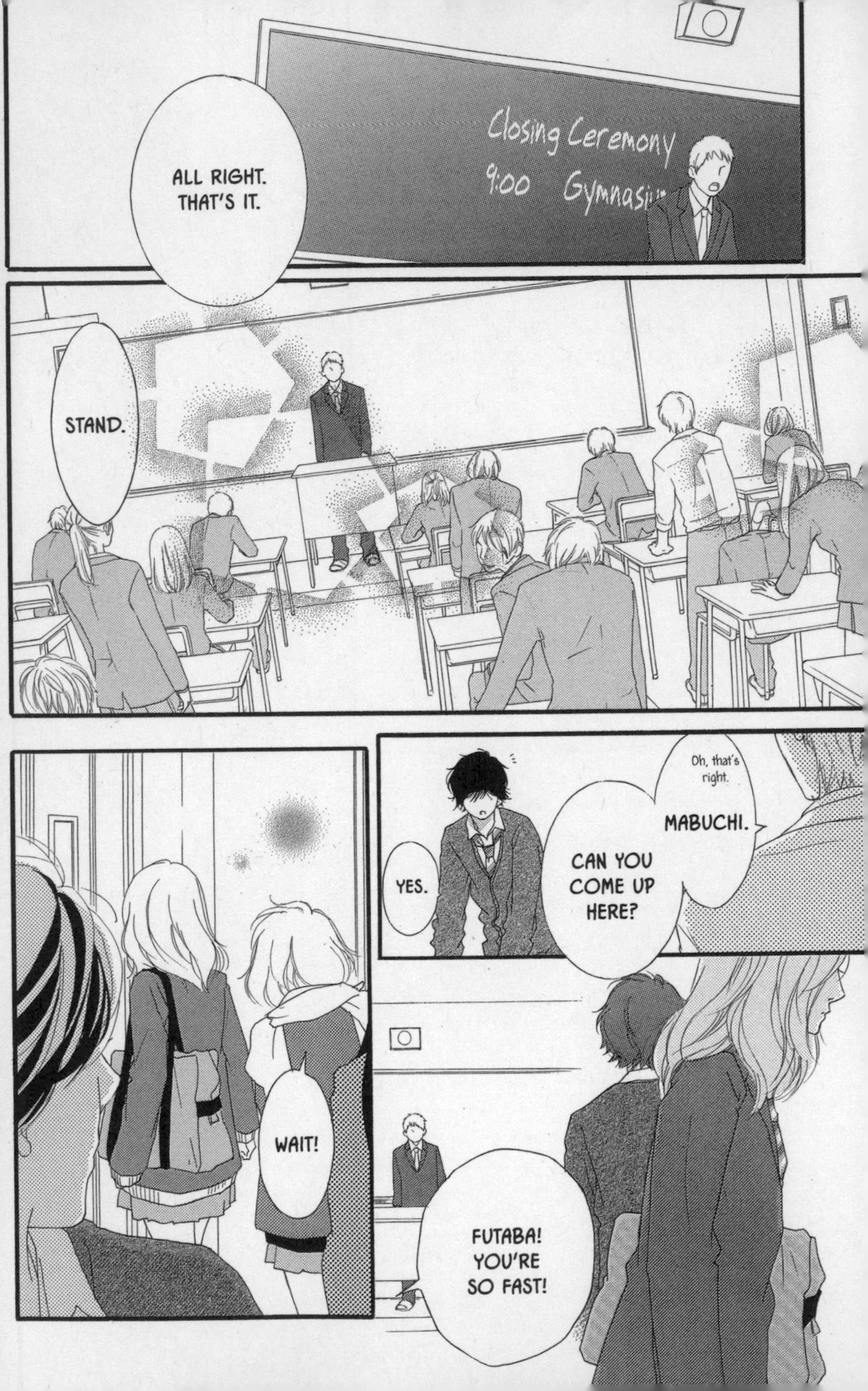
Closing Ceremony
9:00 Gymnasiu
ALL RIGHT. THAT'S IT.
STAND.
Oh, that's right.
MABUCHI.
CAN YOU COME UP HERE?
YES.
FUTABA! YOU'RE SO FAST!
WAIT!

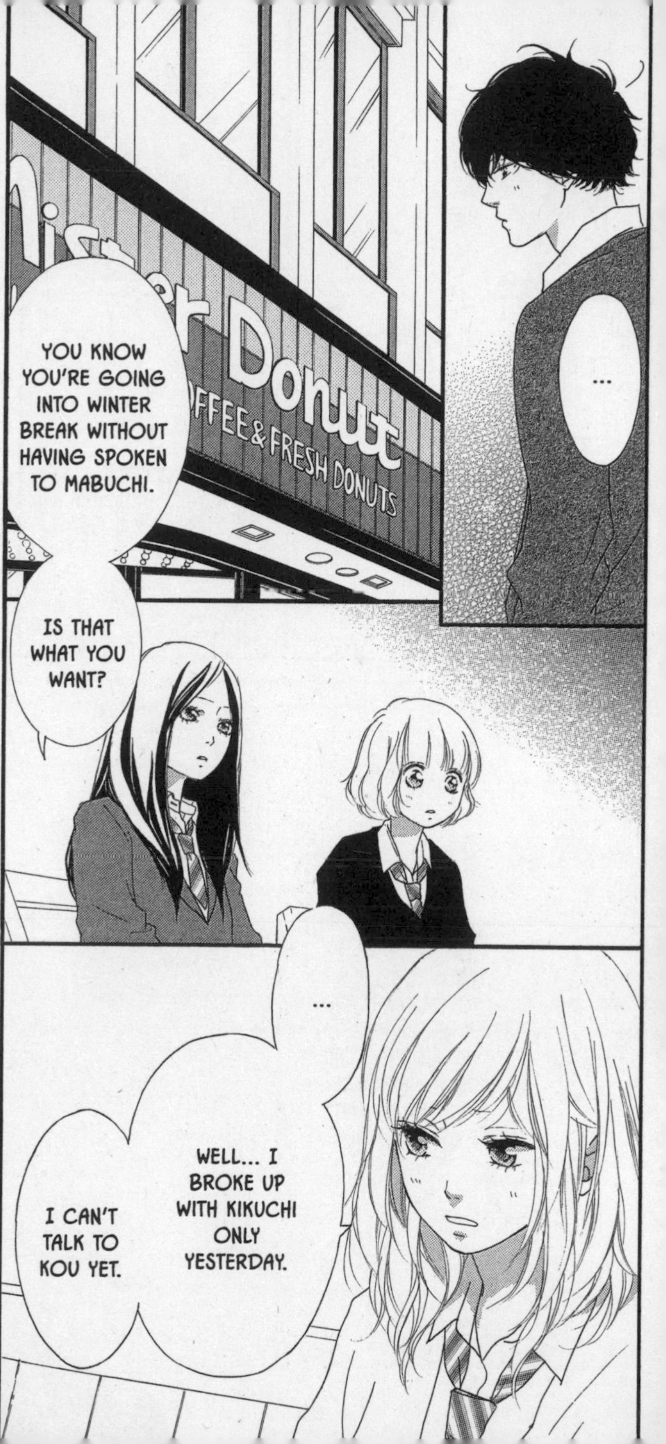
...
YOU KNOW YOU'RE GOING INTO WINTER BREAK WITHOUT HAVING SPOKEN TO MABUCHI.
IS THAT WHAT YOU WANT?
...
WELL... I BROKE UP WITH KIKUCHI ONLY YESTERDAY.
I CAN'T TALK TO KOU YET.

Back to *Romeo and the Black Brothers.* (Yes, I have more to say about Romeo...) I love Romeo, the main character, but my favorite character is Alfred, his best friend. If you haven't seen the series, I'm sure you have no idea what I'm talking about, but I want to get these feelings off of my chest. Please forgive me. I like Alfred so much that I found myself doodling his image without realizing it, and since I'd drawn him, I figured I should color him in too. (I was working on a color illustration at the time.) When I did, I felt so fulfilled. No matter how much I like a series, I usually never draw it. For me to go so far as coloring in Alfred tells you how much I like him. I recommend you check out the series!

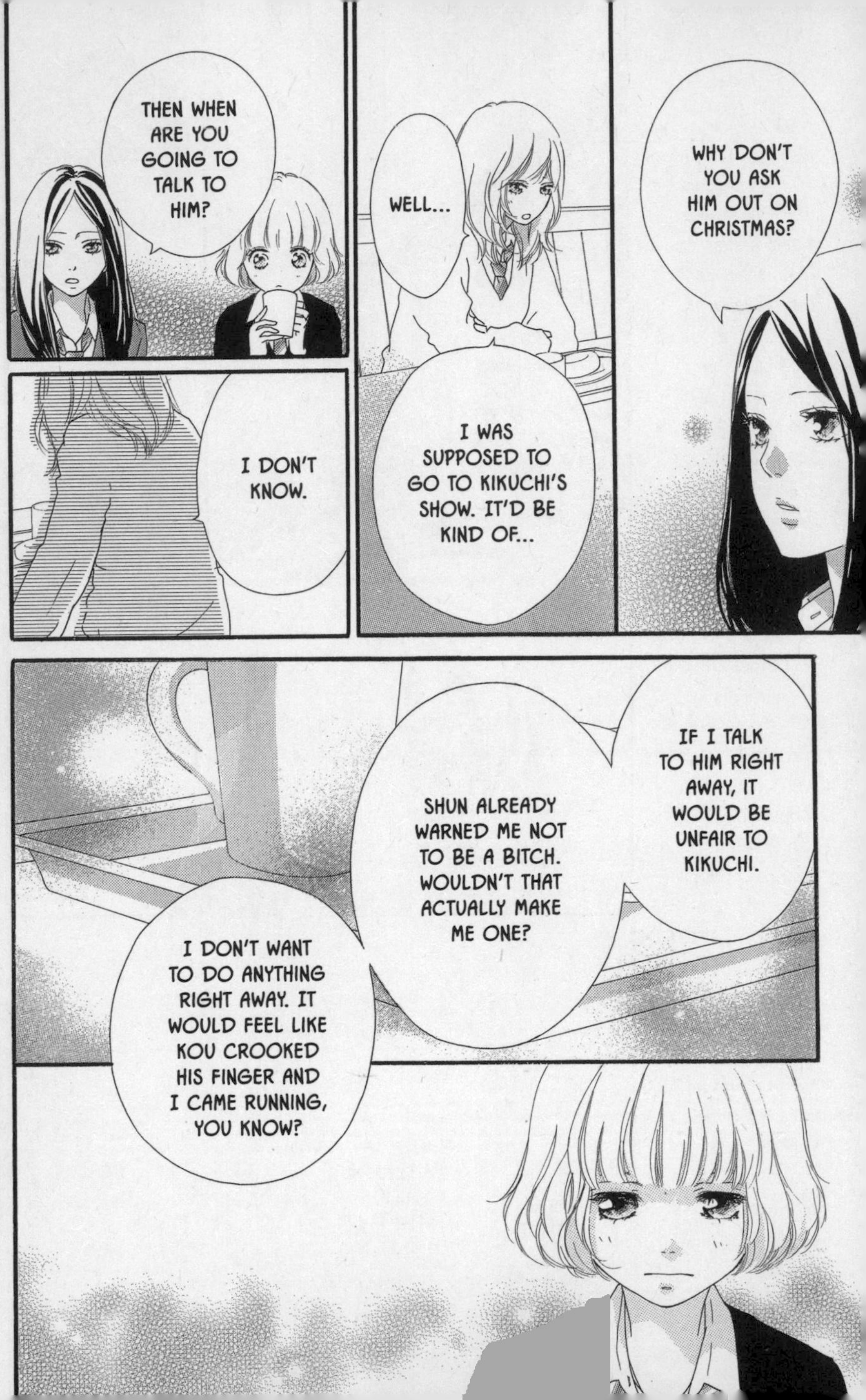
WHY DON'T YOU ASK HIM OUT ON CHRISTMAS?
WELL...
I WAS SUPPOSED TO GO TO KIKUCHI'S SHOW. IT'D BE KIND OF...
THEN WHEN ARE YOU GOING TO TALK TO HIM?
I DON'T KNOW.
IF I TALK TO HIM RIGHT AWAY, IT WOULD BE UNFAIR TO KIKUCHI.
SHUN ALREADY WARNED ME NOT TO BE A BITCH. WOULDN'T THAT ACTUALLY MAKE ME ONE?
I DON'T WANT TO DO ANYTHING RIGHT AWAY. IT WOULD FEEL LIKE KOU CROOKED HIS FINGER AND I CAME RUNNING, YOU KNOW?

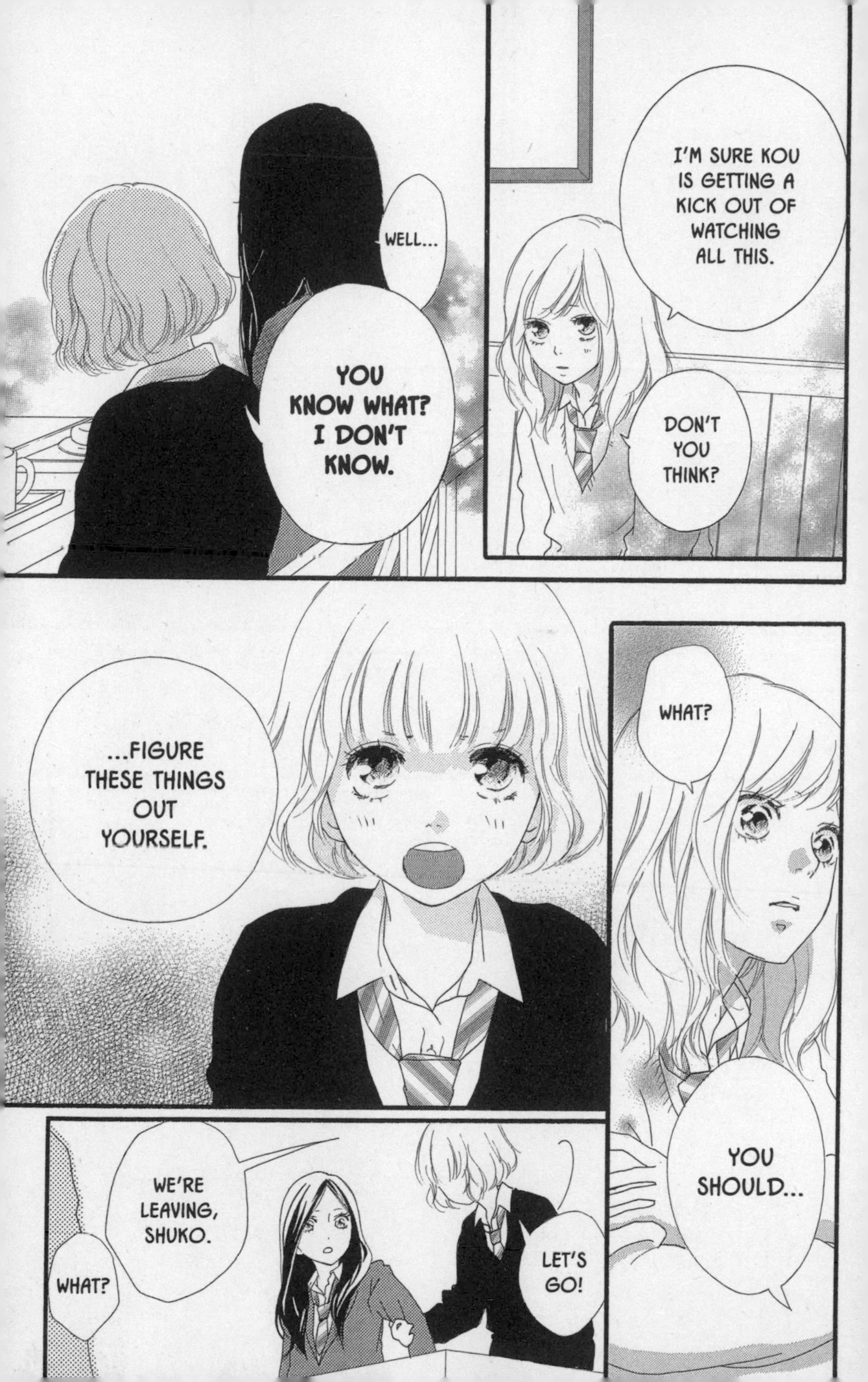
I'M SURE KOU IS GETTING A KICK OUT OF WATCHING ALL THIS.
DON'T YOU THINK?
WELL...
YOU KNOW WHAT? I DON'T KNOW.
WHAT?
YOU SHOULD...
...FIGURE THESE THINGS OUT YOURSELF.
WE'RE LEAVING, SHUKO.
LET'S GO!
WHAT?

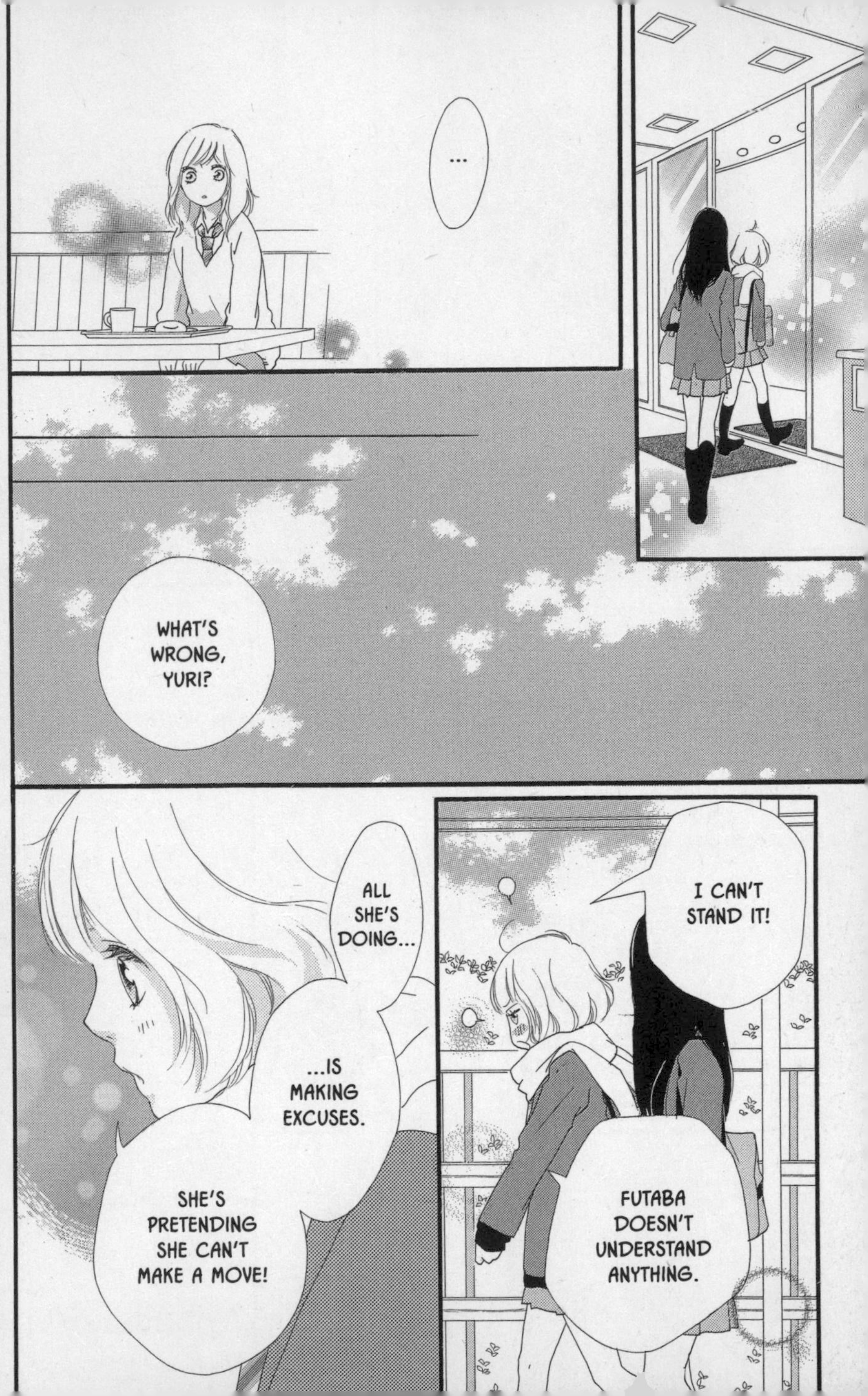
...
WHAT'S WRONG, YURI?
I CAN'T STAND IT!
FUTABA DOESN'T UNDERSTAND ANYTHING.
ALL SHE'S DOING...
...IS MAKING EXCUSES.
SHE'S PRETENDING SHE CAN'T MAKE A MOVE!

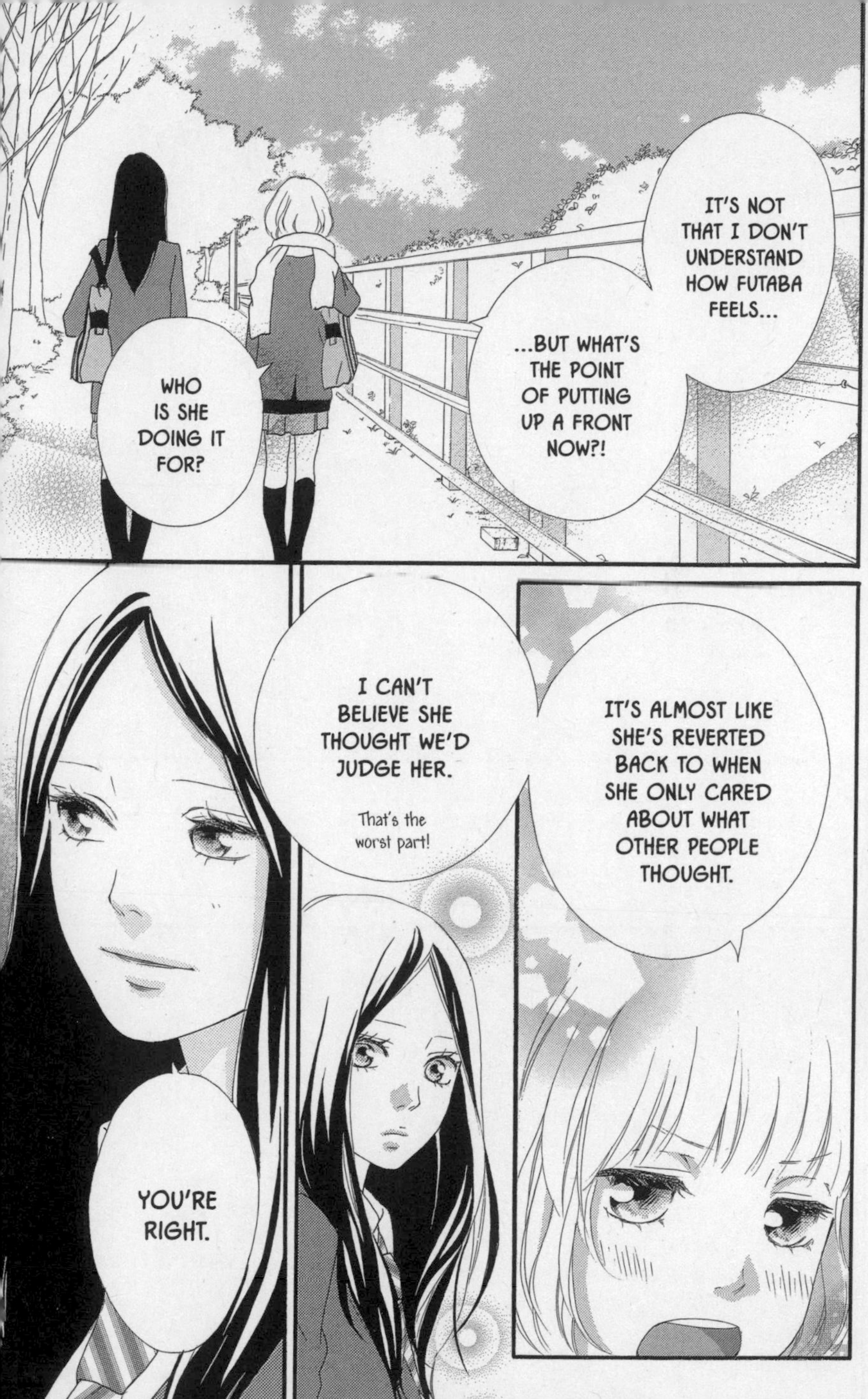
IT'S NOT THAT I DON'T UNDERSTAND HOW FUTABA FEELS...
...BUT WHAT'S THE POINT OF PUTTING UP A FRONT NOW?!
WHO IS SHE DOING IT FOR?
IT'S ALMOST LIKE SHE'S REVERTED BACK TO WHEN SHE ONLY CARED ABOUT WHAT OTHER PEOPLE THOUGHT.
I CAN'T BELIEVE SHE THOUGHT WE'D JUDGE HER.
That's the worst part!
YOU'RE RIGHT.

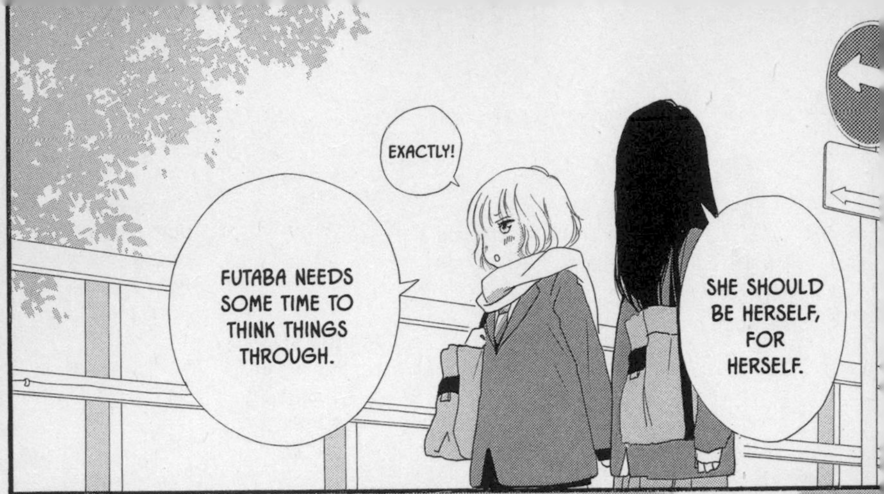
SHE SHOULD BE HERSELF, FOR HERSELF.
EXACTLY!
FUTABA NEEDS SOME TIME TO THINK THINGS THROUGH.

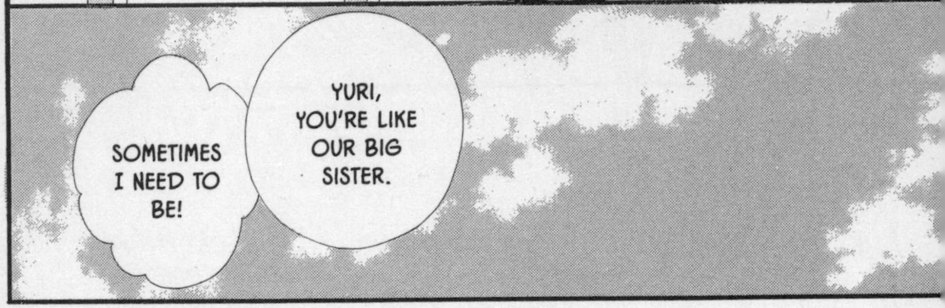
YURI, YOU'RE LIKE OUR BIG SISTER.
SOMETIMES I NEED TO BE!

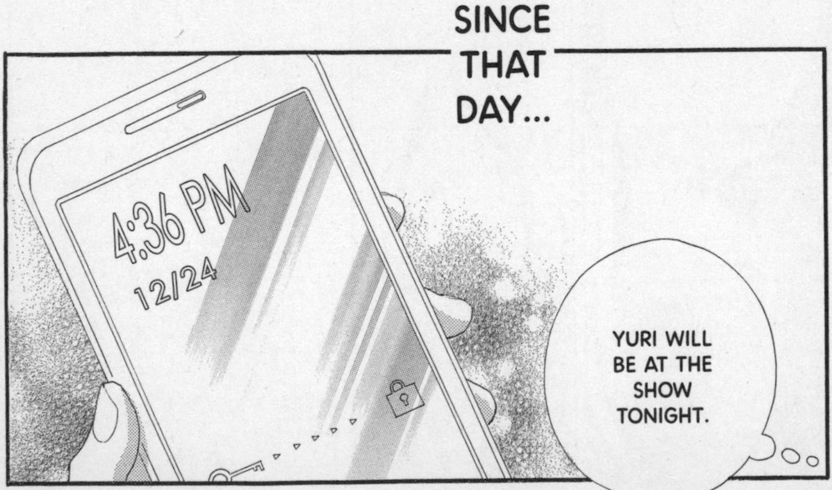
SINCE THAT DAY...
4:36 PM
12/24
YURI WILL BE AT THE SHOW TONIGHT.

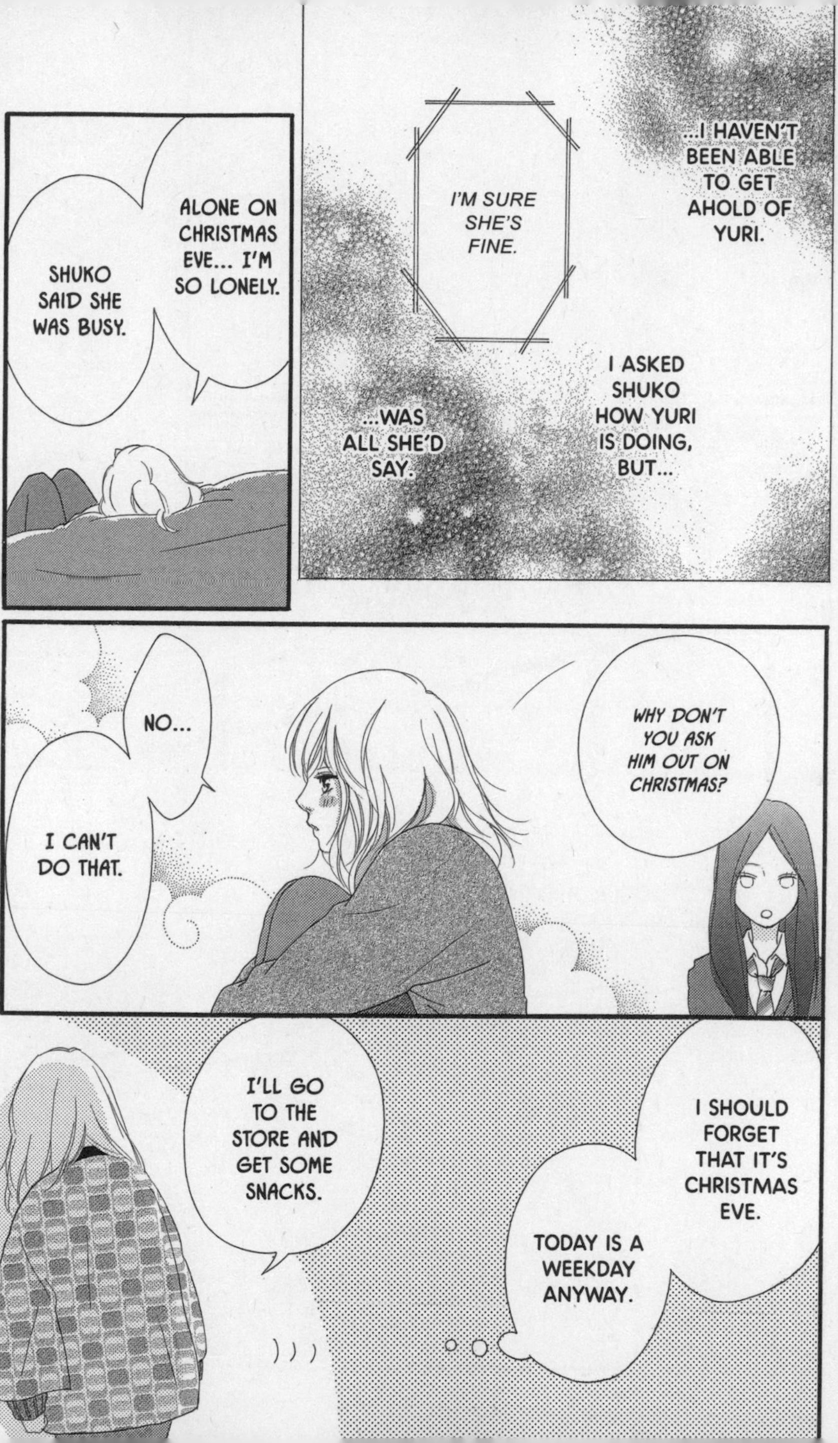
...I HAVEN'T BEEN ABLE TO GET AHOLD OF YURI.
I ASKED SHUKO HOW YURI IS DOING, BUT...
I'M SURE SHE'S FINE.
...WAS ALL SHE'D SAY.
ALONE ON CHRISTMAS EVE... I'M SO LONELY.
SHUKO SAID SHE WAS BUSY.
WHY DON'T YOU ASK HIM OUT ON CHRISTMAS?
NO...
I CAN'T DO THAT.
I SHOULD FORGET THAT IT'S CHRISTMAS EVE.
TODAY IS A WEEKDAY ANYWAY.
I'LL GO TO THE STORE AND GET SOME SNACKS.

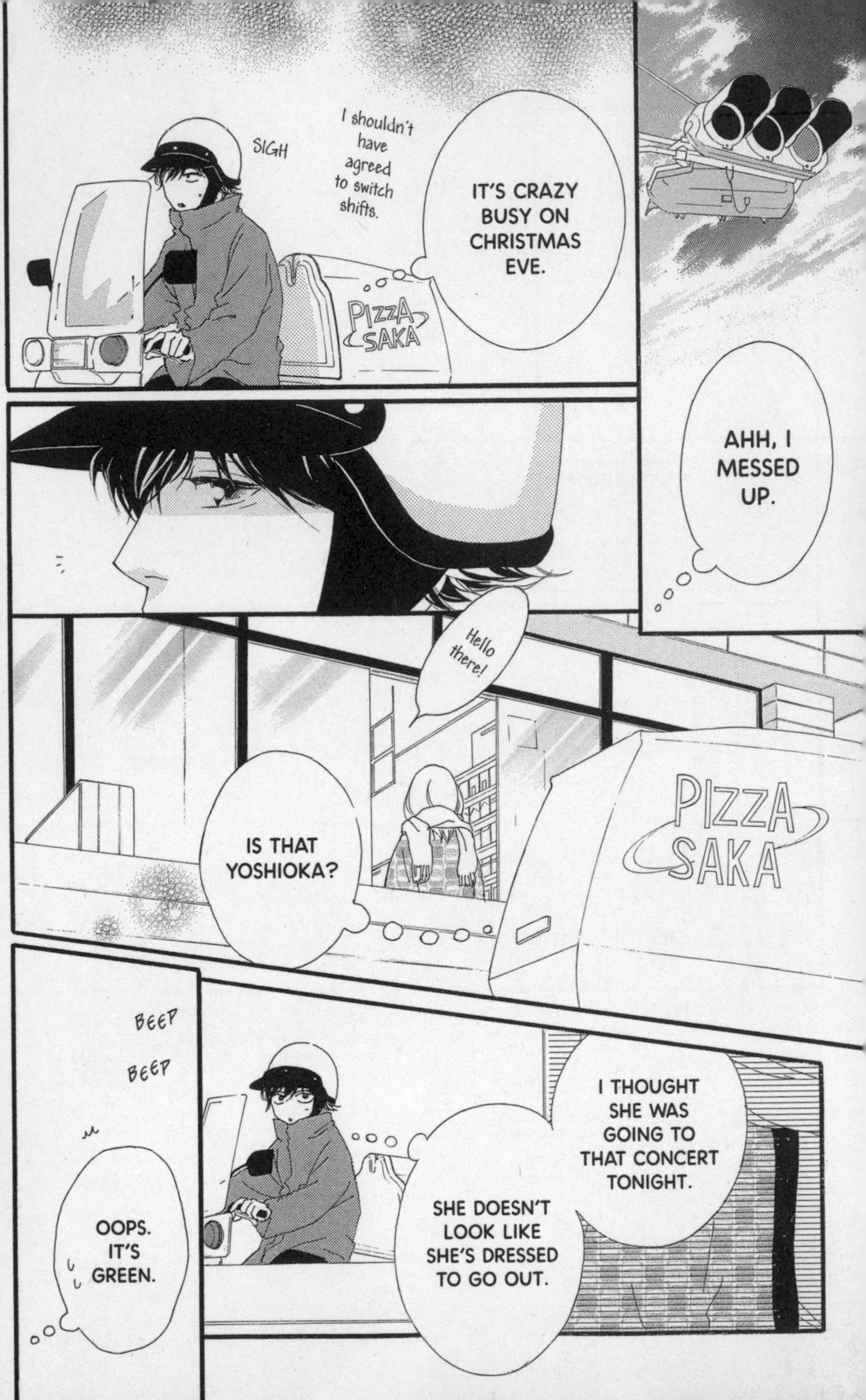
IT'S CRAZY BUSY ON CHRISTMAS EVE.
I shouldn't have agreed to switch shifts.
SIGH
PIZZA SAKA
AHH, I MESSED UP.
Hello there!
PIZZA SAKA
IS THAT YOSHIOKA?
I THOUGHT SHE WAS GOING TO THAT CONCERT TONIGHT.
SHE DOESN'T LOOK LIKE SHE'S DRESSED TO GO OUT.
BEEP
BEEP
OOPS. IT'S GREEN.

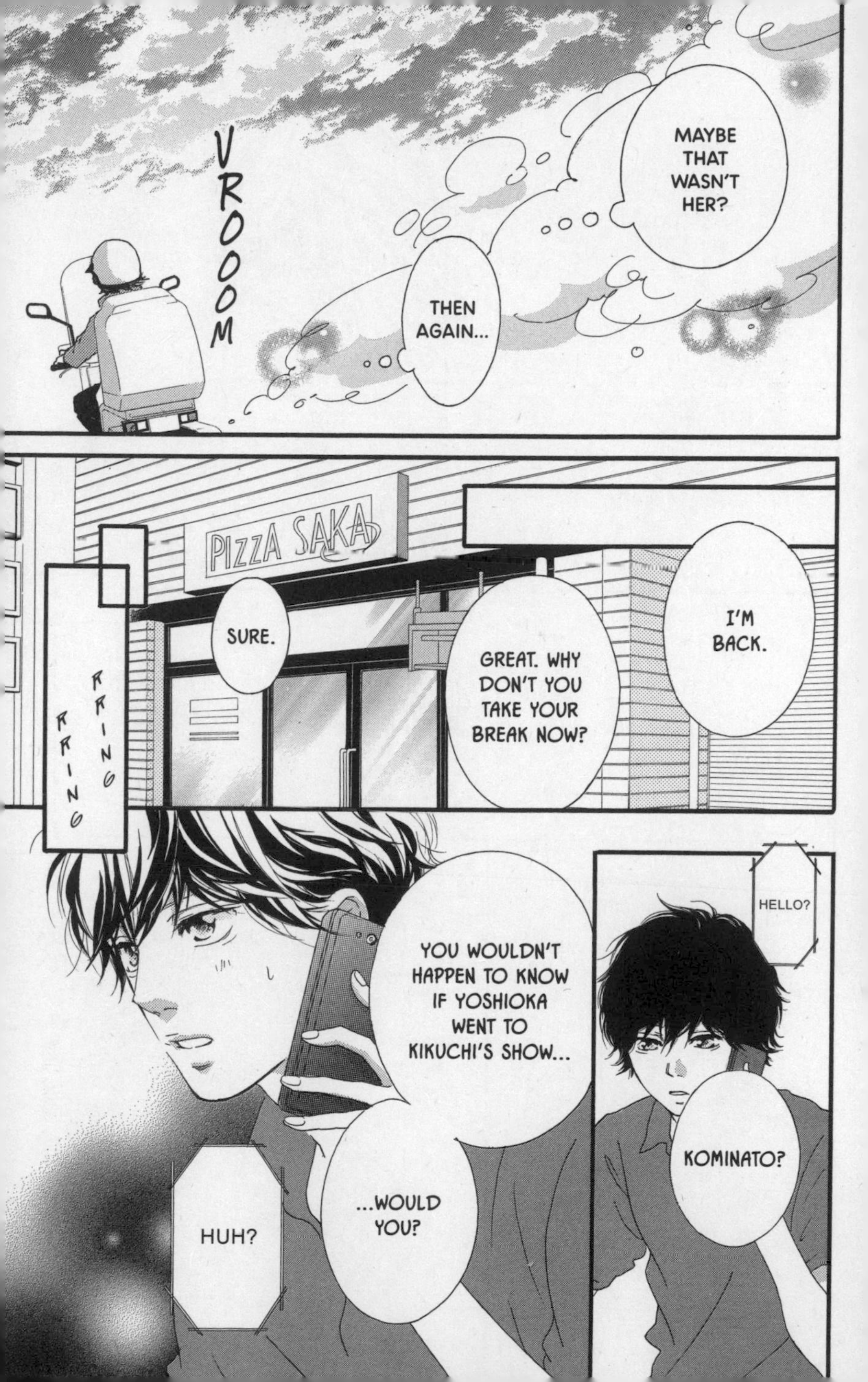
MAYBE THAT WASN'T HER?
THEN AGAIN...
VROOOOM
PIZZA SAKA
I'M BACK.
GREAT. WHY DON'T YOU TAKE YOUR BREAK NOW?
SURE.
RRING RRING
HELLO?
KOMINATO?
YOU WOULDN'T HAPPEN TO KNOW IF YOSHIOKA WENT TO KIKUCHI'S SHOW...
...WOULD YOU?
HUH?

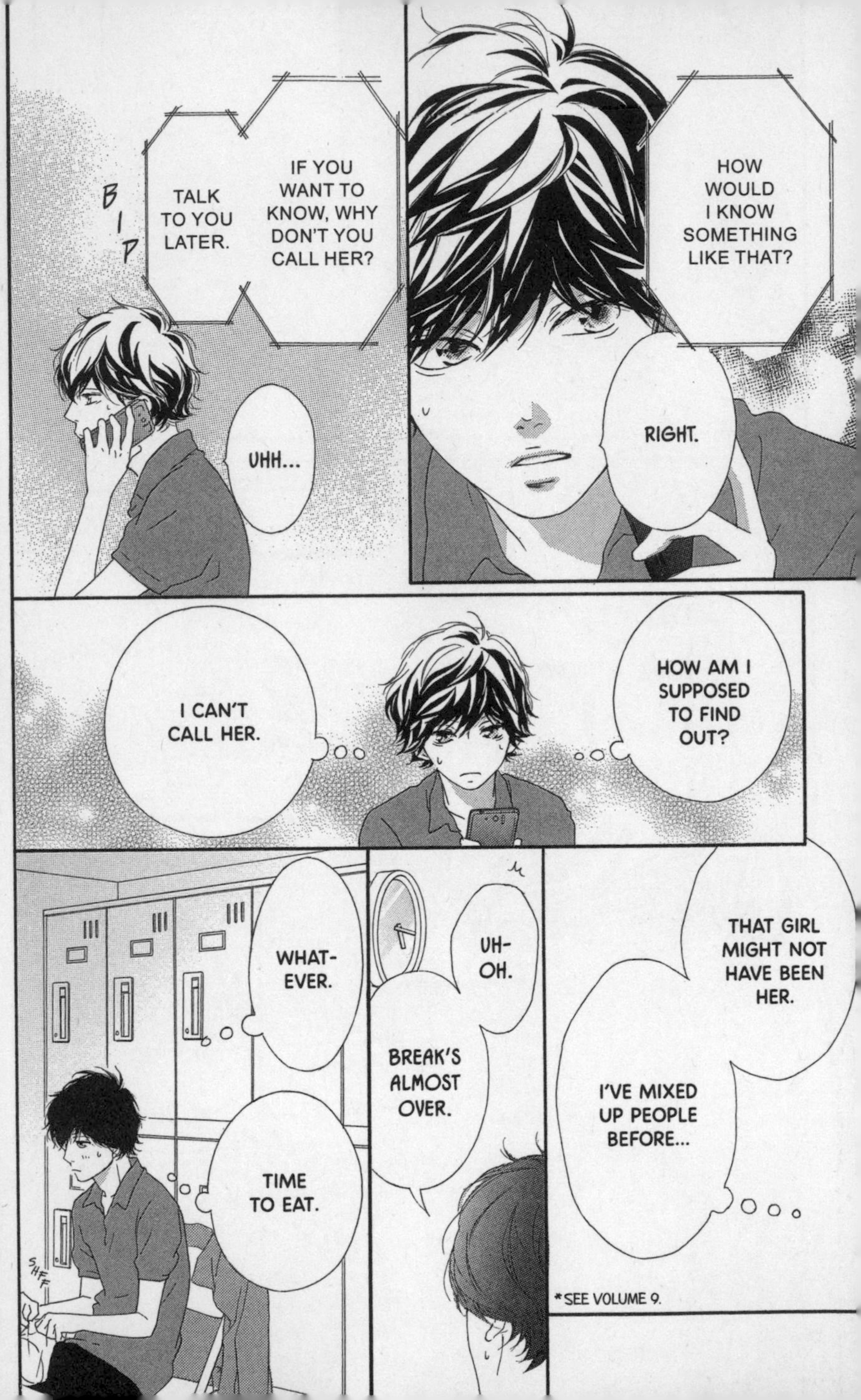
HOW WOULD I KNOW SOMETHING LIKE THAT?
RIGHT.
IF YOU WANT TO KNOW, WHY DON'T YOU CALL HER?
TALK TO YOU LATER.
BIP
UHH...
HOW AM I SUPPOSED TO FIND OUT?
I CAN'T CALL HER.
THAT GIRL MIGHT NOT HAVE BEEN HER.
I'VE MIXED UP PEOPLE BEFORE...
*SEE VOLUME 9.
UH-OH.
BREAK'S ALMOST OVER.
WHAT-EVER.
TIME TO EAT.
SHFF

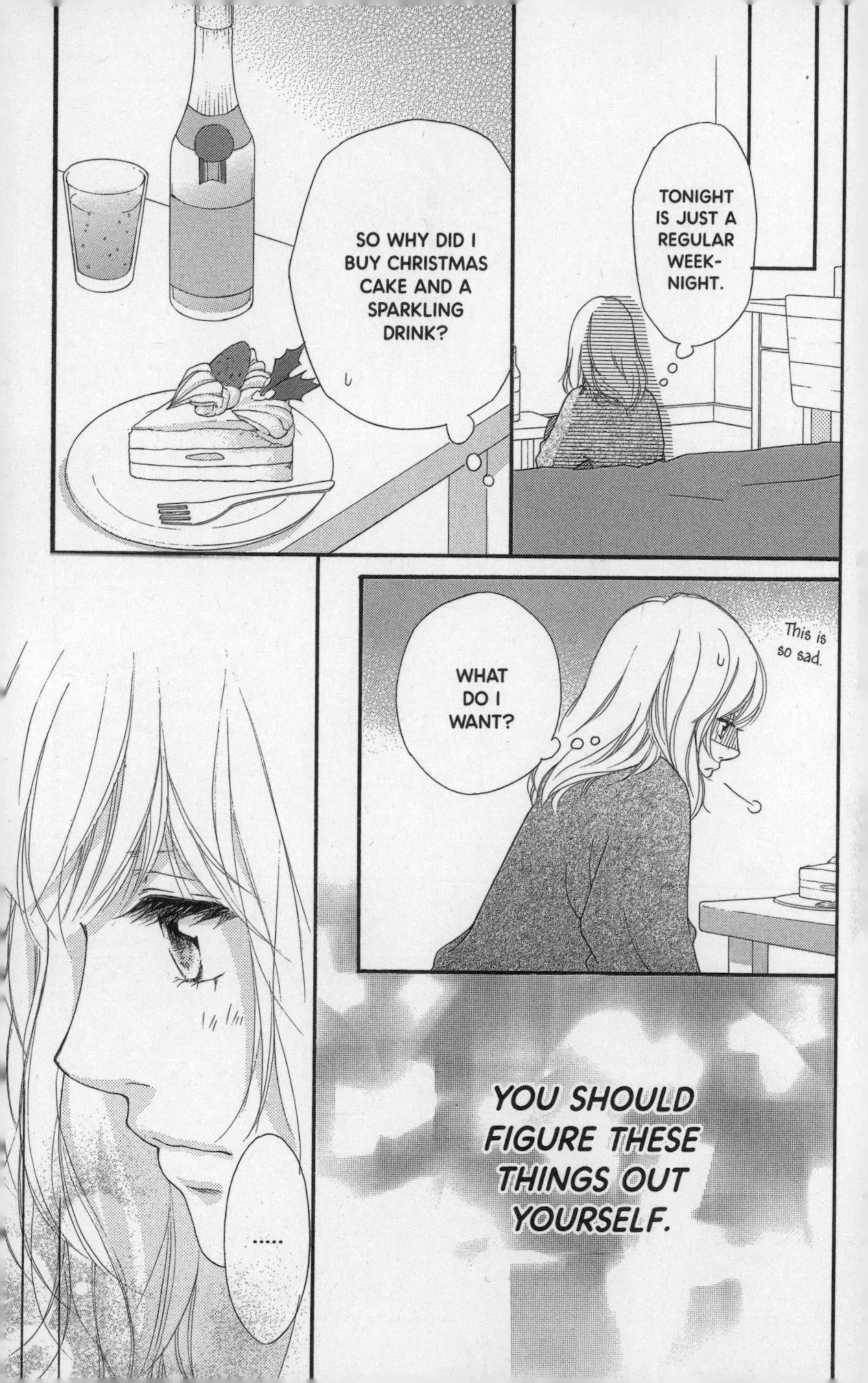
TONIGHT IS JUST A REGULAR WEEK-NIGHT.
SO WHY DID I BUY CHRISTMAS CAKE AND A SPARKLING DRINK?
This is so sad.
WHAT DO I WANT?
YOU SHOULD FIGURE THESE THINGS OUT YOURSELF.
.....

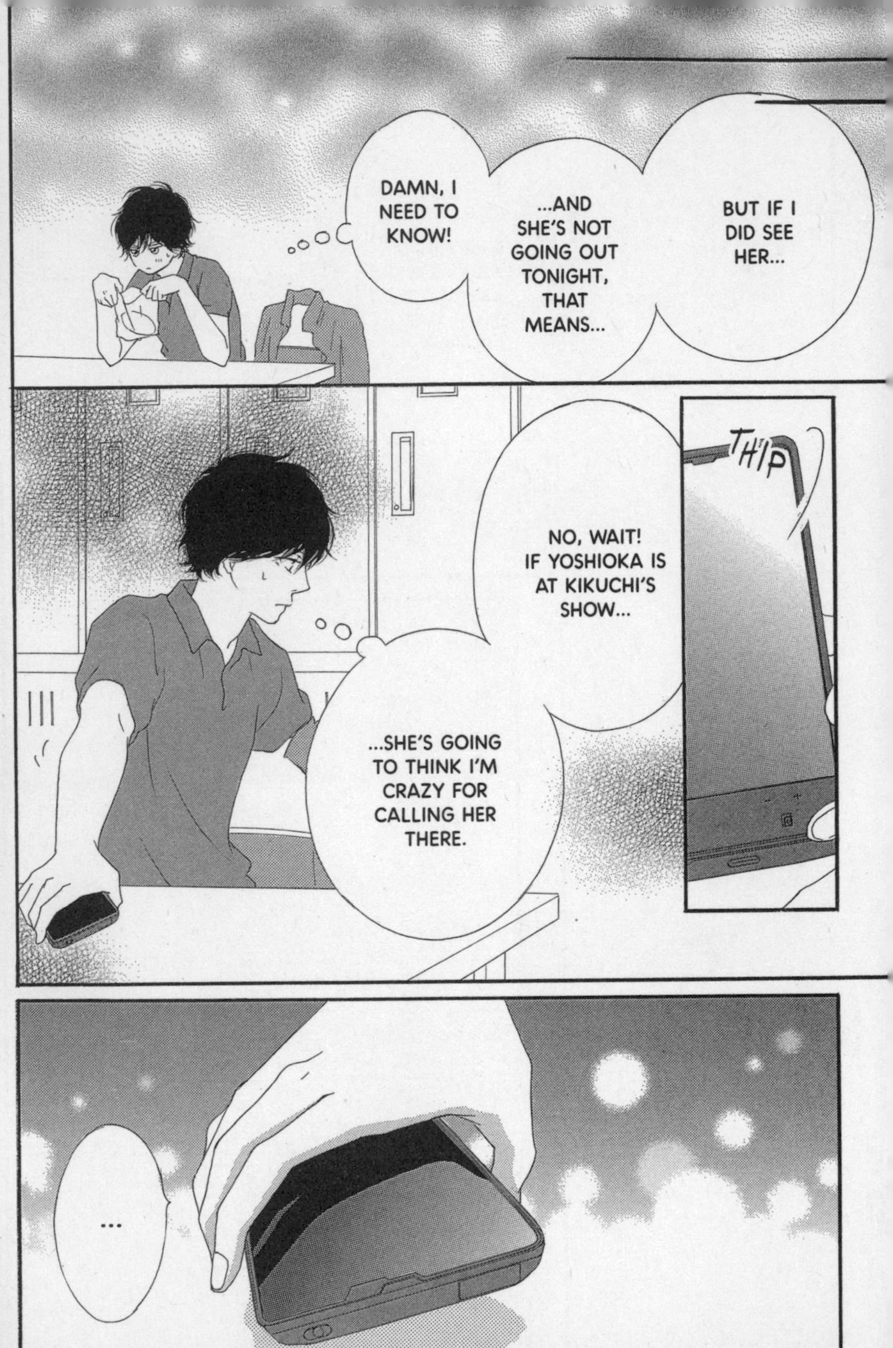
BUT IF I DID SEE HER...
...AND SHE'S NOT GOING OUT TONIGHT, THAT MEANS...
DAMN, I NEED TO KNOW!
THIP
NO, WAIT! IF YOSHIOKA IS AT KIKUCHI'S SHOW...
...SHE'S GOING TO THINK I'M CRAZY FOR CALLING HER THERE.
...

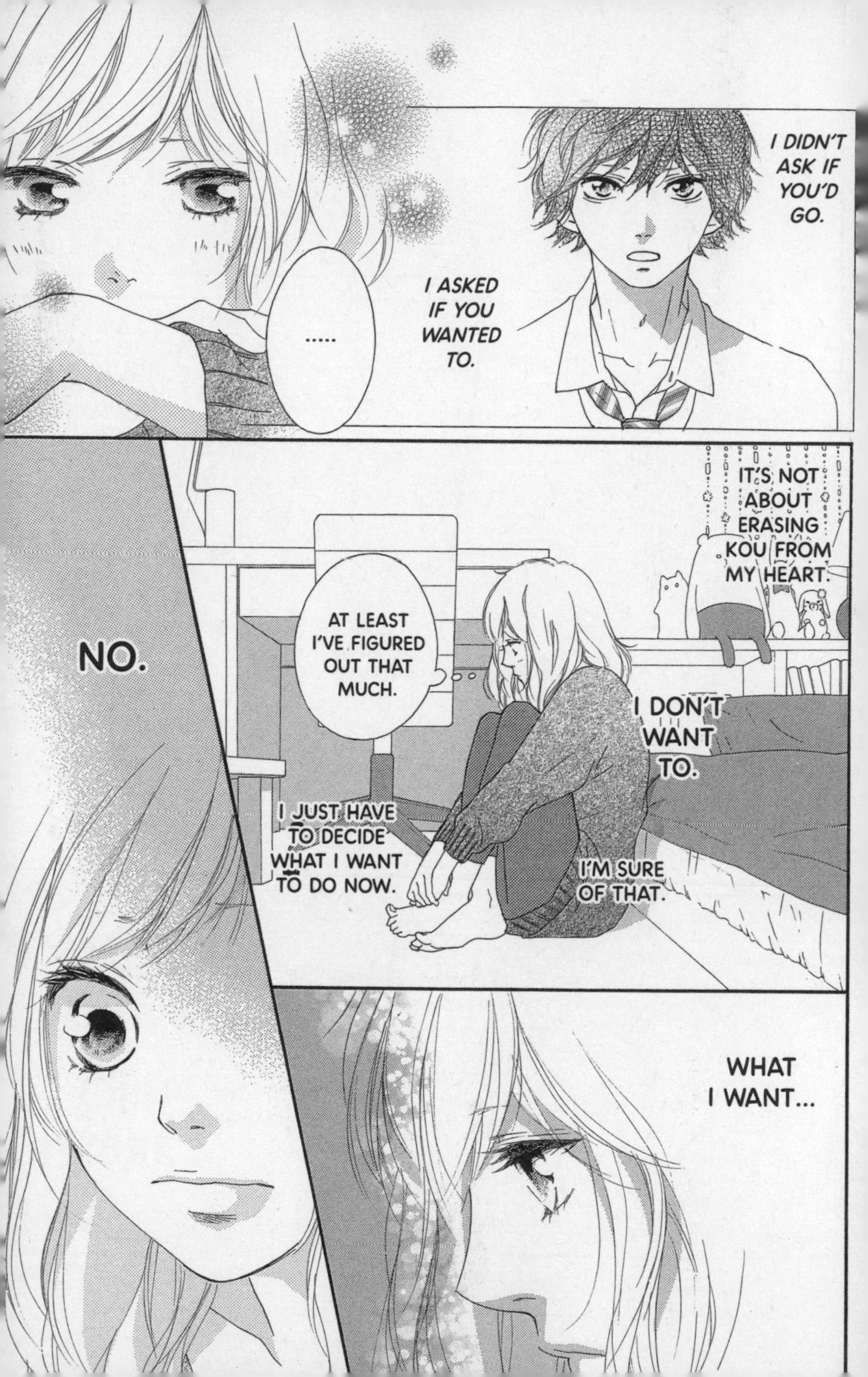
I DIDN'T ASK IF YOU'D GO.
I ASKED IF YOU WANTED TO.
.....
IT'S NOT ABOUT ERASING KOU FROM MY HEART.
I DON'T WANT TO.
I'M SURE OF THAT.
AT LEAST I'VE FIGURED OUT THAT MUCH.
I JUST HAVE TO DECIDE WHAT I WANT TO DO NOW.
WHAT I WANT...
NO.

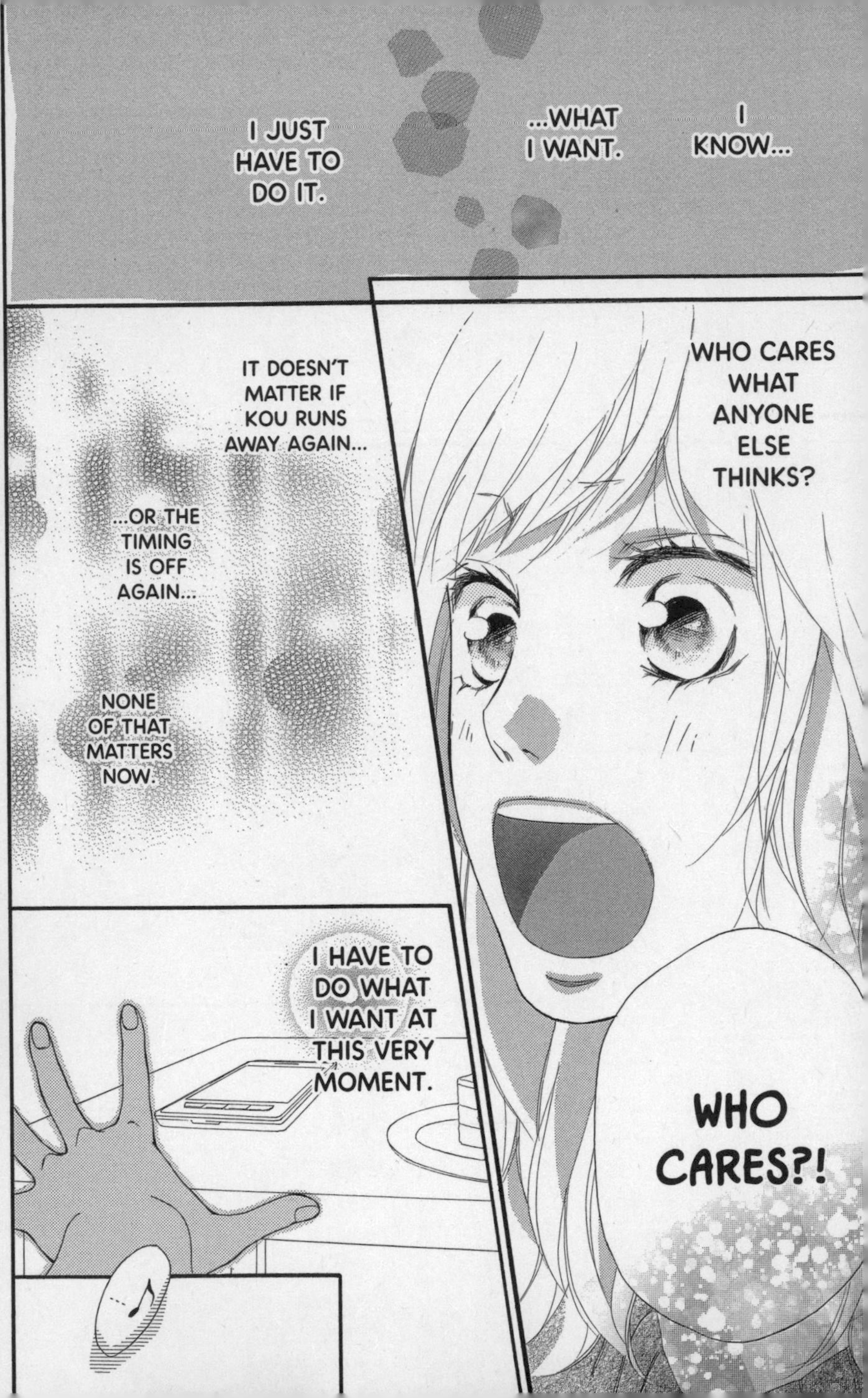
I KNOW...
...WHAT I WANT.
I JUST HAVE TO DO IT.
WHO CARES WHAT ANYONE ELSE THINKS?
WHO CARES?!
IT DOESN'T MATTER IF KOU RUNS AWAY AGAIN...
...OR THE TIMING IS OFF AGAIN...
NONE OF THAT MATTERS NOW.
I HAVE TO DO WHAT I WANT AT THIS VERY MOMENT.

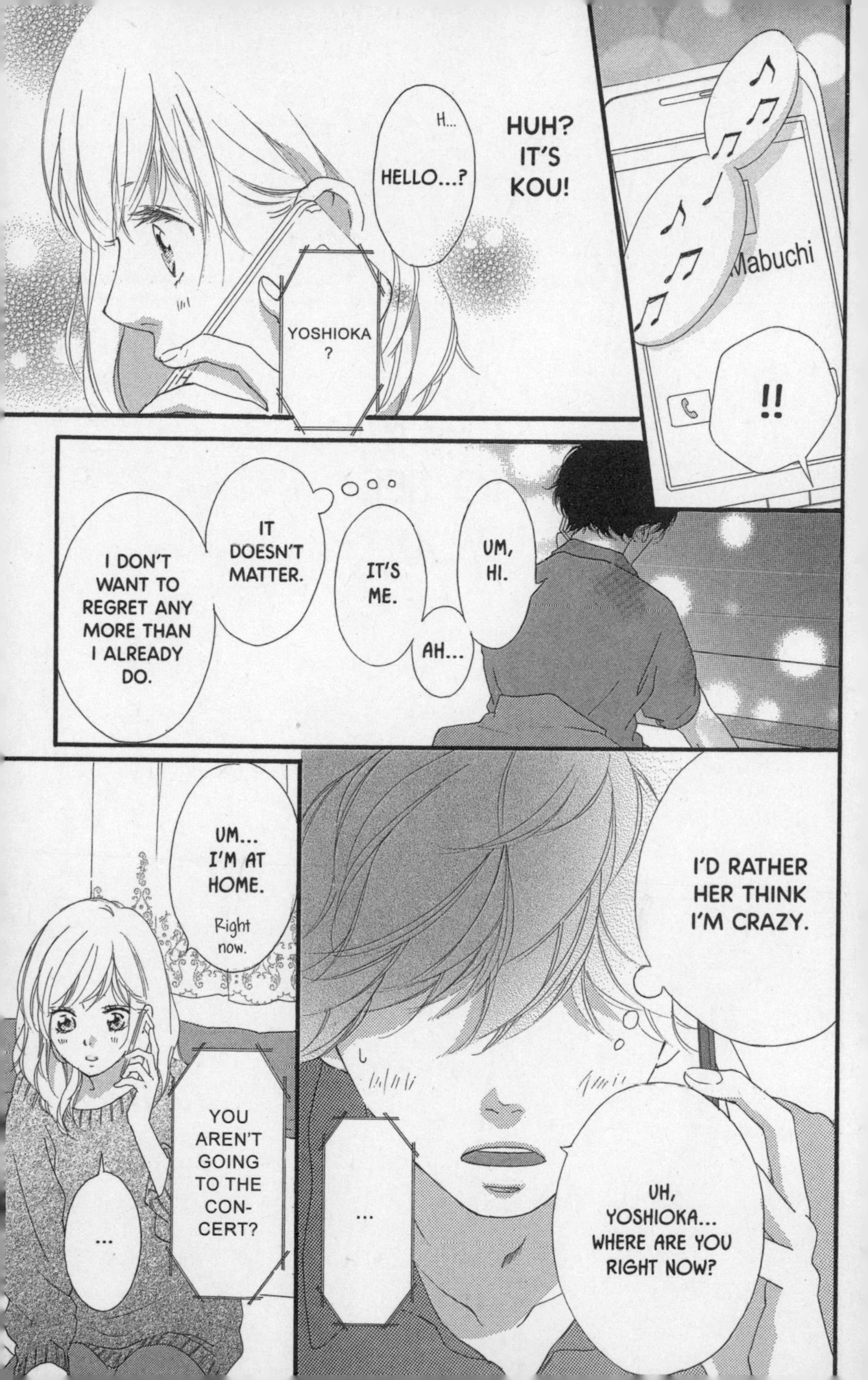
Mabuchi
!!
HUH? IT'S KOU!
H... HELLO...?
YOSHIOKA?
UM, HI.
AH...
IT'S ME.
IT DOESN'T MATTER.
I DON'T WANT TO REGRET ANY MORE THAN I ALREADY DO.
I'D RATHER HER THINK I'M CRAZY.
UH, YOSHIOKA... WHERE ARE YOU RIGHT NOW?
...
UM... I'M AT HOME.
Right now.
YOU AREN'T GOING TO THE CON-CERT?
...

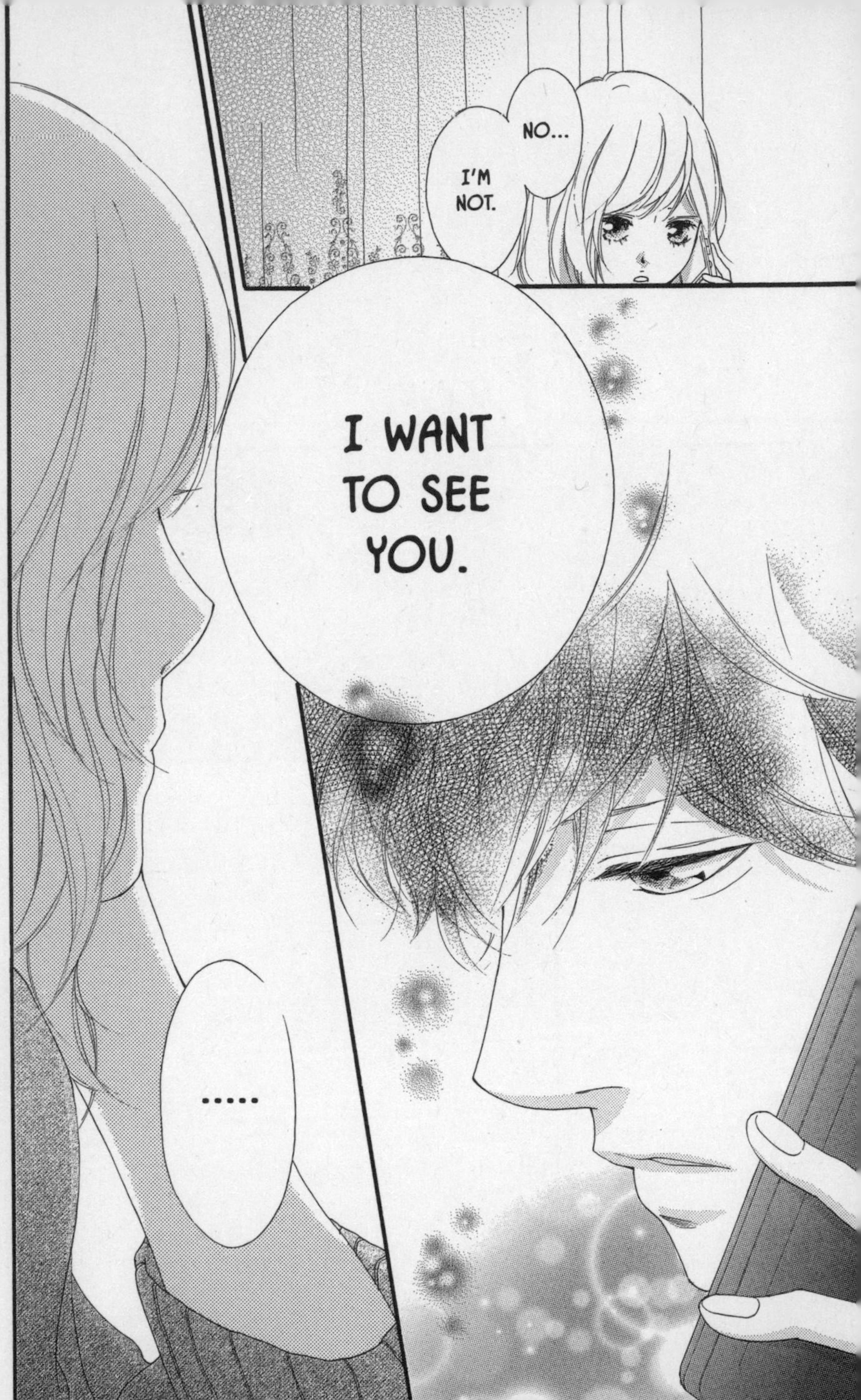
NO... I'M NOT.
I WANT TO SEE YOU.
.....

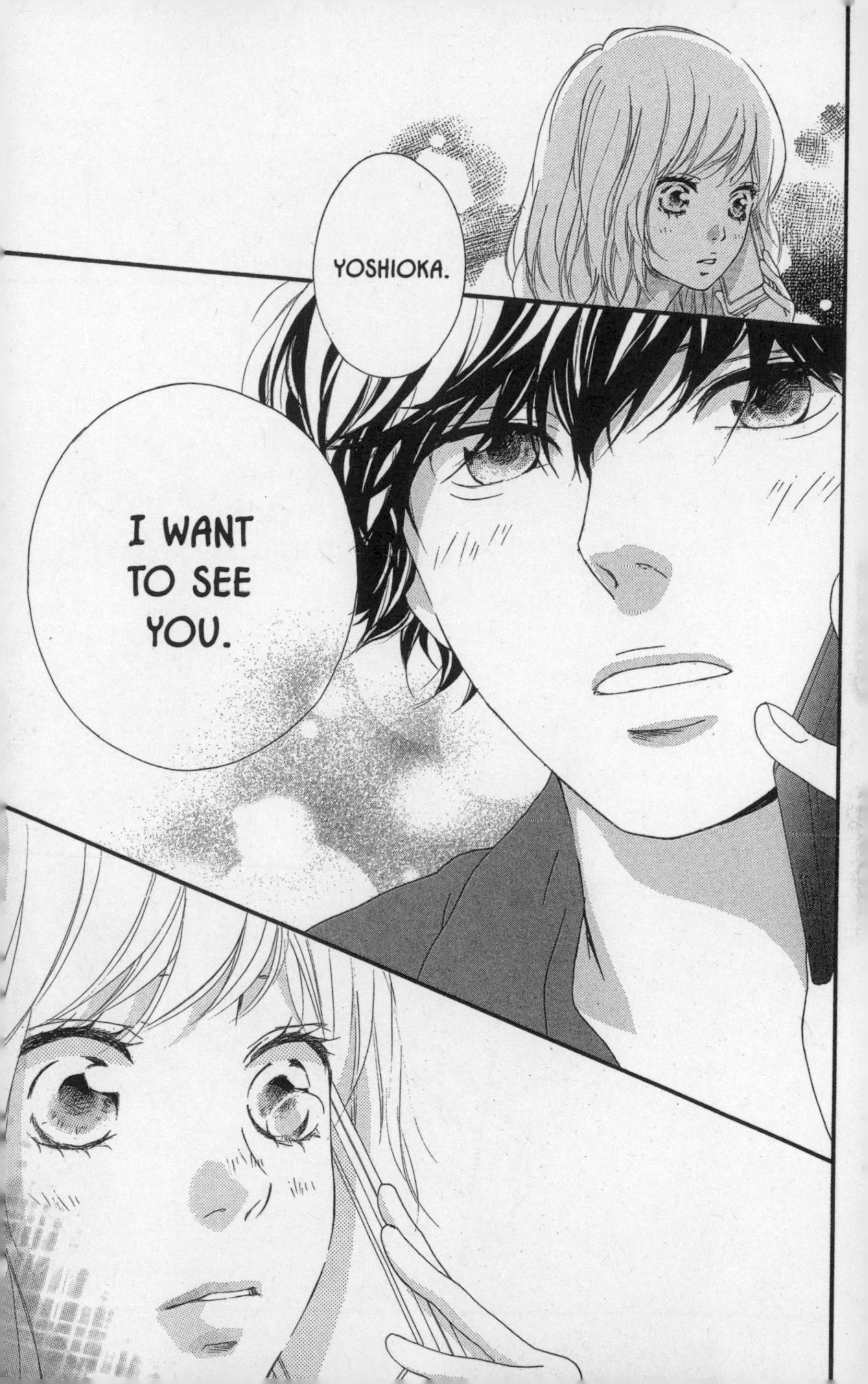
YOSHIOKA.
I WANT TO SEE YOU.

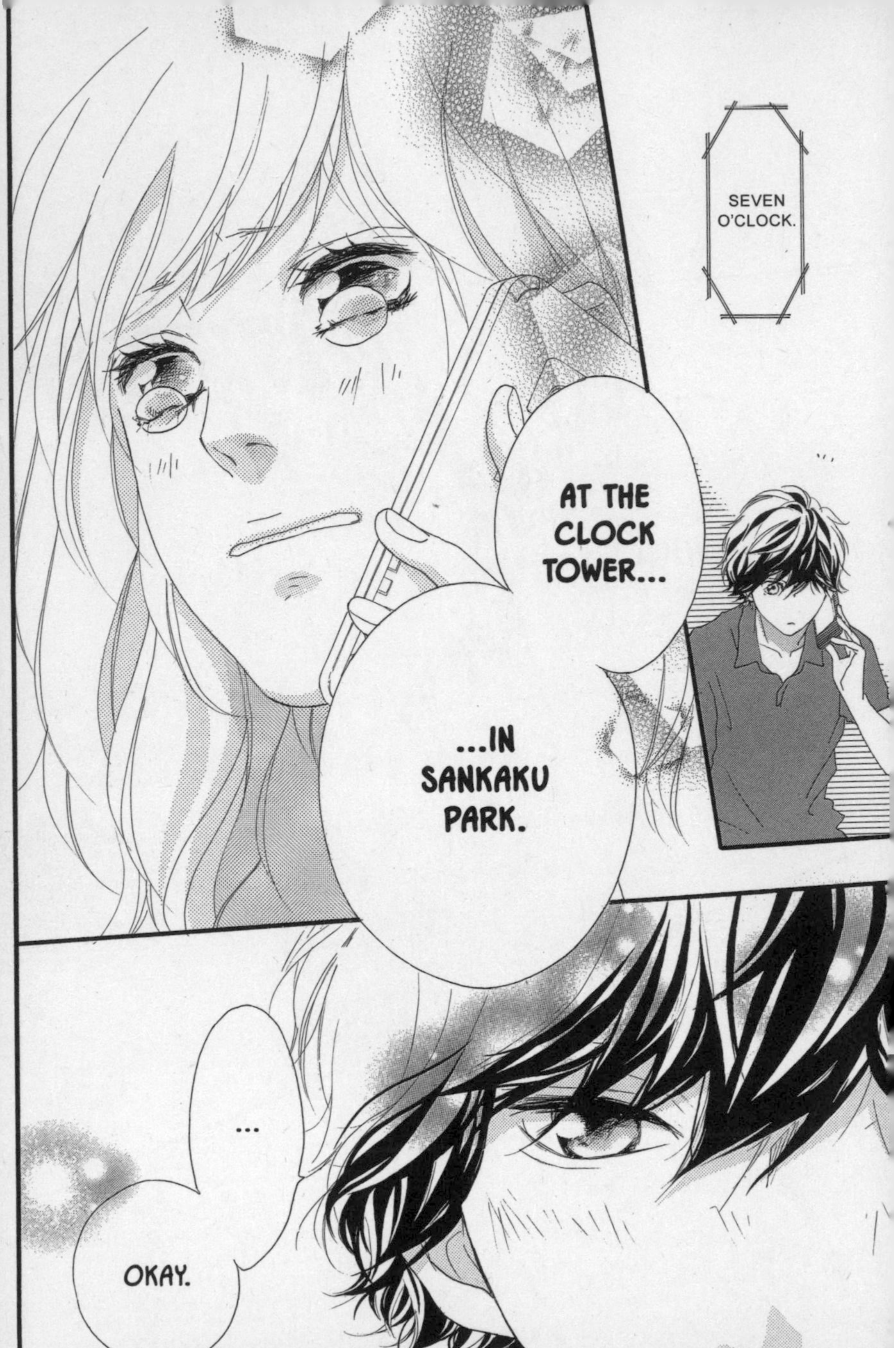
SEVEN O'CLOCK.
AT THE CLOCK TOWER...
...IN SANKAKU PARK.
...
OKAY.

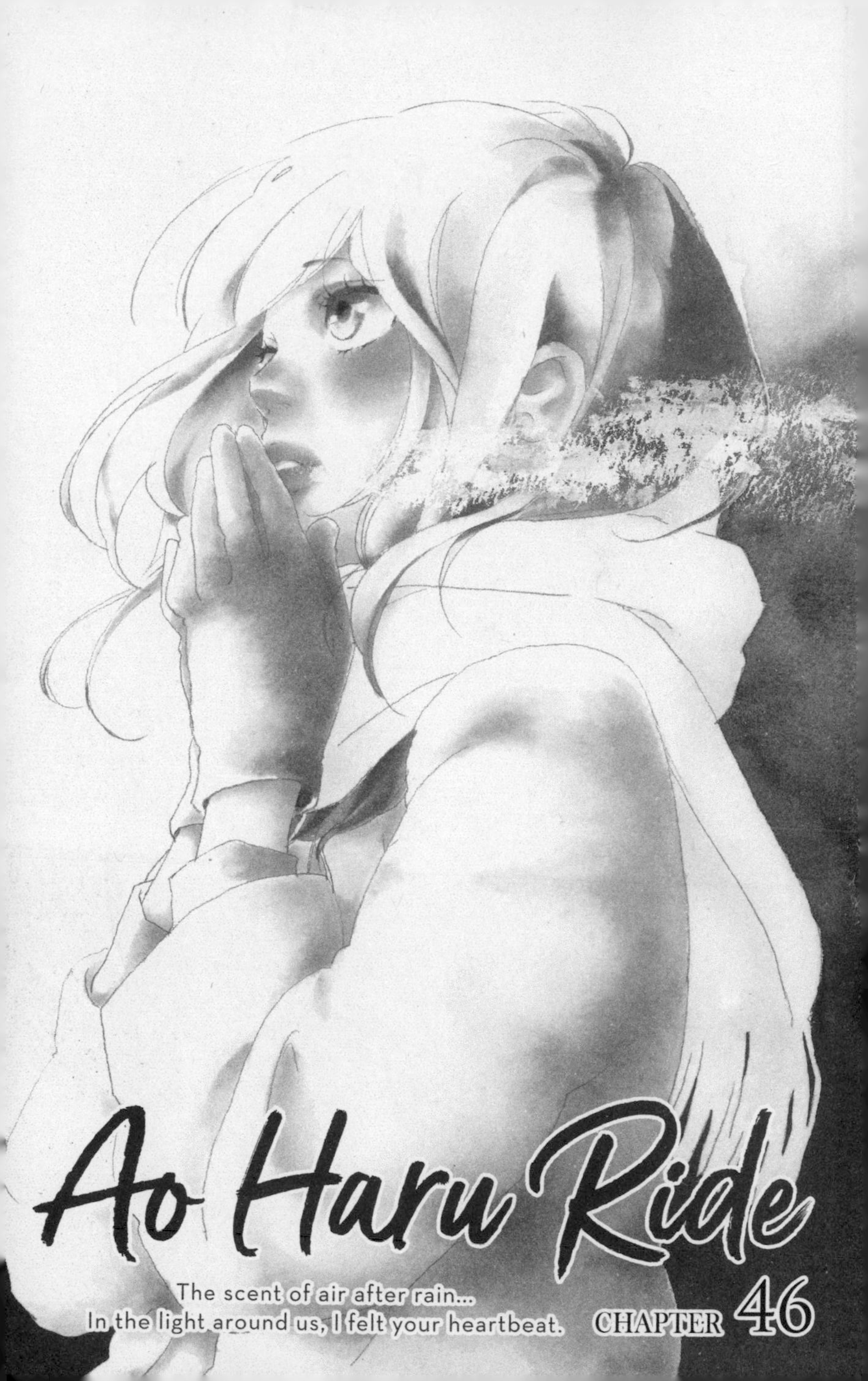
Ao Haru Ride
The scent of air after rain...
In the light around us, I felt your heartbeat.
CHAPTER 46

Thank You Page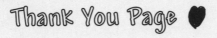

Thank you all for your many letters and messages on Twitter!!
I have to apologize for not being able to reply to everyone. But I want you to know that I do read your letters and messages. I'm so grateful for them.⁺₊
Sometimes I receive words that make me so happy I cry real tears. Then I feel so energized that I want to eat white rice for some reason. (Do you feel me? Do you understand?!)
Many of you replied to my comments about upside down hamburgers. It seems that hamburgers are physically easier to eat upside down. I didn't realize it, but I must've been searching for the easiest way to eat them. I encourage you to try it yourself.
It's so much fun for me to communicate with you through my manga and your letters.
Thank you very much!!!

THANKYOU!

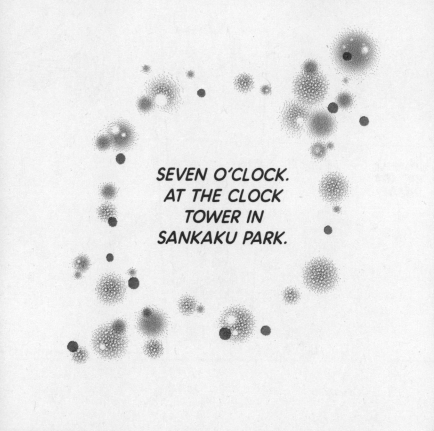

SEVEN O'CLOCK.
AT THE CLOCK
TOWER IN
SANKAKU PARK.

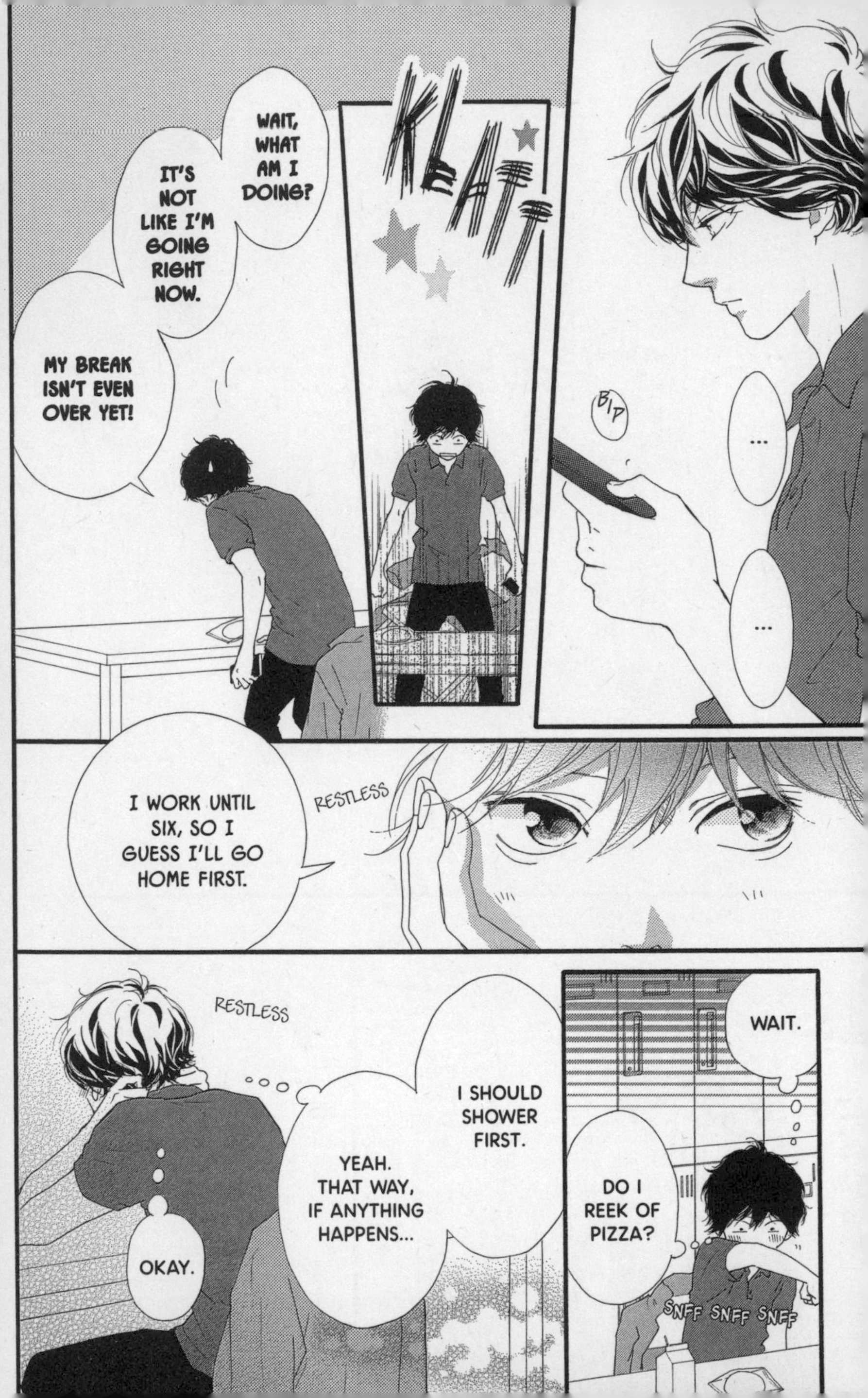
...
BIP
...
KLATT
WAIT, WHAT AM I DOING?
IT'S NOT LIKE I'M GOING RIGHT NOW.
MY BREAK ISN'T EVEN OVER YET!
RESTLESS
I WORK UNTIL SIX, SO I GUESS I'LL GO HOME FIRST.
WAIT.
DO I REEK OF PIZZA?
SNFF SNFF SNFF
I SHOULD SHOWER FIRST.
YEAH. THAT WAY, IF ANYTHING HAPPENS...
RESTLESS
OKAY.

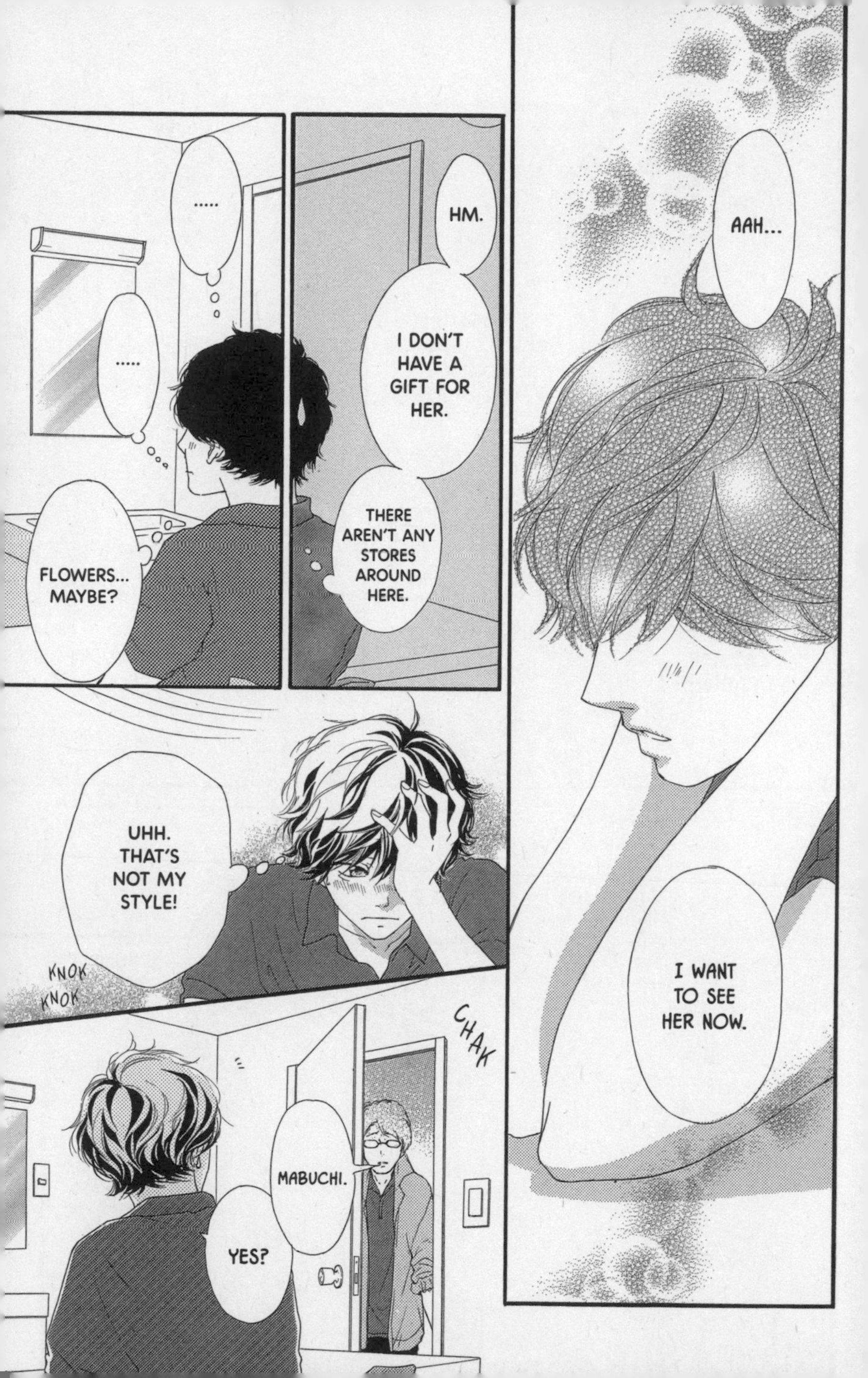
AAH...
I WANT TO SEE HER NOW.
HM.
I DON'T HAVE A GIFT FOR HER.
THERE AREN'T ANY STORES AROUND HERE.
.....
.....
FLOWERS... MAYBE?
UHH. THAT'S NOT MY STYLE!
KNOK KNOK
CHAK
MABUCHI.
YES?

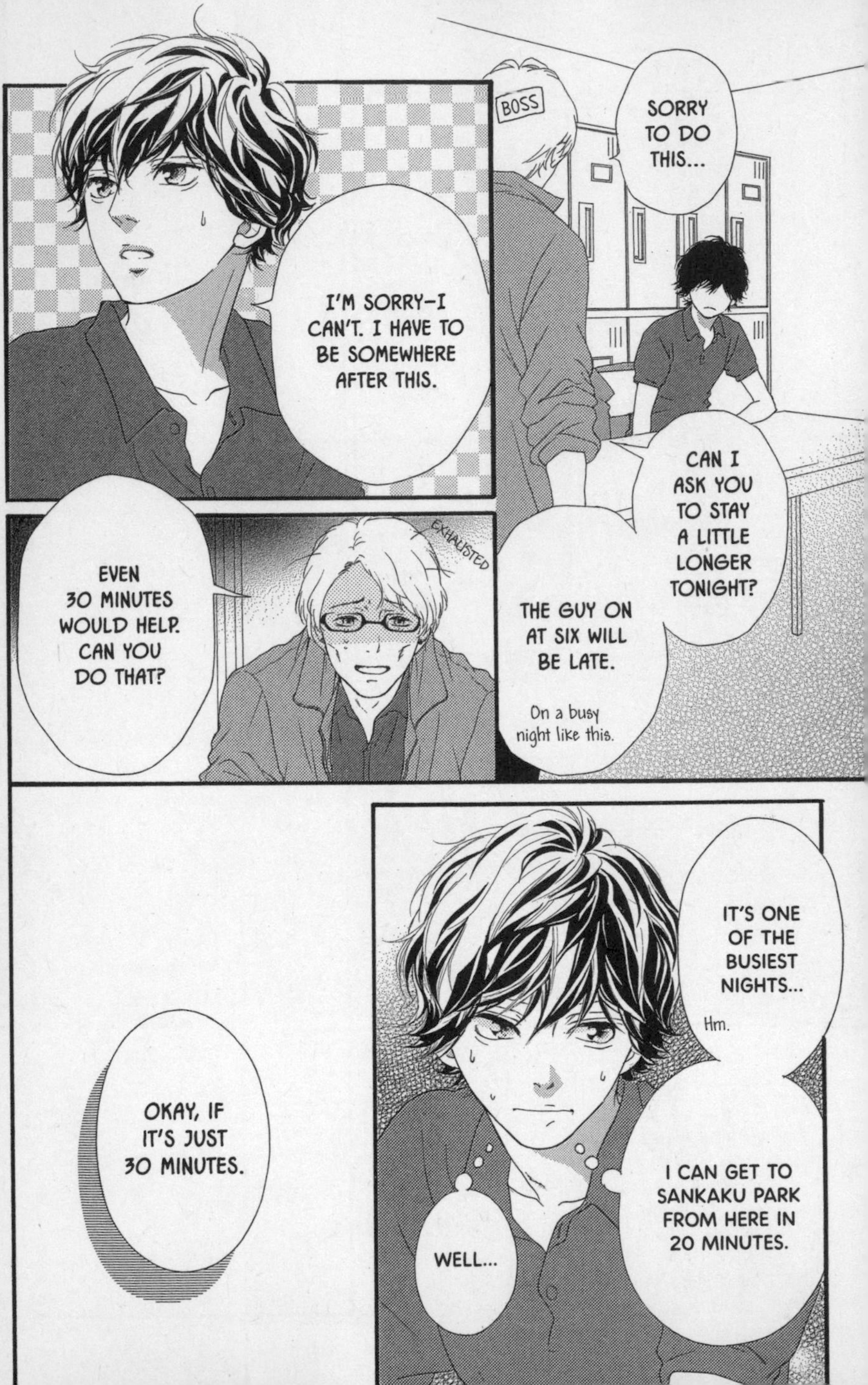
BOSS
SORRY TO DO THIS...
CAN I ASK YOU TO STAY A LITTLE LONGER TONIGHT?
THE GUY ON AT SIX WILL BE LATE.
On a busy night like this.
I'M SORRY—I CAN'T. I HAVE TO BE SOMEWHERE AFTER THIS.
EXHAUSTED
EVEN 30 MINUTES WOULD HELP. CAN YOU DO THAT?
IT'S ONE OF THE BUSIEST NIGHTS...
Hm.
I CAN GET TO SANKAKU PARK FROM HERE IN 20 MINUTES.
WELL...
OKAY, IF IT'S JUST 30 MINUTES.

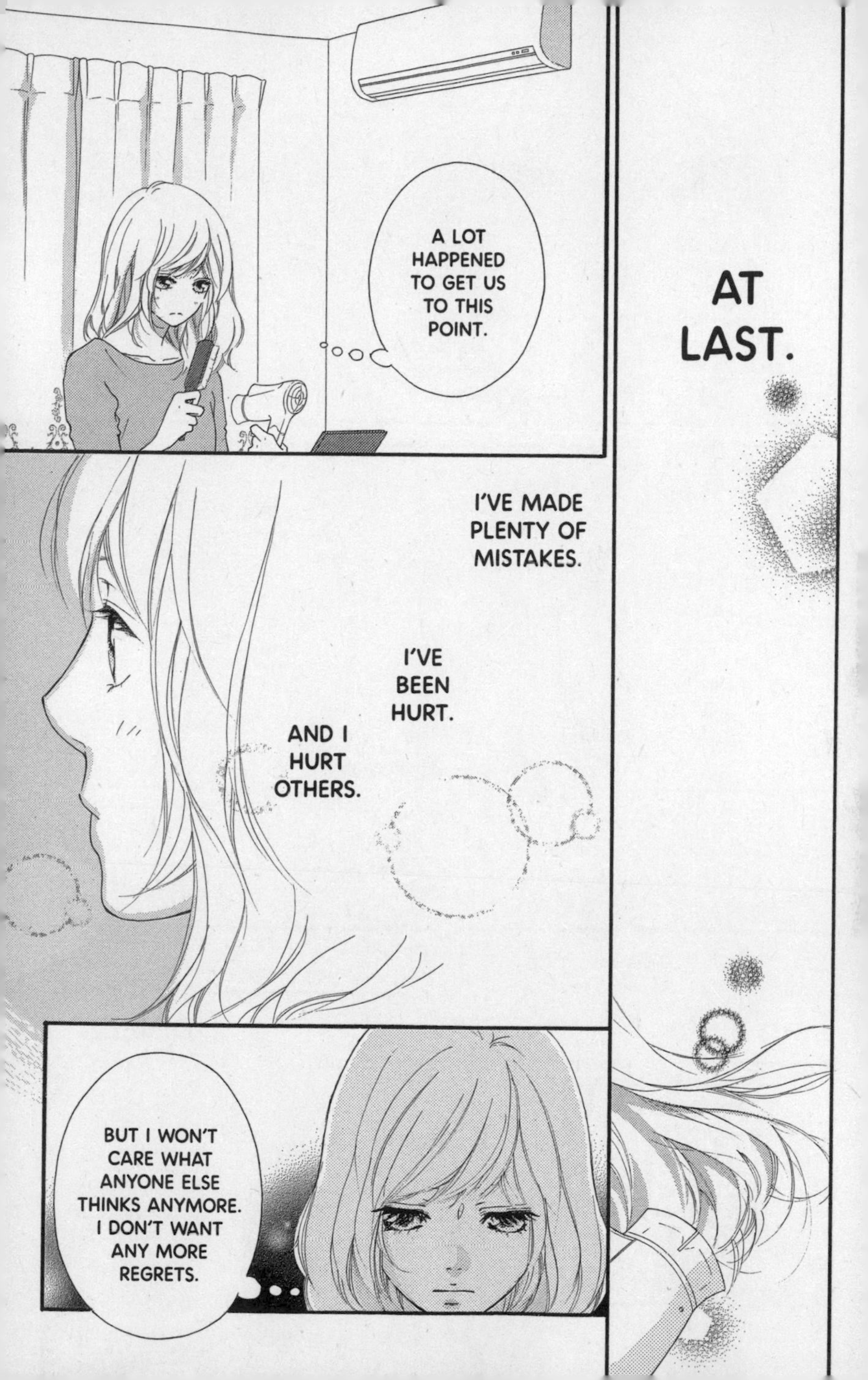
AT LAST.
A LOT HAPPENED TO GET US TO THIS POINT.
I'VE MADE PLENTY OF MISTAKES.
I'VE BEEN HURT.
AND I HURT OTHERS.
BUT I WON'T CARE WHAT ANYONE ELSE THINKS ANYMORE. I DON'T WANT ANY MORE REGRETS.

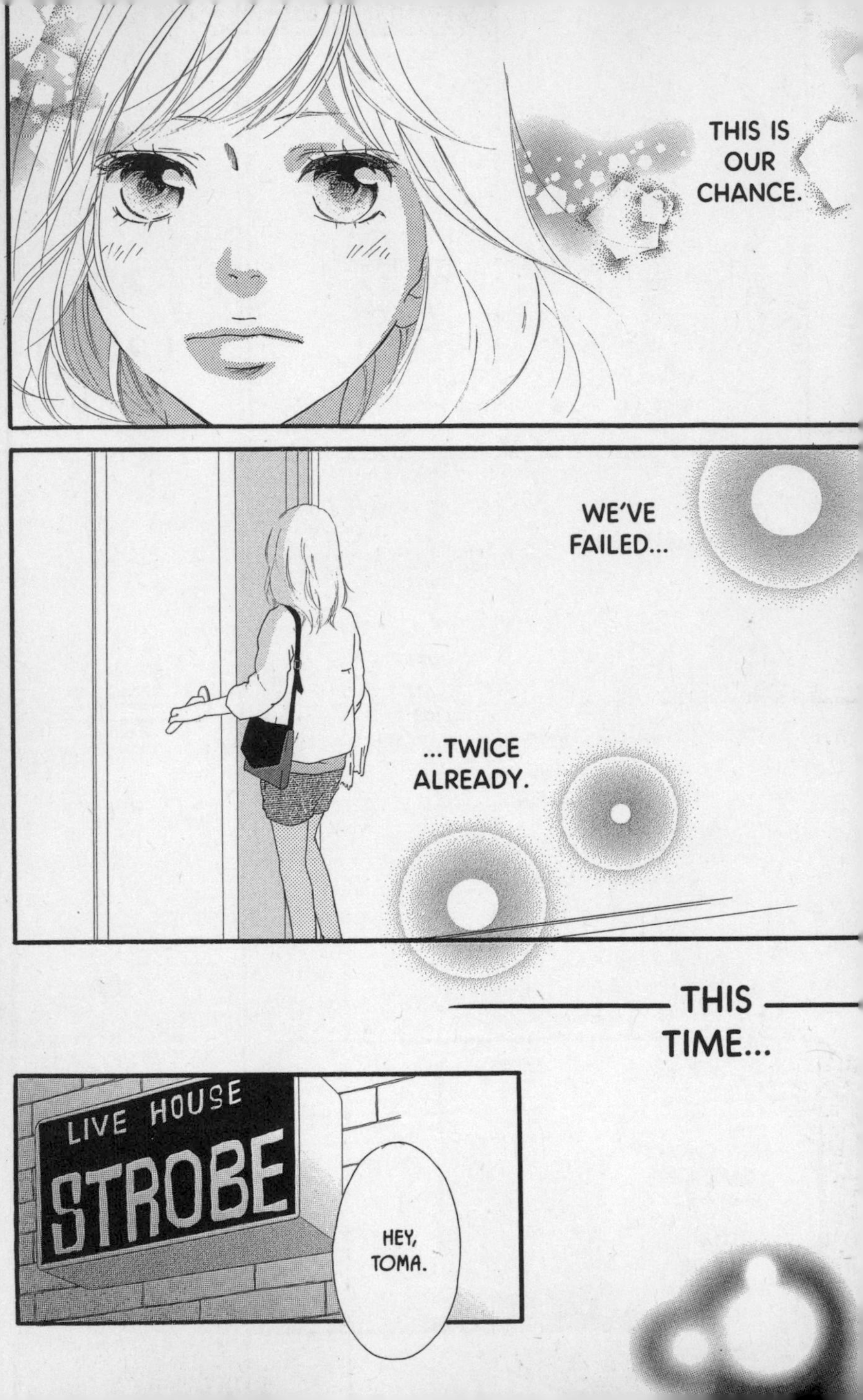
THIS IS OUR CHANCE.
WE'VE FAILED...
...TWICE ALREADY.
THIS TIME...
LIVE HOUSE
STROBE
HEY, TOMA.

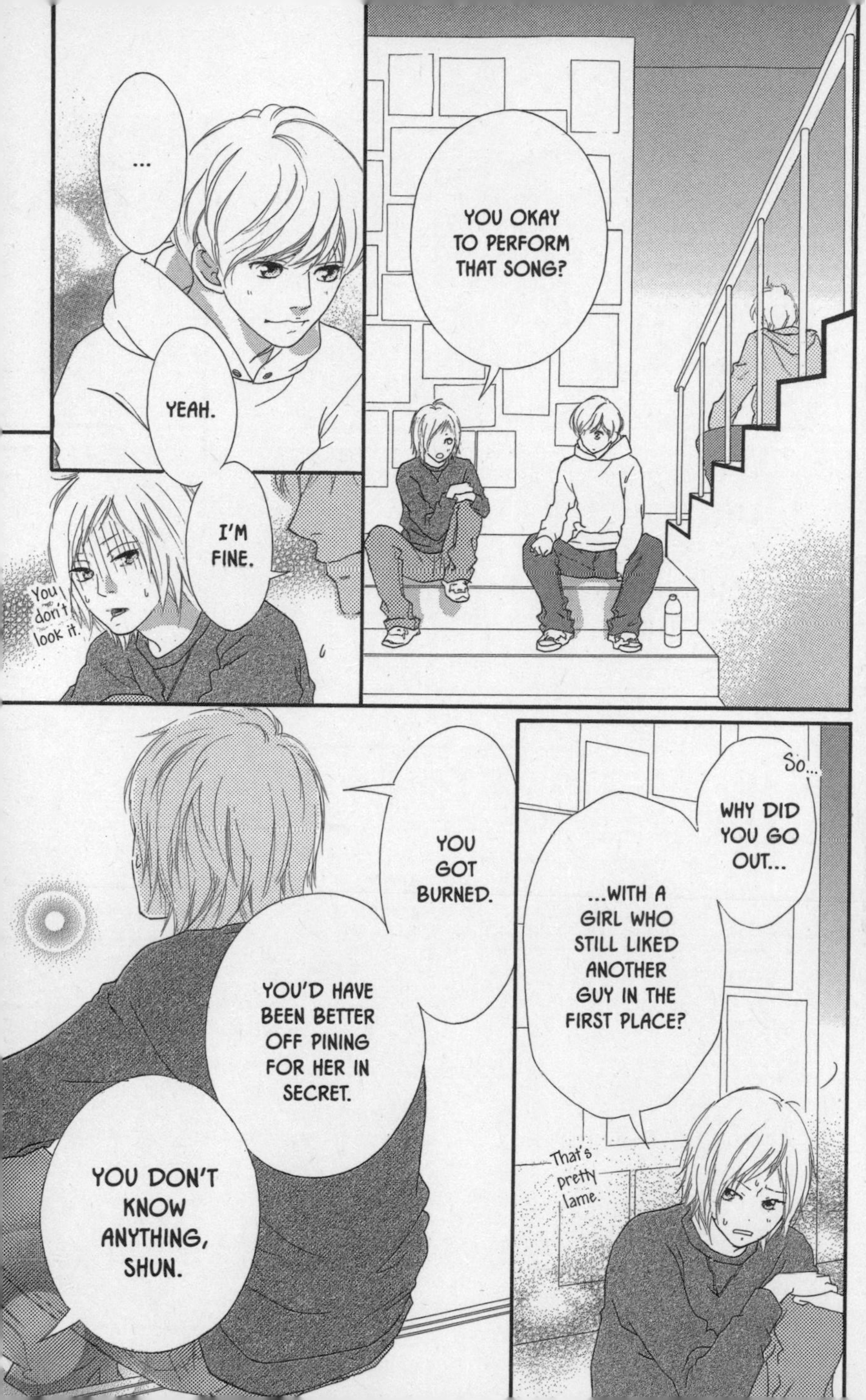
YOU OKAY TO PERFORM THAT SONG?
...
YEAH.
I'M FINE.
You don't look it.
So...
WHY DID YOU GO OUT...
...WITH A GIRL WHO STILL LIKED ANOTHER GUY IN THE FIRST PLACE?
That's pretty lame.
YOU GOT BURNED.
YOU'D HAVE BEEN BETTER OFF PINING FOR HER IN SECRET.
YOU DON'T KNOW ANYTHING, SHUN.

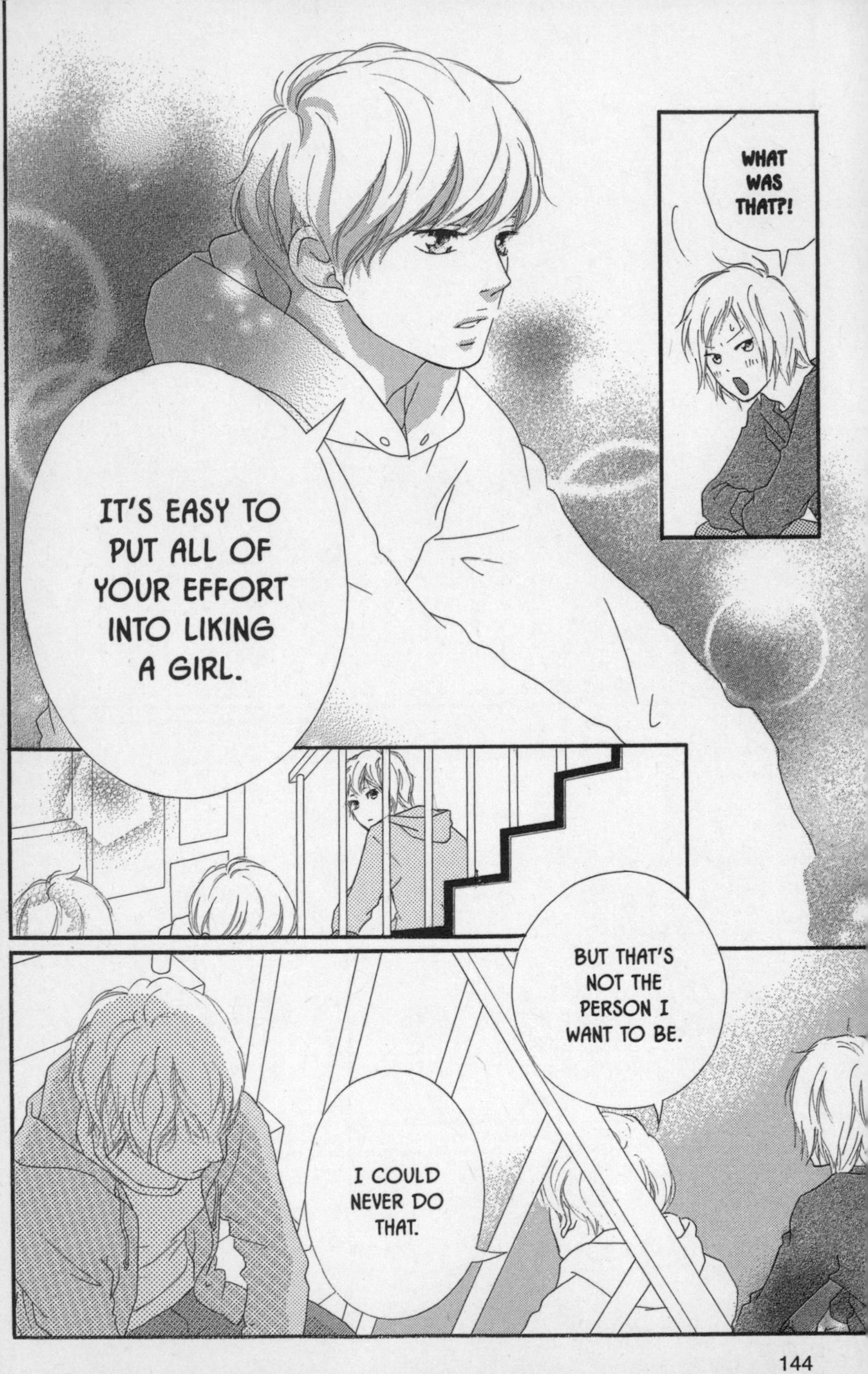
WHAT WAS THAT?!
IT'S EASY TO PUT ALL OF YOUR EFFORT INTO LIKING A GIRL.
BUT THAT'S NOT THE PERSON I WANT TO BE.
I COULD NEVER DO THAT.

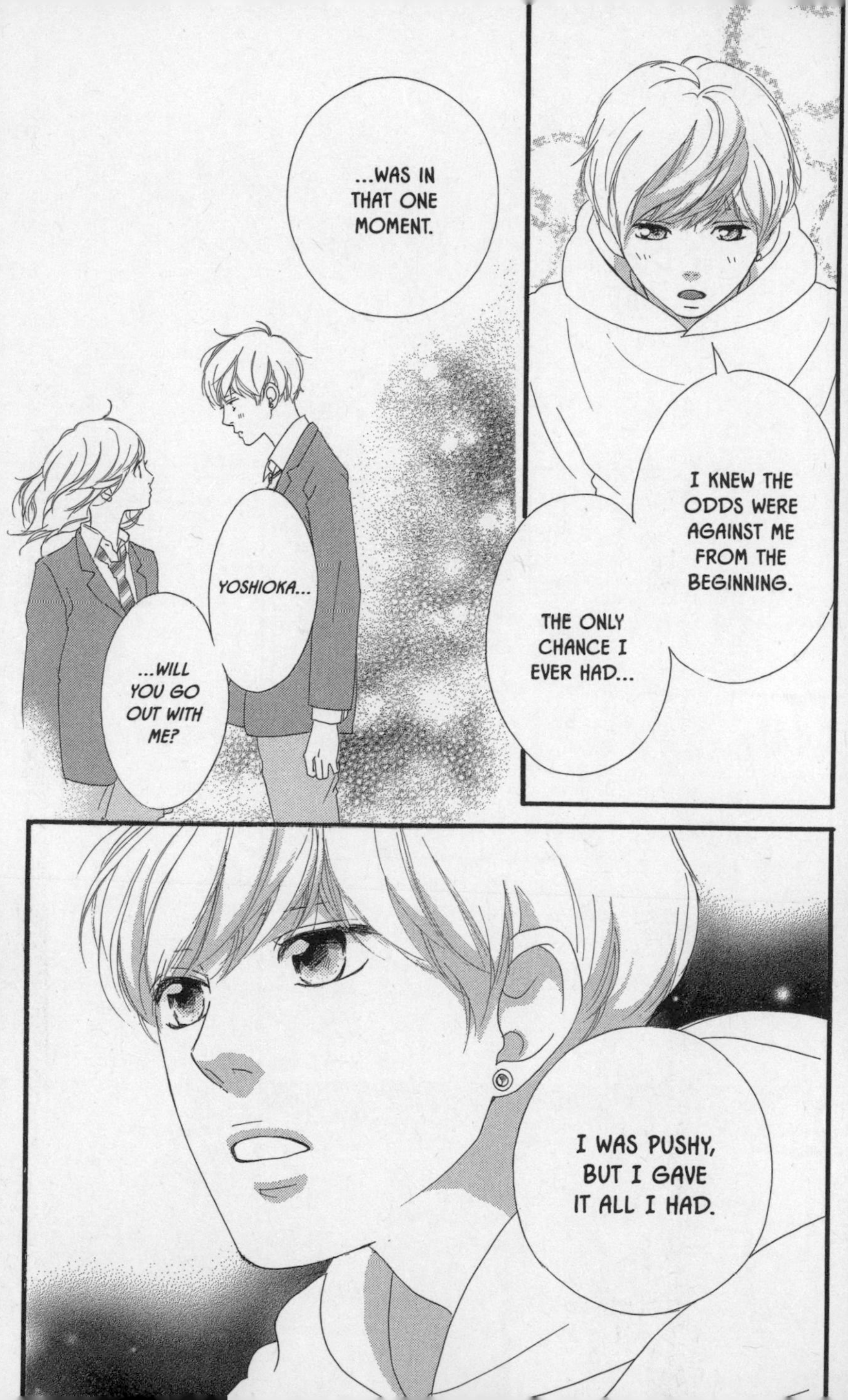
I KNEW THE ODDS WERE AGAINST ME FROM THE BEGINNING.
THE ONLY CHANCE I EVER HAD...
...WAS IN THAT ONE MOMENT.
YOSHIOKA...
...WILL YOU GO OUT WITH ME?
I WAS PUSHY, BUT I GAVE IT ALL I HAD.

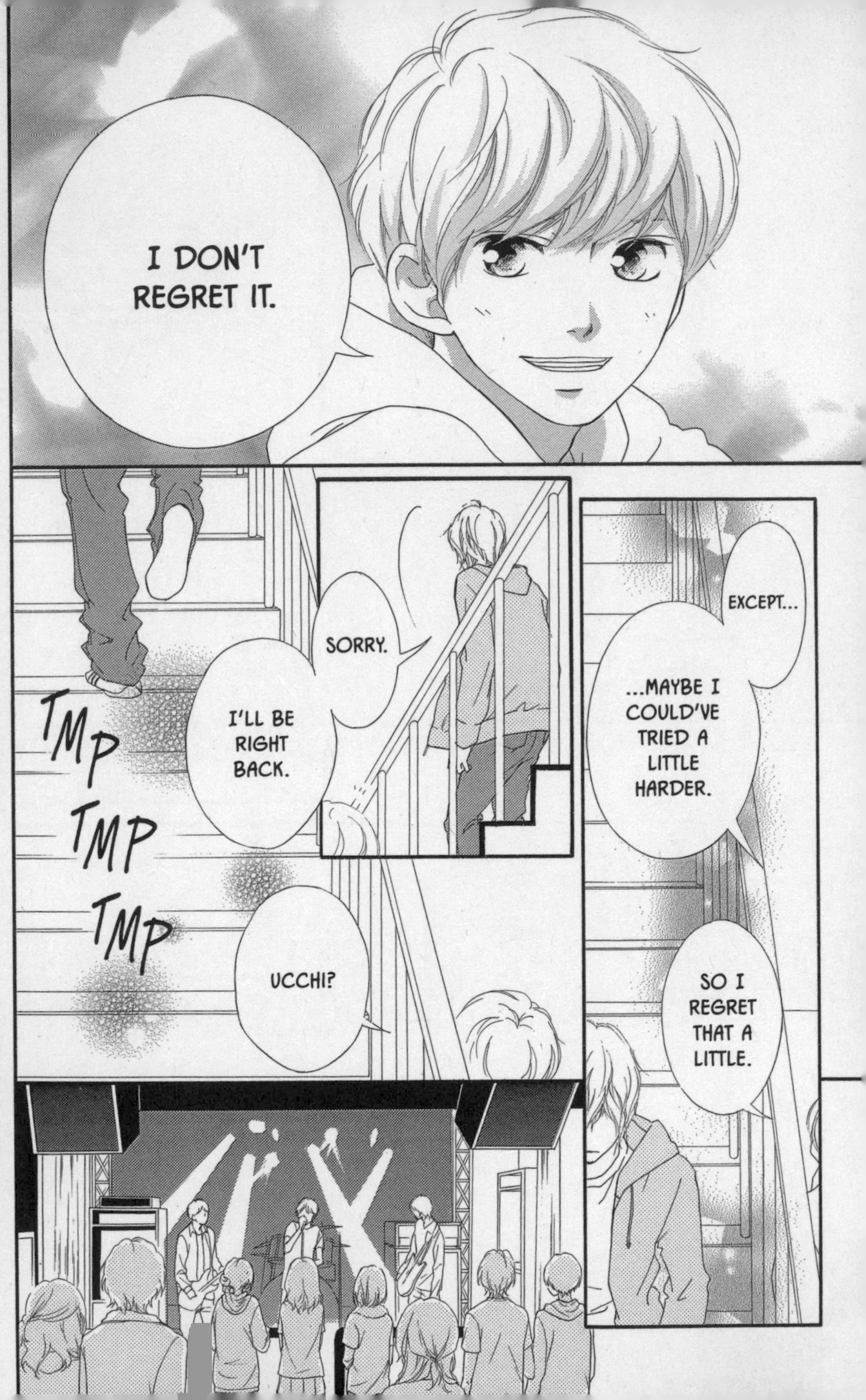
I DON'T REGRET IT.
EXCEPT...
...MAYBE I COULD'VE TRIED A LITTLE HARDER.
SO I REGRET THAT A LITTLE.
SORRY.
I'LL BE RIGHT BACK.
UCCHI?
TMP TMP TMP

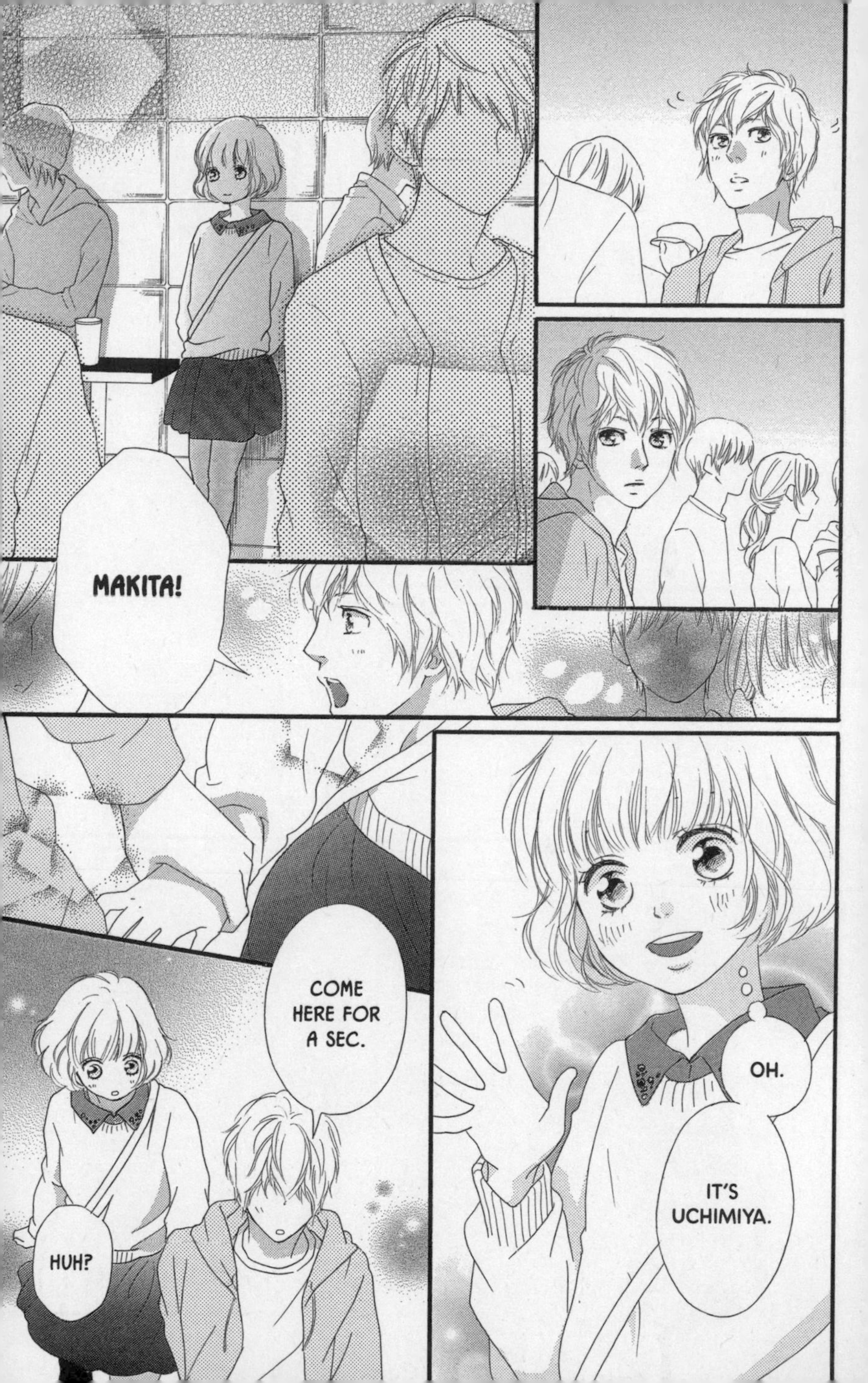
MAKITA!
OH.
IT'S UCHIMIYA.
COME HERE FOR A SEC.
HUH?

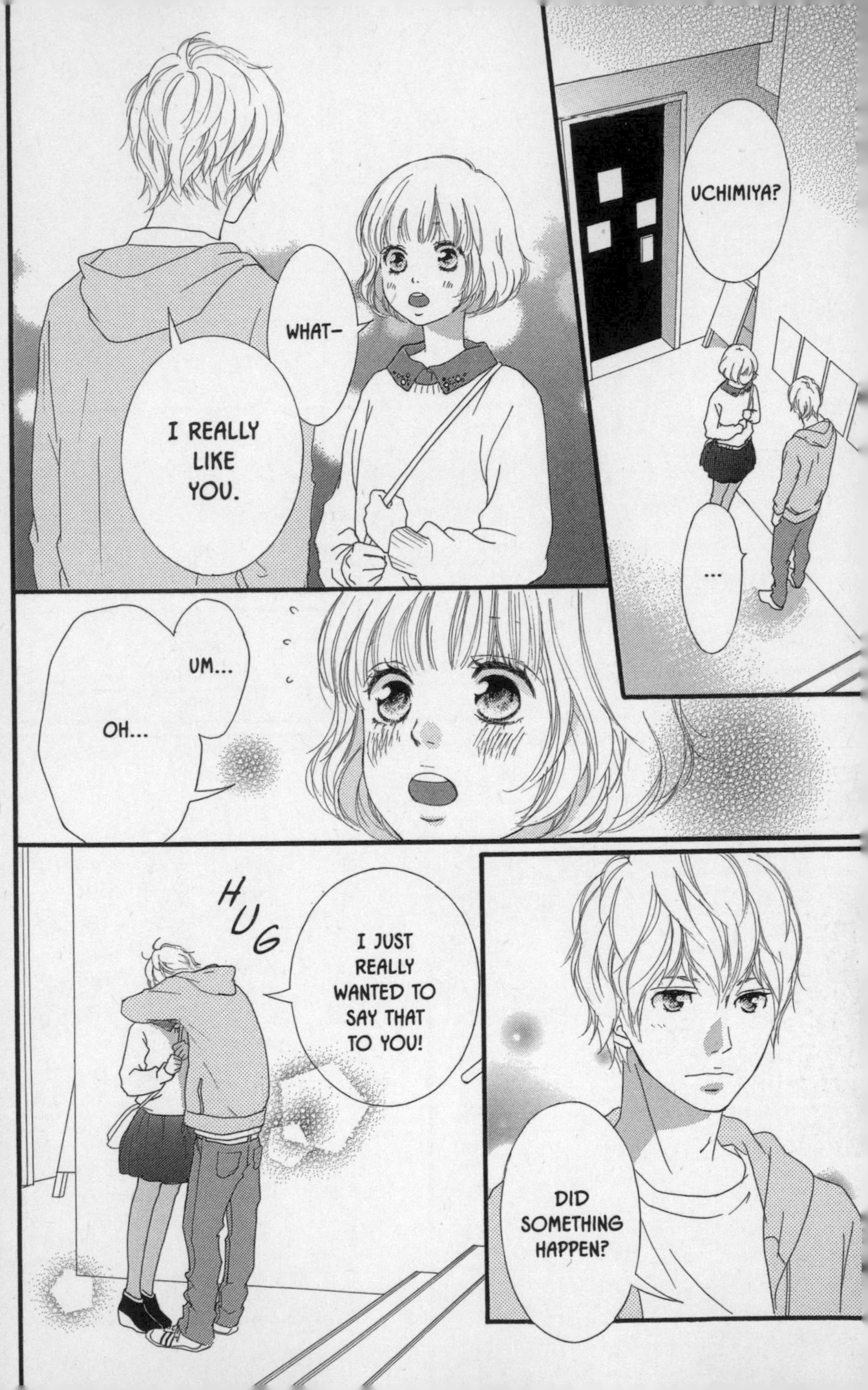
UCHIMIYA?
...
WHAT-
I REALLY LIKE YOU.
UM... OH...
DID SOMETHING HAPPEN?
I JUST REALLY WANTED TO SAY THAT TO YOU!
HUG

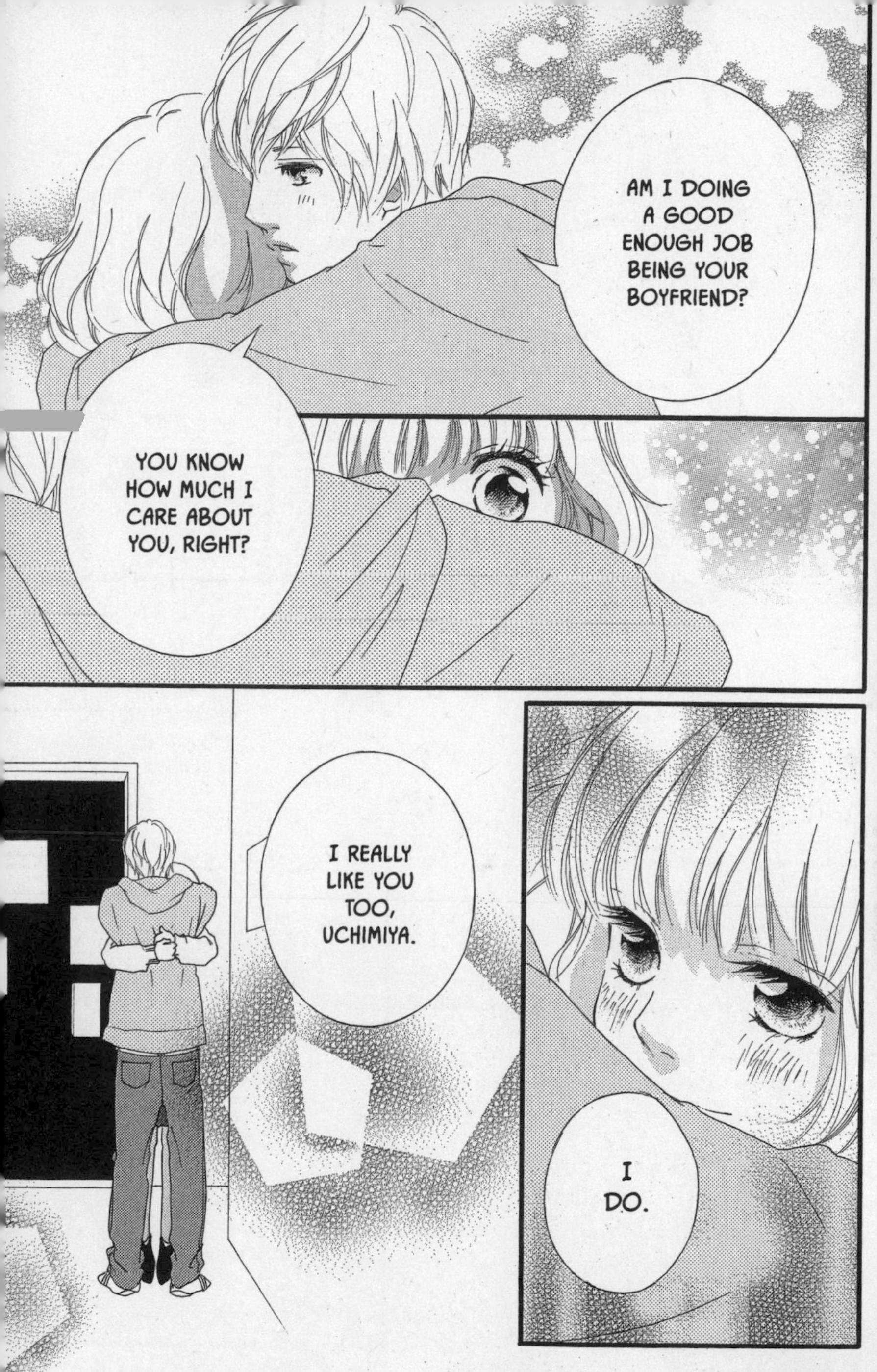
AM I DOING A GOOD ENOUGH JOB BEING YOUR BOYFRIEND?
YOU KNOW HOW MUCH I CARE ABOUT YOU, RIGHT?
I DO.
I REALLY LIKE YOU TOO, UCHIMIYA.

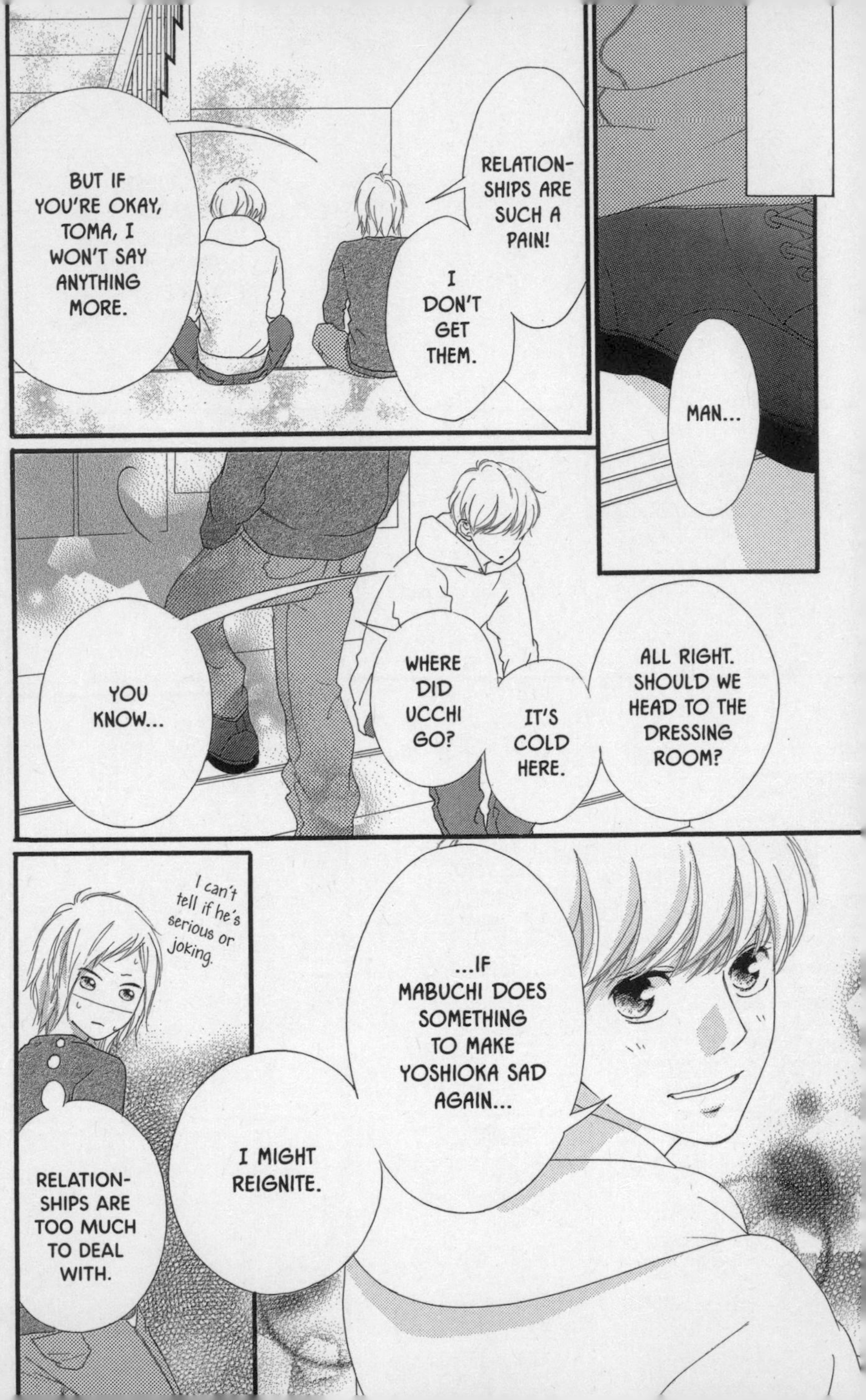
MAN...
RELATIONSHIPS ARE SUCH A PAIN!
I DON'T GET THEM.
BUT IF YOU'RE OKAY, TOMA, I WON'T SAY ANYTHING MORE.
ALL RIGHT. SHOULD WE HEAD TO THE DRESSING ROOM?
IT'S COLD HERE.
WHERE DID UCCHI GO?
YOU KNOW...
...IF MABUCHI DOES SOMETHING TO MAKE YOSHIOKA SAD AGAIN...
I MIGHT REIGNITE.
I can't tell if he's serious or joking.
RELATIONSHIPS ARE TOO MUCH TO DEAL WITH.

Pretty early on I'd decided that Kou's part-time job was pizza delivery, so when someone on Twitter asked what Kou's job was, I gave that answer. I never expected to actually put it in the story. I can visualize Kou making pizza deliveries, and personally I think it's a good choice for him, but what do you all think? In my mind, Aya and Toma also have part-time jobs, and I've even picked those out. Aside from jobs, there are other background story elements I've thought up. Perhaps in the future, one or two of them will make it into the story and become official. Will I be able to work them in? I don't know, but it's fun to think about!

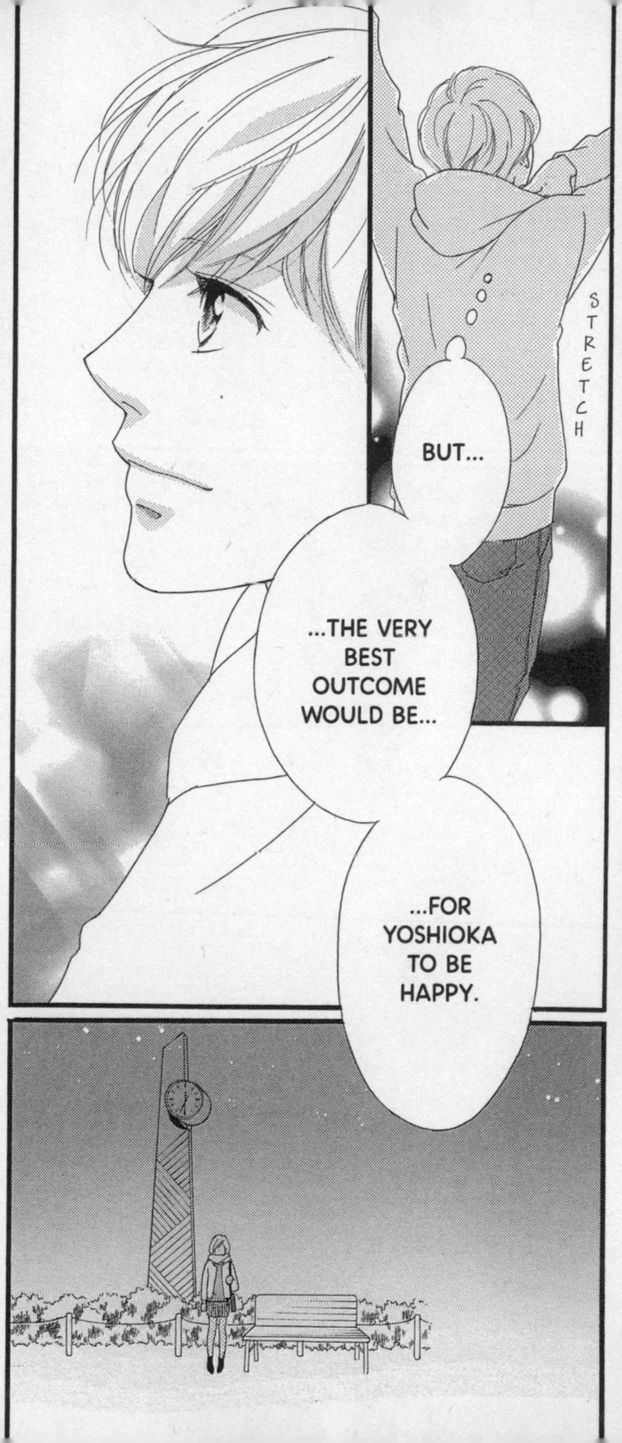
STRETCH
BUT...
...THE VERY BEST OUTCOME WOULD BE...
...FOR YOSHIOKA TO BE HAPPY.

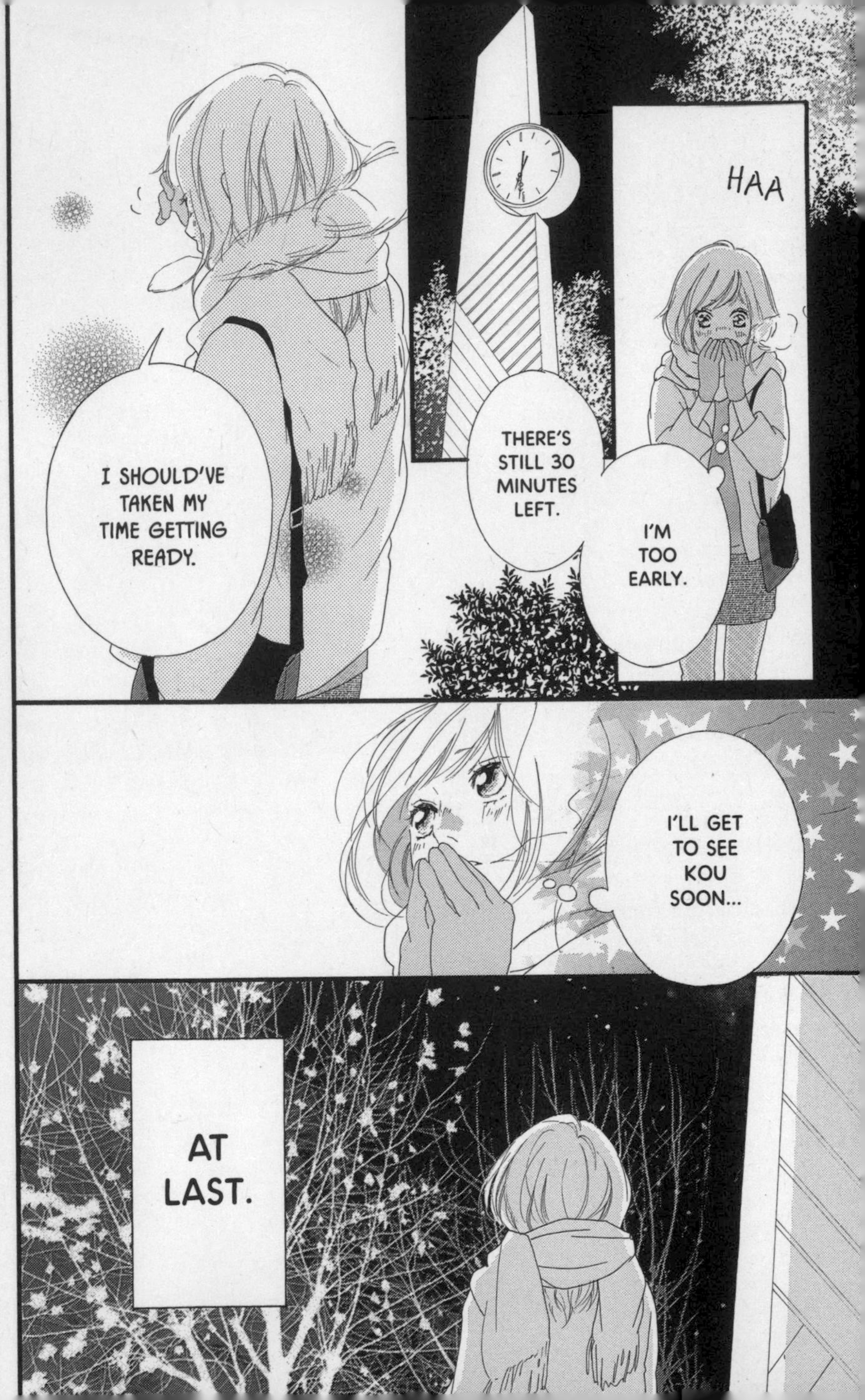
HAA
THERE'S STILL 30 MINUTES LEFT.
I'M TOO EARLY.
I SHOULD'VE TAKEN MY TIME GETTING READY.
I'LL GET TO SEE KOU SOON...
AT LAST.

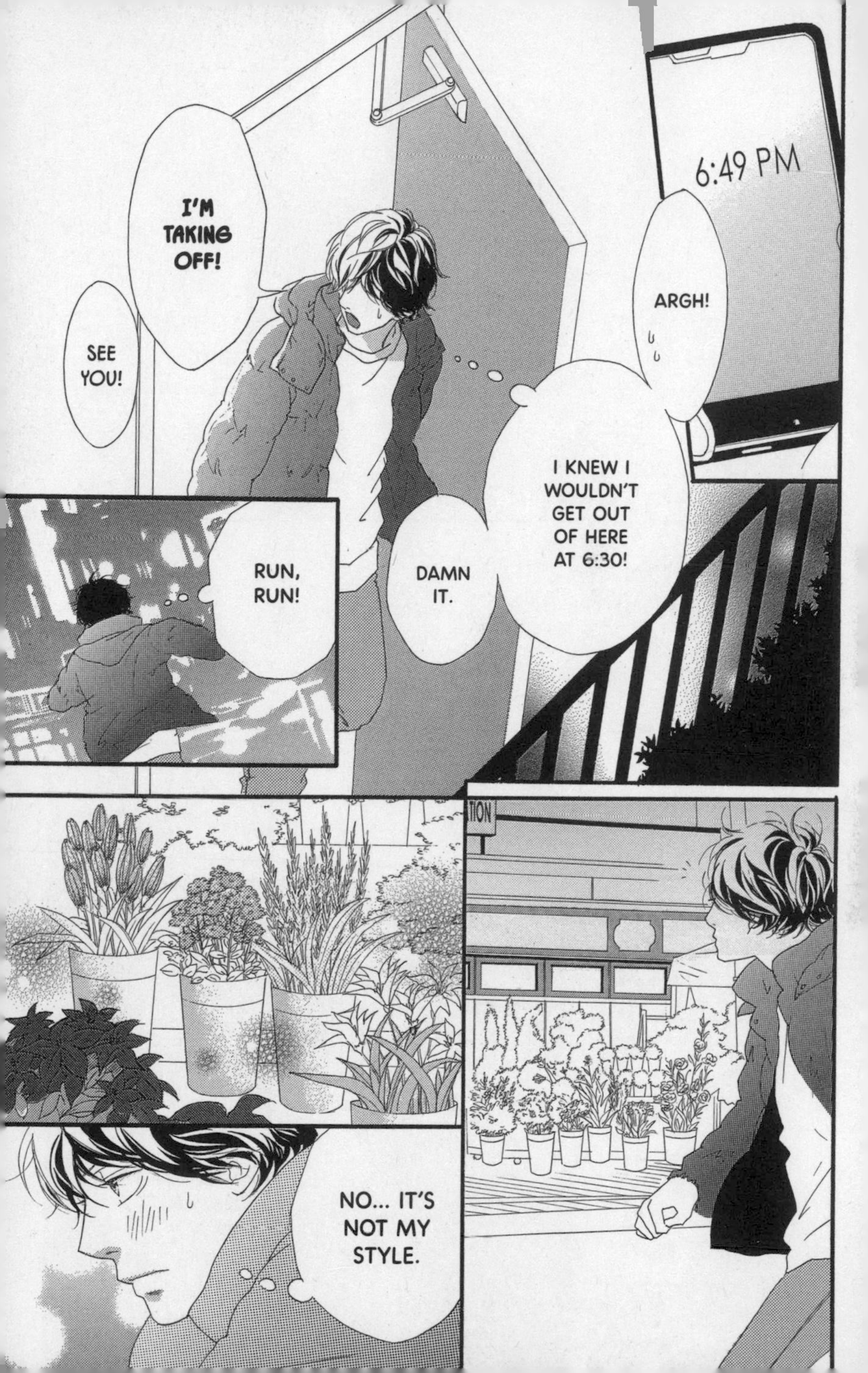
6:49 PM
ARGH!
I'M TAKING OFF!
SEE YOU!
I KNEW I WOULDN'T GET OUT OF HERE AT 6:30!
DAMN IT.
RUN, RUN!
NO... IT'S NOT MY STYLE.

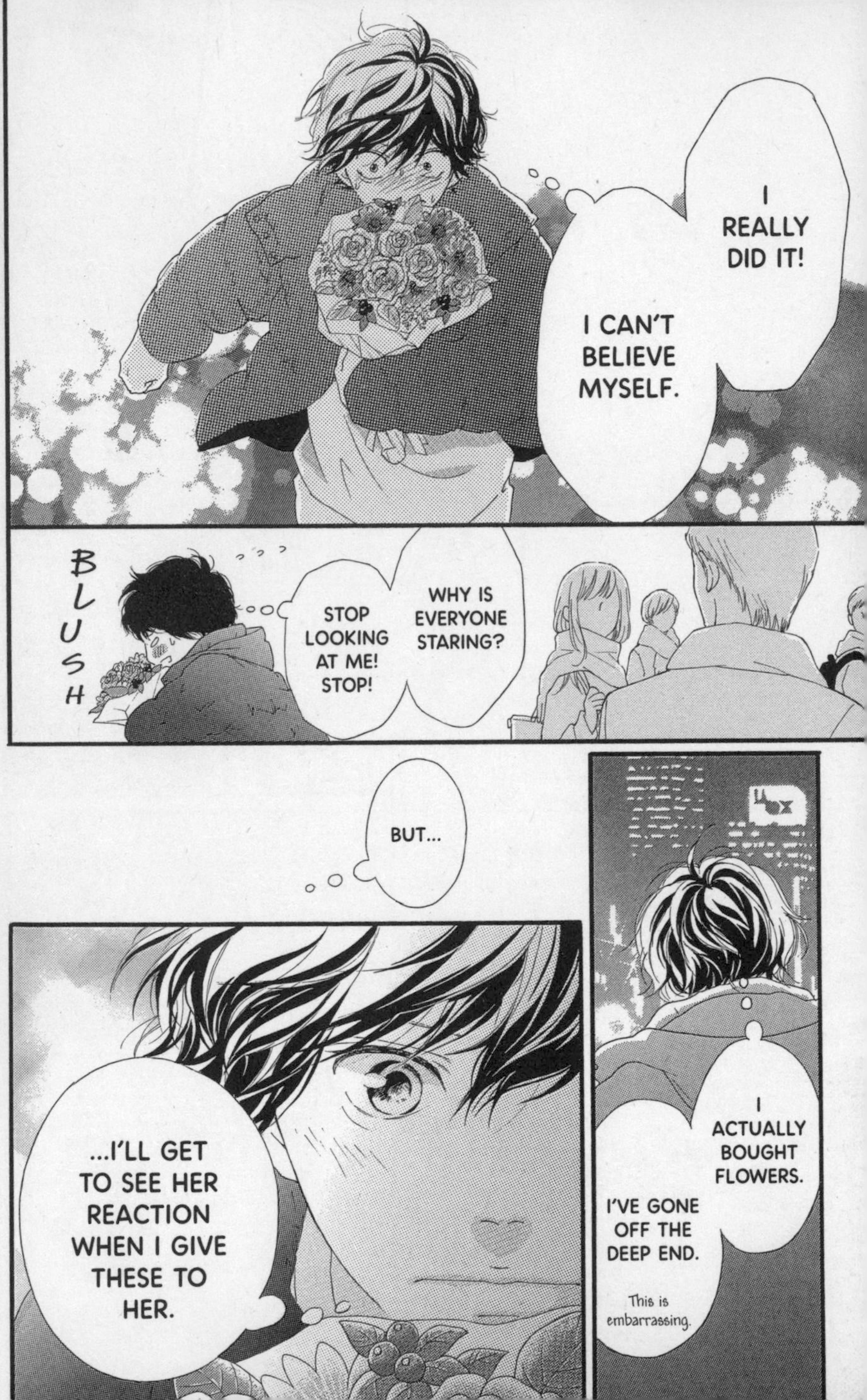
I REALLY DID IT!
I CAN'T BELIEVE MYSELF.
BLUSH
WHY IS EVERYONE STARING?
STOP LOOKING AT ME! STOP!
I ACTUALLY BOUGHT FLOWERS.
I'VE GONE OFF THE DEEP END.
This is embarrassing.
BUT...
...I'LL GET TO SEE HER REACTION WHEN I GIVE THESE TO HER.

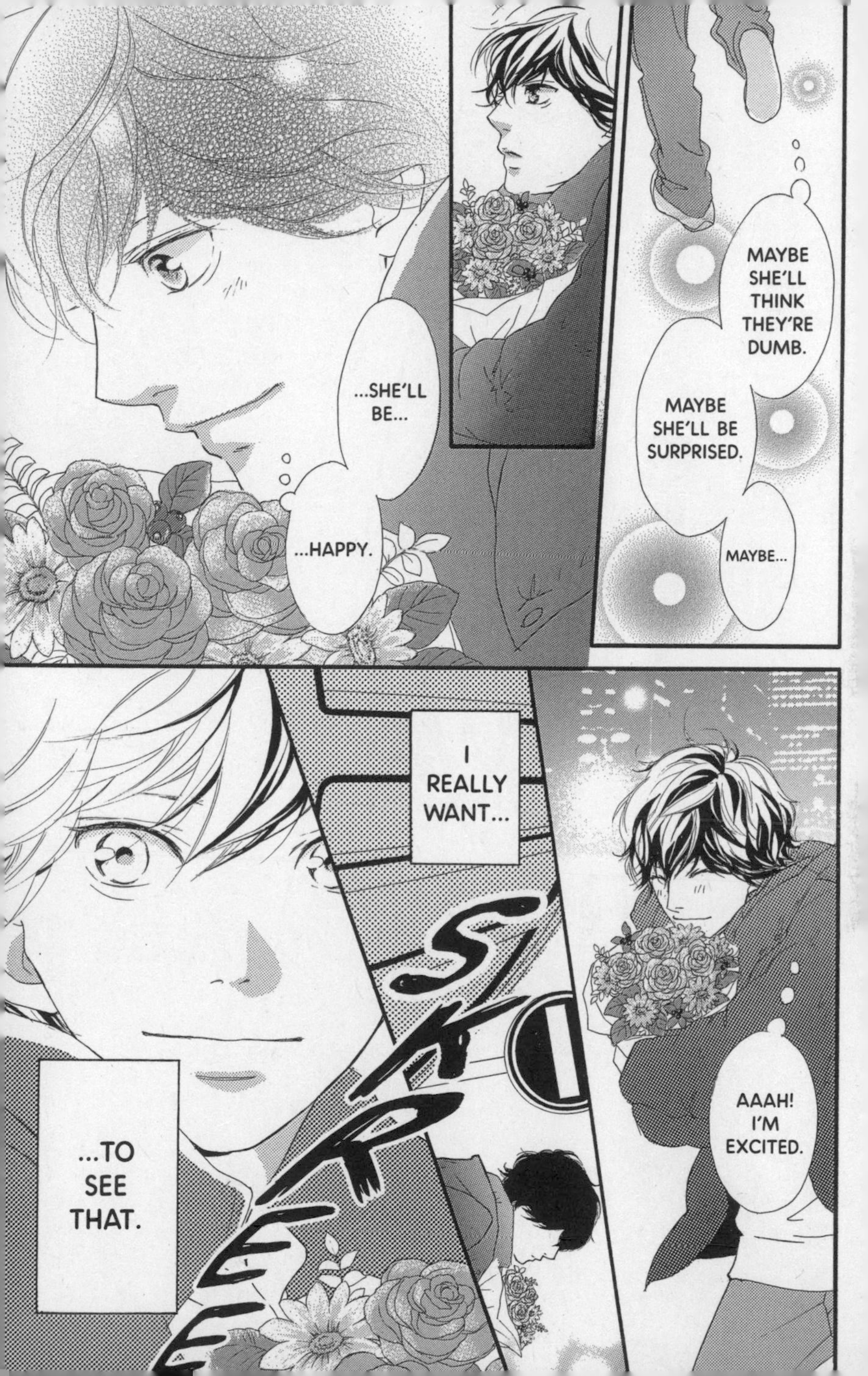
MAYBE SHE'LL THINK THEY'RE DUMB.
MAYBE SHE'LL BE SURPRISED.
MAYBE...
...SHE'LL BE...
...HAPPY.
AAAH! I'M EXCITED.
I REALLY WANT...
...TO SEE THAT.

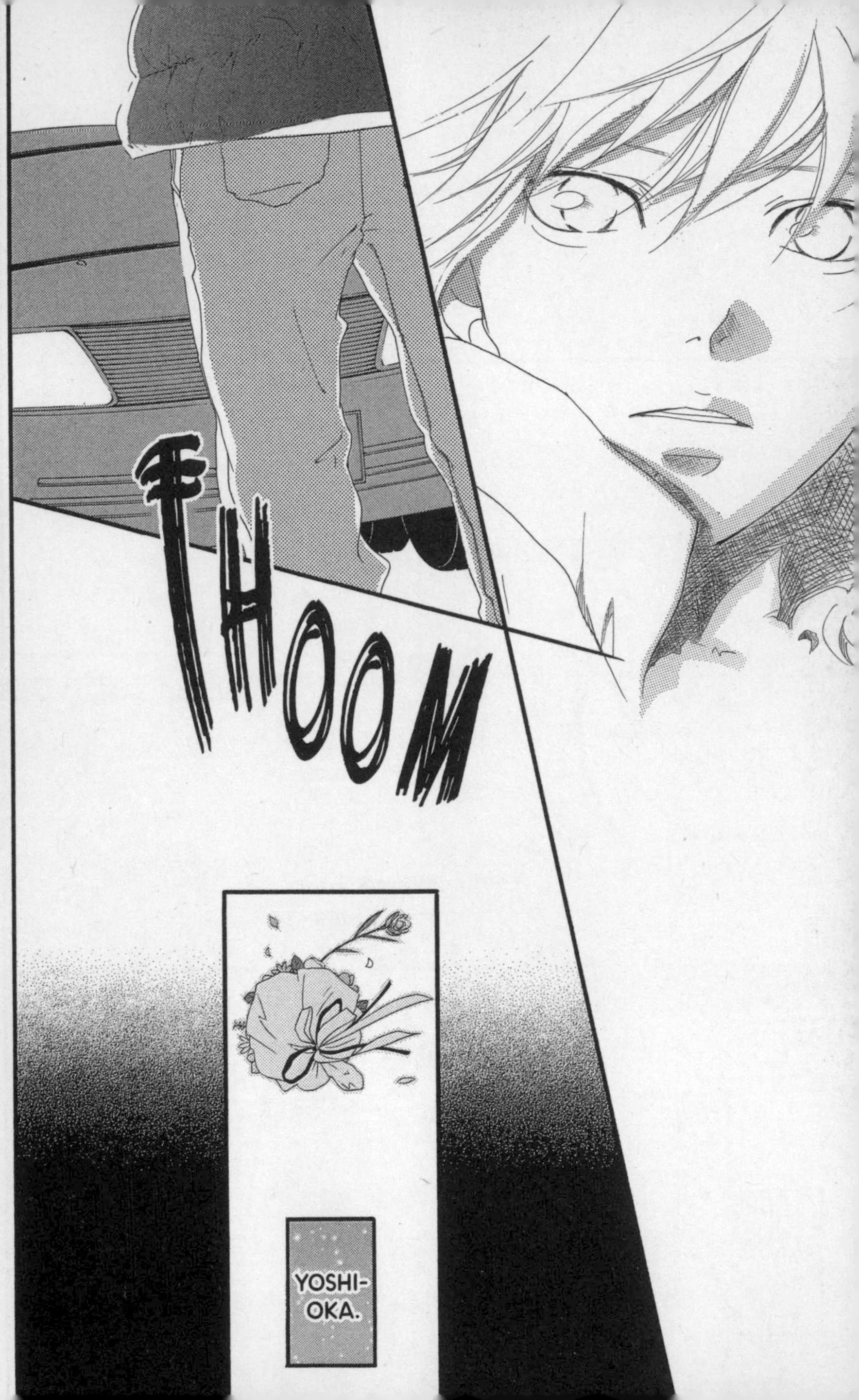
THOOM
YOSHI-
OKA.

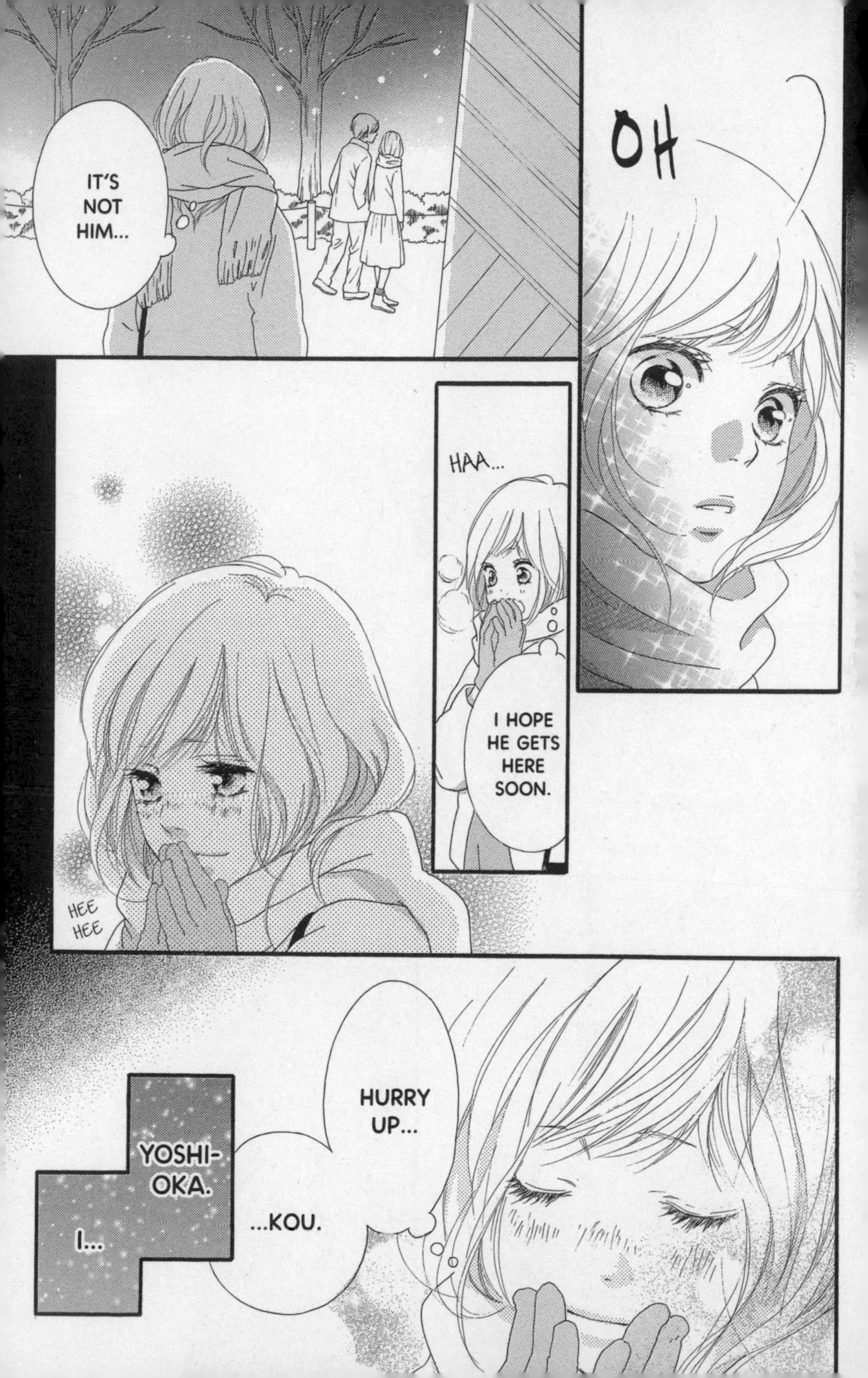
OH
IT'S NOT HIM...
HAA...
I HOPE HE GETS HERE SOON.
HEE HEE
HURRY UP...
...KOU.
YOSHI-OKA.
I...

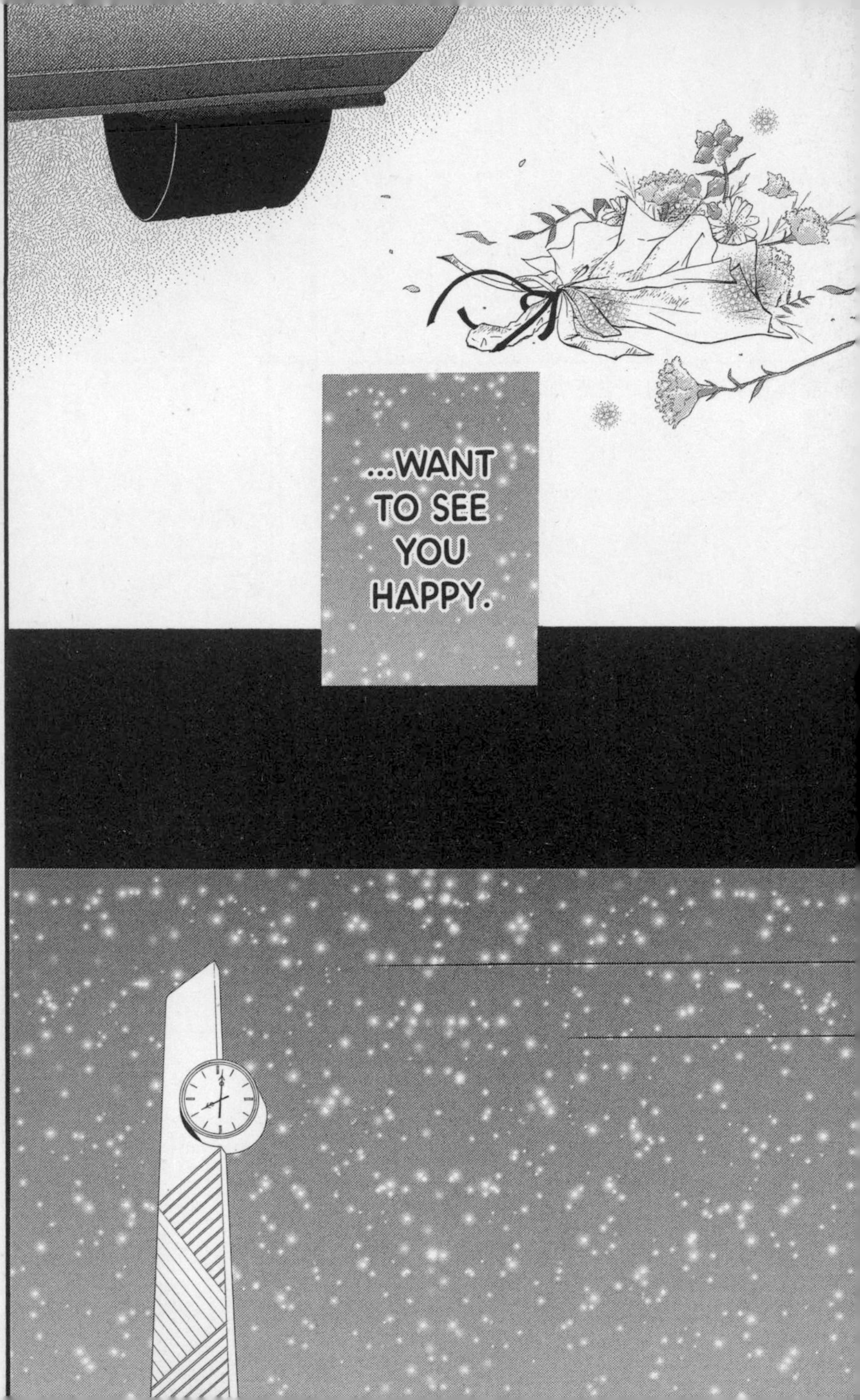
...WANT TO SEE YOU HAPPY.

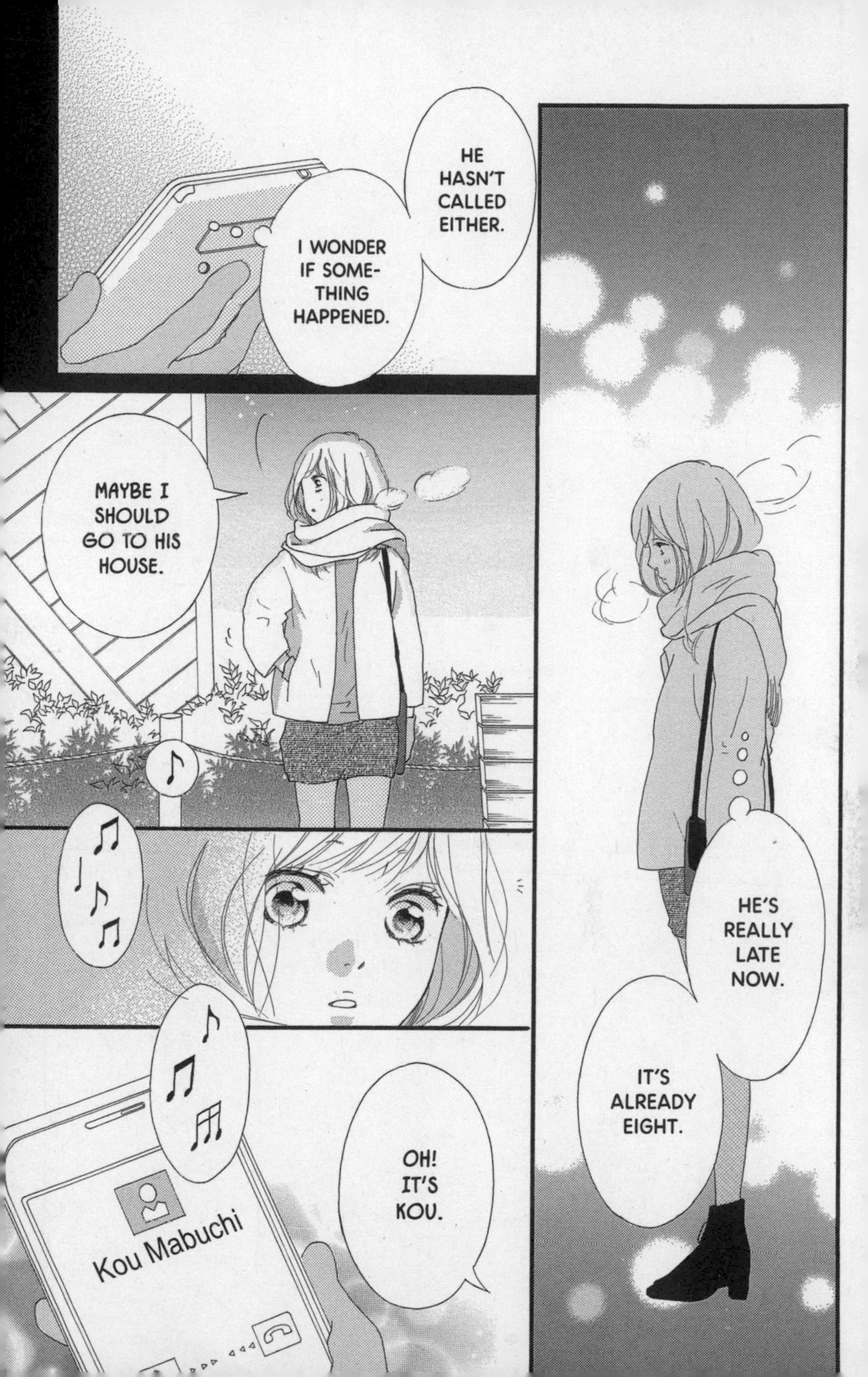
HE'S REALLY LATE NOW.
IT'S ALREADY EIGHT.
HE HASN'T CALLED EITHER.
I WONDER IF SOME-THING HAPPENED.
MAYBE I SHOULD GO TO HIS HOUSE.
OH! IT'S KOU.
Kou Mabuchi

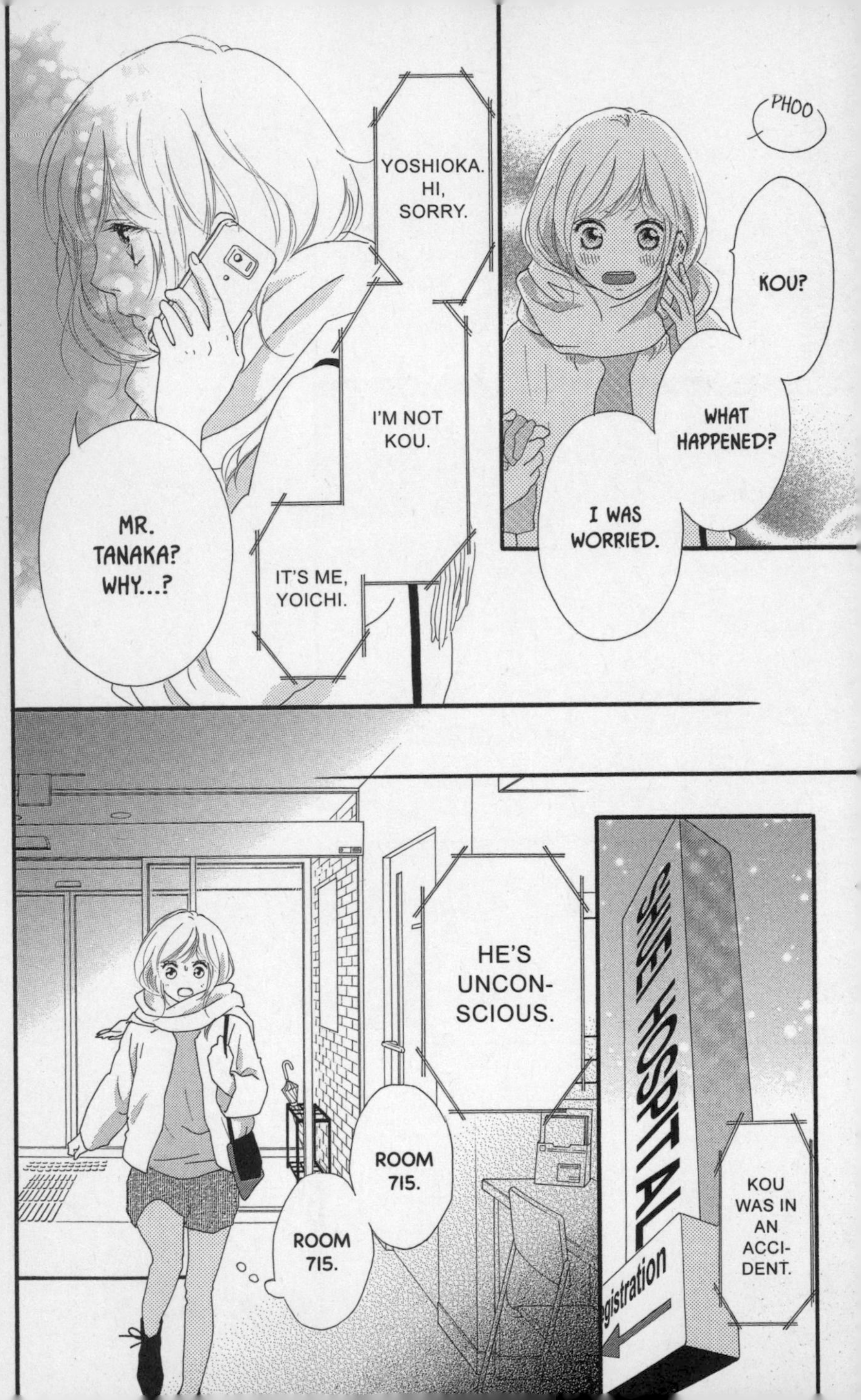
PHOO
KOU?
WHAT HAPPENED?
I WAS WORRIED.
YOSHIOKA. HI, SORRY.
I'M NOT KOU.
IT'S ME, YOICHI.
MR. TANAKA? WHY...?
SHUEI HOSPITAL
KOU WAS IN AN ACCIDENT.
HE'S UNCONSCIOUS.
ROOM 715.
ROOM 715.

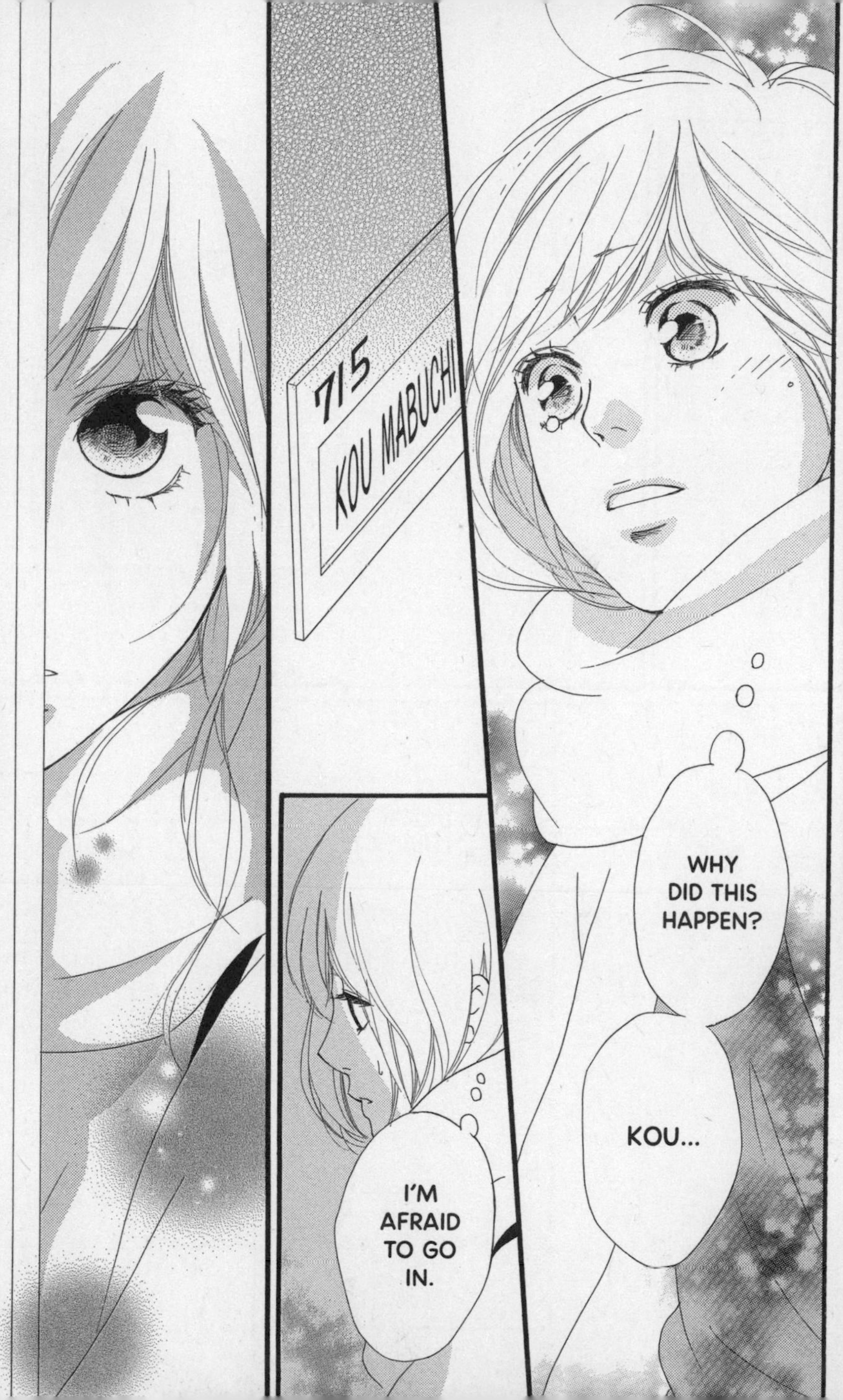
WHY DID THIS HAPPEN?
KOU...
715
KOU MABUCHI
I'M AFRAID TO GO IN.

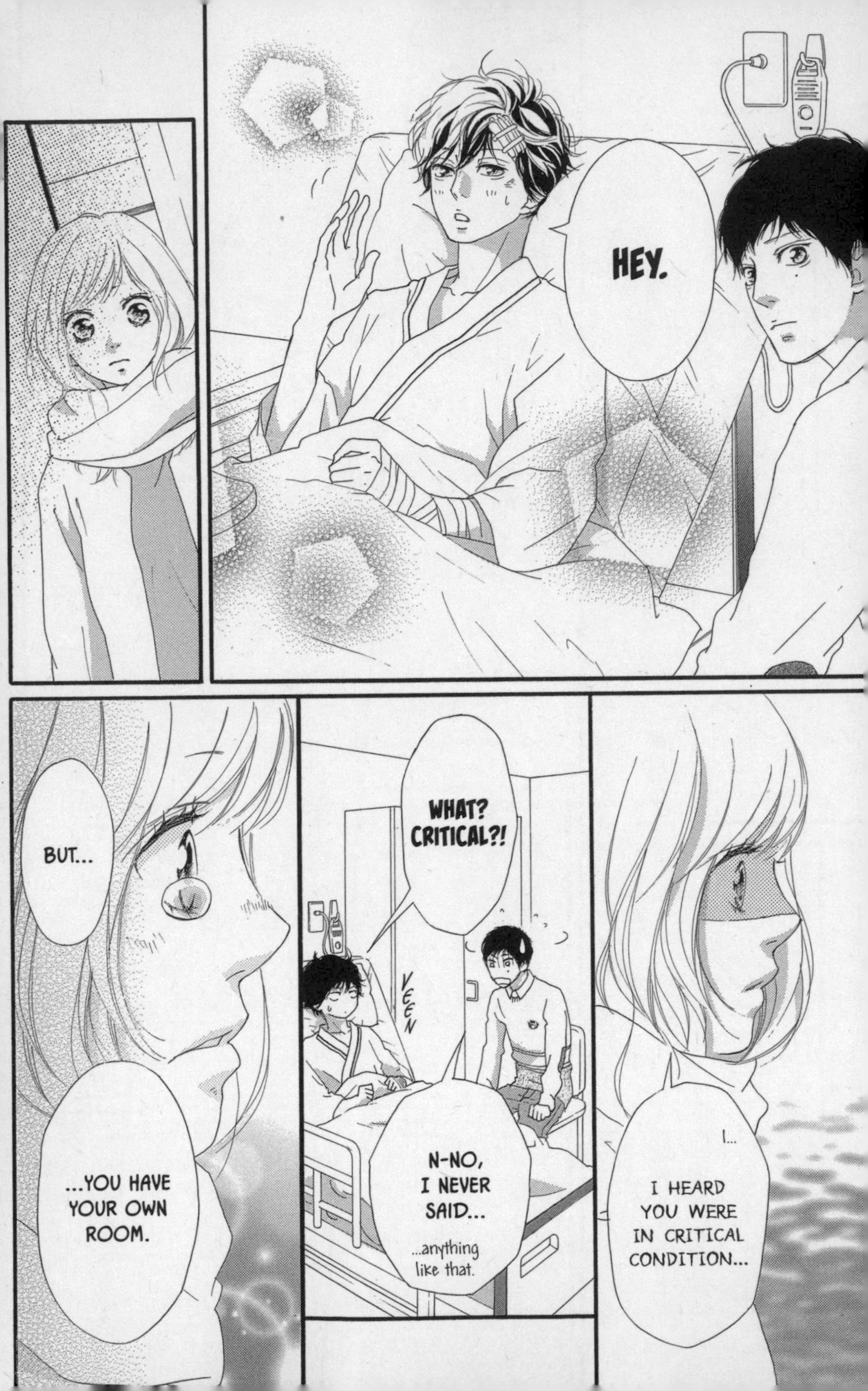
HEY.
I...
I HEARD YOU WERE IN CRITICAL CONDITION...
WHAT? CRITICAL?!
VEEN
N-NO, I NEVER SAID...
...anything like that.
BUT...
...YOU HAVE YOUR OWN ROOM.

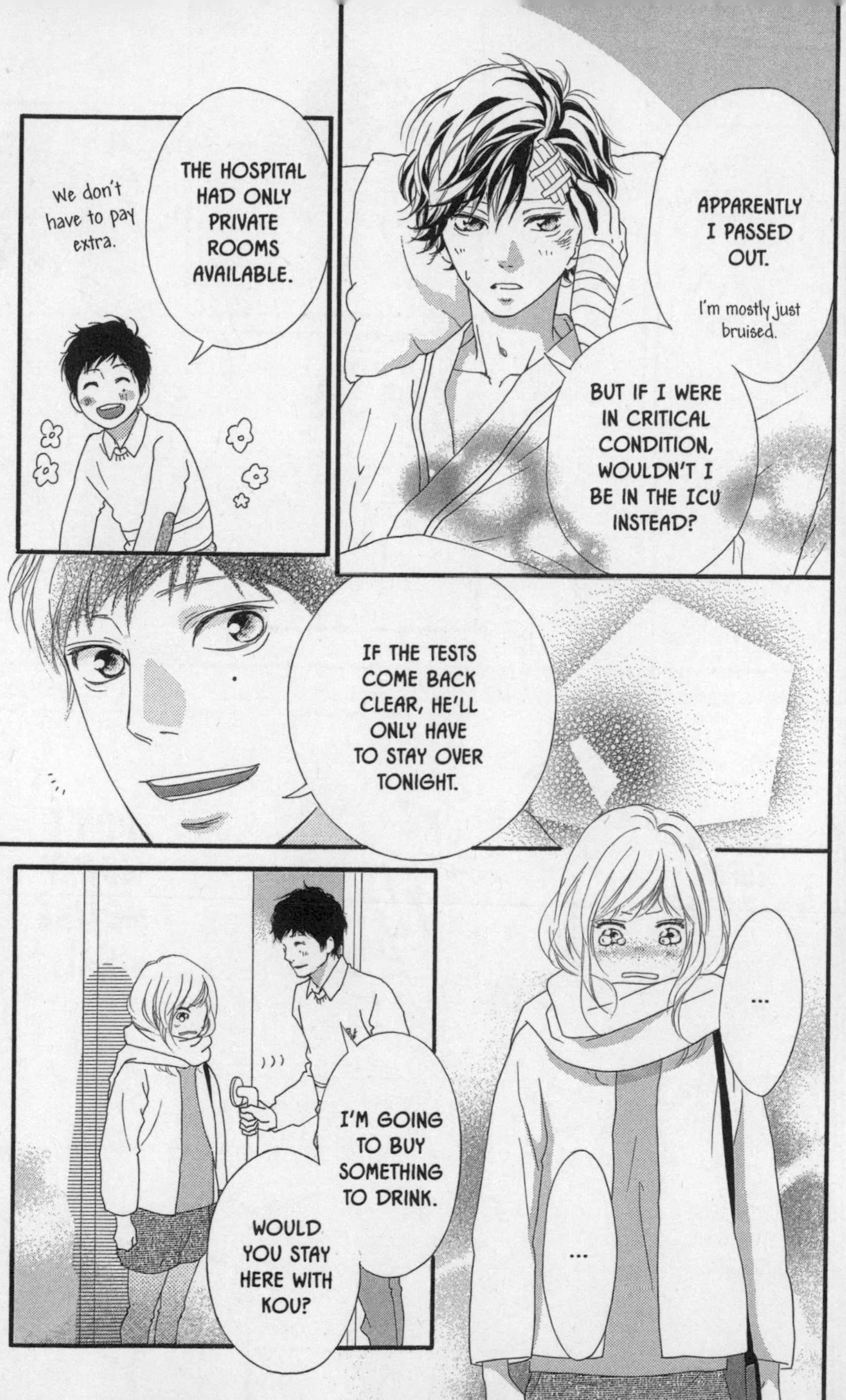
APPARENTLY I PASSED OUT.
I'm mostly just bruised.
BUT IF I WERE IN CRITICAL CONDITION, WOULDN'T I BE IN THE ICU INSTEAD?
THE HOSPITAL HAD ONLY PRIVATE ROOMS AVAILABLE.
We don't have to pay extra.
IF THE TESTS COME BACK CLEAR, HE'LL ONLY HAVE TO STAY OVER TONIGHT.
...
...
I'M GOING TO BUY SOMETHING TO DRINK.
WOULD YOU STAY HERE WITH KOU?

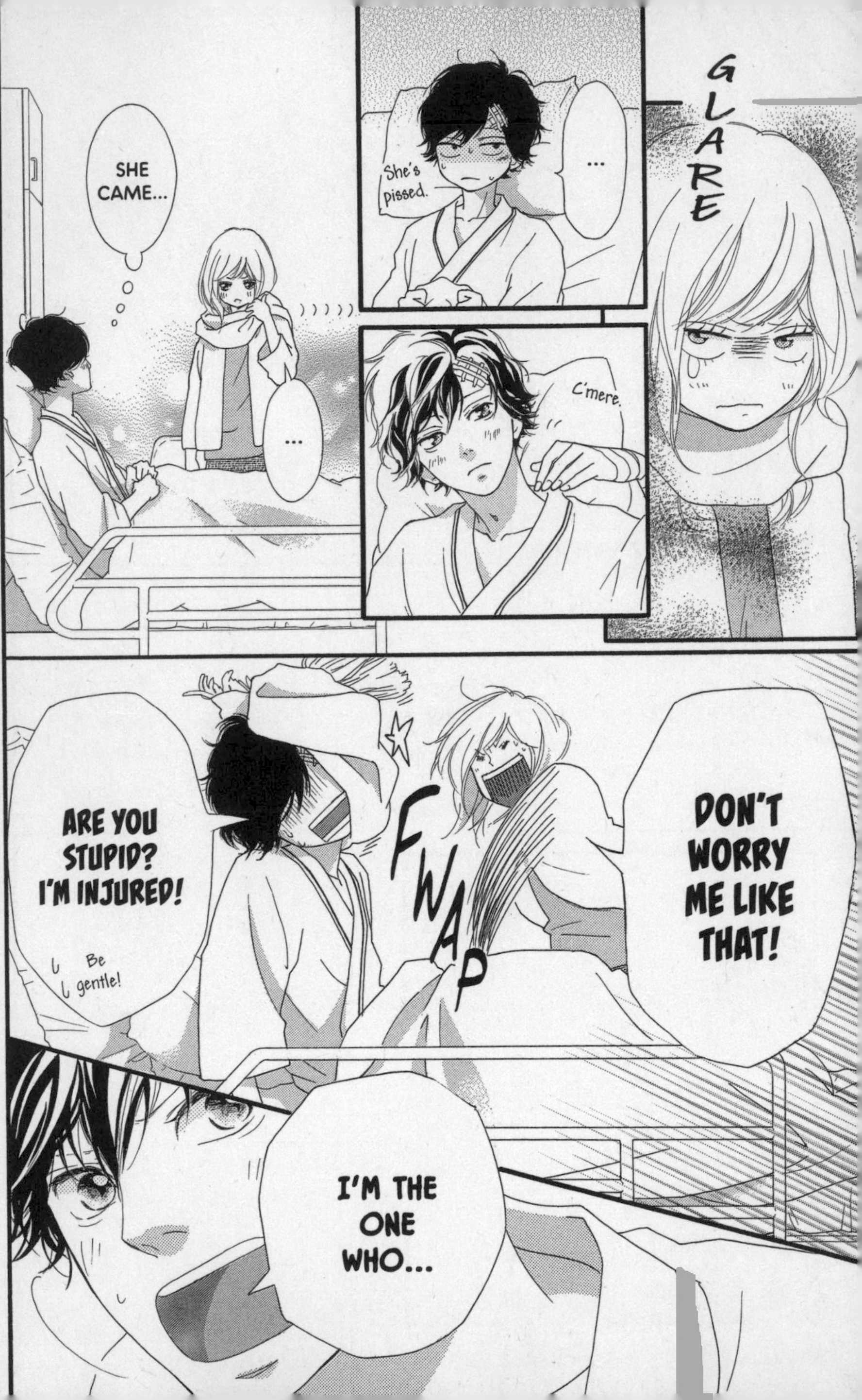
GLARE
...
She's pissed.
C'mere.
SHE CAME...
...
DON'T WORRY ME LIKE THAT!
FWAP
ARE YOU STUPID? I'M INJURED!
Be gentle!
I'M THE ONE WHO...

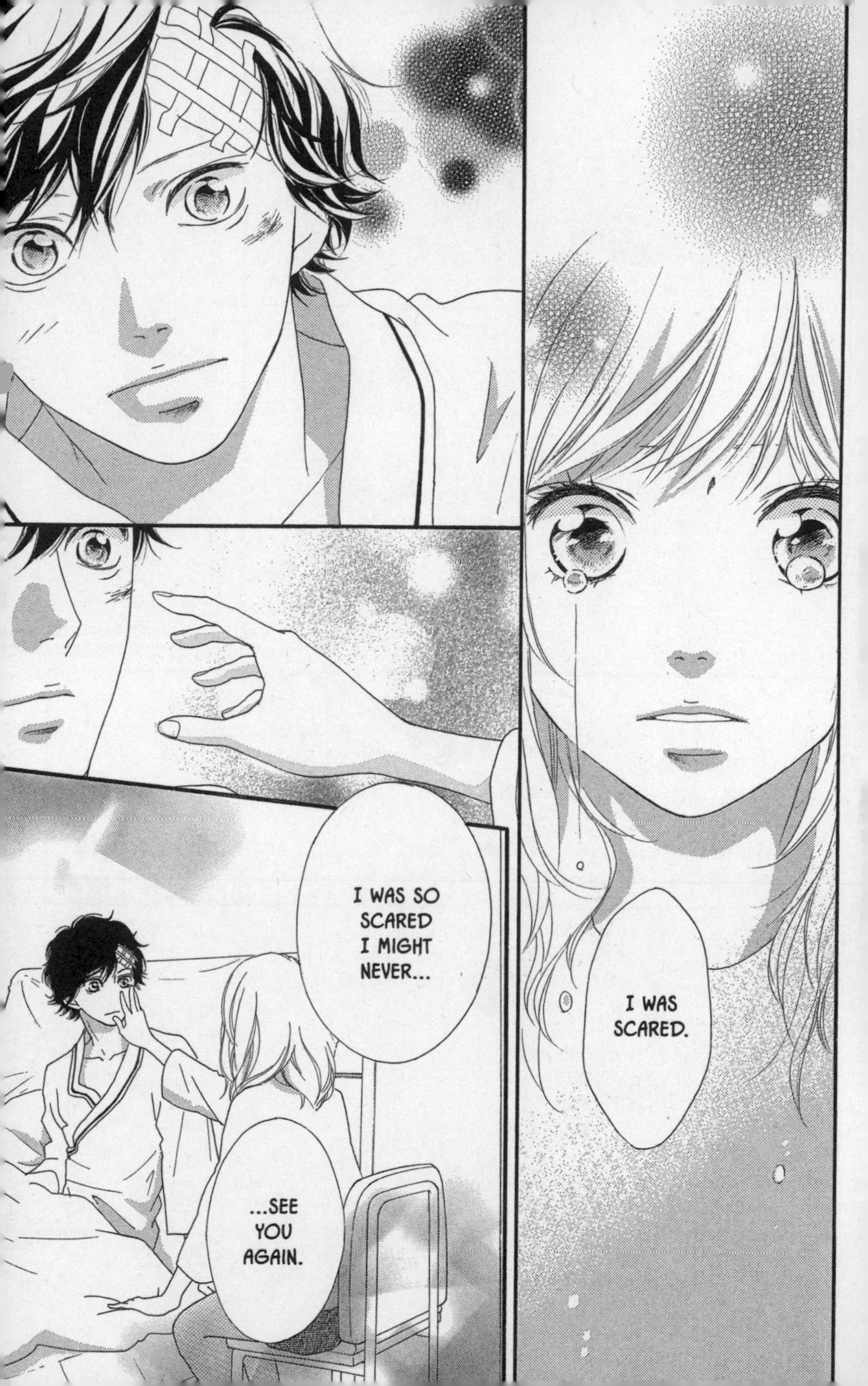
I WAS SCARED.
I WAS SO SCARED I MIGHT NEVER...
...SEE YOU AGAIN.

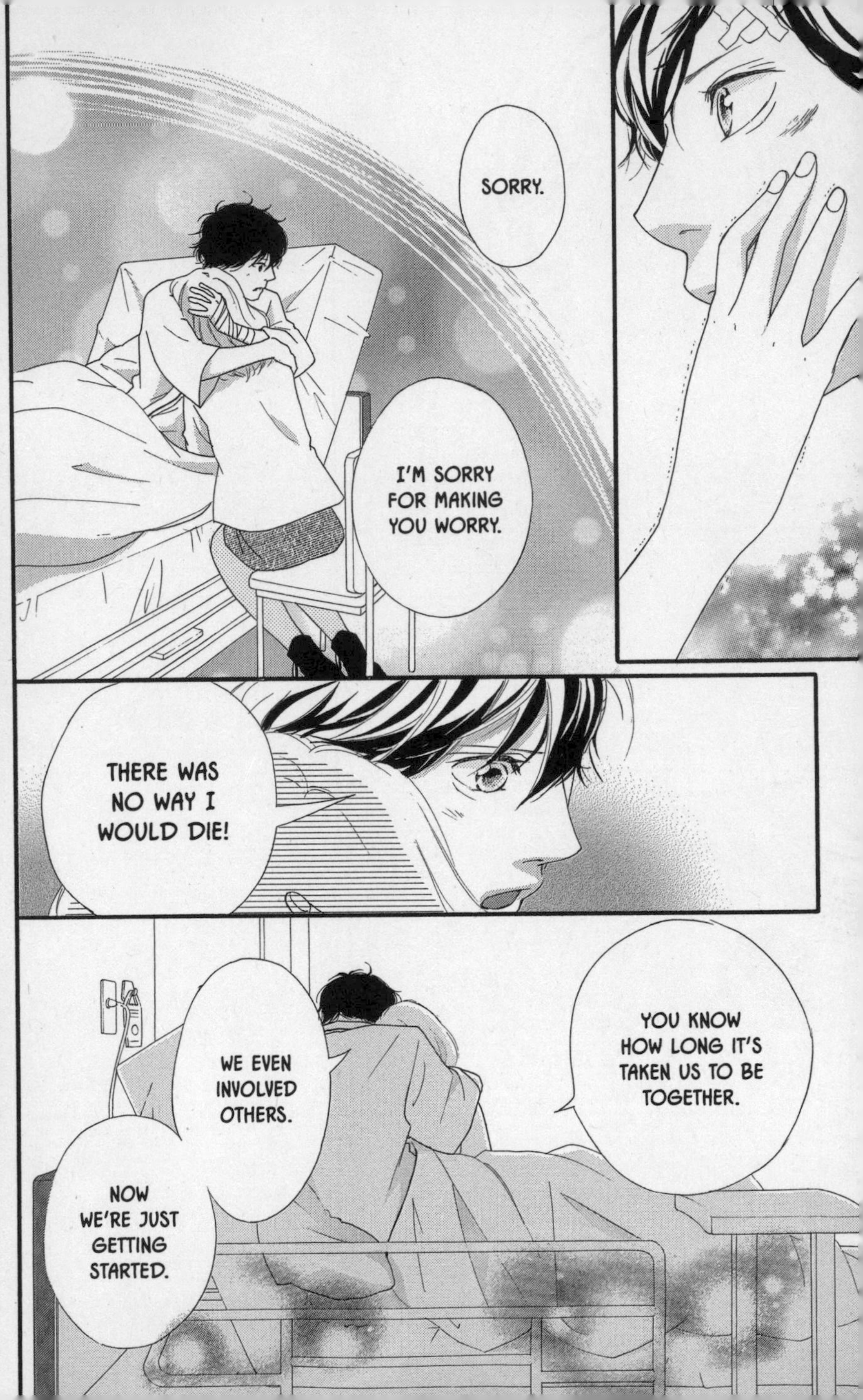
SORRY.
I'M SORRY FOR MAKING YOU WORRY.
THERE WAS NO WAY I WOULD DIE!
YOU KNOW HOW LONG IT'S TAKEN US TO BE TOGETHER.
WE EVEN INVOLVED OTHERS.
NOW WE'RE JUST GETTING STARTED.

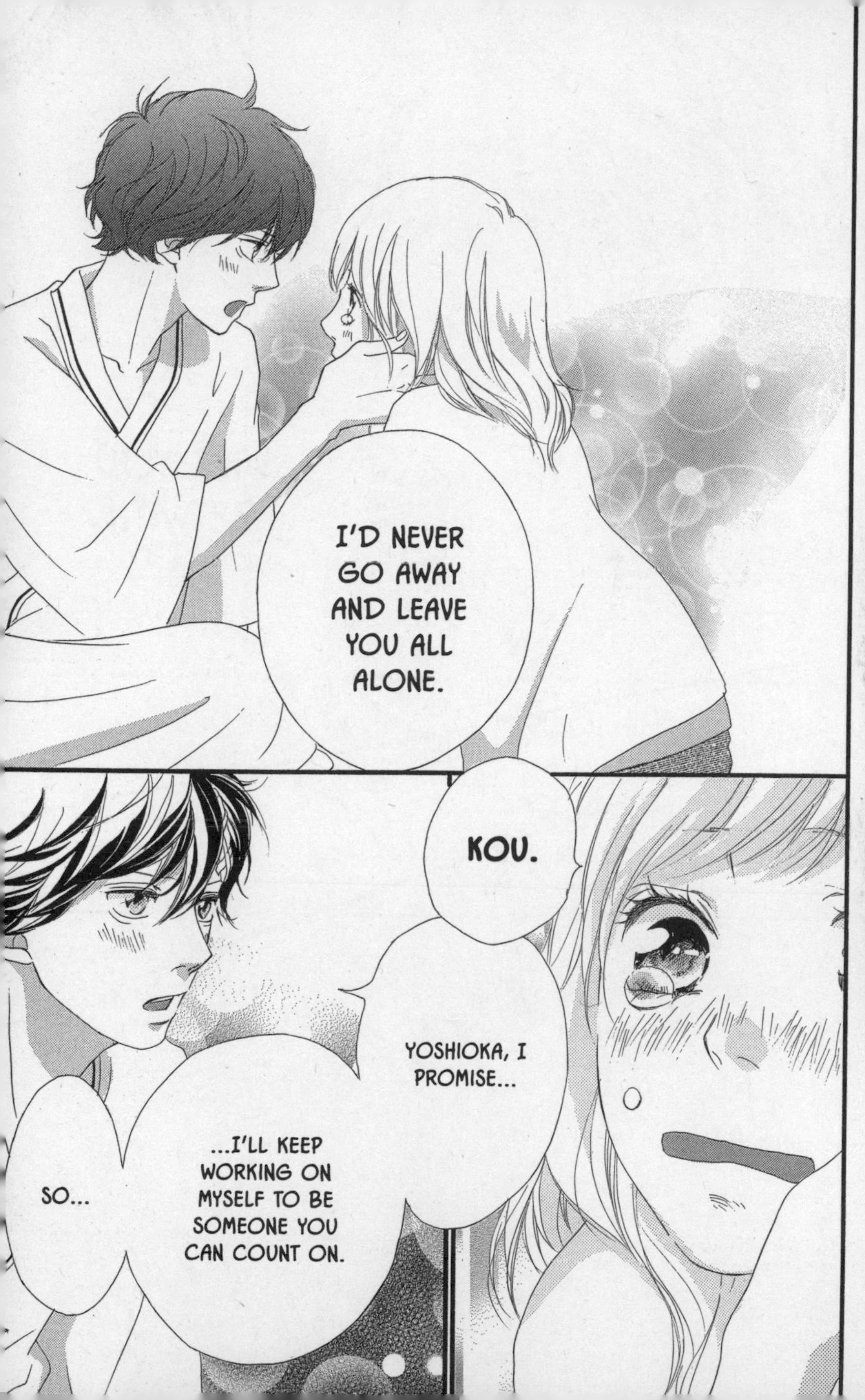
I'D NEVER GO AWAY AND LEAVE YOU ALL ALONE.
KOU.
YOSHIOKA, I PROMISE...
...I'LL KEEP WORKING ON MYSELF TO BE SOMEONE YOU CAN COUNT ON.
SO...

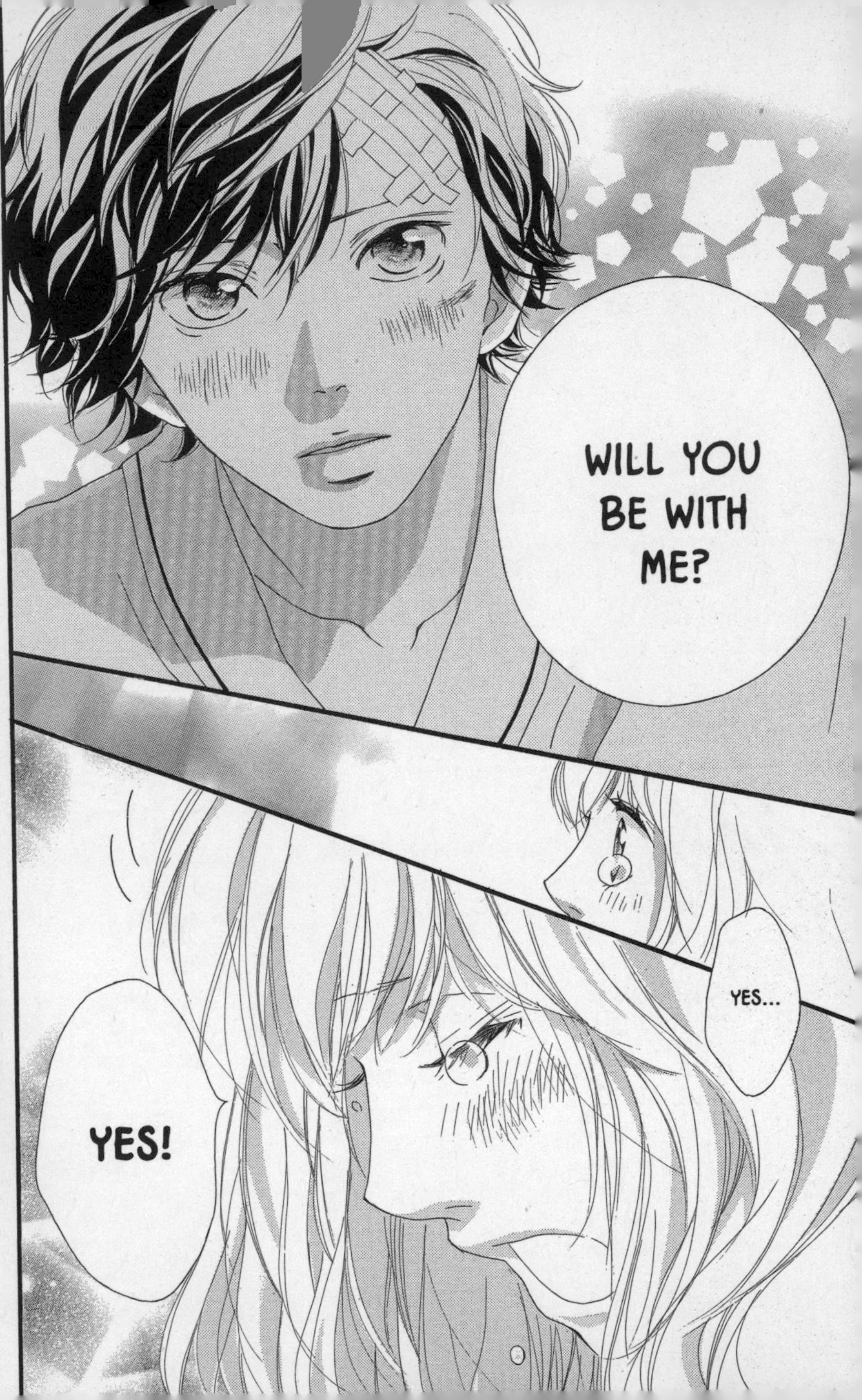
WILL YOU BE WITH ME?
YES...
YES!

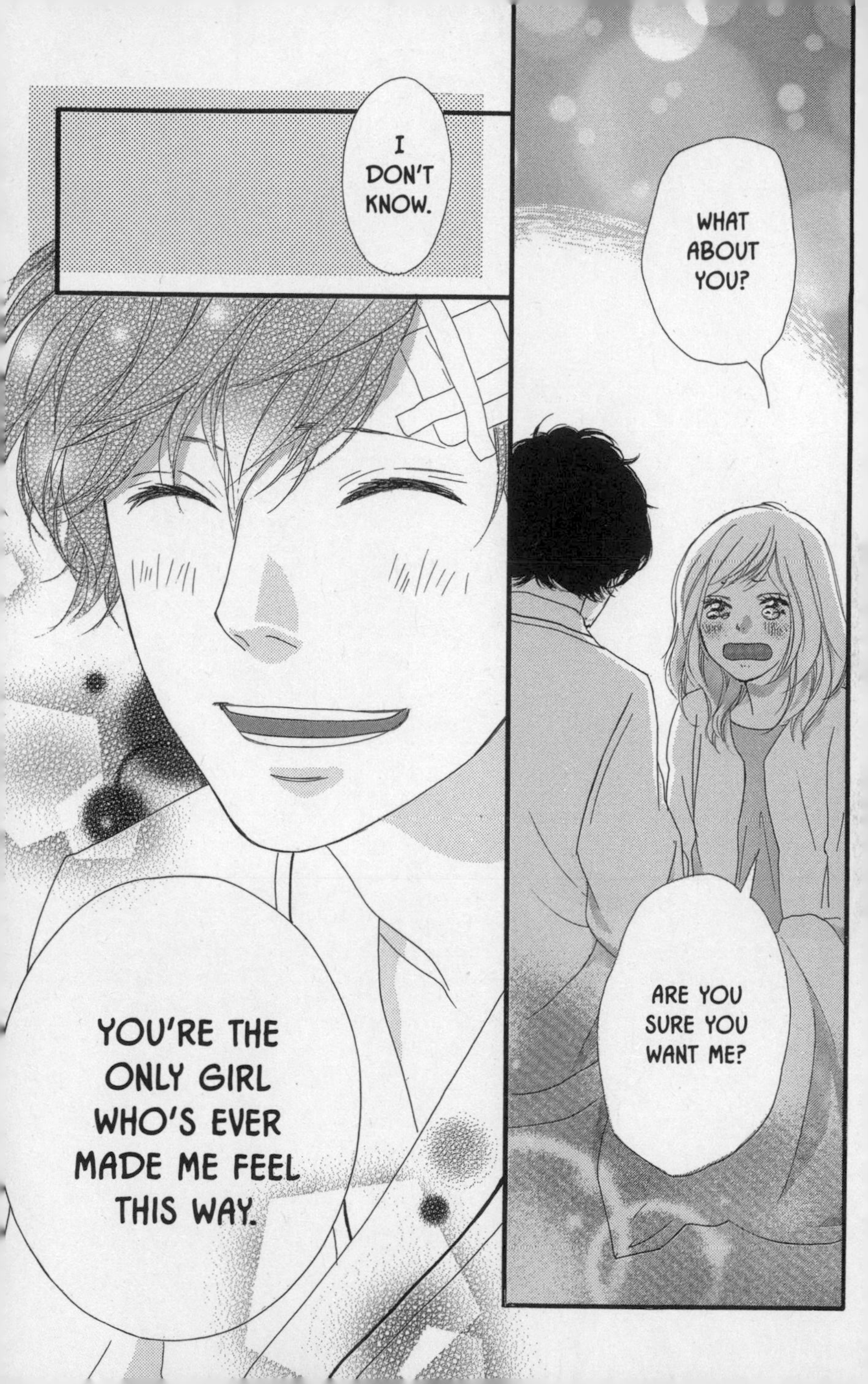
WHAT ABOUT YOU?
ARE YOU SURE YOU WANT ME?
I DON'T KNOW.
YOU'RE THE ONLY GIRL WHO'S EVER MADE ME FEEL THIS WAY.

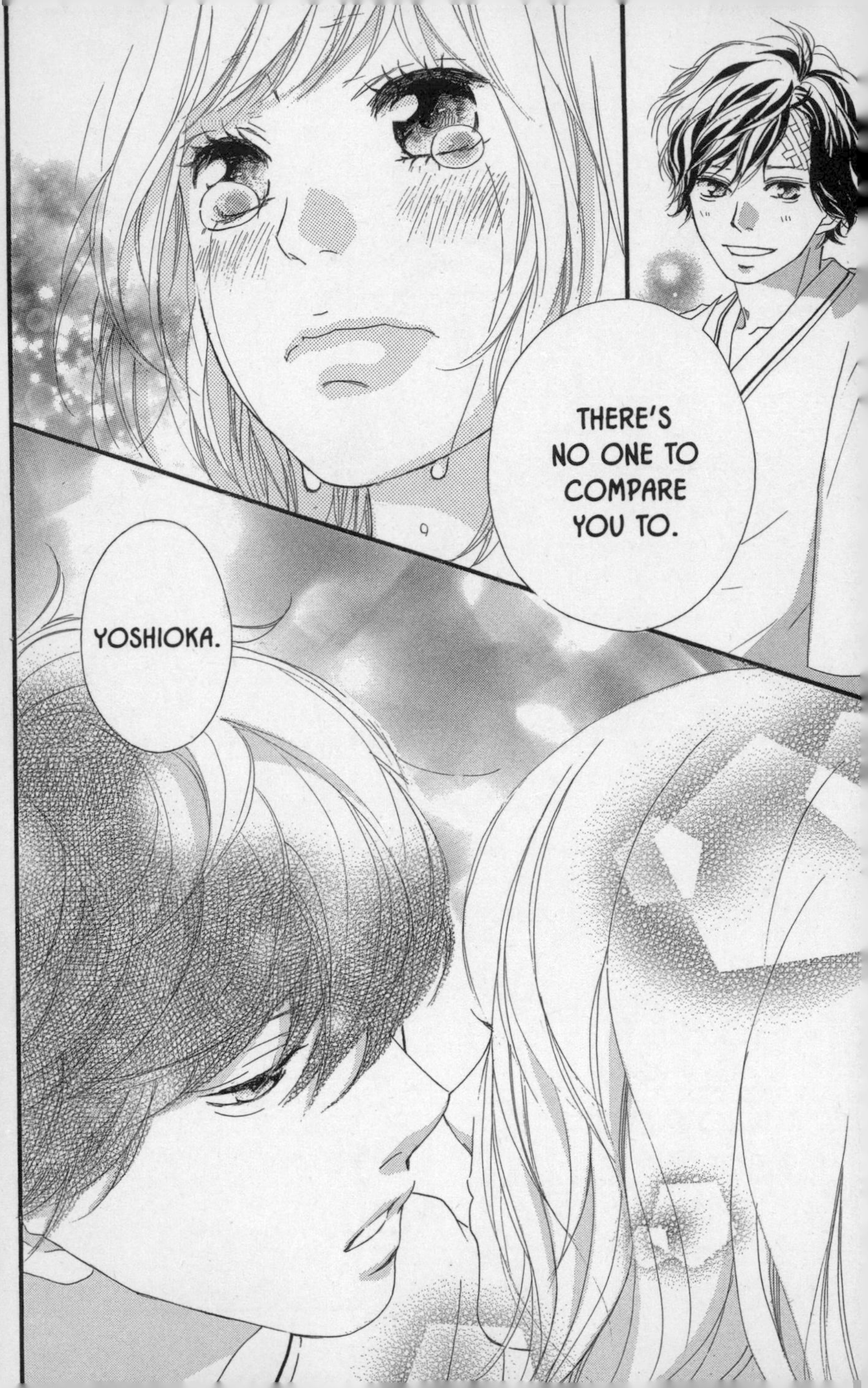
THERE'S NO ONE TO COMPARE YOU TO.
YOSHIOKA.

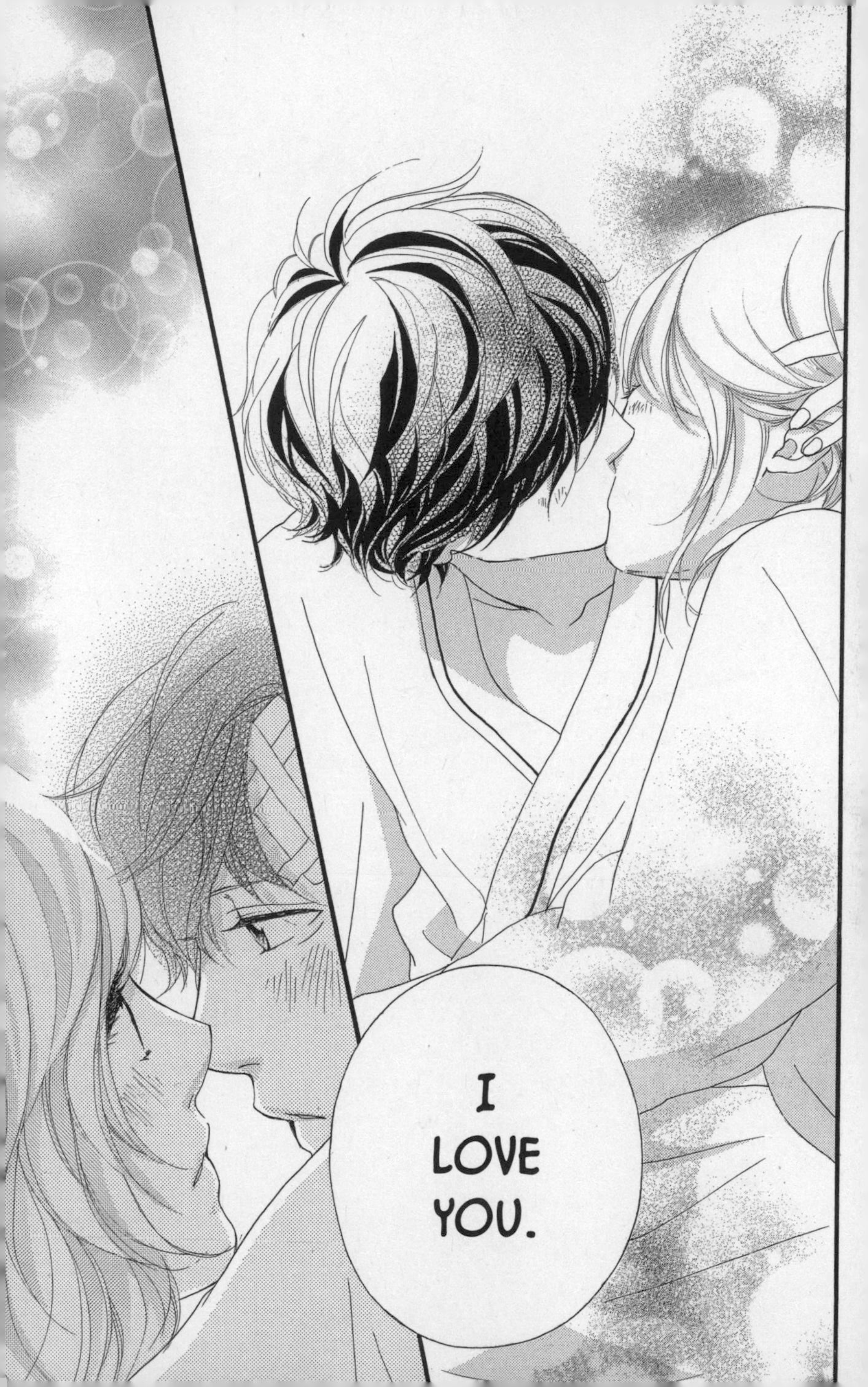
I LOVE YOU.

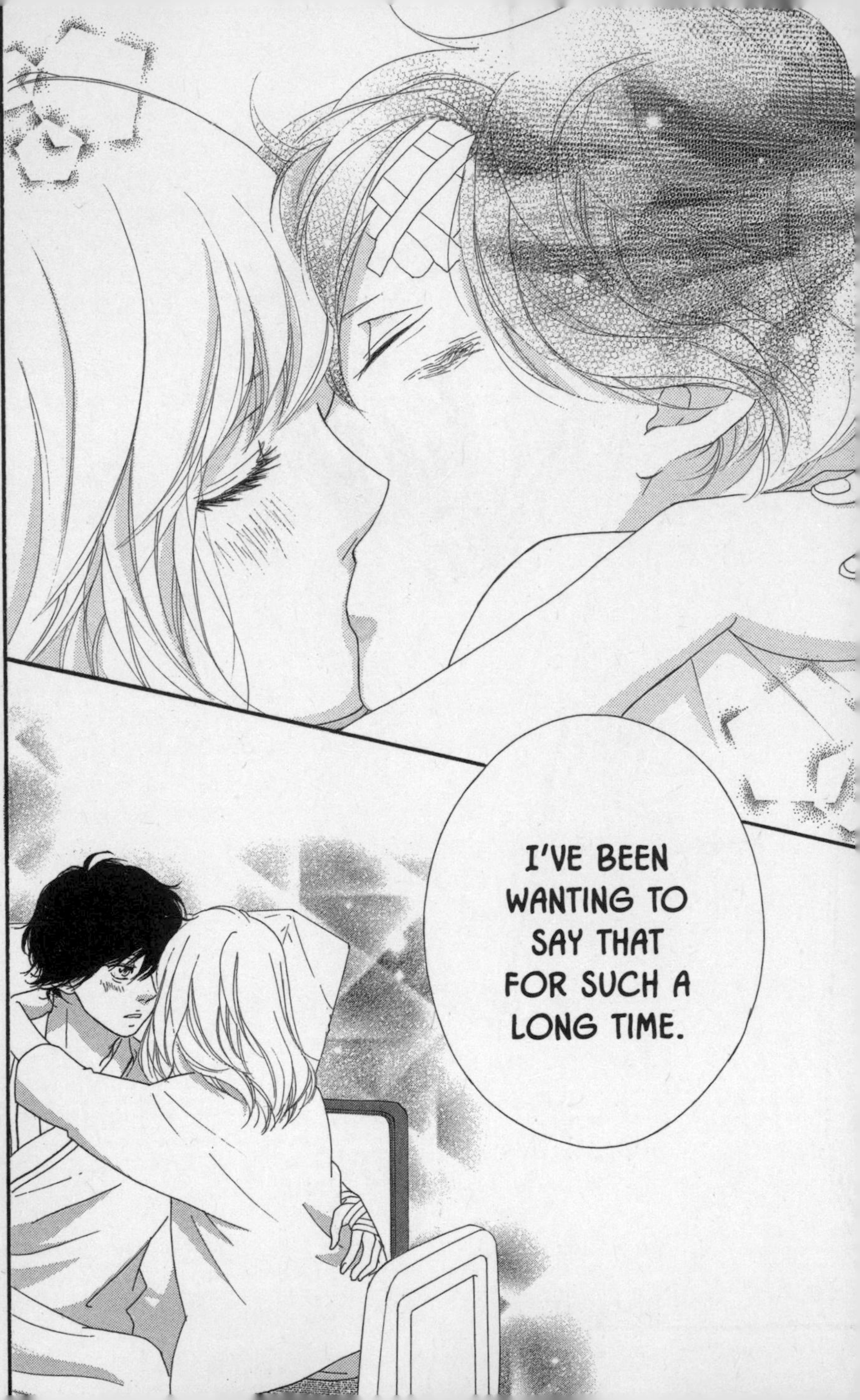
I'VE BEEN WANTING TO SAY THAT FOR SUCH A LONG TIME.

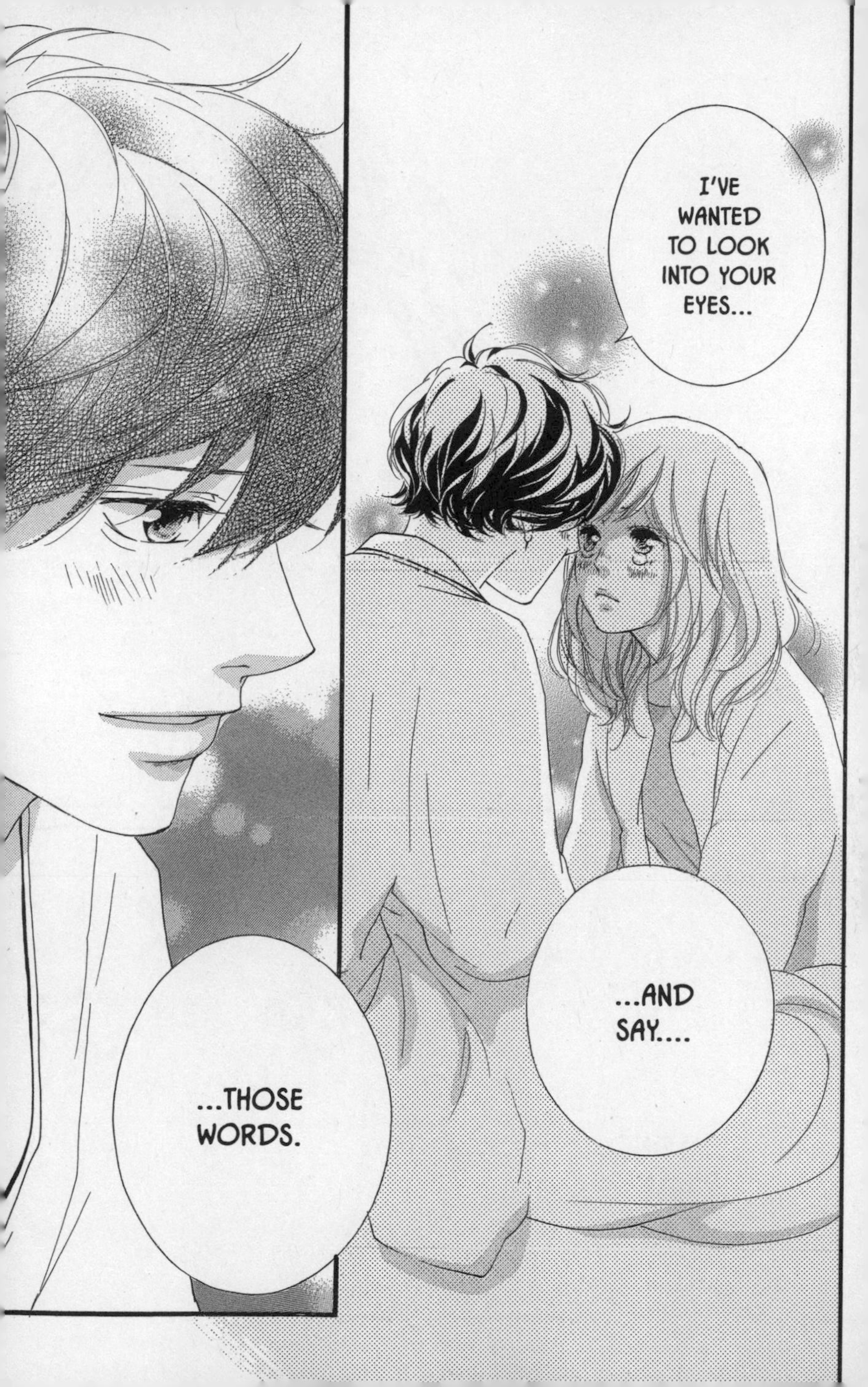
I'VE WANTED TO LOOK INTO YOUR EYES...
...AND SAY....
...THOSE WORDS.

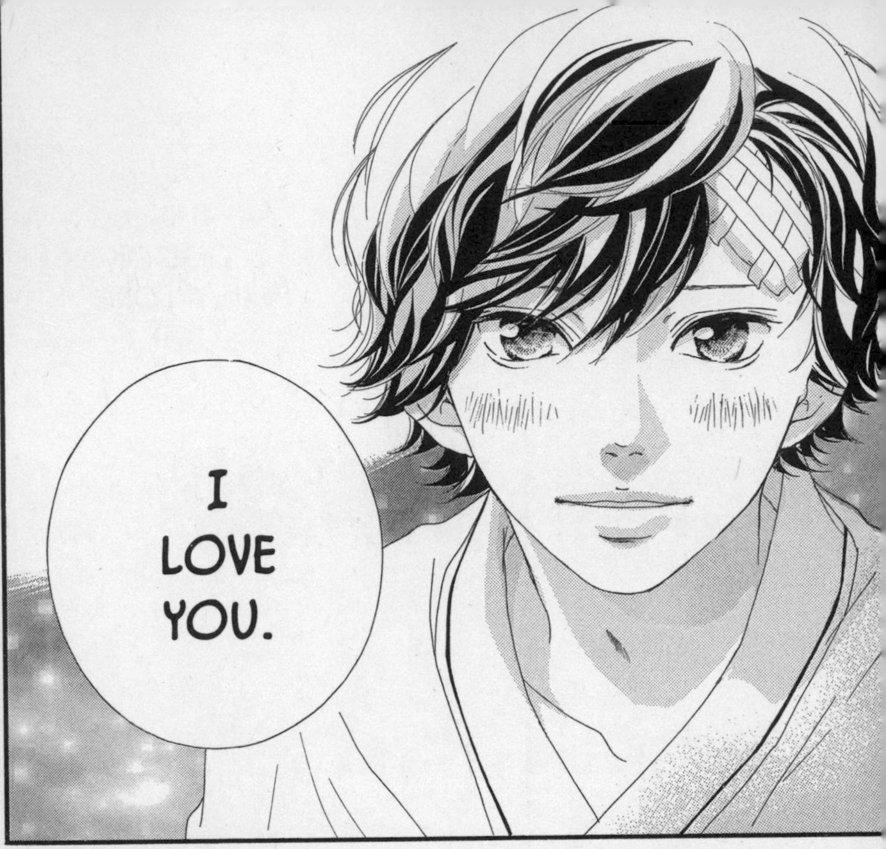
I LOVE YOU.

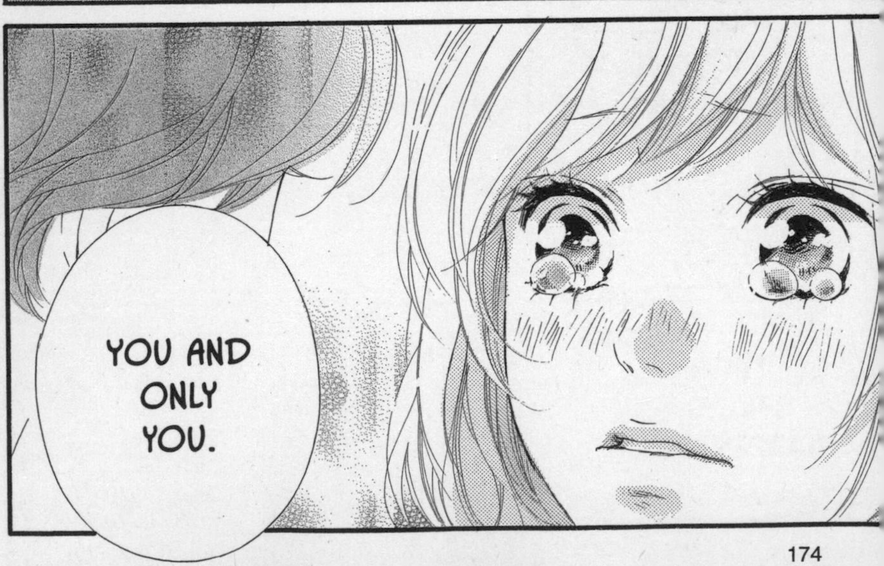
YOU AND ONLY YOU.

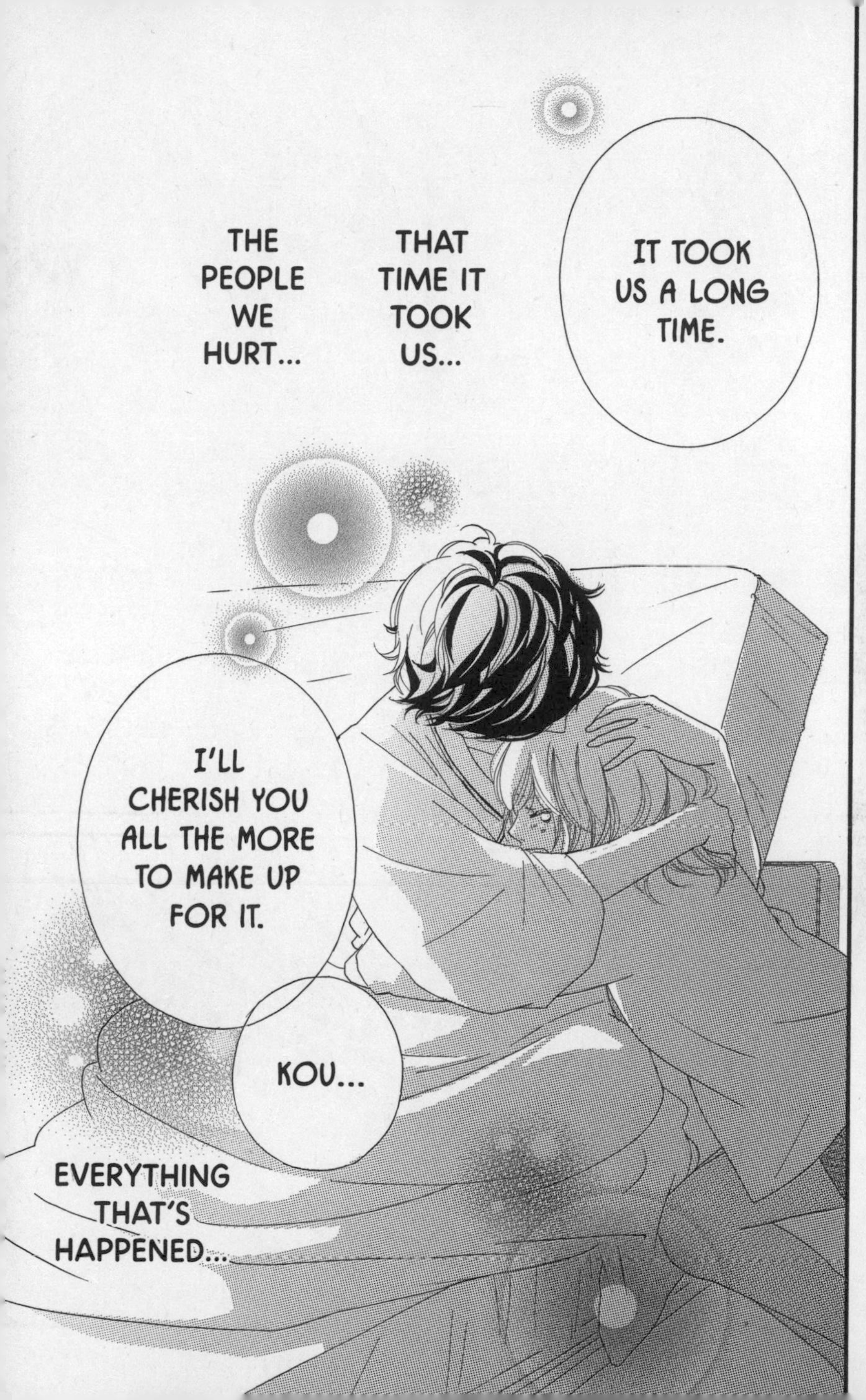
IT TOOK US A LONG TIME.
THAT TIME IT TOOK US...
THE PEOPLE WE HURT...
I'LL CHERISH YOU ALL THE MORE TO MAKE UP FOR IT.
KOU...
EVERYTHING THAT'S HAPPENED...

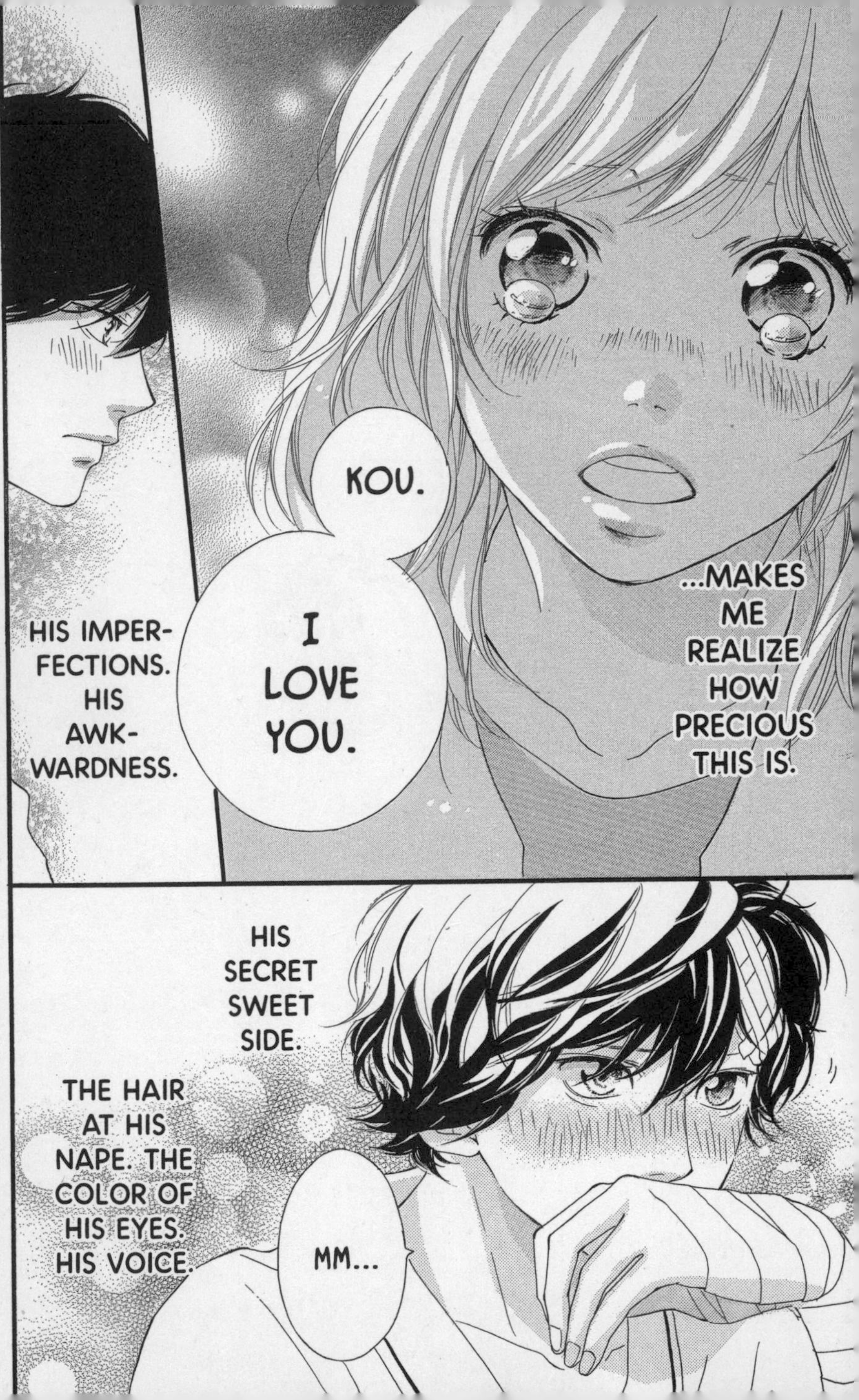
KOU.
I LOVE YOU.
...MAKES ME REALIZE HOW PRECIOUS THIS IS.
HIS IMPERFECTIONS. HIS AWKWARDNESS.
HIS SECRET SWEET SIDE.
MM...
THE HAIR AT HIS NAPE. THE COLOR OF HIS EYES. HIS VOICE.

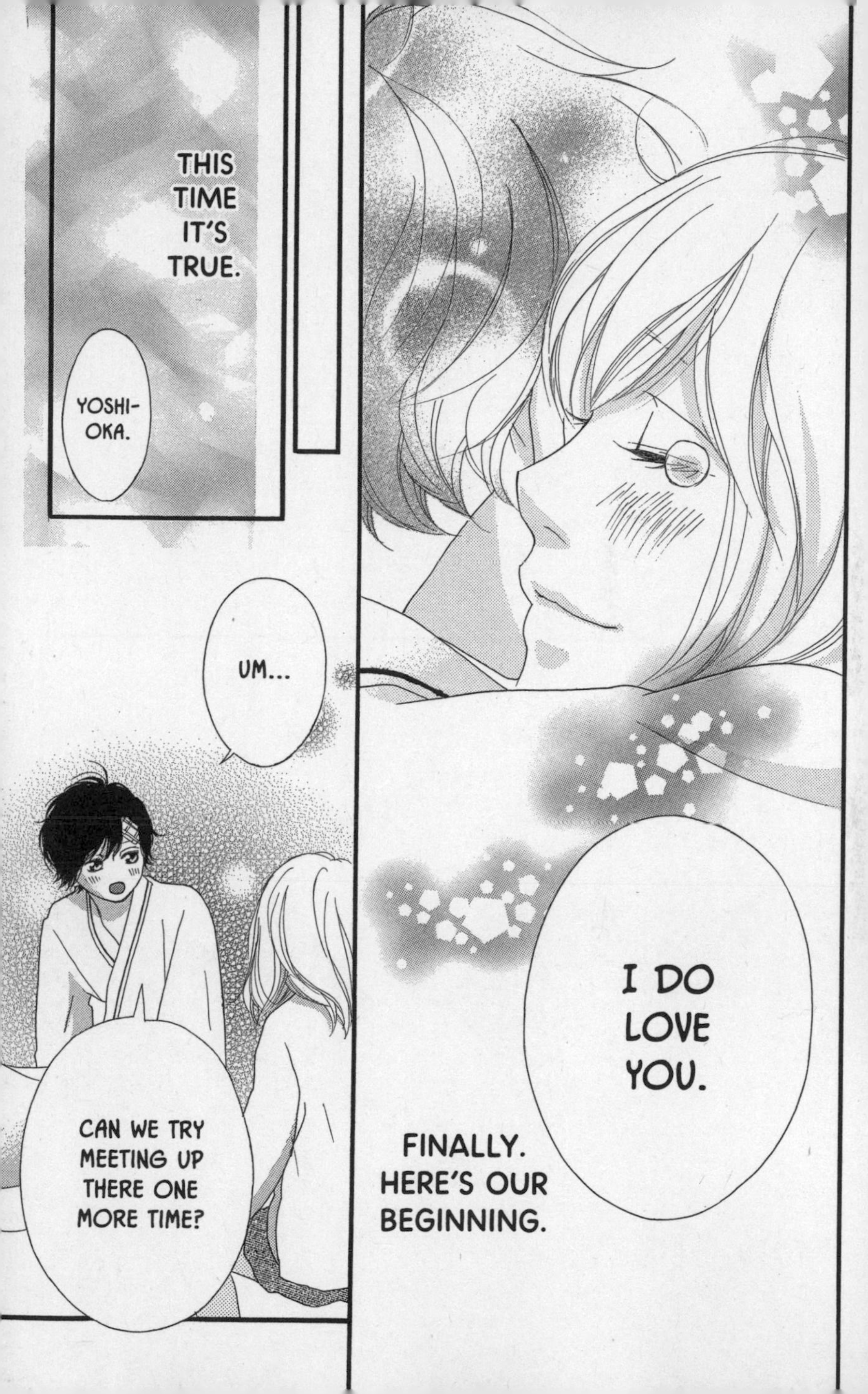
I DO LOVE YOU.
FINALLY. HERE'S OUR BEGINNING.
THIS TIME IT'S TRUE.
YOSHI-OKA.
UM...
CAN WE TRY MEETING UP THERE ONE MORE TIME?

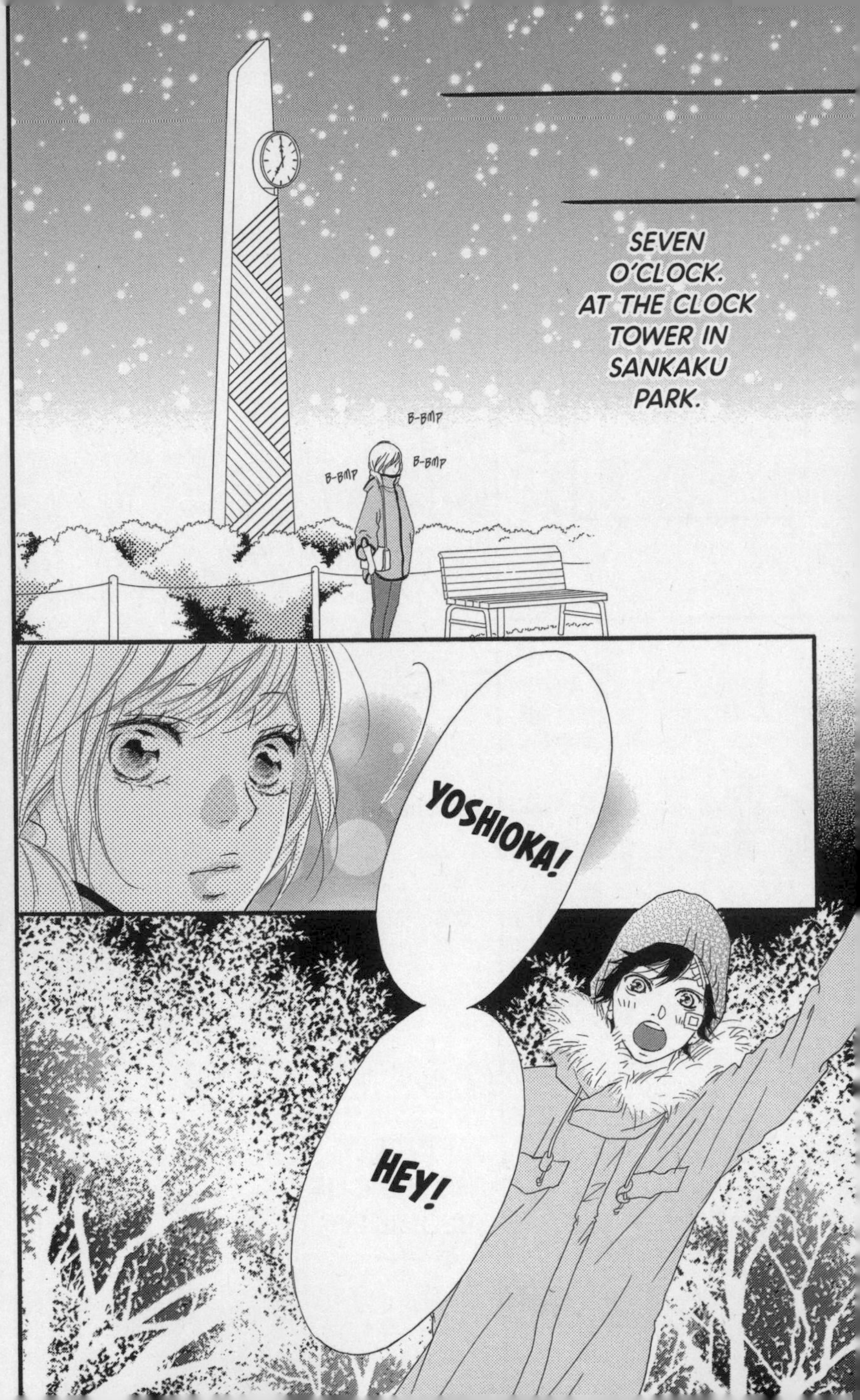
SEVEN O'CLOCK. AT THE CLOCK TOWER IN SANKAKU PARK.
B-BMP
B-BMP
B-BMP
YOSHIOKA!
HEY!

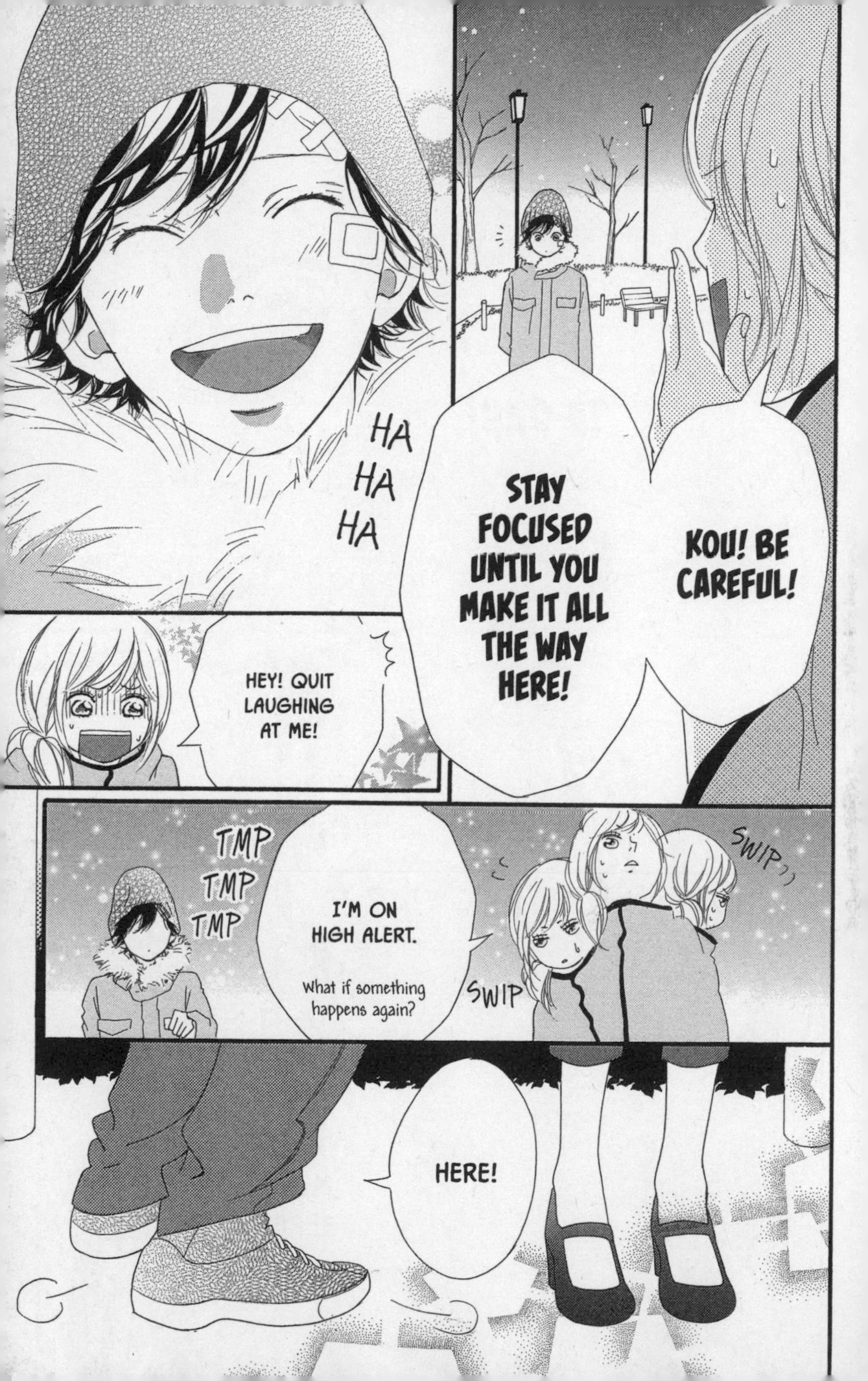
KOU! BE CAREFUL!
STAY FOCUSED UNTIL YOU MAKE IT ALL THE WAY HERE!
HA HA HA
HEY! QUIT LAUGHING AT ME!
SWIP
I'M ON HIGH ALERT.
What if something happens again?
TMP TMP TMP
SWIP
HERE!

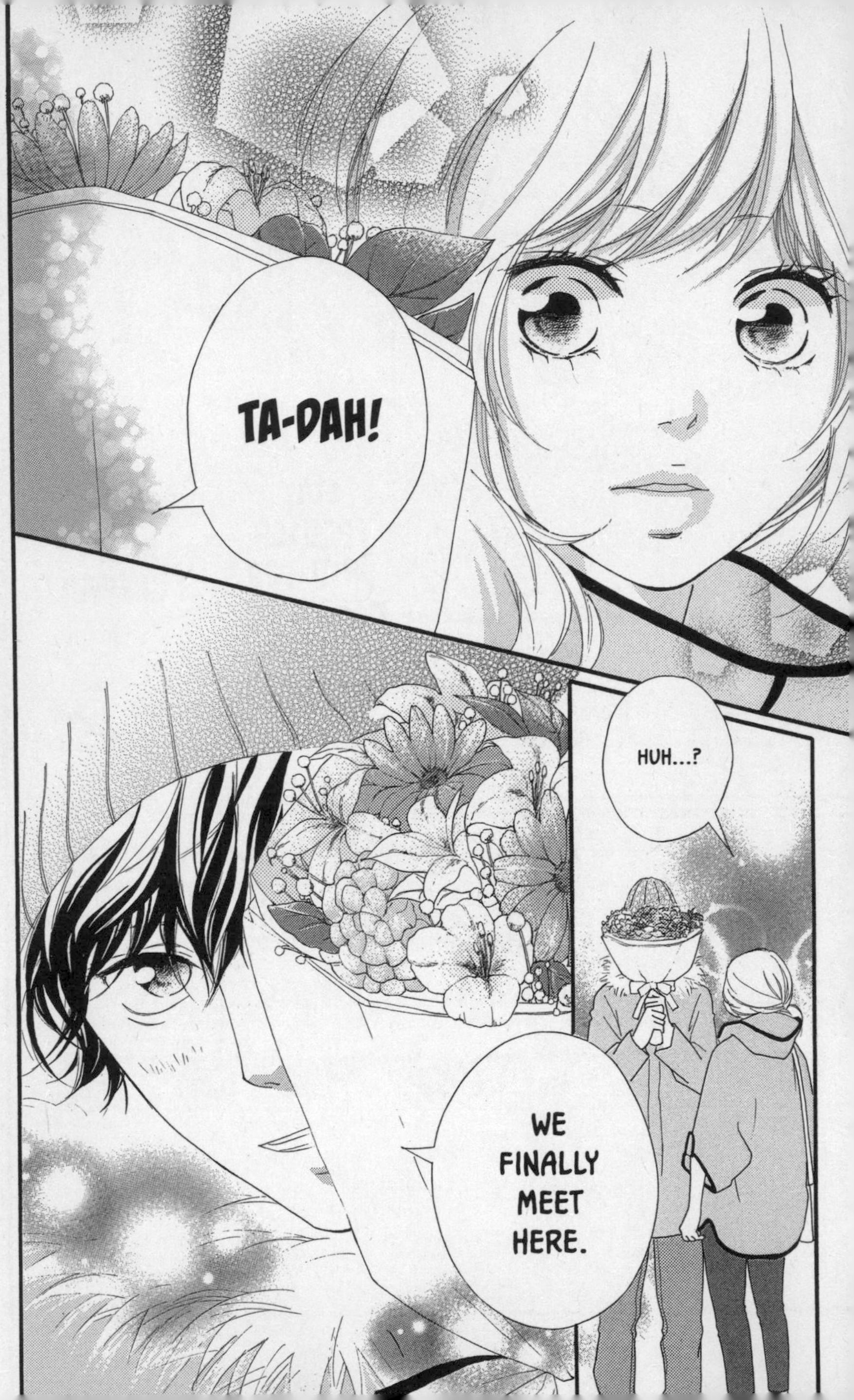
TA-DAH!
HUH...?
WE FINALLY MEET HERE.

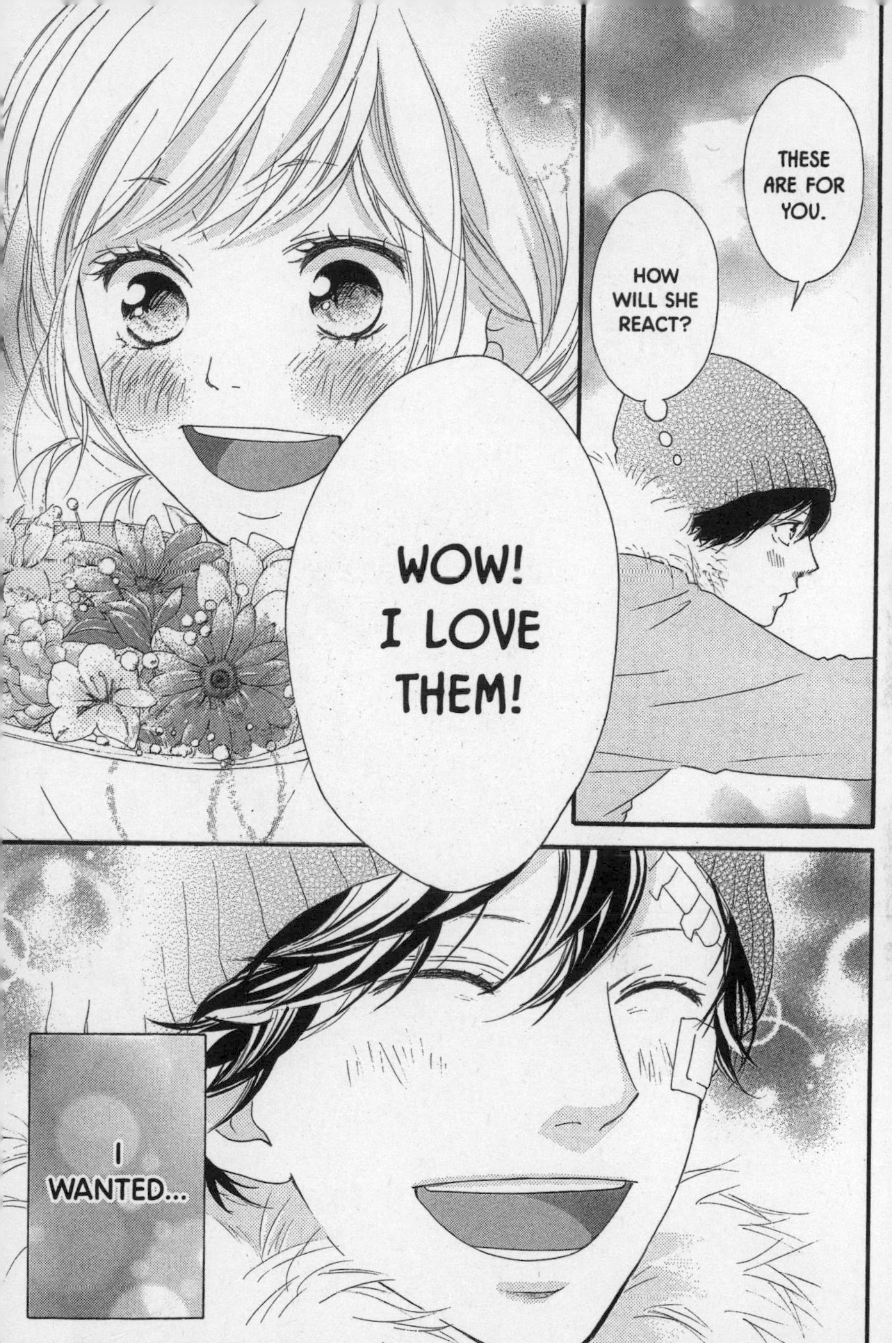
THESE ARE FOR YOU.
HOW WILL SHE REACT?
WOW! I LOVE THEM!
I WANTED...

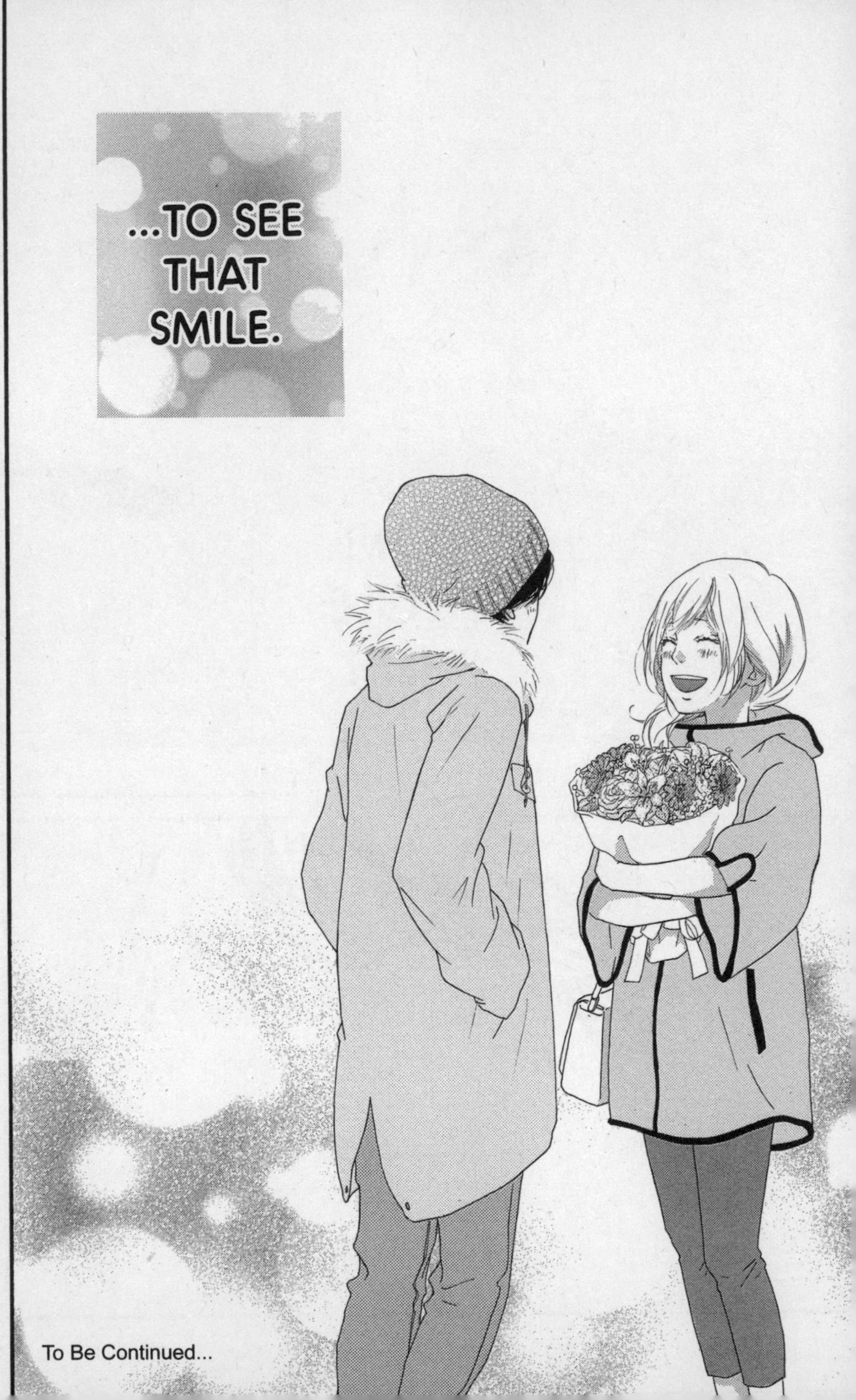
...TO SEE THAT SMILE.
To Be Continued...

Afterword

Thank you for reading through to the end.

If you read *Betsuma* magazine, you may have noticed that I added some pages to volume 12 that weren't in the magazine. It's not that I changed the content, but I wanted to add some subtle, lingering moments. I'm glad I did. I really like those in-between moments, but because I'm working with a set number of pages each month, if I spend too much time on those, the story never progresses. At the same time, I think those moments are the true essence of shojo manga. Maybe that's just my preference, but either way I'm often conflicted. I like the idea of drawing those kind of extra pages specifically for the book because it feels like a bonus. If anyone out there can tell which sections were added, you must be a true fanatic. I wonder if fanatics like that exist... Heh heh heh.

With that, I'll see you in the next volume!

 Io Sakisaka

I finally moved. Two days before the move, almost nothing had been packed, but somehow I pulled it off!

It was absolutely exhausting, and I never want to move like that again. The next time I move, I know I'll have to pack properly.

IO SAKISAKA

Born on June 8, Io Sakisaka made her debut as a manga creator with *Sakura, Chiru*. Her works include *Call My Name*, *Gate of Planet* and *Blue*. *Strobe Edge*, her previous work, is also published by VIZ Media's Shojo Beat imprint. *Ao Haru Ride* was adapted into an anime series in 2014. In her spare time, Sakisaka likes to paint things and sleep.

Ao Haru Ride

VOLUME 12
SHOJO BEAT EDITION

STORY AND ART BY IO SAKISAKA

TRANSLATION Emi Louie-Nishikawa
TOUCH-UP ART + LETTERING Inori Fukuda Trant
DESIGN Joy Zhang
EDITOR Nancy Thistlethwaite

First published in Japan in 2011 by SHUEISHA Inc., Tokyo.
English translation rights arranged by SHUEISHA Inc.

Printed in the U.S.A.

Published by VIZ Media, LLC
P.O. Box 77010
San Francisco, CA 94107

10 9 8 7 6 5 4 3 2 1
First printing, August 2020

ratings.viz.com RATED T TEEN
PARENTAL ADVISORY
AO HARU RIDE is rated T for Teen and
is recommended for ages 13 and up. This
volume contains the heartbreak of youth.

VIZ MEDIA
viz.com

Shojo Beat
shojobeat.com

DAYTIME SHOOTING STAR

Story & Art by
Mika Yamamori

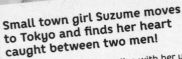

Small town girl Suzume moves to Tokyo and finds her heart caught between two men!

After arriving in Tokyo to live with her uncle, Suzume collapses in a nearby park when she remembers once seeing a shooting star during the day. A handsome stranger brings her to her new home and tells her they'll meet again. Suzume starts her first day at her new high school sitting next to a boy who blushes furiously at her touch. And her homeroom teacher is none other than the handsome stranger!

SHORTCAKE CAKE

CAKE

STORY AND ART BY
suu Morishita

An unflappable girl and a cast of lovable roommates at a boardinghouse create bonds of friendship and romance!

When Ten moves out of her parents' home in the mountains to live in a boardinghouse, she finds herself becoming fast friends with her male roommates. But can love and romance be far behind?

VIZ

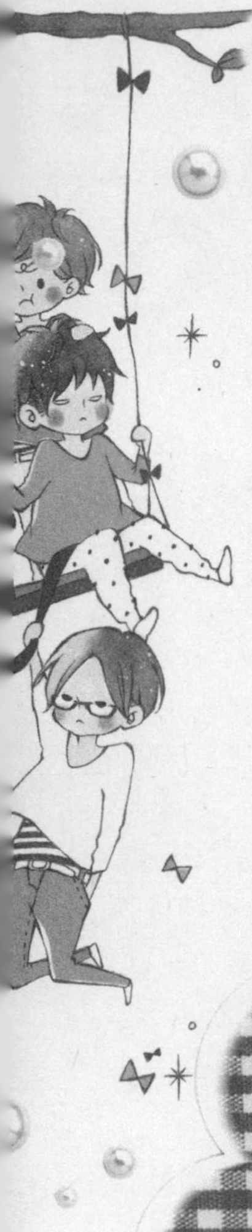

Honey So Sweet

Story and Art by Amu Meguro

Little did Nao Kogure realize back in middle school that when she left an umbrella and a box of bandages in the rain for injured delinquent Taiga Onise that she would meet him again in high school. Nao wants nothing to do with the gruff and frightening Taiga, but he suddenly presents her with a huge bouquet of flowers and asks her to date him—with marriage in mind! Is Taiga really so scary, or is he a sweetheart in disguise?

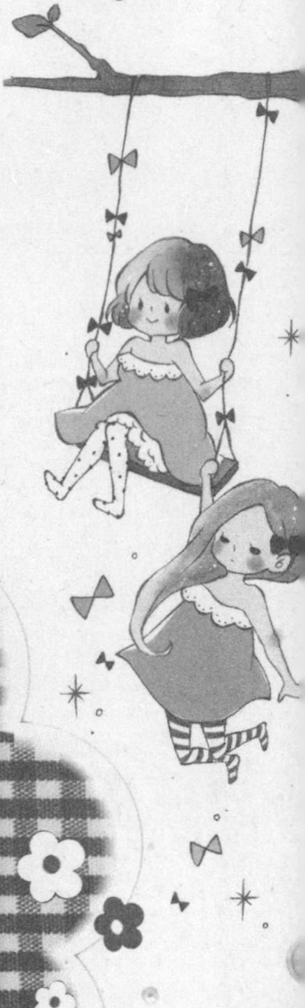

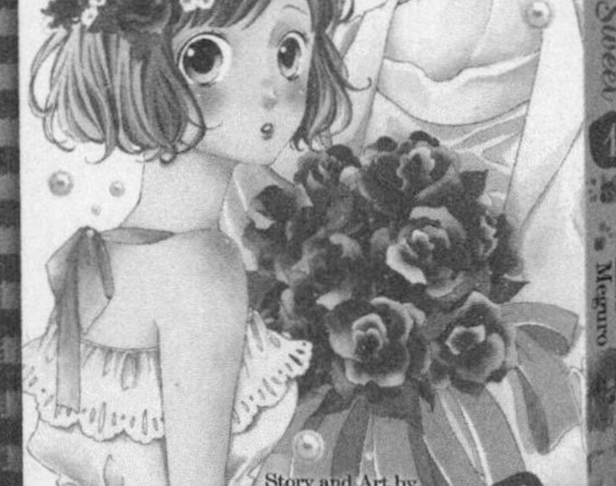
Honey So Sweet
Honey So Sweet 1
Amu Meguro
Story and Art by
Amu Meguro 1
VIZ

Shojo Beat

RATED T FOR TEEN ratings.viz.com

VIZ media
viz.com

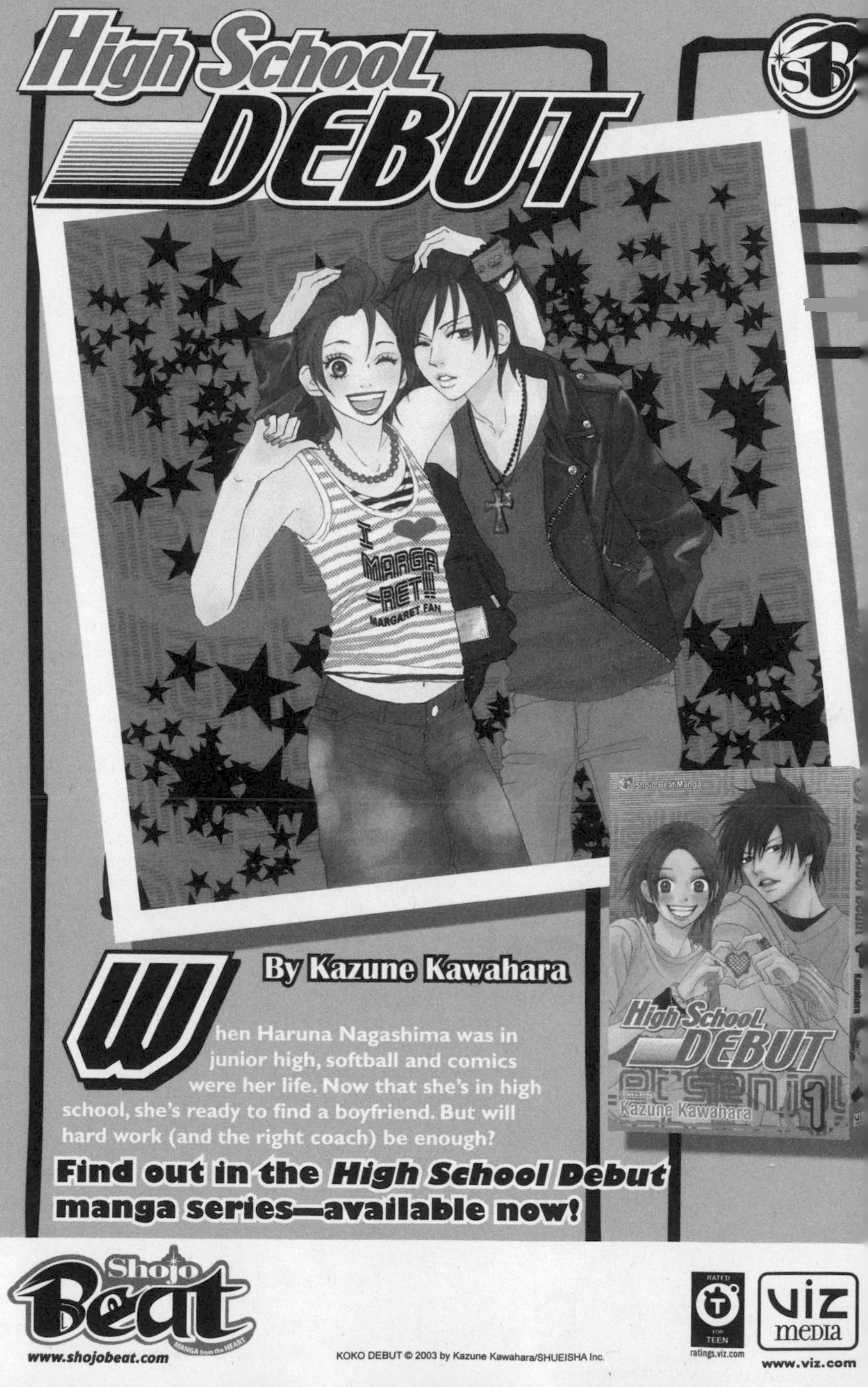
High School DEBUT
By Kazune Kawahara
When Haruna Nagashima was in junior high, softball and comics were her life. Now that she's in high school, she's ready to find a boyfriend. But will hard work (and the right coach) be enough?
Find out in the High School Debut manga series—available now!
I ♥ MARGARET!! MARGARET FAN
Shojo Beat Manga
High School DEBUT
Kazune Kawahara
1
Shojo Beat MANGA from the HEART
www.shojobeat.com
KOKO DEBUT © 2003 by Kazune Kawahara/SHUEISHA Inc.
RATED T FOR TEEN
ratings.viz.com
viz media
www.viz.com

STOP!
YOU MAY BE READING THE WRONG WAY.

In keeping with the original Japanese comic format, this book reads from right to left—so action, sound effects and word balloons are completely reversed to preserve the orientation of the original artwork.